THE ANNEXATION OF MEXICO

FROM THE AZTECS TO THE IMF

One Reporter's Journey Through History

John Ross

Common Courage Press   Monroe, Maine

Copyright © 1998 by John Ross

Cover design by Matt Wuerker
Reprint of "El Tormento de Cuauhtémoc" by David Alfaro Siqueiros authorized
by the Instituto Nacional de Bellas Artes y Literatura and Adriana Alfaro Arenal
Back cover photo: Juan Ramón Martínez León/ *La Guillotina*
Maps by Zoltan Grossman

Library of Congress Cataloging-in-Publication Data is available from the publisher.

ISBN 1-56751-130-9 (paper) — ISBN 1-56751-131-7 (cloth)

Common Courage Press
Box 702
Monroe, ME 04951

207-525-0900   fax: 207-525-3068

First Printing

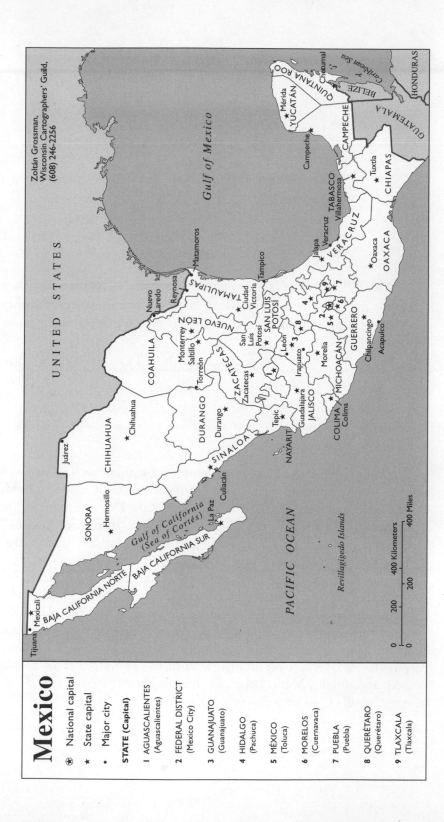

Mexico

⊛ National capital

★ State capital

• Major city

STATE (Capital)

1 AGUASCALIENTES
(Aguascalientes)

2 FEDERAL DISTRICT
(Mexico City)

3 GUANAJUATO
(Guanajuato)

4 HIDALGO
(Pachuca)

5 MÉXICO
(Toluca)

6 MORELOS
(Cuernavaca)

7 PUEBLA
(Puebla)

8 QUERÉTARO
(Querétaro)

9 TLAXCALA
(Tlaxcala)

Zoltán Grossman,
Wisconsin Cartographers' Guild,
(608) 246-2256

UNITED STATES

Gulf of Mexico

Caribbean Sea

PACIFIC OCEAN

Gulf of California
(Sea of Cortés)

Revillagigedo Islands

BELIZE

HONDURAS

GUATEMALA

BAJA CALIFORNIA NORTE

BAJA CALIFORNIA SUR

SONORA

CHIHUAHUA

COAHUILA

NUEVO LEÓN

TAMAULIPAS

DURANGO

SINALOA

ZACATECAS

SAN LUIS POTOSÍ

NAYARIT

JALISCO

COLIMA

MICHOACÁN

GUERRERO

VERACRUZ

OAXACA

TABASCO

CHIAPAS

CAMPECHE

YUCATÁN

QUINTANA ROO

Tijuana
Mexicali

Juárez

Hermosillo

La Paz

Culiacán

Chihuahua

Durango

Torreón

Saltillo
Monterrey

Nuevo
Laredo

Reynosa

Matamoros

Zacatecas

Tepic

Guadalajara

Colima

Morelia

León

Inc

Inrapuato

San Luis Potosí

Ciudad
Victoria

Tampico

Jalapa

Veracruz

Villahermosa

Tuxtla

Oaxaca

Chilpancingo

Acapulco

Campeche

Mérida

Chetumal

0   200   400 Kilometers

0   200   400 Miles

To Doña Teresa García and Tata Gregorio Alvarez Zalpa
who first opened the doors
of México Profundo to me.

"With different flags and languages they came to conquer us...they came and they went and we kept being Mexicans because the only flag we want to walk around under has an eagle devouring a snake on it..."

—Subcomandante Marcos, March 1995

This volume could not have been completed without the kind assistance of Sergio Aguayo, Elizabeth Bell, Padre Francisco Goitia, Carol Mone, Mirabel Gutiérrez, Marcia Perskie, Ernesto Martínez, Kate Doyle, Fernando Jiménez, Doña Rafita Barrientos, Peter Gellert, Trina Kleist, Juan José Quirino, Rocío Mesino, Julian Rodríguez, Lazaro Rodríguez, Betita Martínez, Claude Beagarie, Barbara Belejack, Miguel Angel García, Pedro Fabian Huaruco, Salvador Campanur, Ruth & Clinton, my comadre Arminda Flores, Andrés Barreda, Jaime Aviles, Richard Gibson, my colleagues at *Proceso* and *La Jornada*, Don Lalo and all the Mirandas, Erroll Jones, Jonathan Jones, the Nanas and the Tatas of Santa Cruz Tanaco, my publishers at Common Courage, Armando Peñaloza, Manuel Ruiz, and Don Manolo Cuetara of the Café La Blanca for keeping me fed, Celia Cruz and the staff of the Hotel Isabel for keeping me housed, and, finally, Mario López, for bringing me the news first thing each morning, to all of you *un gran abrazo*—John Ross

CONTENTS

Part Three
Welcome to the First World
The Annexation of Mexico's Economy

Part Four
La Lucha Sigue y Sigue
Contemporary Resistance to the Annexation of Mexico

INTRODUCTION

MY DINNER WITH CLINTON

As usual, the reporters were waiting for the comandantes to come down from the surrounding hills to the Lacandón jungle hamlet with the haunting name of La Realidad (The Reality) which, by June 1995, had become the Zapatista Army of National Liberation's most public outpost. The February military offensive mounted by President Ernesto Zedillo had melted into stand-off by late spring and what would become an interminable series of peace talks, or "dialogues," between the rebels and the government, had just begun. Zedillo unquestionably now held the upper hand—his army occupied EZLN base communities and the ski-masked rebels had been pushed back into the deep bush of the Montes Azules (Blue Mountains) United Nations-sponsored "biosphere."

At a late May session in the highland Tzotzil town of San Andrés Larraínzar (or Sakam'chem de los Pobres on the Zapatistas' map), government negotiators had proposed that EZLN fighters withdraw to special enclaves in preparation for laying down their arms. Although it was quite certain that the EZLN would reject this magnanimous offer from the *mal gobierno* (bad government), Zapatista delegates in Sakam'chem had promised to take the proposal back to their base communities where such matters are decided in general assemblies, in accordance with EZLN structure and the leadership principle of *mandar obedeciendo* (leading by obeying the will of the community). The delegates had even offered to permit the government to witness the village consultations.

But the Zapatistas' brainy, charismatic spokesperson, Subcomandante Marcos, attached certain conditions to the invitation: the government observers could not buzz into the jungle in helicopters, the accepted transportation mode for top-level officials. And the observers had to carry their own gear—no native bearers. Finally, Marcos insisted that the only mode of transportation would be one's own pedal extremities, eliminating the specter of bureaucrats being trundled into the Blue Mountains on sedan chairs. Challenged with hoofing it into the villages like everyone else in this jungle, the government men had, of course, declined the invite and, instead, chastised the Sup for his lack of seriousness.

Despite the Mexican government's rejection of the EZLN offer, the reporters had trekked down to La Realidad anyway, hoping that even if the *mal gobierno* wasn't going to show up, the rebels might want the press to witness the consultations in the villages. The *consultas* would give us a first look at how Zapatista communities in the deep jungle were functioning in the wake of the military's massive February 9th offensive.

The EZLN operates in its own time zone ("Mexican Southeast Time") and the wait for the comandantes stretched into days. The rains had still not broken and the sun was turned up to high broil. Overhead, military aircraft crisscrossed the seamless sky like dull metal horseflies, constantly reminding the Mayan Tojolabales of La Realidad just who was on top now. Closer to the ground, more organic insect life kept the press busily fending off attack. One morning, I arose from a schoolhouse bench and discovered hundreds of ants encrusting my right eye, which was rapidly swelling to the size of a papaya. Meanwhile, our foodstuff, mostly tins of unappetizing tuna fish and sardines, was running as low as our patience. We began scouting out houses where, for a price, we might get fed.

The whitewashed hut was dark and cool, its walls made of boards and packed mud. We scrunched down at a warped wooden table. The very young mother said she had only beans and tortillas. There were no eggs but maybe the chickens had laid one since she last took a look. "Clinton" she yelled at a small pantsless boy in the corner, "go help your sister find an egg." Although the command was made in Tojolabal, the gist was clear, and, indeed, the kid quickly returned, proudly balancing an egg in either hand.

"Clinton?" I asked Ruth, his mama, just to be sure I had heard the name correctly.

"*Sí, se llama Clinton...*" Only she pronounced it more like "Cleen-tone" with the accent on the "tone."

"Like the President of the United States?"

"*¿Quién sabe?*" she shrugged. The boy's father had heard it on the radio and it sounded pretty. By "pretty," she meant it sounded like Tojolabal.

Three decades and more on the ground here told me there was more to the story then just the "prettiness" of the name "Clinton." Mexico's, and particularly Indian Mexico's, relationship with what is not Mexico is infinitely more nuanced and perverse.

My colleagues wolfed down lunch and drifted off, one by one. The discovery of the boy named Clinton failed to excite them. You must have heard it wrong, they scoffed at my scoop. Nonetheless, ten months later when I returned to La Realidad for what Marcos was modestly billing as "The Continental Encounter for Humanity and Against Neo-Liberalism," Clinton had achieved celebrity status. Ofelia Medina, Mexico's premier actress and a staunch Zapatista supporter, posed with the scowling child in her arms and reporters regularly flocked to eat at "the Casa of the Mama of Clinton." I felt vindicated.

The Encounter was a languid event that coincided with Holy Week, providing ample opportunity for reflection on the macro and the micro of Zapatista life. Doubled into a hammock I had hung badly, and swatting at swarms of gnats that flourished in the aftermath of a surprise April shower, I lay awake nights and contemplated two years and more of Zapatista definition. The boy with the pretty-in-Tojolabal name of Clinton weighed heavily on my thoughts.

Why, here at the heart of indigenous resistance to the globalization of practically everything (read "the Annexation of Mexico"), where the bullets and weapons, tanks, Humvees, and helicopters were being supplied to the army that surrounded this village by the Clinton White House, more or less in defense of the Free Market, had a young mother been allowed to impose upon a badly-nourished, brown-skinned child, the name of the portly, very pale-faced President of the *Gringos*? After all, aside from the servile paeans of the tiny Harvard- and Yale-educated clique that, tragically, continues to govern around here, presidents of the United States of North America don't have much of a following south of the Río Bravo—and La Realidad is way south of the Río Bravo, about 20 klicks from the Guatemalan border.

The pathway that led to this absurd infiltration is simple enough. In La Realidad, folks get their news from state radio in Ocosingo, the region's commercial nexus. XEOCH picks up its newsfeeds from AP and Notimex, wire services based in the U.S. With nests of communication satellites girdling the planet, by the autumn of '92, Bill Clinton was on his way to becoming a household name all around the world—and most of those households, like Ruth's, were very threadbare.

I envisioned Clinton's father walking out to his mountain coffee patch with a Taiwanese-made transistor plugged into his ear. The Democrats are on their way to winning a stunning upset and he is thinking about his newborn son...

It is the 500th anniversary of the Conquest of the Indigenous Peoples of America. Both "Cleen-tone" and the Zapatista Army of National Liberation are being born...

The poorly-hung hammock bunched up around me and I considered spreading out on the *ejido* house floor, but it was the scorpion season, as La Realidad's sharp-eyed hammock salesmen never failed to point out at slack moments in the Encounter. I felt trapped by both the hammock and the ironies. Even as hundreds of committed heads and hearts gathered in this jungle to develop a collective cure for the plague that the neo-liberal model has inflicted upon the poorest citizens on the planet, Clinton walked amongst us.

Had the United States at last fulfilled its three-century dream of annexing Mexico?

Not exactly.

The satellites of the New World Communication Order beam in the info-bytes and they are, at first, stoically absorbed and digested by the Mayans down below, often, ultimately, to be spit back with spirited cultural defiance. The name "Clinton" has a Tojolabal ring to it. Besides, taking it is sort of like tak-ing the name of the U.S. President hostage. In this hamlet, fiercely loyal to a rebel army whose uprising dared to spoil the very first hour of the North American Free Trade Agreement, there is a five-year-old boy named for Bill "Bubbah" Clinton!

Zapatista defiance is often edged with such humor, but the joke is one that all Mexico can savor, the sort of graveyard humor that the mordant José Guadalupe Posada told us over and over again in his classic Day of the Dead *calaveras*, in which the skeletal but top-hatted rich eternally flog the ragged, skeletal poor.

In August, 1996, I found myself riding the road from and to La Realidad with the caped urban crusader Superbarrio Gómez. We were charged with res-cuing thousands of delegates who had come from the four corners of the globe to pay obeisance to the Zapatistas at what Marcos was now calling the "Intergaláctica" (a sequel to the Continental Encounter for Humanity and against Neo-Liberalism). The internationals were stuck at a Mexican Immigration Institute checkpoint at the gateway to the jungle and the hard-eyed Migra wouldn't let them through.

As we bumped up the muddy canyon track, I spoke of the boy Clinton and my preoccupation with his name.

"Look" laughed Super, "its simple—they have their Clinton and he's a *panzón* (big belly) (so is Mr. Gómez) *millionario* who lives in the White House. And we have our Clinton and he's a *panzón* too but his belly is filled with mal-nutrition. Like his *tocayo* (namesake), he's a millionaire—with a million worms. And he lives in the Casa Blanca too—only his house is painted white with *cal* (quick lime) to hold the walls together..."

PART ONE

A History of Annexation

Chapter 1

THE FIRST
ANNEXATIONS

Conquest, expansionism, incursion, intervention, invasion, investment, integration, imposition, occupation, absorption, alignment, subjugation, dependency, colonialism, globalization, enslavement, extermination, annihilation, obliteration, and genocide, are some words that describe the process of the domination of one people by another. From investment to invasion, alignment to genocide, there are many steps, each constrained by context and the site-specific histories of the Dominator and the Dominated.

I have chosen to call this process "annexation" in respect to Mexico, because of the word's geographical implications The contiguity of the U.S., and a few centuries of sadomasochistic philandering between the two nations, have most often been expressed on both sides of the 1,964 mile border by an obsession with this word, "annexation." But "annexation" is hardly limited to the territoriality implied by borders. Facilitated by propinquity, the United States of North America seeks to annex Mexico's political, social, cultural and, most of all, its economic turf as well.

But others have sought to "annex" Mexico from a much longer way off, have thrown their long arms across oceans to wrest from this land its riches and its soul. Still others did not have to travel very far...

The truth is that Mexico was first annexed by Mexicans—the Mexicans or "Mexicas" (more popularly known as "Aztecs")—were not even from "Mexico" as defined by modern boundaries of the Valley of Mexico, a 7,000-foot-high basin now occupied, for the most part, by the *mancha urbana* or great urban stain that forms the metropolitan Mexico City area. Rather, they were Chichimeca outlanders from the wild barren lands of the north—conjecturally, Lake Aztlán in Pacific Nayarit state, whose military and political survival skills had been honed by 300 years of ceaseless wandering and rapine.

The Aztecs were hardly the first Chichimecas to stomp into the valley. The fall of Teotihuacan (750 AD), the New World's first great corn-culture city, was occasioned by cyclical drought and the invasion of Chichimeca hordes from the north who collapsed the culture's carrying capacity. The northerners spread throughout the Valley of Mexico, settling around the Texcoco lake system and digging in for the duration. The Toltecs, who flourished at the northeast end of the valley around 1000 AD were acculturated Chichimecas who borrowed Quetzalcóatl, the Plumed Serpent, from the Teotihuacan pantheon, and elevated him to the master of their universe. When Toltec society, crippled by the syndrome of drought in which the history of pre-Conquest Mexico is written, finally crumbled, Quetzalcóatl abandoned ship, fled east into the land of the dawn from whence, one day, he would return to cleanse "Mexico" of sinners, or so his priests divined.

Three centuries later, hauling their voracious hummingbird god, Huitzilopochtli, the wanderers from Atzlán burst into the valley of "Mexico" with domination in their eyes As depicted on Mexico's national flag, Huitzilopochtli prophesied that the Aztecs would establish their city in the place where an eagle was sighted devouring a serpent coiled around a nopal cactus bush. The location, then on the island of Tenochtitlán in the shallow waters of lake Texcoco, is now a very land-locked site, the *Templo Mayor* or Great Temple of Huitzilopochtli and Tláloc, just north of modern Mexico City's Zócalo plaza (or, at least, so the tourist guides swear). The year of the founding is arbitrarily declared to be 1325.

The duality of the deities Huitzilopochtli, "the left-handed hummingbird of the sun," and Tláloc, the bringer of the rain, kept the Aztecs' universe in balance and the people fed. But both gods had to be sufficiently nourished with human blood in order for the formula to function.[1] As the priest class, which trafficked in this balance, grew in influence, the waging of wars and "flower wars" (arranged battles designed to capture victims for blood sacrifice) became the permanent mission of the Aztec rulers.

By 1340, having bullied, threatened, and struck alliances with most of their immediate neighbors around the lake, the Aztecs achieved domination in the valley through the vaunted Triple Alliance with their lakeside neighbors of Texcoco and Tlacopan.

At its apogee, the Aztec model worked well enough. Tenochtitlán, the largest city ever built in pre-Conquest America, blossomed on the island in the middle of the lake. Mindful of the recurring drought that had leveled their ancestors' cultures, the Aztec hierarchy insured nutritional self-sufficiency by exacting heavy tribute from their allies and vassal states, and developing a lake-oriented agricultural system, the *chinampa* (floating island), still functioning in the southern Mexico City borough of Xochimilco. But as Tenochtitlán grew, much like Mexico City today, its needs soon outstripped its abilities to meet them.

From the reign of Xicatl, beginning around 1420—the era in which the Spanish and Portuguese crowns first sought to expand their empires through maritime exploration in the Atlantic—Aztec destiny grew to the limits of

Anáhuac, the One World of the Mexicas, as delineated by the extensions of their conquest. Emperor after emperor dispatched armies of Jaguar and Eagle warriors into the south, crushing and conquering cultures, exacting tribute in the form of taxes, victuals, and sacrificial victims, and imposing their own gods upon local deities. Aztec fighters slammed into the west, overrunning what are now the states of Guerrero and Colima. Motecuhzona I expanded the empire east to Veracruz and parts of Tabasco. The Mexica military machine clanked into Oaxaca, subjugating the Mixtec and Zapotec peoples as far as the Huave territories, south of Tehuantepec.[2] By 1500, the empire extended all the way to Guatemala and the Yucatán on the south, the boundaries of Mayan hegemony. The two great Meso-American empires never squared off, but traded goods and gods instead—Quetzalcóatl became Kukulcan and the cacao bean was common coinage between the two great powers. Shimmering, metallic-green Quetzal feathers formed the coiffures of both the Aztec and Mayan heads of state.

But life down below was not quite so luxurious. When drought struck Tenochtitlán, as it always did, the priests chalked it up to a drop in the blood supply. New tributes were levied upon the annexed peoples. Ordered to produce 25,000 fresh victims willing to be sacrificed to restore the universal balance during the great famine of 1452-1454, the Tlaxcaltecos and the Huejotzingos demurred. Emissaries were sent to Tenochtitlán pleading for exemptions, but the Emperor refused to see the outlanders. The Tlaxcaltecos never forgot the slight—as attested to in the magnificent murals of Desiderio Xochitiozin that now adorn the Tlaxcala government palace.[3]

By the 16th century, the Aztecs had reached the geographical extremes of domination, their lines of control to the most distant annexed territories of Anáhuac were thin and frayed. When the sage *tlatoani* (kingmaker), Tlacaelel, died in 1496, the future suddenly got shaky. Tlacaelel had been the mastermind of Aztec expansionism, welding the priest and the warrior classes together in an instrument of governance that had well served the last five emperors. Now the inexperienced Motecuhzona II, with a tentative hand on the wands of control, declared himself a god in order to bolster his popular stature, an arrogant and graceless gesture crafted to recoup power from the priests.

The Tlaxcaltecos and the Huejotzingos were not exceptions—everywhere in the annexed territories resistance and revolt were afoot. Famine, the flooding of Tenochtitlán and the unexpected sightings of comets and meteors did not much lighten Motecuhzona's deepening moods. When, the chronicles relate, strange vessels with great white wings were sighted off the Yucatán, Tabasco and Veracruz in 1517, 1518 and 1519, Motecuhzona was convinced that Quetzalcóatl had finally returned from the east, to cleanse Mexico of its sins.[4]

Hostile Corporate Takeover

The strangers wasted no time in laying claim to the land. Hernán Cortez dropped anchor on April 21st, 1519, Holy Thursday, and came ashore with 650 men on Good Friday, planting his sword and a cross in the white beach sand of Veracruz (The True Cross) in the name of the Crown and the Holy Mother. Then he convened his crew as an *ayuntamiento* (town council) and had himself elected Captain-General, with full rights to explore and expropriate this fruitful land that was soon to be renamed New Spain.[5] The second annexation of Mexico had begun.

Motecuhzona sent messengers flying down to the beach to bribe Cortez to go away. But the gold with which they gifted him instead whetted the Spaniard's cravings—his men suffered a disease that could only be cured by gold, he explained to the runners, promising that he would soon visit Motecuhzona in Tenochtitlán.

For Hernán Cortez, the Conquest was a make-or-break venture—he was a private contractor who had financed his own expedition on a shoestring, and had sailed from his last port of call, Cuba, without obtaining the proper commissions or cutting the governor in on the expected booty.[6] Now he needed associates to join him in this risky business.

The Totonacos, whose beach he had invaded, were cowed into junior partnership by vigorous displays of cannon and cavalry charges and fanged mastiffs. The locals had little love for Motecuhzona anyway, whose taxes and tributes sucked them dry of sustenance as sacrifice to his own bloody gods.

On August 16th, Cortez, 400 countrymen, and 200 Totonaco warriors set off uphill to network with the Tlaxcaltecos, who harbored similar seething resentments against the Emperor. Just to show that he was serious about this adventure, the Captain General ordered all but one of his ships burned behind him, largely to prevent desertion. There would be no turning back.

Accepting the Machiavellian credo that the enemy of their enemy was their friend, the Tlaxcaltecos readily joined up—not that the Tlaxcaltecos were any less gore-oriented then the Mexicas: 800 human sacrifices were performed each year in their territory, 1,000 every fourth year.[7] But Motecuhzona had been in their faces for a long time, carrying off their own sacrificial victims in one forced "flower war" after another for the last ten years. Now, with 1,200 fighters, Cortez turned on Cholula, only 100 kilometers from downtown Tenochtitlán. "I have seen no city more fit to live in," Cortez noted in a letter after entering Cholula[8]—and then, advised by his Indian consort, Malinche, that the Cholulans were plotting against him, committed maximum atrocities upon its inhabitants, slaughtering 3,000 of their soldiers in the center of the city. Convinced on which side the bread was now being buttered, the Cholulans fell into step, bringing with them neighbors like the Huejotzingos.

Cortez descended between smoking volcanoes into the lake-covered Valley of Mexico with 10,000 men to back him up. Before him gleamed Tenochtitlán, a city-state bursting at the seams with 200,000 citizens—far larger than any urban entity the soon-to-be Conqueror had ever laid eyes upon.

Hernán Cortez's entry into the Aztecs' stronghold could be described as a hostile corporate takeover. Although he brought many hired guns, he did not need to use them. Motecuhzona was only too willing to become a wholly-owned subsidiary of the Spanish Crown. But the Emperor balked a bit at giving up blood sacrifice in return for the One True Cross, a clause, the Captain General underscored, that was a condition of the contract.

Although Motecuhzona eventually came around and accepted Jesús Christ as his Savior, other big machas on the Mexica Board of Directors were not ready for the buy-out. When Cortez physically assaulted the blood-smeared citadel of Huizilopochtli, the priests plotted retaliation. Motecuhzona was taken hostage, kingly collateral against the brewing uprising.

Meanwhile, like so many other go-get-'em business types, Cortez was having difficulties with the home office. His freelance conquest had double-crossed a governor who was to have shared in the spoils, and besides the expedition lacked official seals. 1,400 Spaniards were landed at Veracruz to wrest control of the enterprise from him. Leaving a rump garrison to entertain the Emperor, who, fearful of the wrath of the priests and the people, was grateful for the protection the kidnapping afforded, Cortez descended to the coast to sweet-talk the interlopers into merging forces. After all, they had common interests—he dangled gold gewgaws before their googly eyes and invited them to take "the cure."

The ambiance in Tenochtitlán had turned nasty during Cortez's absence. Motecuhzona was on his last legs and first his brother, Cuitlahuac, and then his brash young nephew, Cuauhtémoc (the descending eagle) had risen up in rancor against the old emperor's betrayal. Cuauhtémoc drove the Spanish from the island in a retreat schoolbooks call *La Noche Triste* or "Sad Night"— although for Cuauhtémoc, the defeat of the hated invaders must have made for a festive evening. Behind them, in the smoldering ruins of their palatial lodgings, the invaders left the corpse of Motecuhzona, punctured by many daggers.

Hernán Cortez was a self-made Conquistador and only the surface of his entrepreneurial skills had been scratched. The progeny of a retired anti-Moorish crusader from dirt-poor Extremadura, he had pulled himself up by his bootstraps, eventually embarking upon and abandoning a promising legal career to freeboot in the New World for fortune and power. Now he retreated to Tlaxcala and fashioned ships to ferry his army onto the island rather than be trapped, as had happened during *La Noche Triste*, on the narrow causeway the Aztecs controlled. He wheedled and threatened and purchased the allegiances of the Aztecs' former trading partners around the lake. Then, assured of their neutrality, he attacked.

The siege of Tenochtitlán lasted 75 days. In addition to their legions outside, the Europeans had a fifth column inside the city: smallpox. The epidemic decimated the populace and dampened resistance, but it was only a taste of the plagues to come. The annexation of the Aztecs by Old World diseases had just begun.

Cuauhtémoc appealed to the outlying Indian nations and was rebuffed. The Purépecha-Tarascans, who had inflicted upon the Aztecs one of the worst drubbings they had ever received in battle when the Mexicas sought to invade their turf, applauded their suffering: "let the strangers kill the Aztecs."[9] Isolated and reviled by its former vassals, ravaged by disease and dissension inside, the inevitable fall of Tenochtitlán came on August 13th, 1521, with the capture of Cuauhtémoc on the adjacent market island of Tlatelolco on what is now the corner of Constancia and Santa Lucía streets in the Peralvio neighborhood. Today a chipped gilt memorial plaque over a heavy-machinery repair shop shares a grimy wall decorated with multiple International Harvester and Spicer logos to mark the spot.

"Señor Malinche," Cuauhtémoc addressed Cortez in surrendering, using the name of the victor's Indian mistress instead of his given Spanish one,[10] "we have chewed dry twigs and salt grasses…we have filled our mouths with dust and adobe…we have eaten rats, lizards, and worms." "Worms are swarming in the streets and the plazas and the walls are splattered with gore," the Aztecs moaned, "they have captured Cuauhtémoc, they have captured the prince of Mexico…weep my people, know that we have lost the Mexican nation."[11]

So the Fifth Sun of the Mexicas was extinguished. The Mexican people have been awaiting the advent of the Sixth Sun ever since.

474 years later, on the eve of the annual commemoration of the fall of Tenochtitlán—an event that brings hordes of Aztec revivalist troupes to the Zócalo of Mexico City—the irreverent Luis González de la Alba added a devastating postscript in his weekly *La Jornada* column: "The fall and destruction of Tenochtitlán which we celebrate [sic] tomorrow was the result of a popular and multitudinous uprising of all the nations between Veracruz and this city, against the fierce repression of the Aztec Empire. By 1521, the Aztecs had inflicted humiliation upon its subject peoples with a ferocity never achieved by the Nazis…"[12]

Despite his defeat, the myth of Cuauhtémoc grew dangerous during his captivity. When he refused to reveal the locations of alleged Aztec treasure troves, Cortez had the Descending Eagle tortured, feet to the fire—a martyrdom exalted by David Alfaro Siqueiros's monumentally muscular mural enshrined in modern-day Mexico's maximum house of culture, the Instituto de Bellas Artes.

REMAINS

There are a few footnotes to this tale of torture and treachery. Three years after he had taken Tenochtitlán, Cortez set off on an expedition south to punish renegade conquistadores who were opening up unauthorized branches of the Conquest in Honduras. Even hobbled as he was by his ordeal, Cuauhtémoc was deemed too much of a troublemaker to leave behind. Paranoia weighed heavily on Cortez's caravan. Finally, in La Venta, on the Tabasco coast, at a spot known as Itzamcanac, in the province of Acalan, the Captain General's mistress, La Malinche, convinced her lover that the former emperor was scheming against him and Cortez had Cuauhtémoc hanged "upon a ceiba tree in front of the house of idolatry" and decapitated.[13] Father Motolinia, the legend goes, subsequently gathered up the Descending Eagle's remains and returned them to Ixcateopán, his designated birthplace in the north of what is now Guerrero state, where they were buried under the altar of the local church and worshiped for more than 400 years by the villagers. Then, in 1940, a drunken priest confessed the town's secret to the *Excelsior* newspaper and the bones were dug up to become a local tourist attraction.[14]

Cortez's own bones suffered an equally disappointing fate. As his worth to the Crown declined from year to year, the Conqueror's standing in New Spain fell precipitously. His arrogance and his failure to divvy up the spoils of the Conquest in an equitable fashion did not enhance his popularity. Accused of a string of mysterious murders, he was summoned back to Spain and, although he later visited the New World as perhaps the richest man in the Americas, the Conquistador had lost all political power and finally returned to the motherland where he expired of excess in 1547. His bones were eventually returned to the land he had "discovered" with little fanfare. Five centuries later, there are no monuments to the Conqueror in Mexico. His dust is walled up in a nondescript niche in the dilapidated Hospital of Jesús on El Salvador Street in the old quarter of the capital.

Hernán Cortez forged one other corporate merger that has long outlived his bones. Before putting in at Veracruz, the Conqueror had touched shore on the coast of Tabasco and bought himself a bargain consort. The high-born daughter of aristocrats from an Aztec vassal state, Doña Marina was possessed of linguistic talents and feminine guile that opened many doors—and treasure chests—for Cortez. Although he never acknowledged her as his wife (he had one, Catalina Suárez, reportedly a harridan, whom he eventually strangled),[15] and dumped her soon after she denounced Cuauhtémoc, Marina or "La Malinche," as she was more popularly known, bore him a son, the first mestizo—"the fruit of two cosmic races" as the Mexican revolution's benchmark intellectual José Vasconcelos would later describe the Blessed Event.[16]

Today, feminist revisionism alternately depicts La Malinche as a victim, or the true power behind Cortez's Pyrrhic throne. But the persona of La Malinche is more loathed than loved in contemporary Mexico—the bottom line is that Cortez's mistress betrayed her people and aided and abetted the most painful annexation of Mexico on the books. La Malinche remains a supreme symbol of submission to forced domination. Whether this submission was consensual, or the most brutal rape in the nation's history is a question that continues to dog the Mexican psyche. Nonetheless, her myth or curse has endured and even flourished, and, as the millennium closes down, La Malinche teaches us much about why Mexico has survived so intact as a culture.[17]

CONQUEST AS ANNEXATION

Having annexed central Mexico to the motherland, the Conquistadores filled in the geographical contours of New Spain with provincial conquests. Pedro de Alvarado and Bernal Díaz del Castillo annexed Indian lands all the way to Chiapas and Guatemala. Other tracked records of Aztec gold and silver tribute to their roots in the Chichimeca north. But Cortez & Company's insolence and brutality grated on Charles V's royal sensitivities. The Conqueror was lured back to the motherland and his dream of ruling New Spain defused.

His sons, however, both named Martín, continued to conspire to regain their authority in the colony. The first Martín, the offspring of a union between Hernán Cortez and a Spanish noblewoman, remained publicly aloof from the conspiracy, but the other Martín, the mestizo, half-Indian son of La Malinche, was seized by authorities and tortured.[18] Great quantities of water were poured down his gullet, a curious trick still practiced by Mexican security forces. The plot was crushed in 1568, and several of its perpetrators drawn and quartered in the Plaza Mayor, once Huitzilopochtli's killing floor and ultimately, the Zócalo. Although both Martíns appear to have escaped with their heads in place, the Age of the Conquistadores was finished. From now on, the King's Viceroy would run the show.

Spain ruled the New World through the Council of the Indies, headquartered in distant Seville. Closer to home, first the Audiencia and then the Viceroy exercised absolute dominion. The *cabildo* and the *ayuntamiento* were instruments of provincial administration. A "Royal Tribunal" imposed and interpreted European law. The Congregacíon allowed for forced relocation of the Indian population and the *repartimiento* provided forced labor. Taxation and tribute rolls were merely expropriated from Motecuhzona's government.

The Inquisition kept dissenters in line—Jews, blacks, rebel Indians, and other heretics were burnt alive in the Plaza of Santo Domingo in some of the most colorful *auto-da-fes* outside of the Iberian Peninsula. Also burnt alive were thousands of Aztec and Mayan codices. The fires of the Inquisition sought to obliterate Mexico's memory. "We found large numbers of these books of characters but since they contained nothing more than superstitions and lies of the devil, we burnt them," boasted Diego de Landa, Bishop of Yucatán, in 1566.[19] New Spain now wrote the history.

Annexation is first a question of land. Out in the countryside, the *encomiendas*, huge extensions ripped from under the Indians, were doled out to the Conquerors. Cortez's own kingdom stretched from southern Mexico City all the way to Oaxaca and he was paid tribute by 23,000 Indians annually. By the end of the 1500s, half the land in the Valley of Mexico had been transferred into Spanish hands through the mechanism of the *encomienda*. Newly-introduced herds of cattle reproduced exponentially, decimating fertile enclaves and munching their way across the landscape, their several stomachs digesting and annexing Mexico.

The Europeans did not hesitate to alter the geography to their liking. The forests on the valley's steep hillsides were clearcut to build up the city. Sediments rushing down the scarred flanks filled up the shallow lake and the newcomers filled in the rest to facilitate wheeled travel. The Spanish, mostly urban dwellers back home, had little use for the elaborate lake and canal system that was the Aztecs' most genuine conquest. Alien spores and seeds, inevitably carried from the old world, blew inland, overwhelming native Mexican vegetation. Today, native species are rare finds, having been annexed centuries ago by the Europeans' weird germ plasma. [20]

What lay under the land was even more diligently annexed. Mineral wealth was excavated by slave labor and loaded onto galleons to swell the coffers of the Crown. Beginning in 1546, just a quarter of a century after conquest, the Zacatecas silver bonanza found shape and weight in the world's major currencies. The Hapsburg kings took a fifth of the share from each ship that unloaded in Seville and financed military expeditions from the Low Countries to Brazil to feed their global ambitions, an arrogance that suffered an abrupt comeuppance with the defeat of the Armada by the British in 1588.

Spain annexed the people it had conquered to work on the lands it had annexed. At first, enslaving the Indians seemed the most expedient procedure: "a man's face, created in the image of God, has become but a piece of paper in this country," wrote the Franciscan missionary Vasco de Quiroga after witnessing the repeated face-brandings of Indian slaves.[21] Church progressives like Bartolomé de las Casas, Bishop of Chiapas, argued that the Indians had souls worth saving—although not quite on a par with *gente de razón* (people of reason). Like children, the *naturales* had to be protected from human predators. A decade and a half after the Conquest, de las Casas urged that African blacks be imported as substitute slaves. By 1600, more blacks than Spaniards were being shipped into the country and, by 1646, 150,000 Africans and Afro-Mestizos were censused, about a tenth of the total population. [22]

Although Indian slavery was outlawed in 1545, the practice continued unabated for centuries and its vestiges still exist on German-owned coffee plantations like Liquidambar in the Sierra of Chiapas.[23] The law was changed to read that only those Indians engaged in rebellious activities could be punished by tribute labor and so the great landowners fomented uprisings they knew they could crush, in order to keep their *naturales* in perpetual bondage.

The *haciendas*, autonomous agrarian complexes with their own resident armies of Indian labor *acasillados*, or attached to, the "big house," proved a much more effective scheme for keeping the urban centers fed than the sprawling *encomiendas*. The *obrajes*, or Indian workhouses, turned out rough cloth and pottery for domestic consumption. Although the Crown expressly prohibited manufacturing in the colony of New Spain, a policy of mercantile imperialism that dictated all consumer goods must be imported from the mother country, the *obrajes* flourished and became the industrial foundations for important colonial cities like Puebla and Vallodolid (later Morelia).

CENTURY OF PLAGUE

The Hapsburg annexation was propelled by death. The whip, the dogs and the sword subdued those who refused to submit to progress. "Who can deny that the use of gunpowder against the Indians is like burning incense to Our Lord?" Gonzalo Fernández de Oveido inscribed in his notes of the day.[24] Those left standing on the battlefield wasted away at home, dying of catastrophic European diseases the Church regarded as divine punishment for Aztec cannibalism.

In the first 100 years of the Conquest, the time it took for the indigenous people of Mexico to develop immunities, 19 major epidemics touched Mexico with their feverish fingers: typhoid, plague, measles, mumps, influenza, pneumonia, and a hemorrhaging disease, "Cocoliztli," unknown in Europe, wracked the poorest of the poor, but it was smallpox that reigned triumphant, killing off 845,000 Indians in just a few weeks in 1545. In retaliation, the Indians infected their conquerors with syphilis, which soon crossed the sea to scourge the Old World.

The dimensions of this annexation by plague are almost beyond human comprehension. An estimated 12.5 million Indians peopled what would eventually become the nation of Mexico on the morning Cortez waded ashore at Veracruz.[25] A century later, only 1.2 million remained. Nearly 12 million indigenous peoples and their cultures died in this holocaust, twice the number who perished during Adolph Hitler's heyday. Only in this century have Mexico's *indígenas* begun to approach their pre-Conquest numbers.

Yet, despite more than half a millennium of genocide, racism, marginalization, and what the United Nations terms "extreme poverty," Mexico's Indians, from the time of the Emperor Cuauhtémoc to the Zapatista Army of Liberation in the jungles of Chiapas today, have never forgotten whose country this really is. In the long run, it is the indigenous peoples who have most fiercely and tenaciously resisted the annexation of Mexico.

LA GUADALUPANA

Thus the annexation of Mexico proceeded on every front—economically, administratively, militarily and environmentally, but of all the annexations inflicted upon Mexico by the interlopers, the spiritual conquest was the most enduring. In a single decade, the Europeans managed to eclipse a 2000-year-old belief system, imposing their "Christian" strictures upon the "Satanic idolatry" that had served the Indians for millennia. But the orgy of conversion never really obliterated the old ways.

The Franciscan missionaries came, trampling on Cortez's heels. The first to arrive called themselves, significantly, The Twelve, and "insisted on walking barefoot the entire 200 miles to Mexico City."[26] By 1523, they were already pulling down the blood-stained stones of the Mexica temples and throwing up Christian churches and monasteries throughout central Mexico. The Church quickly annexed Tenochtitlán's prime religious real estate—the twin temples of Huizilopochtli and Tláloc, which were torn asunder and reassembled as New Spain's first cathedral. The Dominicans, who won the southern franchise, dotted the Oaxaca countryside with enormous hangar-like structures where their gloomy God was said to lurk.

Often, the Christians simply annexed the old gods who had previously been celebrated in these precincts and rechristened them with the names of the saints. Father Motolinia complained that the Indians deliberately buried their idols under the altars and, when, as in Ixcateopán, they prostrated themselves before the Virgin and the Son, they were really invoking pagan deities.[27] Was this heresy?

De las Casas thought not. Where other bishops saw abomination, the Bishop of Chiapas (1540-46) saw Jesús Christ. Defending himself from his detractors in a letter to the Oaxacan Dominicans, Don Bartolomé justified human sacrifice as the ultimate giving of one's self to God.[28]

The most profound example of this syncretic imposition occurred on a December day in the year of Our Lord 1531, the tenth year of the Annexation, upon Tepeyac Hill in what is now northern Mexico City. Juan Diego, an aristocratic Aztec, rumored to be the grandson of Nezahuacóyotl, the poet-king of Texcoco, paused to pray for the health of an uncle at the temple to Tonantzín. But instead of encountering the Mexica earth mother, the Indian was embraced by Her Christian representation. "Give me a space in your heart and in your land," the Virgin, who was impressively dark-skinned, purportedly purred to Juan Diego, instructing him to go straight to the Bishop with a request to build Her a chapel on the top of Tepeyac Hill. But Juan Diego demurred: "I am the last, the tail, a man of the countryside. Who will believe me?"[29]

Thrice the Indian sought out Bishop Juan de Zumárraga, Apostolic Inquisitor and Protector of the Indians, and thrice he was denied an audience.

Trudging back up Tepeyac Hill, humiliated by the Bishop's refusal to listen to an Indian, he wept because he had been unable to fulfill his mission. But the "Brown Madonna" had a new plan and implored Juan Diego to take roses, suddenly blooming on a dry December hillside, to the Bishop and plead Her case just one time more. The Indian obediently wrapped up the roses in his cactus-fiber tunic (*ayate* or *tilma*) and went again to the Cathedral to seek out the prelate. When he unwrapped the garment in de Zummaraga's presence, a perfect image of the Virgin had miraculously imprinted itself upon the fabric.

Four-and-a-half centuries later, the *ayate* hangs under glass high above the altar of Mexico City's modernesque, carousel-shaped basilica, the most visited religious shrine in Latin America. Millions of faithful come to gaze upon the garment yearly, propelled by a people-mover that whisks the worshippers past the relic. Many have crawled here for days on their knees just to pray before the tunic.

The apparition of the Virgin of Guadalupe was the cornerstone of the evangelization of Mexico and Latin America. Yet even the Virgin's name is unadulterated syncretism—Tonantzín's local name was "Coatlatica" or "Coatlazupeo," translated to its nearest Christian cognate, it becomes "Guadalupe."[30] Nonetheless, just as the silver lodes of Zacatecas would soon generate incalculable wealth for the secular kings, the Guadalupana reaped a bonanza of souls for the Lords of the Church. In 1536, five million Indians were converted from heathen idolatry to the Roman Catholic version of Christianity, five times the harvest of the previous 15 years of conquest and annexation. Just how many of the newly faithful expired in the epidemics that accompanied their baptisms, is unknown.

Was the apparition of the Brown Madonna on Tepeyac Hill December 12th, 1531, a trick played by the Franciscan friars on the *naturales*? Rome does not disagree with this interpretation of the "miracle." The Vatican sees nothing at all wrong with such subterfuge, so long as it brings the savages to Mass.

Down the centuries, the charming legend of Juan Diego and the Virgin has proved difficult to defend. For one matter, the Indian's existence is highly suspect. No proof of his physical presence has ever been offered to the Congregation for the Cause of the Saints, which is charged with Juan Diego's canonization—the Congregation has moved cautiously on certifying new saints ever since 1970, when Pope Paul eliminated such venerables as Christopher and George from the roster of the saints because their corporeal being had never been established.

The evidence weighs heavily against poor Juan Diego too. For 117 years after the reported apparition, the Indian's encounter with the Holy Mother received little ink in the chronicles of contemporaries—neither Hernán Cortez nor his Boswell, Bernal Díaz del Castillo, nor the Indianist Bishop de las Casas nor Juan de Zumárraga himself, to whom Juan Diego is said to have presented the miraculous *tilma*, notice his persona in their writings. Only the Friar Bernadino de Sahagún makes passing reference to the Cult of the Guadalupana and then only to sneer at it as "a Satanic invention to applaud idolatry."[31]

Times change. A century and more later, the Náhuatl *Nichan Mopohua*, the first written text to record the story of Juan Diego and the Brown Madonna, struck a chord. Guadalupe's appeal to the darker underclasses, the Indians and Mestizos and Mulattos indentured to the mines and the haciendas and the workhouses of New Spain, was universal. But Her banner was now taken up the by Whites as well—the *criollos* or Americanos who had been born in the New World and chafed constantly under the Spanish-born *Gachupines* (literally, spur-wearers) who ruled colonial society and for whom the fair-skinned Virgin of Remedios was a logo they had first carried into battle against the Aztecs.

By the 18th century, the Virgin of Guadalupe had been converted into the maximum insignia of incipient Mexican nationalism. The Brown Madonna's installation as the official Patrona of Mexico in 1737 ratified the first great fraud perpetrated on a people who have been repeatedly defrauded of their birthright by one swindling set of overlords after another.

Scientific scrutiny bears out the perfidy of the Franciscans' flimflam. Microscopic scans show that the skin tones of the Virgin on Juan Diego's *tilma* have been darkened, and her aureole touched up, by a human hand[32]—without these alterations, Guadalupe experts say, she bears a remarkable resemblance to a virgin from Extremadura, favored by Hernán Cortez. One account has the garment being painted by a talented young Indian named Marcos. This version, promulgated by scoffers like *Proceso* magazine senior editor Carlos Marin, advances that the *ayate* was worshiped during its early years, principally because it had been painted by a live Indian, not by a Christian god.[33]

Unlike the Mexicans, the Church itself questions the Miracle. Such apparitions as Guadalupe, Lourdes, and Fatima are not considered articles of faith and the Vatican has often been the most vocal debunker of the myth. Still, when the 80-year-old abbot of the Basilica of the Virgin of Guadalupe, the hemisphere's most profitable religious showplace, expressed his doubts about the legitimacy of Juan Diego's tryst with the Holy Mother, the roof fell in upon the poor man. *La Jornada* columnist Teresa Jardi, who once watchdogged human rights for the archdioceses of Mexico City, accused Guillermo Schulenberg of "stepping on the dignity of the Indian peoples" for whom Guadalupe is a sacrosanct symbol and a last resort in a time of deepening poverty in Mexico, a time when Her blessing is most needed.[34] Father Enrique Salazar, director of the Guadalupana Studies Institute, and the official promoter of the crusade for Juan Diego's canonization, called upon the Vatican to put an *Odium Plebis* (Hatred of the People) decree upon the head of the wealthy Schulenberg, the son of a bankrupt German count who was a close ally of the long-time arch-conservative, now-ex Papal Nuncio Giralamo Prigione here. "Schulenberg Traitor!" read wall writings in major Mexican cities, always the best barometer of public indignation. The moral of this homily: although belief in the Miracle of the Virgin of Guadalupe is not obligatory for the Holy Mother Church, a lack of faith and enthusiastic devotion in and to the Guadalupana can get one excommunicated from the Mexican race.

Defense of the Dark Virgin is tantamount to the defense of national sovereignty. To this extent, La Guadalupana has provided an antidote to the very annexation she herself once so haughtily imposed upon the true Mexicans.

RECIPE FOR UPHEAVAL

By the third century of European annexation, the balance between the annexer and the annexee was mutating wildly. Spain, battered by global misfortune and at the nadir of Hapsburg administration, was in freefall. New Spain was gathering a full head of steam. Between 1745 and 1810, the population of the colony doubled—from three to six million—as did its landsize, a growth that left the mother country far behind. Emulating their Conquistador ancestors, the Army of New Spain, accompanied by the obligatory missionaries, marched north to subjugate, convert, and annex the distant Indian nations of what is now California, New Mexico, Texas, Arizona, Colorado, Utah and Nevada.

Some of the names of these newly-annexed-in-name-only nations are the Diné (Navajo, in the Spanish tongue), the Hopi, the Zuni, the Ute, the Paiute and the Washoo, the Chemehuevi, the Chiricahua, the Mescalero, the Cocopah, the Walapai, the Yuma and the Havasupai and the Yaveri, the Mohave, the Lipáns, the Papago and the Pima. To the north and the east on the Great Plains were the Cheyenne and Comanche, the Kiowa and the Kaw, the Osage, the Kickapoos, the Pawnee, the Arapaho, the Kiowa Apache, the Jicarilla, the Yavapai and the Ponca. To the west, in California, the Royal Army claimed the nations of the Shoshones, the Monos, the Chumash, the Miwak, the Maidu and the Pomo.

Few of these nations were conquered militarily by the army of the Kings of Spain. By 1735, 7,000 "Mexican" settlers were clustered around the California missions and presidios. The Indians were invited to visit. The settlers, like their conqueror ancestors, had brought with them strange and virulent diseases and the *naturales* succumbed just as quickly as their southern cousins.

The dominion of "Nueva Galicia," (New Spain) stretched into the frozen north as far as Wyoming. Only Brazil occupied more of the Americas than this suddenly gargantuan colony that was soon to declare itself the United States of Mexico. The engine of transformation was trade. During the 18th century, the volume of trade between Mexico and the rest of the world increased sixfold. The Nao routes from the Philippines brought oriental treasures to the port of Acapulco in exchange for Guanajuato silver. On the Atlantic side, trade with the mother country showed a healthy surplus—largely due to silver production, revitalized by mercury refinement techniques. Meanwhile, under maladroit Hapsburg guidance, Spain had become little more than a conduit through which manufactured goods from northern Europe poured into Mexico.

The colony now weighed more then the empire, a poor prognosis for continued Spanish rule, and a change in management style was ordered. The Bourbon dynasty was more enlightened—it was, after all, the Age of Enlightenment—and understood that Mexico must be handled with great dexterity. Despite, or because of, its mercantile success, Mexico had become a tinderbox of class and racial tensions. Anchored deep down at the bottom of the ladder were five million Indian, Mestizo, Mulatto, and black Mexicans—80% of the population was considered non-white. As early as 1600, the Spanish saw the peril to the whiteness of their race: "we are surrounded by enemies who outnumber us," the King's Council Gonzalo de Cervantes wrote the court in abject fear of the darkening masses.[35] Hundreds of thousands of African slaves, hijacked from Gambia and Angola and the Cape Verde Islands, and brought to New Spain to replace the rapidly dying Indians during the 17th century, had ceaselessly intermarried and considerably Africanized Mexican blood lines. By 1819, Africans and Afro-Mestizos numbered 634,000, more than 10% of the total population.

To combat miscegenation and keep the coloreds in their place, the Colony's Spanish and Creole rulers constructed the most rigid racial barriers in all of the Americas—an apartheid that encompassed 16 separate castes with accompanying derogatory nomenclature—"mulattos," "zambos," "zambaigos," "castizos," "moroscos," "lobos," "coyotes" and "cambujos," amongst others—that precisely described the subject's parental mix.[36]

On the other end of the ladder were perhaps 20,000 very white "Gachupínes" and 10,000 upper-crust "criollos," who ran the store. Many had taken to buying noble titles and officer commissions from the Crown, which had put privilege on the auction block in order to raise a treasury against French invasion. A million more creoles ("Americanos") inhabited the rungs just beneath this elite, a standing about which they constantly grumbled.

In 1810, 100 families in the capital, and perhaps a dozen more in the provinces, could be considered the equivalent of millionaires (the peso equaled the dollar back then).[37] The ratio was not radically distinct in 1996 when the nation registered 15 billionaires and 42 million citizens living below the poverty line.

On the eve of insurrection, Mexico had become one of the richest countries on the planet, and also one of the poorest. "This country is divided between those who have everything and those who have nothing" warned the Bishop of

Morelia.[38] "Mexico is a land of inequities," Baron von Humboldt noted in his voluminous diary. The German traveler was as impressed by the 30,000 home-less who slept on the streets of Mexico City each night as he was by the archi-tecture and the urbaneness of this New World Calcutta.[39]

The expulsion of the Jesuits from Spain's New World holdings in 1767 trig-gered riots, led by the lower or secular clergy, that should have set off alarms. After Charles III died in 1788, the Bourbons blundered badly. Centuries of fric-tion between the Crown and the Church over the spoils of New Spain explod-ed with the imposition of the Consolidation, by which the Spanish state took over the collection of all Church loans and foreclosed on those debtors who could not pay up, thoroughly antagonizing the middle class criollos, and, more particularly, the already-disaffected secular clerics, whose families had pur-chased for them parish sinecures through such loans. In their frenzy to raise funds to fend off the French, the Spanish Bourbons squeezed its irritated colony for taxes against which colonists in nearby lands had already revolted. Add into this heady mix the cant of the newly-minted Declaration of Independence of the 13 English-speaking colonies to the north, and stir in the passion and excess of the French Revolution, and the recipe for upheaval was complete.

When, in 1808, Napoleon marched into Spain, the walls of Mexico told the story: "Beloved compatriots, fate has placed freedom in our hands. If you do not shake off the Spanish yoke now, you will be wretched indeed."[40]

¡VIVA MÉXICO! (LET'S GO KILL SOME GACHUPÍNES!)

Uprising, insurrection, rebellion, rejection, expulsion, separation, secession, revolution, independence, liberation, freedom, sovereignty, and nationhood are some of the concepts that define the process of dis-annexation. During the violent, final days of New Spain, a fledgling Mexico stepped from uprising to independence, but true liberation, sovereignty, and nationhood would prove elusive.

Although Spain lost all of the Americas, save Cuba and Puerto Rico, between 1808 and 1821, only in Mexico did separation from the mother coun-try produce cataclysmic bloodshed.

The writing was on the wall long before Napoleon crossed the Pyrenees. The Tumults of 1624 and 1694 had invoked the nightmare of *La Indiada*, that fearful breaking point when the Indians would finally set fire to the big house. The Jesuit expulsion and the famine of 1786 swelled the bad gas that was building up inches beneath the surface of the painfully lopsided Mexican class structure. The first conspiracy was disrupted in Mexico City in 1793, led by a priest, Juan Antonio Montenegro. Over 400 members of the lower clergy would take part in similar conspiracies until independence was won.

Surprisingly, the conflagration did not begin in the capital, but in a country town in the Bajío of Guanajuato, the fertile lowland swath beneath the plateau of the Valley of Mexico that still keeps the federal district fed. Miguel Hidalgo y Costilla was former rector of San Nicolas University in Valladolid. Reputedly the absentee father of three, Hidalgo was secular enough to have lost his job for gambling and wenching.[41] Imbued with the liberation theology of his Jesuit teachers, Hidalgo had been conspiring for months with comrades in nearby Querétaro but the date of the uprising—October 12th, 1810—had been compromised by infiltrators.

Thus, early on the morning of September 16th, the good father clanked the church bells and called the parishioners of Dolores to Mass to proclaim the independence of his nation with hoarse cries of "¡Viva México! Let's go kill some Gachupínes!"—a ritual now repeated with much commercial zest throughout Mexico on the eve of every September 16th ("La Noche Mexicana").

Padre Hidalgo's first act was to free the universally dark-skinned prisoners from the Dolores jail—the Zapatistas' first inclination was much the same during their January 1st, 1994 uprising in Chiapas. Then, with 10,000 enraged Indians, Mestizos, Mulattos, Castizos, Moroscos, and Zambos etc. tramping behind the Banner of the Virgin of Guadalupe, Hidalgo set off for the state capital. But the priest had little control over his "army." The mob rampaged through the Bajío, pillaging towns and butchering unlucky whites in their path.

There were 25,000 enraged poor folks swarming behind Guadalupe's banner when the gates of the silver capital of Guanajuato, the second largest city in all Mexico, were thrown down and the rabble poured into the streets. 300 gachupín and criollo burghers who sought refuge in the Alhondiga granary were slaughtered and the building set on fire by the patriotic arsonist, Juan José de los Reyes Martínez, a local miner, who is remembered by history as "El Pípila," and who, for ever after, has lent his nickname to taco stands specializing in barbecued meat.

The eruption from the bottom up out in the countryside quite terrified the capital. Creole sympathizers of independence were shaken by the volcanic anger of the underclass. The Royal Army, which totaled no more than 23,000 men (21,000 of them criollos) raced out to meet the dusky mob advancing on Mexico City. The battle was joined October 10th at Las Cruces. By now, Hidalgo's hordes had swelled to 100,000 strong, the largest army raised in Mexico since the Aztecs, but they were mostly armed with hoes and machetes, clubs, outrage, and blind faith in the Virgin of Guadalupe whose banner flew before them. 2000 crack Gachupín horsemen cut them down without mercy. When the standard of Guadalupe was snagged by the King's troops, She was lined up as if at a public execution and firing squads Swisscheesed Her image.

When the smoke thinned, Hidalgo was on the run, moving north, but he continued to raise hell and insurrection as he retreated. Finally, in April, just seven months after he had uttered the "Grito" that had unleashed three centuries of bottled-up fury upon the land, Hidalgo was captured in Chihuahua, excommunicated by the Church as a heretic and shot and decapitated by the Crown, which deemed that such double executions insured that the dead stayed dead forever. Hidalgo's head, its wild, white strands of hair tufting his tanned, bald pate, was subsequently hung from the Alhondiga grain house his faithful had sacked back in Guanajuato. As in the case of the Emperor Cuauhtémoc, the overkill backfired. Both martyrs are well-remembered in the Mexican pantheon.

A bloody counterinsurgency commenced. The Royal Army moved like a scythe through the provinces, torching villages and massacring the *campesinos* in a scenario that has been reiterated after failed insurrections throughout the history of Latin America, right up to the Guatemalan and Salvadoran travesties in our own time. But, down below, the revolution had deep scratch. José María Morelos y Pavón, a mulatto priest from the Michoacán hotlands, inherited Hidalgo's decimated army. Breaking the rebel force of less than 2,000 into manageable guerrilla bands, he went on the attack along the southwestern coast, capturing Oaxaca and Acapulco before he was seized and executed in 1815, trying to sever the Veracruz road. Vicente Guerrero, the son of black slaves, took up the torch, punishing the Crown's troops throughout the regions of Guerrero state in which guerrilla warfare has been continuing for nearly a millennium.[42]

Ironically, it was the Royal Army itself that finally called the hostilities off and paved the way for independence. A decade of uprising, massacre, and guerrilla counter-attack had exhausted a once-profitable enterprise and the *criollos* sued for peace. General Agustín de Iturbide, an architect of the brutal counterinsurgency against the *guerrilleros*, and his old nemesis, Guerrero, struck common cause in the Plan of Iguala, jointly calling for independence from Spain and the establishment of a Catholics-only constitutional monarchy in which all Mexicans (except those who refused the Mother Church) would presumably be equal. Iturbide rode triumphantly into Mexico City on September 27th, 1821, precisely 300 years after Cortez had captured Cuauhtémoc and extinguished the Aztec sun. Iturbide immediately crowned himself emperor.

11 years had elapsed since Father Hidalgo had hoarsely screamed "¡Viva México!" into that September Bajío morning and 600,000 Mexicans,[43] most of them poor and dark-skinned, were dead. Mexico had, at last, shaken off annexation, but the freedom that it had won at so exorbitant a price belonged to only a very few.

Chapter 2

AN AMERICAN OBSESSION

From the Founding Fathers to the "Halls of Montezuma"

The paranoid is absolved of his affliction when the worst case scenario comes true. Mexicans have been looking over their shoulders fearfully, anticipating the next incursion from the north, for 150 years now. It is an obsession that does not wear thin despite all the NAFTAs on the Christmas tree.

The annexation of Mexico has been a gleam in the North American eye ever since the Founding Fathers stalked the land. Partially accomplished in 1848, the threat—or promise—weaves its insidious threads into the fabric of daily life south of the Río Bravo. In Mexico, the gringos never go home.

But as obsessed as Mexicans are by the specter of annexation at the hands of the United States of North America, the annexation of Mexico is only one strand (albeit a recurrent one) in the U.S.'s thickly-braided obsession with annexing the known universe.

EXPANSIONIST DELIRIUM

The Founding Fathers broadcast their intentions almost as soon as they disembarked at Plymouth Rock: "God hath thereby cleared our title to this place," wrote John Winthrop in 1633,[1] commenting on a smallpox plague that had "disappeared" Massachusetts' Indian population. By "this place," Winthrop meant everything beyond this place too, north, south, and west.

Cotton Mather's 1699 treatise on "The Faith of the Spanish Christians" reiterated the divinity of the colonists' mission to annex the New World and railed against Mexico as "a fanatically Papist land," laying the spiritual foundation for crusade and forced conversion.[2] A half-century later, Ben Franklin saw national security as a rationale for annexation—expansion to the American nation's natural boundaries would cushion the threat of European invasion.

Although the 1763 Treaty of Paris, which ended the French and Indian Wars and removed the former from the eastern portion of the North American mainland, defined for the colonies their New World neighbors, Franklin remained vigilant. In a conversation with colonial administrator Lord Shelbourne in 1766, as reported in a subsequent epistle to his son, William, Old Ben advocated expanding colonial settlement to the Mississippi River because control of that waterway would permit "strength to be easily poured upon the lower country and into the Bay of Mexico to be used against Cuba or Mexico itself..."[3]

The promulgation of the Declaration of Independence and the victorious six-year war that concluded with British surrender at Yorktown on October 17th, 1781, forcing King George to recognize U.S. sovereignty, seemed to immediately sharpen the new nation's appetite for expansion. "No pent-up Utica constricts your powers/ but the whole boundless continent is yours," waxed revolutionary war poet Jonathan Mitchell Sewell.[4] Conquest is not complete without heroic poetry to lionize it.

"Our confederation must be viewed as the nest from which all America, north and south, will be peopled," Thomas Jefferson, the Father of U.S. Expansionism, informed Archibald Stuart, a fellow Virginia slave-owner in 1986,[5] as they hunkered down to frame the U.S. Constitution. Jefferson set his ambitions south and west. His government shelled out $15 million USD in 1803 to "purchase" "Louisiana" from the French, who had picked up the immense territory as war booty from the Spanish Bourbons. "The Louisiana Purchase" was a little like selling (and buying) the Brooklyn Bridge—neither the old nor the new "owners" actually owned the territory. But a century of systematic massacre of the indigenous peoples of the region, and the annexation of their "purchased" lands by force and trickery soon validated the bogus bill of sale, at least enough to satisfy history's lenient standards.

By 1806, Jefferson was suffering expansionist delirium: expansion to the Mississippi "causes us to broach the idea that we consider the whole Gulph Stream our water."[6] Jefferson's "Gulph scheme" was grounded in a loony, Ptolemy-like reading of geography—that the "gulph stream" was actually an extension of the great river itself. Such an interpretation was purposeful. By 1804, President Jefferson was already poring over maps of Mexico, brought to him by Baron von Humboldt, who had purloined them from Mexico City's College of Mining.[7] The coordinates of annexation were being plotted.

The Louisiana Purchase "provides everything essential to the sovereignty of our country and the peace, prosperity, and happiness of our people," James Madison wrote Secretary of State Monroe in 1804.[8] But even as quill was being pressed to parchment, the gobbling of fresh territories was contemplated. Western Florida was seized from the Spanish in 1808. Six years later, Andrew Jackson, "Ol' Rough and Ready," rode through the eastern portions, annexing the souls of the Seminoles for God and country, erasing their villages and pushing the survivors into the alligator-infested swamps on the pretext of hunting for escaped slaves.[9] "God and Nature destined that New Orleans and Florida belong to this great and rising nation" the Conquistador told a packed press conference.[10] The 1819 Quincy Adams-Onis Treaty formalized the U.S.'s first military annexation of contiguous territory and paved the footpath for future forays south.

Cuba was next on the Founding Fathers' snatch list. Although the isle had been swapped to Spain for Florida by Adams, the Secretary of State now catalogued Cuba as "a natural appendage of North America" and "virtually contiguous."[11] U.S. proprietary stupidity towards Cuba began right then and has not ended yet, perhaps reaching its most absurd decibel of shrillness in 1859 when William Seward, soon to be Lincoln's Secretary of State, claimed the island for the United States because "every rock, every grain of sand, were drifted and flushed out from American soil by the floods of the Mississippi..."[12]

"America's" escalating southern ambitions hardly stopped at Havana. In a July 4th, 1804 editorial, Joseph Chandler's *Journal of the Times* declared the Isthmus of Panama as the U.S.'s natural southern border. "Where is it written in the book of fate that the American Republic shall not stretch from the Isthmus of Panama to the Hudson Bay?" the *Nashville Clarion*, intoxicated by the prospect of continental annexation, asked in 1812.[13]

"Poor Mexico, so far from God and so near the United States" has been an operative lamentation ever since the births of both nations. Ironically, the gestation of Mexico's break with the Mother Country was urged on by the delivery of the 13 colonies from the English Crown. Copies of the insurgents' new U.S. Constitution circulated among the Mexican conspirators as a model for their own. "The United States is almost our guide," confessed the *guerrillero* priest José María Morelos.[14] In 1810, an overly sanguine Miguel Hidalgo, preparing for the victory of his aborted underclass uprising, optimistically dispatched Bernardo Gutiérrez to treat with Secretary of State Monroe. A mutual defense pact, a free trade treaty and a loan were on the envoy's mind, but when he detected the glint of gold in James Monroe's eyes, Gutiérrez promptly resigned his commission and hastened back to Mexico to warn the then-fleeing Hidalgo of U.S. expansionist intentions. Two years later, after the drawing up of Mexico's first rebel constitution at Apatzingán, Michoacán, Morelos sent agents north to plead for Washington's support. Monroe, consumed by the War of 1812, could not find the time to see them.

"America's" Baby Huey-like gluttony for self-aggrandizement reached delusional proportions by the second decade of the 19th century. James Monroe supplied the rabble the rationale for hemispheric annexation. In his annual speech to Congress on December 2nd, 1823, the president bluntly told the world that the U.S. would no longer tolerate European intervention in the Americas: "the

American continents…are henceforth not to be considered subjects for future colonization by any European power," presumably reserving such enterprise for the government of which he was chief of state. Historians label the Monroe Doctrine as the U.S.'s first significant foreign policy initiative, but rather than "the uplifting call for a new world" that apologists such as Robert Pastor postulate,[15] the subtext of Monroe's Doctrine was merely the military and mercantile domination of the Americas.

John Quincy Adams put the true spin on U.S. intentions two years later: "the world should be familiarized with the idea (that) our proper domain is to be the continent of North America. From the time we became an independent people, it was as much a law of nature that this should become our pretension as that the Mississippi should flow to the sea. Spain had possession of our southern border and Great Britain was upon our north. It was impossible that centuries should elapse without finding their territories annexed to the United States."[16]

WESTWARD HO!

No cardinal point on the compass so obsessed the "Americans" as the West. It is the American Direction. As if beckoned by God's finger to a land of milk and honey just beyond the last hills, Americans marched towards the horizon, chopping down forests, taming the wild Indians, and claiming the continent for the White Man and Christianity just as surely as did Cortez when he planted the True Cross at Veracruz several centuries previous and a thousand miles to the south. It has been suggested that the pioneers were only looking for a place to rest—but if their frenetic behavior ever since is any indication, they never found one.

The Louisiana Purchase had opened the spill gates and, as if the nation were expanding into outer space, the western boundaries of "America" kept being pushed back, first beyond the Hudson, then the Ohio, the Mississippi, the Rockies, finally the Pacific Ocean. "The configurations of the earth no longer had any significance—the Rocky Mountains were mere molehills," wrote Massachusetts Congressperson Robert Winthrop, "our destiny is onwards."[17] In 1823, Senator Bayles rose to declare "Sir, our natural boundary is the Pacific Ocean,"[18] but as the century and U.S. ambition for domination matured, the drive west even transcended that pristine puddle. "We are stretching out our hands for what nature meant must be ours"—now Senator Denby was referring to Hawaii and the Philippines.[18] Senator Beveridge was even clearer about annexing this New West. When some upstart reporter pointed out that the Philippines were hardly contiguous to the U.S. mainland, he responded "our Navy will make them contiguous…"[19]

Midway in the "Americans'" mad Westward Ho rush stood the northern half of Mexico. What had been the "Audiencia of Nueva Galicia" under the crown had been transformed into half the Mexican republic following independence in 1821. But whether these vast tracts really represented Mexico's north or the U.S.'s "manifest destiny" to overrun and possess the whole continent ("which Providence has given us for the development of the great experiment of liberty and federated self-government that has been entrusted to us"— John O'Sullivan, editor of the *Democratic Review*, who popularized the slogan[20]) was about to be put to the test. With the American steamroller pushing towards the western horizon, few citizens on either side of the line doubted who would be the eventual victor.

BORDERS

The process of annexation first requires borders that are sufficiently defined to be violated. Skirmishes over which side of the line one's army is encamped upon then become the pretext for taking the entire country beyond. Typically, an incident is provoked to justify an invasion that has long been organized by the aggressor nation. A few shots are fired in "self-defense." War is declared. The plot is a gratingly repetitive one in American history.

The U.S. has a sorry track record of such provocations against resistant Third World countries. The highly-suspect mining of the USS Maine in Havana harbor in 1898 (258 dead) gave William Randolph Hearst and President William McKinley a platform from which to urge the landing of U.S. troops on foreign shores. The 1964 Gulf of Tonkin pantomime ushered in the Vietnam war. But the granddaddy of this nefarious blueprint for conquest and annexation "from the Halls of Montezuma [*sic*] to the Shores of Tripoli" is what U.S. grade school history textbooks term "The Mexican War."

Texas was the border to be defined in blood. The Louisiana Purchase was deliberately ambiguous on this point. Indeed, the territory's inclusion as part of that deal is unclear—first the Spanish and then the Mexicans emphatically rejected this suggestion. The 1819 Adams-Onis Treaty ratified the annexation of Florida, but compromised on Texas. The eastern border of that vast plain (and the western edge of the U.S.) was set at the Sabine River, straddling Louisiana—but expansionists continued to insist the real border began where it is today: at the mouth of the river that is called the Río Grande in the U.S. and the Río Bravo in Mexico, across from the then-lonely outpost of Matamoros, Tamaulipas. Quincy Adams's concession to the Spanish on this issue excited jingoist hyperbole. Representative Trimble made the Capital dome tremble with stentorian rebuke of the Secretary of State: "the Great Engineer of the Universe has fixed the natural limits of our country and man cannot change them!"[21]

For the better part of the next two decades, Texas lay out there, festering under the relentless desert sun, like an enormous wound upon the pride of both nations. The slave owners wanted it desperately for King Cotton, and in 1822, Adams sent Joel Poinsett, a wealthy Mississippi planter, to Mexico City to pry it loose from the self-proclaimed emperor Agustín I (de Iturbide). To make his mission crystal clear, the special envoy arrived on a war ship. The reception was cool: foreign minister Lucas Alamán espoused Bolivarian ideals and linked Mexico's independence to the new nations of Latin America, a south-looking orientation that every succeeding U.S. ambassador through John Negroponte and Jim Jones has sought to turn around.

Poinsett's intrigues were legendary. He founded the York Rite Masonic Lodge, which, because of its anti-Church leanings, attracted radicals like the old *guerrillero* Vicente Guerrero—the York's parent lodge was the Grand Lodge of Pennsylvania. Adams' emissary probably fomented the 1828 Parian market riot, led by Guerrero, that stripped Spanish-born merchants of luxurious oriental wares, engendered massive capital flight and led to the abortive Spanish effort to reconquer Mexico the following spring.[22] Pursuant to President Andrew Jackson's instructions, Poinsett then offered Mexico arms and cash to defend itself, on the condition that Texas be ceded to the U.S. Poinsett was "obsessed" with the task of annexing Mexican territory, wrote then-Secretary of State Martin Van Buren.[23] The Ambassador was so intent on putting the North American imprint on the Mexican landscape that he even imposed his own name upon the nation's botanical nomenclature—the lovely flowering Christmas-time plant that in Spanish is called "nochebuena" (and in Náhuatl "xocoxochitl") is now known as a "Poinsettia."

Texas was a lot closer to becoming an independent slave-ocracy when, at last, Poinsett, a committed slave owner himself, was forced to abandon these exotic shores in 1830. His successor, Anthony Butler, universally panned by Mexican historians as a drunken lout, also had to exit the country hastily after he obstreperously demanded compensation for questionable damages allegedly suffered by U.S. citizens at the hands of Mexican authorities—in one such claim, cited by Josefina Zoraida Vázquez,[24] the Mexican Navy had suppressed a mutiny on an American ship, saving the U.S. captain's life, but Butler demanded damages because U.S. property had been trespassed upon. Despite the spurious nature of his claims, Butler's brow-beating demeanor succeeded in raising the compensation issue to a pretext for invasion (such claims were mentioned in Polk's 1846 declaration of war). Butler also bullied Mexico into granting the U.S. favored nation status—a precursor of the imposition of NAFTA a century and a half later.

Meanwhile, the infant Mexican state was having a hard time keeping a lid on an enormous, under-populated territory 1,200 kilometers to the north of Mexico City, where only 3,400 of the territory's 24,700 residents were of Mexican lineage.[25] Soon after the Adams-Onis treaty was inked, the Crown had relocated settlers from Florida and Louisiana to these deserts, among them the patriarch Moises Austin, around whose son Stephen the settler movement galvanized. The terms of settlement were liberalized by the de Iturbide government which winked at the proviso that the newcomers profess the Catholic faith.

Thousands of pro-slavery southerners streamed into Texas to make their fortune—by 1835, there were 35,000 of them in the territory, outnumbering the Mexican population seven to one. Revolts against Mexican authorities were a dime a dozen—in 1826, Hayden Edwards seized Nacadoches and, long before the Marx Brothers did so in the immortal "Duck Soup," proclaimed the town the Republic of "Freedonia."[26] Mexico City's campaign to increase taxes in the Texas territory sparked furious resistance. The last straw was the 1829 Colonization Law that formally barred slavery in the rebellious region. On March 2nd, 1836, Sam Houston, a Jackson confederate, ex-governor of Tennessee, and the leader of the Anti-Mexican Party, took San Antonio de Bejar, the most important Mexican city in the territory, and proclaimed Texas an independent republic.

In response, General Antonio López de Santa Anna, then in his fourth go-round as Mexico's president, raised a ragtag army, marched it 600 kilometers from San Luis Potosí and fell upon San Antonio to wrest it back from the rebels. "Death to the Gringos!" the Mexicans whooped as they slaughtered 183 mercenaries, cut-throats, and ex-convicts trapped inside the old Franciscan mission known as "El Alamo," now a shrine visited by tens of thousands of Mexicans each year. Amongst those who bit the dust were Jim Bowie, Davy Crockett and Buck Travis, each of them famous Indian killers whom Houston had hired to slap his volunteers into shape.

Days later, the Mexican general repeated the lesson, wiping out 300 Americanos at Goliad—but the two victories were not death blows to the Texas slave-ocrats. Houston regrouped quickly, caught the Mexican Army flatfooted near the city that now bears his name, at the battle of San Jacinto, and howling "Remember the Alamo!," drove "Santy Anny" back into Coahuila with his tail between his legs—not, however, before briefly taking the enemy commander prisoner and convincing him to sign a "secret treaty" (the first of many) which abandoned all Mexican pretensions to Texas. One sign of the treachery to come: Santa Anna returned to Mexico by way of Washington, where he huddled with Jackson, seeking to salvage his good name with the Americanos.

THE REDEEMER OF MEXICO

If for nothing more than inciting the nation's first military coup after "Emperor" Iturbide had refused to appoint him governor of his native Veracruz in 1822, the memory of Antonio López de Santa Anna is permanently framed in the Mexican Museum of Political Absurdities. This paranoiac, supremely self-centered Veracruzano won his spurs against a Spanish exploratory force hell-bent on re-annexing the former colony to the Crown in 1829. When 4,000 Cuban-based Spanish troops took Tampico in the spring of that year, Santa

Anna rounded up an army and swarmed up the swampy Caribbean coast to face a force that was already dropping like flies from Yellow Fever. For his victory over the Gachupínes, the general was dubbed "Conqueror of the Spanish" and *"Benemérito* (well-deserved) of the Republic"—other printable titles that accrued to Santa Anna during more than 30 years of public larceny and treason were "Supreme Dictator," "Perpetual Dictator," "Liberator of the Republic," "Redeemer of Mexico," and, ultimately, "His Serene Highness." Despite his well-deserved reputation for cowardice and betrayal, Mexicans invited him to be their president 11 times between 1822 and 1855—the nation endured 50 different governments during this same period. Some historians count only six actual Santa Anna administrations—but what is certain is that "His Serene Highness" etc. never served very long (only six-and-a-half years total) in any of his avatars as president. Once he had sufficiently looted the treasury, the administration of public affairs bored him silly.

General Santa Anna bounced back from the loss of Texas with typical aplomb. Having retreated to his estate at Mango de Clavo, the "Redeemer" was close at hand when, in 1839, the French shelled the port of Veracruz in the opening (and closing) salvo of the "Pastry War," so named because the invasion was decreed by Louis Felipe to collect an 800-peso bill incurred by the Mexican government when drunken soldiers invaded the shop of one M. Remontal, a French baker. But the dispute had more substance than mere puff pastry—locked in a commercial battle royale with the British, the French used this charade to force a free trade treaty on Mexico that would give France favored nation status, before the Brits petitioned for same. When, following an eight-month blockade of the port, President Anastasio Bustamante continued to resist the imposition and called upon Santa Anna to once again come to the rescue of the country, the French put ashore to take "His Serene Highness" hostage.

Shaken awake by the fighting, Santa Anna rode into the streets to save the *Patria*, reportedly in his underwear,[27] and a French cannonball took off his left leg beneath the knee. The loss of the limb obsessed Santa Anna for the rest of his days—and also hastened his return to the presidency as a national hero, in 1842. One of his first acts as president again was to stage a pomp-filled ceremonial funeral parade to the Santa Paula cemetery where the corpse of his leg was solemnly interred. Two years later, when the "Supreme Dictator" was driven from the capital by public outrage at his wholesale pilferage of the treasury, mobs invaded the graveyard, smashed open the cenotaph, and tore the leg to pieces.

TONKIN GULF ONE

The psychosis of Manifest Destiny north of what very soon would be the border had American politicians hurling acid and brimstone in a Mexican direction. The scapegoating of Mexico and its citizenry by Buchanan and Perot and Clinton and Dole in the 1996 U.S. presidential face-off was sweetness and light compared to the venom spouted both by Henry Clay and James Polk on the 1844 campaign trail.

The count-down to war began with Polk's narrow victory. As his final act in office, in March 1845, President Tyler annexed Texas to the American union and conflict was assured—although with whom was not at first clear. There are Texans who still consider the federal annexation a violation of the sovereignty of the Republic of Texas and are willing to go to war about it, as testified to by the April 1997 stand-off between Texas Republic zealots and that Lone Star state's Department of Public Safety in the Davis mountains, east of El Paso.

Although Santa Anna had acknowledged Texas's independence nine years previous, he now claimed to have done so "under duress"—The Redeemer's "secret treaty" was sealed while he was Sam Houston's prisoner at San Jacinto.

Now Tyler's parting gambit had annexed a big chunk of Mexico's national turf, but beset by Yaqui and Mayan uprisings at both ends of the nation and a treasury Santa Anna had thoroughly cleaned out, Mexico was slow to respond to the U.S. provocation.

The chronicle of the Mexican War is one of invasion foretold. By January, 1846, President James Polk was already drawing up a declaration of war. In February, he ordered General Zachary Taylor to advance his troops from the Sabine to the Río Grande, placing the U.S. Army on what Mexico still considered to be its soil. The maneuver provoked the desired results when, on April 25th, Mexican soldiers crossed the river from Matamoros and engaged in a fire-fight that left 11 Americanos dead. "The hostilities may now be considered to have begun," the general laconically telegraphed Washington.[28] Polk retreated into the Oval Office and added but one line to his previously-prepared war declaration: "American blood has now been shed on American soil."[29] By claiming that the troops had fallen on "American soil," Polk officially inaugurated the U.S. annexation of Mexico's northern half.

There were those who did not buy this hokum. "We don't have a particle of right to be out here. It looks like the government sent a small force on purpose to bring on a war," declared Colonel Ethan Hitchcock, a member of the expedition.[30] A lanky congressman from Illinois promptly introduced a series of "spot" resolutions on the floor of the House, demanding to know the exact "spot" where the U.S. blood had fallen.[31] Abraham Lincoln refused to be hoodwinked by Polk's "Tonkin Gulf" ploy every bit as much as did Alaska's Earnest Gruening and Oregon's Wayne Morse when Lyndon B. Johnson tried to cram the same crap down the throats of the 88th U.S. Congress in August, 1964. "This is one of the most unjust wars that will ever be waged by a strong country against a weak one," the soon-to-be Great Emancipator rumbled, calling Polk's declaration of war "the insane murmurs of a feverish dream."[32] Asked later if opposing the war might damage his presidential ambitions, Honest Abe replied: "would you have voted up what you knew and felt to be a lie?"[33]

Lincoln's basso profundo voice had echo. Up in Massachusetts, a young Henry David Thoreau refused to pay his poll tax in protest and was jailed for the most heinous act of civil disobedience since the Boston Tea Party. When Ralph Waldo Emerson visited the poky in solidarity, and asked what his friend was doing inside, Thoreau shot back "what are you doing out there, Ralph?"[34]

Other famous American authors saw it differently. After Polk carried Congress by 300 votes, the poet Walt Whitman, Lincoln's eventual eulogizer, wrote in the *Brooklyn Eagle* of "miserable, inefficient Mexico—what has she to do with the great mission of peopling the New World with a noble race? Be it ours to achieve this mission!"[35] As usual, U.S. conquest requires a bard to rhapsodize it.

THE HALLS OF MOTECUHZONA

The lopsided mismatch billed as the "Mexican War" was no contest from the opening bell. By 1846, the U.S. population weighed in at 17 million to Mexico's seven. The North American military numbered 104,000. From Manhattan all the way to New Orleans, 60,000 volunteers were recruited for the slaughter. Mexico listed 20,000 troops—and 24,000 officers—but the rosters were probably padded.[36] The Americanos had a count of 70 warships, the Mexicans six. On the day the war was finally declared, there were 1,839 pesos left in the Mexican treasury[37] and a U.S. arms blockade in Veracruz prevented the nation from acquiring arms even if they could find the wherewithal to do so. The "war" about to be waged was the U.S.'s first offensive one and the first in which a president would actually behave like the Commander-in-Chief. For historians of this Manly Art, the Mexican War was a proving ground for techniques, weaponry and manpower soon to be deployed in the U.S. Civil War. Indeed, Robert E. Lee was a member of the war party that took Mexico City and Jefferson Davis led the "Mississippi Rifles." Like Davis, a majority of the recruits hailed from deeply southern slave states where war fever peaked early.

Polk covered his political behind by assuring the American People that the war would be a short one, a matter of months—Democratic Party chances in the 1848 presidential elections depended on the brevity of the conquest. Where have we heard this one before?

To speed settlement along, the U.S. president sought a Mexican patsy. Admiral Alexander McKenzie was dispatched to Havana where Santa Anna was holed up for the winter and offered him $10 million USD to return and throw the war. "In exchange for ceding empty lands in the north," the U.S. pledged to refinance a Mexican government led by the Supreme Dictator.[38]

As always, the Redeemer was eagerly complicit—the U.S. blockade was lifted to allow him to slip back into Veracruz.

The U.S. offensive began in stages, on multiple fronts. Commodore Sloat sailed into San Francisco Bay on a foggy May morning with seven frigates full of marines, and annexed northern California. General Stephen Kearny hopscotched his troops from Las Vegas to Santa Fe to the Los Angeles basin where he and Indian-killer Kit Carson prevailed at the battle of San Pascual in December of '46, despite stiff opposition from the Angelinos. General John Wool moved 3,000 men unimpeded into the deserts of Chihuahua in October. Taylor had advanced south with 8,000 troops and laid siege to Monterrey the month previous. On March 2nd, 1847, the hulking General Winfield Scott landed 10,000 men at Veracruz. Much like Cortez's crews, the rough southern boys who came ashore had never seen such a gleaming, exotic city. The U.S.'s first invasion of a foreign land would be waged by rubber-neckers.

Scott traveled Cortez's path to the Halls of "Montezuma" (the Spaniard took less time to get there), and, like Cortez, Scott found allies amongst a populace highly disgruntled by the failings of its own governments. The *"Polkos,"* said to be Church agents miffed at extravagant war taxes imposed by Santa Anna who, once again, had been called upon to redeem the republic, cheered the progress of the invaders' advance on the capital. From the Yucatán came word that the creole elite, trying to hold off Mayan rebels in a deadly War of the Castes, would be only too grateful to be annexed by the intruders.

But many were disaffected by the invaders. As they marched uphill, the green-clad Americans were said to intone the popular tunes of their country; included among them was "Green Grow The Lilacs, Oh," purportedly the root of the epithet "gringo" which, ever after, has been hurled at the hated interlopers from the north.[39]

By August 20th, Scott—like Cortez, on or about the same date 326 years previous—was encamped just outside the capital. Having severed his supply lines to the coast, sustaining his army on the surrounding countryside (Cortez had burnt his ships to produce the same effect), and outnumbered by Santa Anna's soldiers inside the city, General Scott decided to deal before rushing into battle. His Serene Highness was offered a million dollars to take a dive— Scott raided petty cash and shelled out $10,000 on the spot[40]—but Santa Anna reconsidered his patriotic obligations at the last moment and threw his troops into the fray, taking 4,000 casualties but inflicting 900 dead and wounded on the gringos.

The most celebrated Mexican dead were martyred in battle on September 13th. 50 cadets from the Heroic Military College, soon to be eternally laminated as "Los Niños Heroes" ("the Heroic Children"), were charged with defending Chapultepec Castle, an impressive edifice that now towers over the Mexico City zoo. Legend has it that, rather than submitting to surrender, the lads clad themselves in Mexican flags and leapt to their deaths from the ramparts, perhaps the most poignant moment in the annals of Mexican nationalism. Nonetheless, most of the cadets survived the siege—only six actually took the plunge. Among the survivors was an apple-cheeked officer named Miguel Miramón.

Less fortunate than the defenders of Chapultepec were the San Patricios, 150 Irishmen, who, under the misapprehension that they were defending the Catholic Church from godless Protestantism, joined Santa Anna's army. 50 Of the hapless Irishers were hanged by Scott on the spot, in what is today the ritzy barrio of San Angel.

By nightfall on September 14th, The Redeemer and his government had hotfooted it to Querétaro and the Stars and Stripes flew over the National Palace. The U.S. had annexed the Halls of Motecuhzona.

One hundred years after these traumatic events, Harry Truman became the first U.S. president ever to set foot in the Mexican capital. Invited by his counterpart, Miguel Alemán, to bury the hatchet and cement commercial and military friendships that had been forged during World War II, Truman stood under the balustrades of Chapultepec Castle and returned the battalion flags the cadets had carried that fateful, humiliating day. The war was at last over, but Truman's visit would turn a new page on the annexation of Mexico.[41]

THE GREAT MUTILATION

Accompanying General Scott to Mexico City was President Polk's personal negotiator. Nicholas Trist was a disciple of Thomas Jefferson (he was married to the Virginian's granddaughter and had sat at Jefferson's deathbed). Trist thought he knew exactly what the U.S. wanted—rather than annexing all of this troublesome land, Washington would stake a claim on only the most strategic parts. In addition to the northern territories, Trist coveted the Tehuantepec isthmus, a narrow neck of Mexico that connects the Atlantic and Pacific, but he dropped that demand to speed up the finalization of the agreement. The Treaty of Guadalupe Hidalgo was signed in the Basilica of the Virgin with the same first name, on February 2nd, 1848, a day that will forever live in Mexican infamy. Santa Anna had taken the usual powder and left the humiliating ceremonies up to chief justice Manuel de la Peña y Peña who had been elected temporary president by the rump Congress in Querétaro, and who would soon resign that post so that he could resume his duties as chief justice of the supreme court and so ratify this nefarious document.

Under the treaty's harsh terms, the United States of North America annexed 1,527,241 square kilometers of what had been, for the past 27 years, (although mostly in name only), Mexican territory. The annexed lands were equivalent to the size of western Europe, and included 690,000 square kilometers of Texas and 830,000 in New Mexico and California. The United States acquired 100,000 Mexican citizens and 200,000 Native Americans, all of whom were soon despoiled of their land holdings by an advancing wave of white settlers. All or part of 10 U.S. states were carved from the booty: Texas, Arizona, New Mexico, Oklahoma, Wyoming, Colorado, Kansas, Utah, Nevada, and California—in the latter entity, gold had been discovered at Sutter's Creek in the northern foothills just a few days earlier but news of the find was kept secret from the Mexican negotiators. Between 1849 and 1860, California would produce 27 million ounces of gold.[42]

The terms, writes a bitter Joséfina Zoraida Vázquez, were "among the harshest imposed by a winner upon a loser in the history of world."[43]

In 14 months of active fighting, the U.S. had lost 13,000 men, 14% of its fighting force, an exceptionally high casualty rate—but only 1,700 of these fell on the field of battle (the rest expired due to tropical diseases). It also gained an empire. For the United States, a nation that pioneered such concepts as "body counts" and "cost effectiveness," the price was right. As compensation, Washington obligated itself to pay Mexico $15 million USD but eventually coughed up only about half that much.

Despite Trist's triumphant accomplishments, James Polk was uneasy. The smashing victory had re-stirred the dream that the Isthmus of Panama was North America's true southern boundary and angry voices on the floor of Congress demanded that the whole of Mexico be annexed. General Quitman, the military governor of Mexico City, estimated this would take 50,000 troops and a great many more months. But with the 1848 presidential race upon him, Polk was reminded that he had promised the Democrats a short, triumphal war and time was running out on him. Reluctantly, he sent the treaty on to Congress for ratification. Many were the expansionist voices demanding total annexation that boomed on the floor of the House and the Senate but, surprisingly, one politician who abstained from the fray was the arch-segregationist John Calhoun. The blustery South Carolinian feared that the incorporation of so many brown folks into North America would mongrelize the simple white-black slave-ocratic equation upon which the Confederacy was to be founded.[44]

In the end, the Treaty of Guadalupe Hidalgo easily passed Congressional muster and the gringos abandoned the Halls of Motecuhzona by spring. 150 years down the pike, the "Mexican War" only merits a few lines in U.S. history texts, usually inserted in chapters with titles like "From Sea to Shining Sea" in which U.S. westward expansion is glorified. Although Mexicans remain incensed and obsessed with the armed annexation of its northern territories—the event is still described in catastrophic terms here as "a permanent scar," "the great dispossession" and "the mutilation of the nation"—the cruel truth is that the "Mexican War" was only a pit stop for the American juggernaut as it smashed its way from ocean to ocean to complete the nation's "manifest destiny."

To be sure, the "Mexican War" was one of conquest. The loser lost 51% of its land mass and would never stand up to the Colossus of the North on a military battlefield again. Down the years, there have been gringos like Lincoln who named the annexation of Mexico for what is really was—armed robbery. Military historians, however, warn that the American people should not feel bad about committing this outrage. "We should not be colored (in our view of the Mexican incursion) by the spasm of guilt that seized us after the Vietnam conflict" writes General T. Harry Williams in *The History of American Wars*.[45]

TYING UP THE PACKAGE

The rest of this tawdry history, is still history, even if it only involves the tying up of loose ends. By 1850, for example, the border between the two Californias was marked out in monuments stretching from the Pacific, where Playas de Tijuana now sprawl, to the crossing of the Colorado and Gila rivers. But the markers did not stop freebooter William Walker from rushing across the new border and trying to annex first Baja California and then "the Republic of Sonora" in 1853 and '54. Despite having just swallowed half of the Mexican nation, the U.S., drunk on Manifest Destiny, wanted still more.

Santa Anna returned to the presidency for the 11th and final episode in his venal career in 1853. He arrived just in time to sit down with James Gadsden, a Florida railroad tycoon who had gained land title to half that future state as the government agent charged with removing the Seminoles to the reservations. Now representing President Franklin Pierce in pursuit of more of northern Mexico, Gadsden had been personally selected by Pierce's Secretary of War Jefferson Davis, a fellow southerner. Gadsden's opening offer was $50 million USD for Baja California, Sonora, Sinaloa, Durango, and Chihuahua, but he eventually settled for the Mesilla Valley of lower New Mexico and Arizona (then Sonora and Chihuahua), a tract that would allow for the completion of a U.S. intercontinental rail link from "sea to shining sea." Santa Anna took $10 million off the top for what is called the "Gadsden Purchase" in U.S. schoolbooks and "The Ceding of the Mesilla" in Mexican texts.

Despite the exclusion of Baja California from the Mesilla deal, the U.S. would never stop hankering over it, repeatedly offering to swap it for a write-off of outstanding debts. In the 1980s, one plan reportedly circulating on the periphery of the Reagan administration was a straight-up exchange of that peninsula for Mexico's then $103 billion USD foreign debt, a scenario revisited by Pat Buchanan in 1996.

Although the Tehuantepec isthmus was dropped from the Treaty of Guadalupe Hidalgo by Trist, Washington continued to entertain the dream of digging a canal between oceans from Veracruz to the Oaxaca coast. Finally, in 1857, with Mexico's liberals, under Benito Juárez, being dunned by European creditors for the repayment of certain short term loans, Foreign minister Melchor Ocampo and U.S. Secretary of State Robert McLane struck a dubious bargain. The U.S. was granted the commercial rights to the land bridge and even permitted to station its troops along the right of way to protect the investment, without prior notification to the Mexican government. The agreement itself was signed under the usual threat of invasion—President Buchanan had already asked Congressional permission to move U.S. troops into Mexico's north on the pretext of subduing marauding Indians. Mexico's sovereignty was only saved "fortuitously," as historian Joséfina Zoraida Vázquez notes, because a majority in a U.S. Senate, torn by the debate on slavery and secession, viewed the Ocampo-McLane Treaty as a ploy to expand the South's sphere of influence.[46]

Much as in the case of Baja California, the United States of North America has never lost its ardor to annex the Tehuantepec Isthmus. In 1997, Mexican president Ernesto Zedillo put the nation's maritime terminals and railways on the block and bidding was initiated for the ports of Salina Cruz, Oaxaca and Coatzacoalcos, Veracruz and the rail line that traverses the isthmus between them. Among the possible recipients are U.S. transportation giants like the Union-Santa Fe-Southern Pacific, now the biggest freight carrier in the world.[47]

The obsession of annexing Mexico still burns strong in the boardrooms of North America.

Chapter 3

ANNEXATION
BY COMIC OPERA

The gift of Guadalupe Hidalgo and its sequelae of "acquisitions" did not much abate the U.S. mania to absorb all of Mexico. A *New York Times* editorial, run under the no-nonsense rubric of "The Annexation of Mexico" in December 1860, argued that "The Mexicans, ignorant and degraded as they are," might welcome a U.S. protectorate "founded by free trade [even then the *Times* endorsed NAFTA], and the right of colonization so that, after a few years of pupilage, the Mexican state would be incorporated into the Union under the same conditions as the original colonies..."[1]

But, distracted by its brewing civil war, the United States could not yet consolidate these aspirations. The next chapter in the Annexation of Mexico would be written by old pretenders, the Hapsburgs, whose comic opera crusade to reestablish a resurgent royalist reign over the New World blossomed at precisely the hour that Mexico's powerful northern neighbor was torn asunder by secession and civil war.

TWO CIVIL WARS

Mexico's civil war (1857-60) is dwarfed by the prodigious bloodletting that began on the far side of the Río Bravo less than 20 months after its own had terminated. The self-preoccupied sense of destiny with which history is engraved in nations like the United States of North America, with little history of their own of which to boast, elevates U.S. fratricide to near biblical proportions. But civil war was just as traumatic for the life of the young republic to the south.

The run-up began in 1855 when the liberals, grouped around former Oaxaca governor Benito Juárez, overthrew Santa Anna for the last time—the old fox took refuge in Venezuela and never hoodwinked his troubled *Patria* again. Juárez, a Zapotec from the Sierra of Oaxaca, had once been called "an Indian of low degree" by Santa Anna in a Oaxaca city restaurant where the young law student was then waiting tables. Years later, following the Texas debacle, Benito Juárez took his revenge, denying the Redeemer of Mexico sanctuary in Oaxaca, a state which the Zapotec now governed.[2]

Now, with the Supreme Dictator on the lam for good, Juárez, a fierce anticleric, was free to move on the Church, an institution he considered to be at the root of all Mexico's demons. Four reform laws were promulgated to curtail the Church's power and confiscate its landholdings—the Catholic Church was purported to possess fully a quarter of the nation's land wealth. Although the Laws of Reform were incorporated in the Constitution of 1857, Juárez would have to wait eight years before they became fully operative, and then under the reign of a foreign emperor.

Benito Juárez and his team were classic liberals, even by neo-liberal definitions. They did not want to nationalize Church property, but rather to sell it off to private speculators and, indeed, many colonial church buildings in the capital's old quarter were bought up and leveled by speculators, a deed that Jonathan Kendell, a *Wall Street Journal* editor and presumably a champion of neo-liberal expediency, does not at all appreciate in his consummate history of the capital.[3]

The Liberals were "free thinkers," championed free enterprise and free market strategies such as free trade. They even sought, as President Carlos Salinas would 13 decades later, to "free up" Indian communal lands for private concessionaires—a process which, much as Carlos Salinas's 1991 revision of the land reform provisions of a constitution that borrows much from Juárez's, incited indigenous rebellion among the Yaquis of Sonora. Moreover, the liberals believed unflinchingly in what Luis González y González terms "the tutelage" of the United States.[4]

Despite the Liberals' aggressive defense of private property, the Conservatives, led by old Lucas Alamán, sensed that this Indian upstart threatened ancient privileges, and felt compelled to foment bloody insurrection. The civil war dragged on for three years and, for a conflict that was billed as being an ideological one, was marked by exceptional brutality on both sides. Not only were patients murdered in their hospital beds by marauding troops but so were the doctors who rushed to treat them.

Finally, the Conservatives, commanded by General Miguel Miramón, the survivor of the gringos' furious fusillade at Chapultepec Castle, grew weary of the slaughter and Juárez rode unimpeded into the capital in January 1861, declaring himself president of the Mexicans. His freshman counterpart, Abraham Lincoln, the upset winner of the 1860 U.S. election, recognized the Juárez government immediately and never wavered in his support of the Zapotec, a rough-hewn back-country attorney like himself, who had fought his best battles on behalf of the underdog.

But, like Lincoln, Juárez's convictions outshone his political skills. He immediately stirred the fury of the Church by trying to reinstate the Reform Laws—the Vatican labeled him a "heretic" for stripping priests of their clerical garb. Mexico was flat broke as usual and "the Indian" (as Lincoln's cohorts always referred to him) did what few other Mexican presidents have dared to do since, even when the nation has been forced to grovel at the toes of its foreign creditors—he suspended payments on the foreign debt for two years.

The British press responded by calling Juárez "a savage" and an "Ojibbaway."[5]

MONARCHIST INTRIGUES

The debt moratorium soon became the pretext for a bizarre crusade, orchestrated by Emperor Napoleon III, to brake the U.S. locomotive, now grossly puffed up by the annexations of 1848, before it gobbled up all of Mexico and the lands below. But Napoleon's ultimate goal was even more problematic: the restoration of monarchist rule in the Americas, a lunatic misreading of history made possible only by the Emperor's royal megalomania and the coming Union-Confederacy butchery in the U.S.

As a wise contemporary, Karl Marx, inscribed in *The 18th Brumaire*, history the second time around invariably invokes farce.[6]

Lincoln's surprise election was a catalyst to the monarchists' schemes—they correctly suspected that he would polarize the slavery-abolitionist debate, force the eleven states of the Confederacy to secede, and considerably weaken the Union's commitment to defending the Monroe Doctrine. Napoleon (Bonaparte's nephew), his empress Eugénie, Archduke Franz Josef of Austria, Isabella II of Spain's restored Bourbon dynasty, Queen Victoria, and even Alexander of Russia concurred that the moment was fortuitous for royalist reinstallation. The blueprint was drafted by Prince Klemons von Metternich, Henry Kissinger's role model,[7] and centered on the occupation of Mexico and the restoration of an imperial regime; material and economic aid and eventual recognition of the Confederacy as an independent state; the gradual re-introduction of monarchism in America; and the suppression of all republican regimes in the western hemisphere.[8]

The bedfellows in this international conspiracy were strange ones. The interests of southern Protestant planters and Mexican Catholic conservatives coincided with those of European royalists. The American groups shipped delegates to the continent to hammer out the shape of the arrangement. José Gutiérrez de Estrada, a Mexican nobleman ousted by Juárez, courted the southern slave owners, suggesting that Negro slavery might be reinstated in Mexico—you will remember that it was banned in 1829 to keep these same southern slaveowners out of Texas. De Estrada appealed to Napoleon to send the beleaguered Mexican people a European emperor to save them from god-less liberal debauchery.

In October, 1861, representatives of the Spanish, French, and British Crowns (Queen Victoria was already building iron ships for the Confederate Navy) met in London to organize a tripartite debt-collecting mission to Mexico. Spain jumped the gun when, in December, Count Juan Prim, who had ambitions of becoming the first reconstituted Viceroy of Mexico, landed 4,000 Cuban-based troops in Veracruz.

Benito Juárez, like Motecuhzona centuries before, sent envoys to treat with the European invaders. Britain and Spain were appeased with promises of priority payoffs and withdrew. France, which had both an ulterior motive and a penchant for belligerent debt collection (recollect the Pastry War), demanded immediate settlement. Now the debts were more outstanding than in 1838. Among the collectibles was a 3.7 million-franc-loan to Conservative General Miguel Miramón, granted just days before Juárez seized the capital, at 2,000% interest. Because the Swiss banker who had underwritten this usury did not have a navy to sail out and dun the Mexicans, he had offered Napoleon a 33% share upon collection.[9]

THE ITINERANT REPUBLIC

The French invasion began in earnest in the spring of 1862. In the war-ravaged United States, the Confederacy had won the Battle of Bull Run and seemed invincible. Southern cotton was baled high on the piers of Matamoros where foreign ships carried it away, around the Yanqui blockade, to European markets.[10] In those first exhilarating days of victory, it was not untowardly optimistic to consider a victory by the South and the establishment of a contiguous slave-ocracy extending all the way from Washington D.C. to Mexico's southern border. Meanwhile, Lincoln, committed to fighting "one war at a time," had no ships to spare to extend his blockade of Confederate ports to Matamoros, Tampico, and Veracruz to defend both his ally Juárez and Monroe's Doctrine.

The French army followed the route of Cortez and Winfield Scott up from the beach, but on the morning of May 5th ran into heavy resistance by unexpectedly tough Mexican troops on Guadalupe Hill, just outside Puebla. Under the command of Generals Ignacio Zaragoza and Porfirio Díaz, the Mexicans— the majority were barefoot *indígenas* from the Zacapoaxtla Sierra who, under the Law of the "*leva*," had been press-ganged into action—held the day, and forced the invaders to pull back to Córdoba and Orizaba. The Battle of Puebla is, of course, still celebrated each May 5th in Mexico by colorful re-enactments of the rout, and, in the United States, by Chicanos, as a sort of Mexican-

American national holiday, with conspicuous sponsorship from both Mexican and U.S. beer companies.

Napoleon III played the patriotic panic card and converted the defeat at Puebla into a call for recruitment—30,000 troops came over during the winter of '62-'63 to avenge the stain the Zacapoaxtlas had inflicted upon French national honor. Under General Achilles Bazaine, the invaders swept through Veracruz, launched a 70-day siege of Puebla, and rolled down into Mexico City, taking the capital a little more than a year after the much-celebrated Mexican victory. Juárez, resolved to save the instruments of governance, declared the republic an "itinerant" one, and retreated north, pursued by Miramón and Bazaine. Borrowing a page from Hidalgo and Morelos and his own civil war campaign against this same Miramón, the president broke up the federal army into guerrilla units that would punish the French for the next four years and eventually repel their flawed crusade to annex Mexico and reestablish monarchy in America.

THRONE OF MOTECUHZONA

The French entry into the capital should have awakened the invaders' suspicions. "The people are attracted by curiosity, not enthusiasm," wrote Captain Pierre Henri Lozillon. "The few demonstrations [of support] are organized by the police."[11] Church bells pealed eerily day and night throughout the otherwise silent city. French troops enjoyed the same icy reception as they fanned out into the provincial capitals.

Despite the unappetizing welcome, the stage was being laid for the *piece de résistance* in this intercontinental comic opera: the return of monarchy to the Americas. Groomed for the starring role was Archduke Maximilian, Franz Josef's troublesomely liberal sibling (Maximilian was forced to renounce his right of succession to the Austrian throne before he sailed off on his Mexican adventure). A thin, blonde, ascetic chap of 32 who subscribed to the "Noble Savage" school of the Americas, Maximilian was not, on the face of things, the most absurd candidate for the Crown of Motecuhzona: had not the Hapsburgs once conquered and ruled the mighty Aztecs?

Maximilian had even bigger plans for the new world. Not only would he restore the Hapsburg dynasty in Mexico, but he would create a league of American royalty stretching from the Confederacy to Brazil, where his distant relative, Dom Pedro, reigned as emperor. The Archduke's accomplice in this fairy tale enterprise was Carlota, the daughter of Belgium's King Leopold and granddaughter of Louis-Philippe, a high-strung, ambitious disciple of the Empress Eugénie, Napoleon III's consort. One of the royal couple's first political collaborations was to compose a book of etiquette for their new Mexican court.

But Maximilian's liberal leanings and needy ego demanded that the Mexican people first conduct a plebiscite on the establishment of a monarchy. Favorable results were dutifully arranged (electoral fraud even then was a local art form) and Maximilian and Carlota were officially invited to crown themselves Emperor and Empress of Mexico.

After a bumpy, insect-plagued journey up from Veracruz, the royal couple entered Mexico City in May 1864 from the north, passing through the Basilica of the Virgin of Guadalupe where Archbishop Labastida, taking no chances on a repeat of the cool welcome extended the French army the previous year, drummed out tens of thousands of worshippers to celebrate their arrival. "These Mexicans are so strange. For anyone who does not know them and is foolish, their ovations and their flatteries are intoxicating. They will sweep them off their feet and then destroy them," Juárez, who had moved his "itinerant republic" all the way to the city that now bears his name on the northern border, remarked knowledgeably.[12]

TROUBLE AT THE CASTLE

By Spring 1863, the tide was beginning to turn in the U.S. Civil War. Grant seized Vicksburg in May and the Union held at Gettysburg in June. Juárez hurried south too, occupying towns as soon as the French abandoned them. Meanwhile, Maximilian had no sooner settled in than Napoleon began to pester him for the 260 million francs still due France. The French Emperor also demanded that he be given the mineral-rich state of Sonora as his own personal duchy. Maximilian disaffected the Confederacy by refusing to recognize the secessionists, choosing to remain neutral in the civil war up north. The Throne of Motecuhzona offended the Church too, by refusing to nullify the reform laws. Archbishop Labastida lamented that Maximilian was no better than the Liberals—a perception the Emperor confirmed one September 16th when he traveled to Dolores, Guanajuato to cry out Padre Hidalgo's grito "¡Viva Mexico!" (Let's go kill some Gachupínes!) One added insult to the Conservatives: Maximilian also had cast the first statue of the martyred guerrillero José María Morelos y Pavón.

There were ugly scenes at the royal court too. The Austrians were offended by the Mexicans' lack of punctuality. Mexican courtiers were not allowed to use restrooms reserved for the Europeans. The word "nigger" was uttered at royal balls. Maximilian seemed immune to such mundane matters. He and Carlota were sprucing up Chapultepec castle and redecorating the entire city. Still the malaise extended into their love nest—Carlota moved into a separate bedroom. Both had taken lovers—Maximilian, the gardener's wife, and Carlota, a dashing Austrian officer whose child she most probably bore.[13]

CRUMBLING CONFEDERACY

By 1865, the Confederacy was on the run and whining for Europe and Mexico to come to its rescue. A desperate Jefferson Davis, despite having been a gung-ho "Mississippi Rifle" volunteer for the Americans' annexation expedition, now pledged respect for Mexico's pre-1848 territorial integrity and renounced the pretensions of the Monroe Doctrine. If a southern victory could be pulled out of the fire, both the Confederacy and the European emperors suggested the 1.5 million square kilometers that had been separated from national territory by the gringos would be returned to Mexico.

In a remarkable letter, reprinted in the invaluable *Lincoln and the Emperors*, E.L. Hardy, Austrian vice consul in Richmond, endorses Mexico's domain as extending from Honduras to Oregon. California would be returned to the Empire rather than be allowed to fall into the hands of the hated Abolitionists. Hardy even mentions buying out the Mormons and re-incorporating Utah in the new, re-enlarged Mexico.[14]

But the Confederacy's tormented struggle had run its course. At the last second, Napoleon considered replacing Davis with a "Southern Crown" but could stir little Confederate support for the concept. Lee surrendered at Appomattox on April 9th. A week later, Lincoln was dead.

In the aftermath of defeat, panic-stricken Confederate officers—"gentleman soldiers"—fled to Mexico and pleaded for sanctuary from Emperor Maximilian who granted them their own colony near Córdoba, Veracruz, modestly baptized Carlota. Among the first refugees were General John Magruder and California supreme court justice David Terry—Mexicans in the region still claim descent. The southern gentlemen sipped juleps at the Confederate Hotel in Córdoba and planted cotton and tobacco, but soon went bust without sufficient slave labor.[15] At the other end of the South's social ladder, ragged rebel troops streamed across the border, were fed by Juárez's army, and joined up to fight their former commanding officers. Lincoln's successor, Andrew Johnson, free of the burdens of civil war, sent arms and ammunition to Juárez's revitalized army.

THE FAT LADY SINGS

Just as it did for Mr. Lincoln, the Union's victory sounded the death knell for the French re-annexation of Mexico and thoroughly cooked Maximilian and Carlota's geese. By late 1865, Juárez occupied most of the countryside, pinning the Emperor down in the capital where he was not happy. Across the Atlantic, Bismarck's Prussia was goose-stepping on the eastern front and Napoleon was forced to re-think his pledge to maintain 20,000 French troops in Mexico through 1867. U.S. Secretary of State Seward's thinly-veiled threat reminding France of the existence of the Monroe Doctrine settled the matter.

In December 1865, Napoleon III informed the Mexican emperor that he wanted his army back. So eager was Napoleon to guarantee an equitable French withdrawal that he even offered Washington Sonora and Baja California, two Mexican states that the ever-hungry U.S. sorely coveted but which Bonaparte's heir hardly owned.

Carlota literally went nuts when she heard of Napoleon's betrayal, flying off to Europe in a rage to confront the French emperor and Eugénie. Rebuffed, she rushed south to the Vatican and appealed to the Pope to save both her crown and her head, but when the Pontiff offered the distraught empress a cup of chocolate, she accused him of poisoning her (not an unknown Papal strategy) and fled, collapsing on the Vatican steps. She never recovered her senses, babbling away incoherently into the next century. Every year, until she finally gasped her last in 1927, she was said to re-enact her departure for the New World by stepping into a rowboat on a pond at her moated Belgian estate. The loss of a Mexico she never owned had driven her quite mad.[16] It is an oft-repeated tale in Mexico and, subversively, her tragedy never fails to stir sympathies here—this is a nation hopelessly addicted to such *telenovelas* (soap operas).

With his wife careening madly around Europe and the French army pulling the rug out from under him, Maximilian feebly sought to fix things up with Washington. Writing President Johnson, he extolled his own good works and complained, much as president Ernesto Zedillo did when the *New York Times* ran an unfavorable piece in July 1996, that "the U.S. press never tires of publishing malicious interpretations of events in this country."[17] Johnson responded by ordering General Sheridan and 50,000 troops to the Mexican border in the defense of national security and the Monroe Doctrine.

The last French troops exited Mexico City in April 1867 under safe conduct granted by Juárez General Díaz and the Emperor fled to Querétaro where the Zapotec's troops finally cornered him. Despite pleas from Seward to spare Maximilian's life, Juárez was determined to demonstrate to the world that whoever attempted upon Mexico's sovereignty would suffer "the ultimate consequences." Maximilian was executed June 19th, 1867, on Campana Hill above the old mining capital. Another who met the firing squad at the Emperor's right hand: General Miguel Miramón, his multi-million-franc loan still unpaid.

THE LAST LAUGH

The colorful pageant of the failed French Annexation cost at least 50,000 mostly poor and mostly Mestizo and Indian Mexicans their lives. Today, the defeat of the French forces is celebrated as a reminder of Mexico's struggle for sovereignty each May 5th, although, curiously, more on the northern side of the Río Bravo than on the southern. There is an intriguing political reason for this anomaly. In 1967, the Chicano Student Union at Cal State-Los Angeles was looking for a date on which to honor Mexican American pride and ground the growing Brown Power movement. But the obvious choice, Mexican Independence Day, which falls on September 15th-16th, came much too early in the school term to organize a proper party so the *"Cinco de Mayo"* was selected in its stead.[18] The success of the event attracted commercial sponsorship—first from Corona Beer, whose sales soared in the U.S., and then by North American breweries. Civic proclamations followed, legitimizing the date as a kind of Chicano national holiday. Even the *gavachos* are invited in now. Bill Clinton wolfs nachos as Gringolandia goes Mexican each May 5th, in an annual marketing frenzy that nets millions for the snack and beverage giants.

But, for this reporter, the real celebration of the victory over French annexation takes place not on May 5th but at pre-Lenten carnival festivities in the Nahua Indian municipality of Huejotzingo, Puebla, under the Ixtaccihuatl volcano, not far from the actual site of the Battle of Puebla. An entire fantastical French army, replete with contingents of *Zapadores* (sappers) in woolly busbys, "Zuavos"—infantrymen in fake blonde muttonchop sideburns, "Turcos" in turbans, "Negros" in practically nothing but black greasepaint, and be-ribboned "Zacapoaxtla" Indians square off with fanciful homemade muskets for five days and nights, blasting off 20 tons of gunpowder in the process—in addition to multiple hands and fingers (38 in 1994, I was told, when I visited the local hospital.)[19] An ocean of beer and a continent of roast meat nourishes this boundless fandango. Like the holy day it marks on the Christian calendar, Carnival in Huejotzingo brings catharsis and renewal, a great smoky dance celebrated by these speakers of the Aztec language each year to encourage the seeds they are about to insert in the ground and to mock that eccentrically-garbed army of strangers who, once upon a time, tramped through town on the way to annexing Mexico and lost their pants in the process. Every once in a while, the Indians of Mexico enjoy the last laugh.

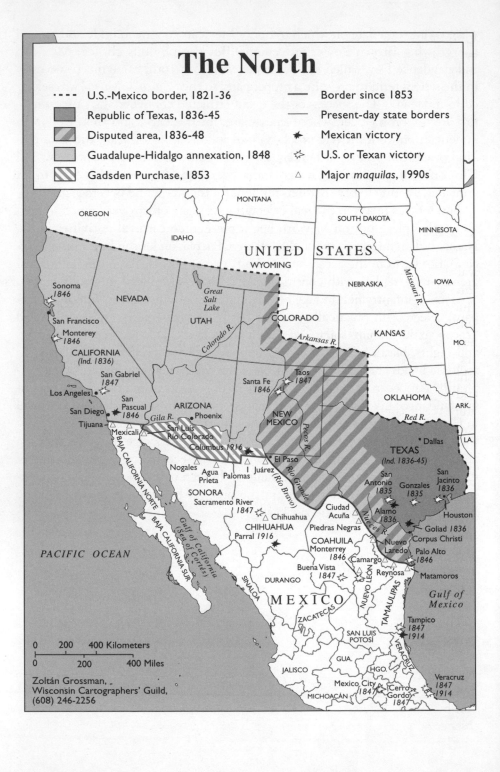

The North

- - - - U.S.-Mexico border, 1821-36   —— Border since 1853

▨ Republic of Texas, 1836-45   —— Present-day state borders

▨ Disputed area, 1836-48   ✦ Mexican victory

▨ Guadalupe-Hidalgo annexation, 1848   ✧ U.S. or Texan victory

▨ Gadsden Purchase, 1853   △ Major *maquilas*, 1990s

MONTANA

OREGON

IDAHO

UNITED STATES

WYOMING

SOUTH DAKOTA

MINNESOTA

NEBRASKA

IOWA

Missouri R.

Sonoma
1846

NEVADA

Great
Salt
Lake

UTAH

Colorado R.

COLORADO

Arkansas R.

KANSAS

MO.

San Francisco

Monterey
1846

CALIFORNIA
(Ind. 1836)

San Gabriel
1847

Los Angeles

San Diego

San
Pascual
1846

Tijuana

ARIZONA

Phoenix

Gila R.

San Luis
Rio Colorado

Mexicali

Santa Fe
1846

Taos
1847

NEW
MEXICO

Pecos R.

OKLAHOMA

ARK.

Red R.

Dallas

LA.

TEXAS
(Ind. 1836-45)

BAJA CALIFORNIA NORTE

Columbus 1916

Nogales

Agua
Prieta

Palomas

El Paso

Cd. Juárez

Rio Grande
(Rio Bravo)

San
Antonio
1835

Alamo
1836

Gonzales
1835

San
Jacinto
1836

Houston

SONORA

Sacramento River
1847

Chihuahua

CHIHUAHUA

Parral 1916

Ciudad
Acuña

Piedras Negras

COAHUILA

Monterrey
1846

Nueces R.

Nuevo
Laredo

Goliad 1836

Corpus Christi

Palo Alto
1846

PACIFIC OCEAN

Gulf of California
(Sea of Cortés)

BAJA CALIFORNIA SUR

SINALOA

DURANGO

ZACATECAS

Buena Vista
1847

Camargo

Reynosa

MEXICO

NUEVO LEÓN

TAMAULIPAS

Matamoros

Gulf of
Mexico

SAN LUIS
POTOSÍ

Tampico
1847
1914

0   200   400 Kilometers

0   200   400 Miles

GUA.

JALISCO

Mexico City
1847

HGO.

Cerro
Gordo
1847

VERACRUZ

Veracruz
1847
1914

Zoltán Grossman,
Wisconsin Cartographers' Guild,
(608) 246-2256

MICHOACÁN

Chapter 4

Pax Porfiriana, American Dream

The National Museum of Interventions is housed behind stolid stone walls on a shady Coyoacán street in the south of the capital. The site has long been one for worship: under the Aztecs' domain, a temple of Huitzilopochtli stood here and the gunnels of the sacrificial wheels ran thick with the blood of local offerings. The convent of Churubusco became the headquarters for the National Guard during the invasion of '47—its defenders momentarily stopped the gringo army as it swept northwest towards Chapultepec Castle. Nearly a century and a half later, in 1981, riding the end of the oil boom, José López Portillo, a president with anti-imperialist pretensions, refurbished the historic old halls and christened the site the National Museum of Interventions.[1]

The designation of the Museum was in keeping with the locale's religious antecedents. Anti-interventionism is the bedrock of Mexican foreign policy and the bitter experience of repeated foreign invasion has elevated it to a near-religious principal. By "anti-interventionism," Mexicans refer, almost exclusively, to U.S. intervention, and López Portillo's museum did not at all amuse then-U.S. ambassador John Gavin.

Visitors to the museum's 13 galleries tiptoe through airless, well-guarded rooms stuffed with flags and battle standards, old maps and cannons, muskets and ammunition chests and portraits of the perpetrators of, and resisters to, a century of intended annexations of Mexico.

The interventions are meticulously charted on wall plaques. Between 1817 (when time begins for the Museum) and 1876, the first year of the presidency of Porfirio Díaz, interventions are recorded in 34 out of 59 years. During the first six years of the Díaz era, interventions occur every year. Then, for the next 29 years, between 1882 and 1911, the charts go blank—except for one incursion by the Arizona Rangers to quell a copper strike in 1906. Yet, despite the absence of invasion and intervention, the annexation of Mexico by the United

States of North America became a fact of daily life during the three decades and more of General Porfirio Díaz's mandate.

"ORDER AND PROGRESS"

Two roughshod boys born into the sierra of Oaxaca dominated Mexican politics during the second half of the 19th century. Benito Juárez combined an inflexibly liberal vision of how Mexico should be governed with Indian persistence, as he rose from the Zapotec mountain town of Guegalatao to become, in turn, that rugged southern state's governor, the chief justice of the supreme court, the framer of the nation's Constitution, and, ultimately, Mexico's president for a crucial make-or-break decade.

Porfirio Díaz's vision of the nation, on the other hand, was clouded by ruthless ambition. The mestizo son of marginal innkeepers from the state capital, 40 kilometers from Juárez's birthplace, Díaz was the Zapotec's cohort in the Ayutla revolution of '55 which finally toppled Santa Anna. His military skills were honed in the civil war and the young general's exploits during the resistance to the French were the stuff of legends—and an interminable telenovela, *The Flight of the Eagle*, broadcast nightly by the Televisa entertainment conglomerate at the zenith of Carlos Salinas's popularity. Salinas was often compared to Díaz by his critics.

After the French retreat in 1867, Díaz ushered President Juárez back into the capital, but three years later, when the Zapotec chose to ignore the very constitution he had devised and opted for reelection, the general turned against him. Exiled to his Oaxaca hacienda, Porfirio Díaz waited for his moment—which came after Juárez's death in 1872. Defeated once again in his bid for the presidency, Díaz launched an armed rebellion that engulfed Mexico in two more years of internecine bloodshed. Finally, in 1876, Porfirio Díaz emerged on top of the corpse heap and proclaimed himself President of Mexico.

Porfirio's position was a precarious one. The United States refused to recognize his government and Mexico seemed so unstable that it became a convenient target for the annexationists. President-elect Rutherford Hayes stoked up the war chant, seeking to deflect attention from his fraudulent 1876 election. On the morning of Hayes' inauguration, major newspapers in Washington, Philadelphia, and New York ran editorials that revived the "protectorate" concept of Mexican annexation.[2]

Constant scrapes agitated the borderlands between the two nations. Cattle rustlers like Richard King, founder of the King Ranch dynasty, zigzagged their stolen herds between Mexico and Texas with impunity.[3] Apache bands, dislocated by America's march west, fled into Mexico and raided north into the U.S. When Hayes declared hot pursuit, Díaz resisted—today, "hot pursuit" (of trans-border drug traffickers) remains an equally incendiary topic for Mexican nationalists. Pragmatic as Santa Anna, Porfirio Díaz parlayed anti-gringo sentiment that continued to seethe south of the Río Bravo into a popular mandate to become first provisional president and then the virtual dictator, for the next 34 years.

"Order & Progress," in that order, were the buzzwords with which Porfirio Díaz ran the show. After 60 years of bottomless carnage, the country hungered for order and Díaz dedicated his first years to establishing same. His model of governance was necessarily authoritarian: the President acted in the best interests of the Fatherland, the Congress approved the President's initiatives, and the Public was compliant because it, of course, understood that the President was acting in its best interests. Such a schema necessitated a large repressive force to maintain the stated order. Díaz retained the federal army in this capacity and created the rural police (*"rurales"*) who adorned themselves like *charros* (ostentatious Mexican cowboys) and terrorized the countryside into submission on behalf of large, urban-based, absentee landowners. At the grassroots, Díaz enlisted the allegiances of local *caciques* (rural bosses) and their private armies of gunsels (such armies survive in Chiapas today as *guardias blancas* or white guards) to keep the peace. Penal colonies were established in remote corners of the country, such as the Valle Nacional of Oaxaca, a malarial enclave where political prisoners performed slave labor on feudalistic tobacco export plantations.[4] "Monterías" flourished in Chiapas's great untrammeled Lacandón jungle—rebellious Mayan Indians were rounded up and press-ganged to toil in the logging camps where the precious mahogany and cedar was clear-cut and shipped north to floor the great mansions of New York and London.[5] Jails and lunatic asylums—both of which Díaz eventually sought to privatize (Wackenhutt proposes to do the same under Zedillo)—were filled to the brim.

The "Pax Porfiriano" promoted the image of stability. Díaz controlled the Mexican press with an iron hand and no mention of social disturbance was ever published. To burnish his international profile, the Dictator granted Associated Press the wire monopoly on the proviso that he controlled what went out on it.

The consistency of Díaz's rule eventually won the United States's admiration—the general himself served as president for 30 years, ceding the office only once, from 1880 to 1884, in accordance with Juárez's constitution, to his confidant, General Manuel González. After '84, Díaz ordered a constitutional amendment to insure seven subsequent electoral victories. The Dictator's foreign minister, Ignacio Mariscal, matched his Jefe's longevity, serving 30 years. Matías Romero, who, as Juárez's foreign minister had been an architect of

Mexico's new and improved relationship with the U.S., was ambassador to Washington for 16 years, until his death in 1898.

The "Progress" part of the Porfirian equation was delegated to the *Científicos* (the Scientists). The dictator, an unschooled military man, assembled this technocratic braintrust to promote economic "development." Entranced by European and American science and technology, the *Científicos* advocated opening up Mexico to massive foreign investment in order to springboard the *Patria* out of dire poverty and into the 20th century—a policy not unlike one that would be entertained by Salinas a hundred years later. Everything was put up for sale. Romero was reported to keep a "blue book" on his Washington desk, listing available concessions with the dollar prices affixed to them.[6]

The *Científicos* were Social Darwinists with a predatory understanding of the nation. "The weak, the unprepared, those who lack the necessary tools to triumph in the evolutionary process, must perish and leave the field to the strongest," the elegant José Ives Limantour told the National Science Conference in 1901.[7] Such racist attitudes (read "white" for "strong") did not presage relief for most Mexicans (about 98% of the population) upon whom the renovating drops of first world science and technology would never rain.

"SO CLOSE TO THE UNITED STATES..."

From the outset of his eight presidencies, there is evidence that Porfirio Díaz, who had experienced the annexation of half of Mexico in *carne propio* (his "own flesh") understood the dangers of having a ten-million-ton U.S. gorilla sitting on his northern border: the axiom "Poor Mexico, so close to the United States and so far from God" may be the Dictator's most lasting contribution to Mexican nationalist thought. Throughout his long rule, Díaz sought to counterbalance the threat of U.S. annexation by courting European investors.

Despite the gross insult the Maximilian escapade had inflicted upon national honor, diplomatic relations were reestablished with France, which came to own 21% of all mining interests in Mexico.[8] The French founded the National Bank, built textile factories, opened department stores and set the Porfirian style—Díaz even had the Paseo de la Reforma remodeled to resemble the Champs-Elysées. Frenchified mansions lined the neighborhoods running off the boulevard and interior decoration was just as frilly. Comic Opera became a favorite entertainment of the elite.

The Germans too were invited to invest and bought mineral rights in the northern Sierra Madre and settled Chiapas's Soconusco on the Guatemalan border where they still retain huge coffee plantations. Germans dug mines and built breweries and played their accordions, from which has evolved the popular, rollicking "*Norteña*" music of the U.S.-Mexican border.

British bankers and traders ruled the world and Latin America was no exception—the Anglos were granted concessions to run electric power companies, the Mexico City tram system, and 4,500 miles of railroad.[9] Díaz contracted Weetman Pearson, later First Viscount Cowdry, to build Puerto México (now the port of Coatzacoalcos), designed exclusively for European clients. Between 1885 and 1910, British entrepreneurs opened 210 mines in Mexico.[10] Pearson brought in Mexico's first oil gusher. But, despite the deluge of concessions to assorted European investors, Díaz was never able to neutralize the U.S. gorilla.

Then, as now, the United States dominated investment in Mexico—55% of the total boodle. The Land of the Aztecs was the only one on the continent in which the U.S. share of the market outstripped that of the Brits. So extensive were British holdings in the late 19th century that they actually owned nearly a billion-dollar share of the United States itself.[11]

Famous American fortunes were made in Porfirian Mexico. Rockefeller's Standard Oil bought in on the ground floor of petroleum development. The refined, art-loving Guggenheims befouled the air of El Paso-Juárez with their ASARCO refinery for a century. J.P. Morgan established banks and annexed great swatches of Mexican countryside with greenbacks. Railroad tycoon Jay Gould hooked up with Ulysses Grant, but went broke on the Mexican Southern Railroad to Díaz's home state of Oaxaca. The Hearsts claimed enormous tracts of Mexican forest lands in the Chimilapas on the Oaxacan Isthmus and the Tarahumara Sierra of Chihuahua.

The volume of business U.S. entrepreneurs were doing in Mexico jumped 14 times during Díaz's immense tenure—from $9 million in 1870 to $36 million by 1890 to $117 million in 1910.[12] The U.S. dominated commercial trade, with 51% of the market (the British had only a 17% piece).[13] By 1910, the Dictator's final year in office, the United States had a total $646 million USD investment in the continuing stability of the Mexican economy.[14]

THE ENGINE OF ANNEXATION

The railroad was the engine with which Díaz opened Mexican resources to global exploitation. It also helped Don Porfirio rush troops into back country hotspots whenever the natives got too restless. Díaz never tired of pointing out that when he came to power in the putsch of '76, Mexico had only 200 miles of track (concessioned by Juárez, also a true believer in the future of rail travel)—when the Dictator was finally forced to flee to Europe, 12,000 miles of railway knitted the nation together.

The biggest giveaway came in 1880, just three months before Díaz deferred to González: the Mexican Central and the Mexican National routes that would link the capital with the border at El Paso-Juárez and the two Laredos, were concessioned to a Boston combine, represented by rail baron Hiram Nickerson, owner of the Atchison (later the Santa Fe). E.H. Harriman and Brown Brothers would soon be in on the deal. The two concessions "were to seal the fate of Mexico to that of the United States," writes Joséfina Zoraida Vázquez, "ever since, the Mexican economy has been complementary."[15] If this distinguished historian's analysis holds water, the U.S. annexation of Mexico, begun as a gleam in Franklin's and Jefferson's and Monroe's eyes, and carried all the way to the Halls of Motecuhzona by Scott's Army in '47, became, under Porfirio Díaz's hard hand, a palpable reality from which Mexico would never ever escape.

To be certain, Díaz tried to rectify the advantage he had given U.S. investors. Pearson got the Veracruz-to-Mexico City route ("Every turn associated with the thrilling history of the Conquest" read a contemporary travel brochure).[16] The soon-to-be Lord Cowdry finally built the Tehuantepec line—Hawaiian sugar was now unloaded at Salina Cruz, stacked on Pearson's flat cars and hauled over the hump of the Isthmus for reloading at Puerto México, upon ships bound for Philadelphia. Díaz had lured Pearson from building tunnels under New York's East River to dig Mexico City's Profound Drainage System: "an eternal pedestal and glory of our country," the Dictator waxed grandiose at the inauguration of the new sewer system.[17] Weetman Pearson enjoyed vast holdings all over Porfirian Mexico, ranging from a burlap bag factory to electricity generating plants (Mexican Light and Power) to his several rail lines, to the Eagle (El Aguila) Petroleum Company.

British and American-owned rail companies imported their own workers and English was the official language of the roads. Orders were given in the gringo tongue, which much galled the Mexican peons hired to lay the tracks. One of Francisco Madero's first acts of state after the Dictator's downfall was to reestablish Spanish as the language on the railroads. Today, the stiff British presence on the Veracruz-Mexico City line is still burlesqued in Tlaxcala country towns like Contla where young couples, dolled up in tophats, frock coats, long skirts, and parasols, cavort in wild Indian dances at Carnival time.[18]

"THE MOSES AND THE JOSHUA OF HIS PEOPLE"
Annexation is primarily a territorial thrust. The U.S., which had been repeatedly foiled in its bid to annex Sonora and Baja California, simply obtained what it could not get by conquest via government concessions. Between 1882 and 1895, 70 million acres of Mexican real estate fell into foreign hands—by 1910, the acreage had soared to 134 million.[19] The

International Corporation of Mexico, headed by Michigan attorney George Sisson and German immigrant investor Lewis Husser, snapped up 14.6 million acres of Sonora (the Yaquis had to be subdued before they could move in), Baja California, two Pacific Coast islands, and 340,000 acres in Chiapas. Edward Doheny, the California oil magnate, bought 620,000 acres in the Poza Rica region. Pearson received 800,000 acres for his Aguila Oil company in the Tampico-Tuxpán corridor. The Mexican Land & Colonization Company, a joint venture between J.P. Morgan and several members of the British House of Lords, purchased 3,000,000 acres in Chiapas and Baja's San Quintín Valley (now leased to transnational tomato growers).

In southern Mexico, U.S. and British speculators dominated export agricultural production—*henequén* (sisal) from the Yucatán, rubber (Pearson had a 300,000-tree plantation), chicle, precious hardwoods and coffee from Chiapas. Up north, the great Hearst ranch in Chihuahua abutted the Creel-Terrazas holdings. Together they were larger than the kingdom of Belgium.

What was under the land was annexable as well. Between 1884 and 1898, the mining law was altered four times to give foreign investors incentive to dig. The mines were often remote enclaves of foreigners, serviced by costly rail lines built by the owners to haul out prime material. El Oro Mine & Railroad Company, north of Mexico City, a joint British-U.S.-French-German venture, featured its own golf course and polo field. Spurred by Díaz's concessions, subsidies and low tariffs, Mexico recaptured world leadership in silver production. Gold output rose from one million pesos in 1877 to 40 million in 1911, and black gold gushed along the northern Veracruz coast, propelling Mexico to seventh place on the global production charts. Rockefeller's Standard, Pierce Oil, and Royal Dutch were players but the two giants, Doheny and Pearson, dominated the burgeoning industry, bringing in major strikes at a moment in history when the world's great economies would take a qualitative leap by converting to petroleum to power commercial production.

Annexation by concession was excellent for business. Under the Díaz dictatorship, Mexico's Gross National Product grew 380%.[20] Díaz paid off the foreign debt for the first time ever—one of his first acts as president was to settle outstanding reclamations with the U.S. By the turn of the century, Mexico was running its first trade surplus since the Conquest. Porfirio's *Científicos* had no trouble obtaining long credit lines from the world financial community. Like Carlos Salinas a century later, Porfirio Díaz was eulogized by the captains of international capitalism: "He is the Moses and the Joshua of his people," trumpeted Andrew Carnegie.[21] The Anglo-American Mining Guide compared the general to "Alexander, the Caesars, William the Norman, the Great Napoleon..."[22]

THINGS FALL APART

While the macro of the Mexican economy boomed under Díaz's firm hand, the micro fell apart. There was and is no trickle-down in the Mexican class structure as the extraordinary historian Daniel Cosio Villegas explains: "The idea [of trickle-down], largely confirmed by the experience of the United States and England, was inoperative in Mexico for two good reasons—first, Mexico's social pyramid was not tall with a narrow base so that fertilizing waters drained down an almost vertical slope. In Mexico, the pyramid was squat, with a very broad base, so that the flow was slow and almost horizontal. Moreover, separating each of the three levels, was a thick, impenetrable slab that caused rainfall to stagnate on the crest with little or no flow below." [23]

At the tip of the pyramid were the neighborhoods running off Reforma where the mansions sported French maids and British butlers and the residents wore bowler hats and carried parasols and played at croquet. It was where the white-haired, walrus-mustachioed Díaz lived and, as he grew older, the only world he ever saw as he drove each day to the National Palace, his chest blazing with medals like some European archduke in exile.

But just outside this walled, well-policed precinct, most of Mexico was sinking in dire poverty. In the capital's slum barrios the average life span was 24 years (it was 45 in Paris). 43 out of 1,000 adults died each year (compared to six in a not very spick-and-span London), making Mexico City the most insalubrious urban center on the planet. 50% of all babies born did not survive their first year. [24]

Misery in the city was matched by gnawing hunger in the countryside where 80% of the population was still tied to agricultural production—although less than 3% of Mexicans owned land. 7,000,000 Indians and Mestizos were bound to 834 haciendas and land development corporations. [25] Rural wages in 1910 were 35 centavos a day, precisely the same as they had been in 1810 when Padre Hidalgo rang the church bells and yelled "¡Viva Mexico! (Lets go kill some Gachupínes!) [26] Indeed, the Mexico that lived outside of Díaz's dream world was no better off than it had been at Independence a century before— and now those same bedraggled Mexicans watched helplessly as the independence won by Hidalgo and Morelos and Guerrero and all their subsequent martyrs was sold off inch by inch to the despised gringos.

The bad gas seeped in in stages. The 1907 worldwide economic downturn wreaked havoc in Porfirian Mexico—henequén prices plummeted, copper collapsed, and the textile market disintegrated. In May, panicked banks called in all loans and the Guggenheims shut down their smelters. "The panic of 1907 was most trying. No one escaped from it, great or small," wrote John D. Rockefeller. [27]

Labor troubles spilled over. In May, 1906, the Díaz governor in Sonora gave the green light for Arizona Rangers to cross the border to repress a miners' strike at Colonel William Greene's great Cananea copper pit—a score of Mexican workers were slain. Washington, fretting that the strike had been ignited by IWW (Wobbly) agitators, offered to send backup troops.

In June 1907, 6,000 striking textile workers at Río Blanco, Veracruz were beaten and gunned down by the rural police. John Kenneth Turner reported between 200 and 800 dead—their bodies stacked on flatcars and fed to the sharks in Veracruz port.[28] Both incidents sparked the cohesion of the Mexican labor movement. Work stoppages on the railroads all the way from Chihuahua to Mexico City moved the Díaz government to merge the British and U.S. rail lines into one system—the creation of the National Railroad Corporation irritated Díaz's foreign associates. Although the corporation's board of directors sat in New York where Harriman could keep an eye on them, the Mexican government retained 51% of the stock in the new enterprise. Such behavior was strangely out of character for Washington's old associate.

In 1908, the Dictator confirmed what had already been rumored in Washington. In an interview with James Creelman, of *Pearson's Magazine*, Díaz, then 78, announced he would not be a candidate in the 1910 presidential election and would "welcome an opposition party in Mexico."[29] The Creelman interview was soon on the front page of Mexican newspapers and encouraged a power struggle for succession between Secretary of Finance Limantour and Secretary of War General Benjamín Reyes. Díaz became so enraged at the vulture-like antics of his underlings that he withdrew his pledge of never running for the presidency again, and declared himself a candidate for one more term.

Despite the Dictator's backstepping, the Creelman interview had excited the nation's long-quiescent political opposition. Galvanized by the circulation of the Flores Magón brothers' *Regeneración*, 5,000 Liberal clubs blossomed in Mexico between 1908 and 1910.[30] But while the middle class organized itself, the dispossessed continued to stew in abject poverty. It would take a few more years of social disintegration for their fury to fully explode into the first great social revolution of the 20th century.

MADERO'S MICROBE

The most significant challenger to Díaz's long-lived rule came from an unlikely direction—Francisco Madero, the scion of Coahuila *hacenderos* who had reaped their fortunes in export agriculture, copper mines and steel and textile mills during the Porfiriato. A diminutive vegetarian, practicing spiritualist, and Lenin look-alike, Madero had studied abroad at Berkeley and in Paris and had returned to his homeland brimming with democratic fervor. Barnstorming the land on the Anti-Re-election ticket and in defense of Juárez's 1867 constitution, Madero triggered the lingering discontent of the bourgeoisie, increasingly cut out of the action by Díaz's encrusted old guard. Although the little man himself characterized his chances as those of "a microbe against an elephant,"[31] the pachyderm was soon infected as years of repressed political frustrations coalesced around Don Porfirio.

The dictator responded by clapping Madero and 5,000 supporters in jail. The June 21st, 1910 election was as bogus as all those that had come before (and would come afterwards, too) and the 80-year-old dictator was returned to the presidency by a stunning margin.

To celebrate his "triumph," Don Porfirio programmed a splendiferous celebration of Mexico's 100th year of independence in September of that year. The budget for the gala affair equaled the nation's education outlay for 1910 and poor people were energetically discouraged from attending the festivities, exacerbating unrest.

Díaz's downward spiral had just begun. Madero bribed his way out of San Luis Potosí prison and, fleeing to Texas (as the Dictator himself had done 35 years earlier), he called for Mexicans to gather in the plazas of their towns and cities on November 20th, 1910 at 4:00 in the afternoon and rise up in rebellion. Few dared. But the aging Díaz, exhausted at the prospect of having to beat off Madero's challenge, had little fight left in him.

"THE WILD BEASTS ARE LOOSED"

Idols crumble fast when they finally begin to fall here—perhaps it is the climate. The nose-dive of Carlos Salinas, who outdid Díaz by selling off the nation's banks, highways, airlines and public utilities, and privatizing agriculture in only one sixth the time it took the Dictator to do so, is a contemporary case in point. Salinas's image as the new Redeemer of Mexico collapsed just three weeks after he left power in December 1994 as peso devaluation set off a chain reaction that started the nation on the deepest economic slide since the Great Depression. Today, *ambulantes* (itinerant street vendors) brave Reforma Boulevard traffic to hawk comic latex heads of the self-exiled ex-president. Like Santa Anna's leg, Salinas's head is passed from hand to hand and scorned on the streets of the capital.

The Dictator's own head took a few months longer to fall. Madero's *grito* was heard south of Mexico City in Morelos state where Emiliano Zapata mounted first his horse and then an army of campesinos to punch up Díaz's "*federales*." Achilles Serdán formulated conspiracies in Puebla. Doroteo Arango, aka Francisco Villa, an alleged bandit, and Pascual Orozco, said to be a mule skinner, harkened to the call in Chihuahua. In Sonora, Alvaro Obregón, a garbanzo bean farmer, threw his lot in with the rebels. Appointed by Madero as Governor of Coahuila, Venustiano Carranza assembled an Anti-Re-election army. Spurred on by Villa, a wily tactician who transported his fabled *"Division del Norte"* on Díaz's crackerjack railroads, the rebels took the border at Juárez and headed south to where Zapata was already laying waste to the federal army. The old man, weary of defending the indefensible, threw in the towel fast. Less than six months had elapsed since Madero's revolution had begun.

The dictator's pretext for abdication was prescient: he was stepping down to avoid "international conflict,"[32] i.e., U.S. intervention, always a scenario at moments of Mexican turmoil. Leaving his Washington ambassador Francisco León de Ibarra behind as a caretaker president, the old man hobbled up the gangplank of the Ypiranga and sailed off to Paris with one last warning to those for whom he had governed so long: "The wild beasts have been loosed. Now let us see who can cage them…"[33]

Chapter 5

MEXICAN REVOLUTION, U.S. NIGHTMARE

After three decades plus of unimpeded access to Mexico's land, resources, industry, and financial markets, the Americans, and their British competitors, were thoroughly discombobulated by the fall of Porfirio Díaz. Not that the outcome was unexpected. In 1909, the Dictator and U.S. President William Howard Taft had joined hands at the border, in El Paso-Juárez—the first meeting ever between heads of these two distant neighbor states. But, for the Americans, uncertainty about the future weighed heavily upon this historic huddle: how much longer could Díaz survive and who would be his successor? An El Paso police report that anti-Díaz bombers awaited him in that city shortened the Dictator's visit and added to the U.S. preoccupation.[1]

The U.S. demanded from Don Porfirio a contiguity of succession that would assure access and privilege in Mexico for its citizens and guarantee the protection of their lives, property and investments in the wake of the social upheaval that was bound to accompany the impending transition of power. Fresh from putting the wogs in their place as ambassador to the Philippines, Henry Lane Wilson was dispatched to Mexico to implement this policy—although there are some (the Dictator's son, for one) who suggest that the Ambassador played an active role in toppling the Díaz regime because that regime "no longer responded to the expectations of U.S. dollar diplomacy."[3] The Dictator's favoring of German and Japanese investment over the Anglo-American axis in the last years of his regime is cited as the motive for the U.S. rancor.

Whatever the depths of Lane Wilson's complicity in Díaz's downfall, there is little question that the Ambassador, an arrogant racist who had been in Mexico for only a year, was a master at meddling in this, the first stage of what historian Berta Ulloa labels "the Intervened-in Revolution,"[4]: "At every decisive moment, U.S. influence was exerted to alter the course [of the Mexican Revolution]."

If the Ambassador had finally mistrusted Díaz, he cottoned even less to Francisco Madero. Lane Wilson bluntly informed Taft that the little man would fail to control anarchy, would even encourage it, and predicted a lengthy period of upheaval that would be bad for the U.S. business interests it was his obligation to protect. From the moment Madero took office in November 1911, replacing de Ibarra, Henry Lane Wilson needled the new president about his failure to protect U.S. citizens and their property. 17 gringos had allegedly been killed in Mexico since Díaz's departure and Madero's fledgling administration had been "apathetic and cynically inefficient" in bringing their murderers to justice (several of the 17 were later shown to be walking around, apparently still quite alive).[5] In a note made public in August 1912, the Ambassador hinted that the U.S. might have to land troops in order to safeguard its own citizens—perhaps 50,000 Americanos were estimated to be living and working in Mexico at the time. Taft ordered 20,000 troops to the border to back up Lane Wilson's not-so-veiled threat.

The Ambassador's disdain for Madero was stoked, at least partially, by the U.S. oil companies—Doheny was incensed by the export tax hike of five to 20 cents a barrel that the strapped Madero government had imposed on foreign producers. Lord Cowdry remonstrated similarly with his own government.

But U.S. business interests were not monolithic, as points out Frederick Katz, author of the magnum opus on intervention in the revolution (*The Secret War in Mexico*).[6] Agricultural concessionaires feared that Madero would be pressured by peasant leaders like Zapata into expropriating their plantations and their ranches and wanted him out of the way. On the other hand, Rockefeller's Standard Oil stood accused of financing Madero's 1910 election campaign with the expectation that the corporation would get a better deal from the new president than the arrangement it had with the old Dictator.

THE ALMIGHTY'S BLACK GOLD

The petroleum players each sought advantage for their own distinct agendas and differences flourished between them. But, collectively, their influence was decidedly in the ascendancy—and would exert great influence on U.S. policy for the next four decades. In 1910, Pearson brought in his Potrero I gusher, spouting 100,000 barrels a day, and was immediately topped by Doheny's Tampico finds—Cerro Azul spouted 1.4 million barrels before it was capped. Between 1910 and 1912, precisely the span of Madero's moment in the world spotlight, Mexico's annual oil output grew from 3.5 million barrels to 16 million and the nation leaped from the seventh leading producer on the planet to the third, eclipsed only by the U.S. and czarist Russia. "The great oil area of the world now stretches from Kansas to the Tehuantepec," wrote *Wall Street Journal* correspondent Clarence Barron,[7] later chairman of Dow Jones and a Doheny apologist.

"One can but reflect that the Almighty permitted the tapping of His reserves of oil only when the world was coming into line to receive the benefits," Barron muses in a perverse little volume, *The Mexican Problem*, that invests Doheny with almost divine authority.[8]

"Mexico has so much to give us, fruit of the tropics, minerals, oil, the wealth of a continent compressed into an isthmus," Barron drools, "and we have so much to give her—the fruit of our political and social mantle, machinery, progress..."[9] Edward Doheny was a "pioneer" who had cleared the jungle and brought the future to the "backward" Mexicans who are "good people but children who want to be in debt and, at the same time, free."[10] The neighbor republic's troubles the soon-to-be Dow Jones chairman of the board attributed to "IWW agitators and German agents."[11]

Barron's paean to the California oil man also provides an insight into life behind the heavily guarded fences of the private oil reservations that Díaz had allowed the companies to annex. Unlike the *México Bronco* (Wild Mexico) outside the enclaves, Ebano, a Doheny camp near Tampico, was a model of efficiency where thousands of Mexicans and Americans worked in peace and harmony. Americans, however, had been forced into supervisory roles in Ebano because Mexicans "did not work very well under their countrymen." Barron wasn't sure whether to attribute this phenomenon to "jealousy or a desire to learn from the Anglo-Saxon race or the innate recognition of our superior leadership."[12]

THE AMBASSADOR'S BLACK HAND

Francisco Madero was less a flaming radical than a Juárez liberal (and a timid one at that) who worshiped the sanctity of private property. Madero desired neither to upset class distinctions nor to disturb the existing privilege into which he himself had been born. But the U.S. reading of Madero was blurred by the myopia of its ambassador.

The new president's stay in office was troubled from its first days. When it became evident that Madero did not intend to expropriate and redistribute the great sugar cane *haciendas* of Morelos among the *campesinos*, despite the strong support offered him by the entity's agrarian poor, Emiliano Zapata rose against the man whom he helped to bring to high office. The Plan of Ayala, Zapata's agrarian program, declared on November 11th, 1911, in the plaza of the hacienda which had swallowed his home village of Anenecuilco, at the same hour that Madero was being sworn in up in the capital, also announced an eight-year guerrilla war against whoever ruled in Mexico City, no matter what his revolutionary pretensions, that, three-quarters of a century later, continues to galvanize contemporary agrarian struggle.

Madero disregarded the Indian Zapata's rebellion and the brutal half-Indian General Victoriano Huerta was sent forth to put this country ruffian in his place. Huerta, who had won his stripes slaughtering the Yaquis under Díaz, was not a wise choice. Francisco Madero's errors were pathologically self-destructive. Not only would Huerta come back to haunt him, but the new president's failure to fathom the depth of the class enmities his halting, by-the-book insurrection had unleashed was fatal. Whether Madero was so abstracted by his aristocratic mindset that he failed to notice the apocalyptic anger and frustration of the underclass or he simply, studiously, avoided this unpleasant subject so as not to alarm his middle class constituents, the result was just as disastrous. By New Year's 1913, the nation was fast spinning out of his control.

The president committed other political blunders too that cost him dearly. Although Díaz had sailed off, the political class that had perpetuated the Dictator's grotesque stay in power remained free to intrigue towards a coup, to be headed by General Reyes or the old man's nephew, Félix. The federal army was also left intact, a fact that ultimately signed the president's death warrant.

Riots exploded in seven Mexican cities following the lynching of a Mexican in Texas during the summer of 1912—Mexicans were frequent victims of lynchings in Texas. In *They Called Them Greasers*, Arnoldo DeLeón describes multiple incidents between 1865 and the turn of the century in which Mexicans were burnt alive, sexually mutilated, and had their ears hacked off during Texas lynchings[13]—a state where "it cost $25 to kill a buzzard and $5 [the cost of the rope], to kill a nigger or a Mexican."[14]

Despite the mounting anti-American sentiment south of the border, Henry Lane Wilson, just like every U.S. ambassador from Poinsett through William Weld (unconfirmed at this writing), continued to intervene in Mexico's internal affairs on behalf of both Washington and the investors whose interests he was sworn to uphold. The Ambassador did not hesitate to provide assurances to Reyes (then imprisoned by Madero) and Félix Díaz (whom Lane Wilson was heard to address as "the Savior of Mexico")[15] that the United States would look favorably upon a substitution in the office of the presidency—the Ambassador later boasted that he had informed President Taft that such a coup was imminent. But when the moment came, it was Victoriano Huerta, not Díaz, who responded to the call.

The coup began February 8th, 1913 with a mob attack on Lecumberri Prison to free General Reyes. Fighting raged in the capital for ten days and the *"Decena Trágica"* ("10 Tragic Days") killed hundreds and left the center of the city in smoldering ruins. On February 18th, Huerta and Díaz met with Lane Wilson at the U.S. embassy, which served as the operational base for Madero's overthrow and subsequent liquidation. The president was arrested hours later. Four days later, the man who had dumped Díaz, and his deposed vice president, José María Pino Suárez, were murdered in cold blood by Huertista officers outside the Lecumberri "Black Palace" in the east of the city. The official explanation was the famous Porfirian *"Ley Fuga"* (Fugitive Law)—the two men were allegedly gunned down when they sought to escape.

Huerta's responsibility for the assassinations is aboveboard. "I did to Madero what he wanted to do to Díaz. How is my act worse then his?" he purportedly confessed to the wife of Lane Wilson's eventual successor.[16] The Ambassador's complicity is more circumstantial—on the afternoon of the killings (February 22nd), Huerta attended a Washington's Birthday gala at the U.S. embassy, during which he was closeted with Lane Wilson for several hours. Madero's mother protested that she had pleaded with the Ambassador to deliver a message to Taft asking guarantees for her son's life, but that the envoy had refused to transmit it, cynically explaining that he "had no right to interfere with the regime" to save the ousted president's neck.[17] The day after the coup, Lane Wilson convened the diplomatic corps, and instructed the ambassadors assembled at the U.S. embassy to seek quick recognition from their governments for Huerta's bloody seizure of the Mexican presidency. When his own government waffled, Lane Wilson encouraged U.S. industrialists like the Speyer & Company banking firm and E.N. Brown, operator of the Mexican Central Railway, to petition Taft in favor of the new regime—Doheny, miffed at Huerta because of the general's developing friendship with Lord Cowdry, was an exception to the high pressure lobbying.

Huerta's "*golpe de estado*" and the ambassador's black hand in Madero's murder infuriated the rebel chieftains who, two years previous, had brought the late little man to power. Zapata sicced his Liberating Army of the South upon the usurper. Venustiano Carranza, the long-bearded patrician governor of Coahuila, reactivated the Constitutionalist Army and Villa pledged his subordination to "First Chief" Carranza, an arrangement which proved a transient one.

Within a week of the Madero assassination, Lane Wilson sent an emissary north to advise Carranza that he was rebelling against "a lawfully constituted government." The governor of Coahuila grew apoplectic. The *gringo* ambassador was the cause of the problem, Carranza snapped, and sent the envoy packing, resolved to continue fighting until the revolution had been won.

Rather then stemming "anarchy," Henry Lane Wilson's malevolent meddling plunged Mexico deeper into revolutionary chaos. His intervention, as historian Lorenzo Meyer concludes "hastened the arrival of of the real revolution."[18]

WHITE MAN'S BURDEN

Huerta's future was not assured. Although Britain, encouraged by Lord Cowdry, had granted swift recognition to the general and his gang, Taft, defeated for reelection in 1912, ceded the issue to his successor.

Like Madero, Woodrow Wilson was hardly a radical, but came to power in radical times. The President of Princeton University and a hardcore Christian moralist descended from a long line of preachers, Wilson had risen to power as the result of one of the last Leftist surges in U.S. history—the Progressive movement, out of which radical labor and populist farmers had conjured up enough class hatred of Wall Street and big business to dominate electoral options. The 1912 ballot pitted Democrat Wilson against the Progressives of "Bull Moose" candidate Teddy Roosevelt (really a lapsed Republican)—Wilson won easily, 6 million to 4 million votes, with Taft a distant third.

Secretary of State William Jennings Bryan, whose "Cross of Gold" speech and eccentric demand for the free coinage of silver had electrified the electorate in a presidential bid lost to mega-expansionist William McKinley in the 1896 balloting (Bryan ran thrice), was the idol of American populism. Together, the odd couple of Wilson and Jennings Bryan revamped U.S. policy in Mexico. "There are those who wish to possess Mexico, who wish to use her, who regard her people with condescension and contempt, who believe they are only fit to serve and not for liberty—such men cannot and will not determine the policy of the United States," the president declared,[19] and Jennings Bryan forthwith recalled Ambassador Henry Lane Wilson. Reviled by the Mexicans and regarded by the new administration as an accomplice to murder, Ambassador Wilson packed his bags for good.

In his stead, Wilson appointed envoys to talk sense to the warring Mexican factions and cajole them into smoking the peace pipe. Former Minnesota governor John Lind, a teetotaler, met with Huerta and was offended by the swilling dictator. He advised Bryan, whose populist, free silver philosophy he shared, that Mexico's problems were such that only radical agrarian reform could stave off universal chaos. Wilson's efforts to talk Carranza into taking over as provisional president were equally disastrous—the First Chief rebuffed the overture as one further proof of Yanqui interventionism and grew furious when a U.S. military attaché reportedly pledged to guarantee a favorable relationship with Washington, if only northern Mexico were ceded to North America.[20] Villa was more receptive, vaguely promising to safeguard U.S. investments should he come to power.

From the inception, Woodrow Wilson's messianic mission to bring U.S. style "democracy" to Mexico was sabotaged by an imperialist paternalism whose real message was embarrassingly evident: to maintain the United States' commercial domination over its southern neighbor. The bottom line for Wilson, wrote Katz, was "to fight off expropriation and the limitation of privileges enjoyed under the Díaz regime." [21]

Woodrow Wilson's rhetoric smacked of the White Man's burden—the U.S. president wanted to make "the backward nations" part of "a universal commercial world." He would show them "order and self-control in the face of change."[22] Wilson's benchmark for bringing democracy to the heathens was free elections, explained Walter Page, his ambassador to England—"we'll make them vote and live by their decisions" and if they failed to do so "we'll go in there and make them vote again." [23]

"We're going to teach the Latin Americans to elect good men," the president declared[24]—and General Victoriano Huerta had neither been elected nor, by the American president's definition of decency, was he a good man.

DEMOCRACY'S GUNBOATS

Although General Huerta promised new Ambassador O'Shaughnessy that elections would be held in the fall of 1913, he abruptly called them off and, in October, dissolved Congress. Wilson now declared what he termed a period of "watchful waiting" and instructed General Leonard Wood to draw up a contingency plan for the invasion of Huerta's Mexico.

To this reporter, leafing through contemporary accounts of Wilson's preparations for invasion, the build-up seems oddly reminiscent of George Bush's push for the Persian Gulf slaughter. Months of blood-curdling editorials (Hearst was, as usual, belligerently cooperative) and tooth-rattling Congressional debate prepped the American people for the coming Mother of All Battles. The U.S. oil companies, stung by the General's fondness for Lord Cowdry, clamored for the usurper's immediate ouster. American rail barons demanded that the president "reestablish law and order" south of the border. Senators Fall and Lodge jointly introduced legislation calling for the occupation of major Mexican cities in order to save U.S. lives—none of which had yet been proven lost in the escalating Mexican civil war.

The charged atmosphere excited old annexation ambitions. When Huerta collaborator Emeterio de la Garza traveled to New York to meet with Speyer & Company's John Hammond, he was advised that the General's term in office might well be extended if Mexico would only turn over Baja California and the top half of the nation all the way to Matamoros, to the gringos. On October 24th, 1913, Otto Kahn, J.P. Morgan's associate, met with Wilson liaison Colonel Edward House to tout his scheme "to guarantee free elections in northern Mexico," suggesting that U.S. troops be sent over the border as far as the Sierra Madre where they would set up a buffer zone that would separate that part of the country from the rest of the republic.[25] By January, U.S. troops were on alert along the border. White House intelligence reports indicated that a German ship would soon be arriving in Veracruz, bearing arms for the Huerta regime. In classic gunboat diplomacy fashion, Wilson ordered a Naval blockade of Mexico's Caribbean coast to prevent delivery.

The required Tonkin Gulf scenario began on April 9th when the gunboat USS "Dolphin," patrolling off Tampico, sent a crew ashore to reconnoiter fuel from a warehouse in the port that was owned by a U.S. citizen. But the city was under siege from the Carranzistas and martial law was in effect—when the sailors tied their whaleboat to the pier, they were taken into custody by Huertista officers for being in the wrong place at the wrong time.

Although the detention of the seven swabbies lasted no longer than an hour, Rear Admiral Henry Mayo, a protégé of Navy Secretary Josephus Daniels, later Roosevelt's ambassador to Mexico (FDR was then assistant secretary of the Navy), blew a gasket. The Mexicans were ordered to honor the Stars and Stripes with a 21-gun salute within 24 hours or face the consequences. The provocation had been impeccably rehearsed: Admiral Mayo felt free to issue his ultimatum without even consulting Daniels or Roosevelt, his superiors.

Huerta's first reaction was to demand reciprocity—if the American flag was to be saluted, the least the U.S. could do was salute the Mexican flag in return. The American president was not amused. "If the salute is not fired, I will go to Congress and ask for such action as may be necessary to enforce respect for the nation's flag," Wilson retaliated April 15th.[26] William Randolph Hearst, suspicious that the peacenik president would quickly chicken out, baited him in his flagship *San Francisco Examiner*: "Has the magnificent American fleet been assembled just for the ridiculous purpose of making the Mexicans salute the American flag?"[27] Decrying the "Mexican Problem" as one of U.S. "national security," Hearst demanded nothing short of invasion, occupation, and annexation.

Wilson's military advisors concurred, advocating armed intervention to reenforce the United States' global position, strengthen control of the Panama Canal, and safeguard the oil flow from Mexico. "Our world power status is infinitely more important than the murder of Madero, a bloodthirsty Huerta, or any other usurper in the Mexican presidency," declared General McIntyre of the War Department's Insular Bureau.[28] On April 20th, Wilson went before Congress and asked permission to land U.S. troops in Mexico, a request that was wholeheartedly granted by the House 323 to 29, considerably better than Bush would do eight decades down the congressional pipeline, when he persuaded the legislature that Operation Desert Storm, was "like shooting fish in a barrel." (Bush won the House 250-183 and the Senate 52-47.)

After nine months of foreplay, Woodrow Wilson chose the historic route for penetration. Following in the footsteps of Cortez, Napoleon, and Scott's army, 4,000 troops were put ashore down the coast at Veracruz on April 22nd, 1914. Their ostensible mission was to seize the customs house and confiscate a shipment of arms just delivered by the Ypiranga—the same ship that had hauled Díaz off to Europe four years earlier. As it turned out, the weapons were really of American origin, purchased by Huertista gun-runners in New York.

Military advisers warned President Wilson that trying to take just one building in the port of Veracruz was liable to lead to resistance from the Mexicans the U.S. troops might encounter along the way, but the caution had little resonance. One is reminded of the disastrous 1980 landing of troops in Iran by another Christian moralist president.

17 Americans were killed in the assault on the customs house—the largest number of U.S. military casualties since the Yanquis stormed the shores of Cuba and the Philippines at the end of the last century—the U.S. had subsequently landed troops in Panama, the Dominican Republic, Honduras, and Nicaragua, before putting in to Veracruz.

At least 123 defenders of Mexican sovereignty lost their lives in Wilson's assault—but U.S. troops reportedly burnt many bodies at public pyres, a sanitary measure to forestall disease, and no accurate count is yet known. The American president's twisted liberal gunboat diplomacy had carried the day— although the Huerta government was ultimately successful in unloading the Ypiranga down the coast, at Puerto México.[29] The U.S. flag once again flew over Veracruz.

TIPTOEING THROUGH THE MINE FIELD

Woodrow Wilson's muddleheaded intervention instantly united a warring Mexico against the gringos. Within hours, Huerta handed the U.S. ambassador his walking papers and broke off diplomatic relations with Washington. American flags were torched throughout the land, a statue of George Washington was toppled in Mexico City and the U.S. consul taken hostage in Monterrey. Huerta sanctimoniously called for volunteers to fight the Yanqui invaders. The wound of '47 still smarted on the southern flank of the Río Bravo.

Huerta's enemies were no less inflamed. "If the Americans send a million soldiers, we will fight them, one man against hundreds. We may have no army or no ammunition but we have men who will face their bullets," Emiliano Zapata proclaimed from the hills of Morelos.[30] Venustiano Carranza virtually declared war on Wilson: "The invasion of our territory, the stationing of American troops in Veracruz, the violation of our sovereignty, could provoke us into an unequal—but just—war..."[31] Villa, on the other hand, refused to condemn the Yanqui invasion, remaining silent for weeks. In May, he and Carranza entered into a pact not to attack the Americans unless Wilson moved against rebel-controlled territory. Both vowed to continue to carry the fight to Huerta.

Carranza, in particular, made it clear that he was not going to put aside his differences with the usurper in Mexico City just to face the hated gringos. The decision not to join forces in the face of foreign aggression was a crucial one in gaining military advantage over Huerta, Ulloa suggests.[32]

Wilson had been stunned by the 17 American deaths at Veracruz, the first American blood shed on his watch (the Mexican dead apparently did not trouble his Christian conscience), and ordered his troops kept on a short tether in

Veracruz. Rather than marching to the Halls of Motecuhzona, Admiral Frank Fletcher busied himself tidying up the port city. Prostitutes, who freely plied their trade along the *malecón* (seawalk) were relocated to a red light zone outside of town. Public urination was prohibited and the U.S. Commander ordered regular garbage collection, even providing the locals with garbage cans (reportedly at $2 USD a can).[33]

After Veracruz, President Wilson would tiptoe more cautiously through the Mexican minefield—but he never relinquished his crusade to impose a "final solution" on the "Mexican Problem." "The renunciation of plans for an extension of the intervention in no way mooted the American government's intentions of imposing on the country a government (acceptable to Washington)."[34]

The U.S. president unilaterally convened an inter-American conference to mediate the Mexican dispute, in, of all places, Niagara Falls, New York, the honeymoon capital of North America. Huerta was obligated to attend and sent a delegation of top-drawer diplomats—the counsel for the Mexican delegation was a crusty oil company lawyer with extensive business holdings in Mexico, one William F. Buckley, the father of the aging *enfante terrible* of the American right.

Carranza, as expected, declined the invite but asked his political lieutenant, Luis Cabrera, to eavesdrop from the sanitary distance of Buffalo. The First Chief's position was straightforward: the only points to negotiate were the date of the U.S. pull-out and the separation of Huerta from the office that the U.S. had stolen for him. The conference groaned to a halt at the end of June with no resolution in sight—which led wags to jibe that "Niagara falls faster than Huerta."[35]

The Niagara negotiations were disrupted by sobering news from the continent—On June 27th, Archduke Francis Ferdinand was assassinated in Sarajevo by Serbian nationalists, a shot that laid the logs of world war on the fire. The conflagration began in August. From that date forward, the "Mexican Problem" would move to a back U.S. burner, although the unstanchable revolution caused many unpleasant moments at the White House for several years to come.

GENERAL HUERTA'S LIVER

Huerta's plunge from grace was as brusque as Díaz's. On June 23rd, Villa's 18,000 *"Dorados"* ("Golden Ones") smashed the Huertista army at Zacatecas—a short train ride from Mexico City. Carranza, fearing that he would be upstaged by the Centaur of the North, ordered the Chihuahuan to halt and refused to send coal to fuel the advance. Wilson reminded Britain of the doctrine that bore Monroe's name and, despite objections from the merchant princes that the U.S. was seeking to extend its commercial "suzerainty" over all of Latin America, His Majesty's government now withdrew its support for

Huerta. By now, Cowdry and Doheny were both furious at the general for again raising the export tax from 20 to 65 cents the barrel—Doheny was, in fact, paying his taxes to Carranza.

General Huerta abandoned Mexico City on July 15th with an appropriate metaphor: "I am depositing the honor of a private man in the bank known as the conscience of the world."[36] He was also depositing a sizable chunk of the public treasury in foreign banks. German and British ships rushed to Puerto México, vying for the privilege of ferrying the general and his boodle to Europe. At the White House, Bryan and Secretary of the Treasury McAdoo "embraced and danced around like a bunch of boys."[37]

But the Huerta saga had not yet run its course. By the summer of 1915, the general was rendezvousing with his faithful supporters in El Paso and raising a fresh army, supposedly with German backing. Historian Barbara Tuchman insists that Huerta met with the Kaiser's men in Barcelona in February of that year.[38] Although no solid evidence of collusion has ever emerged, at this stage of the European conflict the Germans were intent on cutting off British oil deliveries from Mexico and a new Huerta counterrevolution presented possibilities.

The General's resurgence did not at all please Wilson—who needed to settle the Mexican Mess before he could turn his full attentions to global conflict. Huerta was arrested in El Paso by the FBI on July 4th for violation of the Neutrality Act. "I am enjoying the novel experience of being in jail in liberty-loving America on the day you celebrate your independence," he told reporters.[39] Housed at Fort Bliss, Huerta began drinking heavily—his guards apparently facilitated the booze deliveries, and on January 15th, 1916, cirrhosis claimed his liver and his life. Just across the border the Mexican Revolution continued to defy Wilson's efforts to contain it.

DANCING WITH THE CAUDILLOS

The warclouds massing over Europe made it imperative for the Wilson White House to impose an end to the revolution, but the wrath of Mexico's underclass and the ruthlessness of its leaders was, for once, beyond North American restraint.

Francisco Villa began 1915 as the U.S.'s favorite to cool the revolution off. Villa's image north of the border had been burnished by popular mythology and the eyewitness accounts of adventuresome U.S. journalists. The acid-dipped Hearst man, Ambrose Bierce, the "Old Gringo" of Carlos Fuentes' novel,[40] ambled south to join Pancho Villa and was never heard from again—Bierce probably bit the dust in 1911 at the Battle of Ojinaga and was buried on the spot in a common grave. Jack Reed's heroic dispatches on the move with Villa in 1913-14 spread the legend of this ruddy, robust, hard-drinking rebel who had begun life as Doroteo Arango in the badlands of Durango, rustling cattle from the great *haciendas*.[41] Impressed by Villa's apparent neutrality after the U.S. landing at Veracruz, Wilson's advisers saw this shrewd opportunist as less stridently anti-American than Carranza. Villa also enjoyed the unlikely support of conservatives who reasoned that "if Mexico was a nation of bandits, it might as well be governed by one" (Katz, La Jornada, April 15th, 1997). Both the Hearsts and the Chandlers offered editorial support—Otis Chandler, brother of the *Los Angeles Times* publisher, was even arrested in a Villista conspiracy to overthrow Carranza's governor in Baja California.[42]

Woodrow Wilson did not hide his antipathy towards Venustiano Carranza. The sentiment was eminently mutual. The towering (6' plus) First Jefe, his gaze shaded by creepy smoked glasses and always fingering his flowing white beard like some sort of Mexican Mister Natural, did not hesitate to hide his hatred of the gringos. Despite—or because of—his prickly anti-Americanism, Carranza won fans on the U.S. left. The invasion at Veracruz had sparked widespread protest by labor and peace organizations across the U.S. Samuel Gompers even urged Wilson to recognize a Carranza government. Muckraker Lincoln Steffens, who had influence at the White House, lobbied the president on Carranza's behalf and John Kenneth Turner, whose *Mexico Bárbaro* had torn the mask from the Díaz dictatorship for American audiences, published "Hands Off Mexico," a pamphlet that demanded the withdrawal of U.S. troops and Carranza's recognition.

But Carranza was not looking to the Colossus of the North for moral support. His vision was much more Bolivarian. The First Chief saw clearly that Mexico's struggle against oligarchy and annexation was a Latin American one: "Our example will save other Latin nations from these same ills and create the respect of powerful nations for the small," he wrote in a document later to be labeled "the Carranza Doctrine," in pointed juxtaposition to Monroe's.[43]

Of the three key revolutionary leaders (Obregón was about to make it a foursome), Emiliano Zapata was the most difficult for the Wilson White House to size up. Though his guerrilla army operated in the strategic center of the country—Morelos, Puebla, northern Guerrero—and had easy access to the capital, the Caudillo of the South was the most remote of the rebel chieftains. A proud man whose Indian blood percolated distrust at the White Man, be he Mexican or North American, Zapata rejected discourse with Wilson's agents. Although his city-bred advisors eventually sought to open channels to protest possible U.S. recognition of a Carranza government,[44] the Horseman of Anenecuilco was never a factor in Wilson's frustrated crusade to resolve "the Mexican Problem."

THE REAL REVOLUTION

In spite of the U.S. diplomatic campaign to impose a speedy settlement, the revolution took its own time and followed its own course. Obregón's Army of the Northwest, slashing down the Pacific Coast, overran Guadalajara and was the first to reach the capital after Huerta abandoned the city in mid-July. Carranza and the Constitutionalists arrived in August and summoned Villa and Zapata to a convention that would determine the shape of the revolutionary regime. But the Centaur and his southern counterpart bridled at the patrician Carranza's authoritarian pretensions and retired to the state of Aguascalientes instead, then rebel-held territory, to stage their own convention and formulate their own revolutionary government—an event celebrated by the Neo-Zapatista Army of National Liberation during its mythic, if rain-shortened, "National Democratic Convention" in August 1994.[45]

Even if the revolution continued on high boil, at least Huerta was gone from the set, and, by October, Wilson was ready to cut his losses—7,000 U.S. troops were withdrawn from Veracruz. The port was immediately occupied by Carranza's army. Under fire from Villa and Zapata, the First Chief packed up and moved his government to that coastal city in November, where he took up residence in a lighthouse, purportedly to stand sentinel against renewed Yanqui aggression, a lesson Wilson had not yet sufficiently digested.

To this day, U.S. presidents, in their boundless arrogance, continue to deceive themselves and their nation, that they know what is best for their southern neighbors when they don't have a clue. Washington's blessing is the kiss of death in Mexico and by leaning towards Villa, Wilson guaranteed that he was betting on the wrong horse.

In December 1914, Francisco Villa and Emiliano Zapata galloped into the capital. A murky photograph of the two rebel legends lounging under an ahuehuete tree in Xochimilco is the only evidence left of a summit that might well have been the apogee of the Mexican revolution. But both Villa and Zapata were local *caudillos*, with regional agendas, who felt uncomfortable on the throne of Motecuhzona and yearned to return home as soon as possible. By January, 1915, both had drifted out of the capital, leaving a provisional president, who soon fled to the provinces too. The city was free for the Constitutionalists to re-occupy.

Widespread fighting surged across central Mexico that spring. In despair, Wilson tendered an ominous message to all of the warring armies: the U.S. might have to intervene "to save Mexico from itself."[46] The battling generals did not even flinch at the White House warning.

Obregón and Villa went nose to nose in April in the Bajío of Guanajuato, not far from Padre Hidalgo's hometown, first twice at Celaya and then León. Villa was trounced each time. The Centaur lost 4,000 men and his fabled Division del Norte was left in tatters. Obregón lost 150 men and his right arm which, like Santa Anna's leg, was entombed in a shrine in the San Angel district of the capital—decomposition led to the limb's cremation in 1989.

The tide had turned at Celaya and as Francisco Villa limped back to his native Chihuahua, Wilson decided he could live with Carranza after all. By October, it was a done deal.

THE ULTIMATE TREACHERY

The ultimate treachery took place November 1st on the Agua Prieta (Sonora)—Douglas (Arizona) border. As Villa prepared his assault, Carranzista General (and later president) Plutarco Elías Calles huddled with U.S. General Funston and won safe passage for his soldiers north of the dividing line. Men and heavy weaponry were transported by rail through Douglas, allowing the Carranzistas to confront the patched-up Division del Norte on three sides. Eyewitnesses describe Villa's troops throwing themselves at Calles' barbed wire defenses where, much as in the shadowy death ballets then being danced on Europe's Western Front, they were cut to ribbons in the crossfire from the Gatling guns.[47] The artillery that evening was under the command of a young Calles protégé, Lázaro Cárdenas.

Villa's fighters were masters of the night, but, testify survivors, the Agua Prieta battlefield was brightly illuminated by arc lamps, reportedly a gringo special effect.[48] The defeat at Agua Prieta shattered the Division del Norte forever—from now on Villa's forte would be the war of the flea.

For a few days, it appeared that Wilson had at last achieved a victory in this interminable conflict. On November 3rd, Pancho Villa met with General Funston on the border and was offered political asylum in the United States—which he categorically rejected. The conversation was the last a Wilson agent would have with the wily ex-rustler. Two weeks later, the Wilson administration recognized the de facto government of Venustiano Carranza, but the long-anticipated betrayal failed to extinguish the hostilities.

Driven out of Sonora, Villa moved east back towards his Chihuahua redoubt, pausing in Juárez to "borrow" $25,000 from Guggenheim's ASARCO smelter. Weeks later, Villistas hit the Hearst ranch at Babicora, executing a bookkeeper and setting off a panic-stricken evacuation of U.S. mines and ranches in the region. Villa issued a manifesto condemning the Wilson-Carranza pact and accused the First Jefe of having annexed Mexico to the United States of North America, all the way to the Tehuantepec Isthmus—which, he fibbed, Carranza had leased to the Yanquis for the next 99 years. Pancho Villa, on the other hand, swore he would stand up to the gringos. In spite of Wilson's persistent meddling, the Mexican Revolution was not quite over yet.

VILLA VOTES EARLY

For his next act, the bandido in the desert would play Woodrow Wilson like a *conjunto* (combo) sawing through a *corrido* (ballad) in a border *cantina* (bar). Not a few of these tunes were already celebrating Villa's feats of bravery.

Francisco Villa's plan was nothing less than to provoke a U.S. invasion that would force Carranza to strike back, divert the First Chief's army from attacking his own bruised ranks, and, eventually, unite the Mexican people behind the Chihuahuan's audacious leadership to take on the gringos.

1916 was a presidential election year on the other side of the Río Bravo and Villa voted early. On January 10th, yelping "Death to the Gringos!" Villistas assaulted a train at Santa Ysabel, Chihuahua carrying 16 U.S. engineers who had been invited back into the state with Carranza's assurances, to reopen an evacuated mine. Lincoln Steffens heard of the massacre when he strolled into the American Club down in Mexico City later that afternoon and discovered his compatriots popping champagne corks with great glee. But why are you celebrating this butchery, he inquired? Because U.S. intervention in the Mexican inferno was now assured, reasoned his colleagues.[49]

Thunder rumbled over Washington. Ex-president Teddy Roosevelt urged Wilson to use the Big Stick: "If we don't do our duty in Mexico now, someone else will seize it for themselves" (a nod to the Kaiser who was now an active player in the Mexican Game).[50] Senator Works and Senator Fall, the latter of whom never missed an occasion to threaten invasion, introduced legislation that would sanctify still another incursion. By 1916, the U.S. Army, building steadily for war in Europe, topped 175,000 regulars (65 infantry and 25 cavalry regiments, 21 field artillery units, and eight air squadrons).[51] Much of this weaponry was, for its day, cutting edge—the U.S. had never fought a gasoline-powered war and the military badly needed a theater in which to test its newly-acquired capabilities.

The stage was being set for yet another Yanqui stab at annexing Mexico when, on March 9th, an hour before dawn, Pancho Villa preempted Washington's mighty military machine by attacking the United States of North America.

COLUMBUS

Several years ago when I visited Columbus, New Mexico, memories of Villa's raid on this quiet border outpost were fast fading. Most of the residents were snow bunnies who had fled to southern New Mexico to escape winters in the frozen north. The curator of the cluttered Pancho Villa Museum was himself a native of Three Mile Island, Pennsylvania, from which he had been driven by the 1979 near-meltdown at the local nuclear power plant.

But one resident who remembered the incident quite clearly was the former postmistress, Margaret Epps, then in her late 70s. What the old woman remembered best were the flames shooting from the burning storefronts as she trotted towards town in her father's milk wagon. "It was awful. There were bodies in the street," she gasped in the kind of mechanical horror that folks who have been telling the same story most of their long lives affect. "That Pancho Villa was a bad man!"

We were swaying on antique rockers in the postmistress's sunny front room. She leaned forward and launched into an invective-splattered diatribe about the naming of nearby Pancho Villa state park: "Its a damn shame! They brought this crappy statue down from Tucson because no one wanted it there. Why do we want a statue of Pancho Villa here? He almost burnt the damn town down!" The old woman said she was always waiting for Villa to come back and finish the job, had been waiting for 70 years for the worst to happen.

"Mexico is just over there"—she pointed south down the dirt road. "I see these Mexicans come walking past here everyday and I lock my front gate now," she frowned, "any one of them could be Pancho Villa…"[52]

PUNITIVE EXPEDITION

History is magnified in the re-telling. The truth is that the Columbus raid lasted little over an hour and one warehouse, a handful of storefronts, and the U.S. garrison were attacked and/or torched. "Viva Villa!" the ragtag invaders yipped and fired off their pistols like extras in a wild west extravaganza. 17 gringos gasped their last, but Pancho Villa lost at least a hundred. For the Centaur of the North, the Columbus raid was a gamble and, for once, it had paid off. As shrewd a poker player as Yasir Arafat, another desert fox, Villa knew the Yanquis would pursue him back across the border and that the stubborn, gringo-hating Carranza would refuse the U.S. permission to do so— which would hardly halt the American advance. Tensions between the First Jefe and the White House would be screwed up to the breaking point.

Villa's hunch paid off. General Calles was ordered to mobilize on the border to resist the imminent invasion from the north and Carranza placed the garrison in Veracruz on red alert. War was in the wind.

With both an election and the bloodshed in Europe dominating his desk, Wilson was compelled to act forcefully to rescue North American honor. On March 15th, General "Black Jack" Pershing, 4,000 troops (the number would grow to 10,000 before the "Punitive Expedition" was terminated) and two airplanes crossed the border on a manhunt right out of Wyatt Earp: Bring Back Pancho Villa Dead or Alive! Not until George Bush went after Manuel Noriega in Panama City in 1989 would the U.S. launch so massive an expedition south of the border to bring one man to justice. "It does not seem digni-

fied for all of the United States to be hunting for one man in a foreign country," General Funston, Pershing's superior, wrote to his cousin.[53]

Pershing's "Punitive Expedition" was doomed from the moment he planted
his boot on Mexican soil. By going after the gringos in their lair at Columbus,
Villa had fulfilled, for millions of Mexicans, the fantasy of revenge against the
hated mutilators of the Patria. The raid once again inflated Francisco Villa's
stock as a leader of the revolution. While Carranza sought to annex Mexico to
the gavachos, Pancho Villa boasted that he had not only stood up to them but
punched them square in the nose.

Villa's star rose fastest over his home turf of Chihuahua—through which
Pershing had to march if the Yanqui general was to stay on the Centaur's track.
But as the U.S. convoy rolled from settlement to settlement through the high
desert, it was met with stony silence from the villagers. No one would talk.
They had seen nothing. *No, Señor, lo siento...* Although Funston had cau-
tioned Pershing "to convince the Mexicans of our justice and humaness,"[54] the
Americans grew irritated at the silent reception and their bellies growled with
hunger because no one would feed them, either.

When Funston requested permission from the fuming Carranza to run supply trains across the border to keep his men in rations, the First Jefe flatly
refused, returning a note oozing with irony that feigned surprise at the request,
which, he pointed out, was the first official notice he had received that U.S.
troops had entered Mexican territory.

By now, Villa had become a ghost, plying the sierra and hiding out in mountain caves even as the "Punitive Expedition" trooped by yards away. "I feel like
I'm looking for a needle in a haystack," Pershing whined to Funston.[55] The
trouble began in April. A U.S. unit tried to cross through Parral, Villa's adopt-
ed hometown, and was set upon by a furious mob whooping "Viva Villa!"
Black troops from the 10th Cavalry (Pershing had commanded them at San
Juan Hill in the decisive battle of the so-called "Spanish-American" war), were
summoned to rescue their Caucasian brethren, and opened up "in self
defense."[56] When the gunfire ceased, there were 40 dead Mexicans and two
defunct U.S. soldiers on the AP wire out of Chihuahua City. The massacre was
reprised on June 20th at El Carrazal when nervous troops responded to a pro-
Villa throng with machine gunfire—this time the score was 74 Mexicans
killed—and a dozen U.S. soldiers.

The fresh carnage elevated national blood pressures. Pershing now demanded 50,000 troops to occupy all of Chihuahua and permission to requisition the
state's railroads. Washington mobilized 150,000 National Guardsmen and posted them at the border. Carranza General Jacinto Treveño responded with a
curt warning, instructing Pershing that the only direction his troops could pro-
ceed, if they wanted to avoid the armed wrath of the populace, was north.

Mexico was on fire by July. Americans were shot in Mazatlán and Tampico. Meanwhile, the U.S. steamed into full-bore presidential election mode.

The First Jefe was a master at brinkmanship. He stared down Wilson from behind those creepy little glasses and Wilson blinked first. General Obregón was dispatched to the border to discuss a suitable date for Pershing's departure. The talks were inconclusive. The inconclusive talks were continued in U.S. summer vacation spas at Atlantic City and New London, Connecticut. Meanwhile, on the ground, Treveño kept Pershing pinned down at the Mormon beachhead of Colonia Dublin.

Then, on September 1st, despite Carranza's claims that Villa's troops had been dispersed, the Centaur of the North reappeared, storming down into Chihuahua City, attacking the fortress-like prison and riding back into the hills, enriched by 1,500 recruits and a refurbished arsenal. On November 23rd, the revitalized Villa repeated his daring exploit, scattering Carranzista defenders and exacting cruel revenge upon the state capital's Chinese community. On Christmas eve, Pancho Villa struck once more, this time further to the east, at Torreón, where he had won a smashing victory over Huerta in 1913. Again, the rebel chieftain butchered the Chinese with unrepentant hatred.

Why Villa so hated the Chinese has not been brightly illuminated by historians. The Centaur of the North reportedly despised orientals more than North Americans, whom he called "white Chinese." It is said that the Torreón massacre was the sequel to a previous murder spree, when Villa's boys, influenced by "dubious brandy," "tied Chinamen to horses by their pigtails" and tore them apart.[57]

Flabbergasted by Villa's comeback, Pershing appealed to Wilson for a half-million troops to occupy the entire country. "We must take the whole of the country and keep it," echoed his lieutenant, George Patton. There seemed to be no bottom to the Mexican quicksand.[58]

ZIMMERMAN'S TELEGRAM

Despite the day-by-day revolutionary drama that gripped Mexico, Woodrow Wilson was understandably distracted. Although he had won the election by an ample margin from Charles Evans Hughes, the mounting body count in Europe and on the high seas assured him that world war was inevitable. The Germans had unleashed what they cheerfully defined as "unlimited submarine warfare" and had taken to sinking British ocean liners like the *Lusitania*, with a horrendous loss of lives—over 1,000 passengers drowned in the 1915 tragedy, including 128 Americans. Fighting wars on two fronts, particularly one involving eternally squabbling *caudillos*, would not be the direction of Wilson's foreign policy, no matter what fresh outrages the Mexican revolution had in store.

By 1917, anti-German paranoia had infected every nook and cranny of the American brain. The Kaiser was suspected of orchestrating the unending shenanigans in Mexico. Both Villa and Carranza were German proxies. Carranza's constitution had been written by Germans. Pancho Villa had been financed by German gold to attack Columbus—the proof was heavy coverage of the raid in the German press. "Villa is a tool operated by an unseen hand," charged the staid *Christian Science Monitor*.[59] The commanding officer at Parral suddenly recalled the presence of a German agitator on the scene.

But, for the Germans, Carranza was a more valuable prize and the flirtation with the U.S.-loathing First Chief was intense. With the White House on the verge of plunging into the European bloodbath, German foreign minister Arthur Zimmerman telegraphed his ambassador in Mexico the following message, to be delivered the day Wilson entered the war: "We make Mexico an offer of alliance on the basis of make war together, make peace together. We guarantee generous financial support (to be conveyed through a Japanese conduit) and the understanding that Mexico is to recoup its lost territories of Texas, New Mexico, and Arizona" (if, of course, the Germans won the war.)[60] One can imagine how tantalizing the offer must have appeared to Carranza, a northerner raised on the myth of the "Great Dispossession." But the First Chief never got the opportunity to take the Huns up on the proposition (although Tuchman claims he had an inkling).[61] The "Zimmerman telegram," in a classic espionage fiasco, was sent through Washington where British Intelligence intercepted it.

On April 9th, Wilson, motivated by the same Christian moral principles and enthusiasms for the free market that had caused him to intervene in Mexico in the first place, joined America's European allies to make the First World War a truly global event. Immediately, as would occur 23 years down the road when the U.S. marched off to World War II, hostilities with Mexico cooled down, and Villa drifted off into extraneous belligerence. Mexico sank to the bottom of the American agenda.

BOLSHEVIK CONSTITUTION

Pershing's withdrawal began in January 1917. He was still holed up with the Mormons, having long since ceased to hunt Pancho Villa. As the "Punitive Expedition" retreated towards the border, the hassled Chinese begged for protection from Villa's pogrom and some were allowed to return to the U.S.— from which they had been driven by the anti-Chinese laws a decade earlier. The last American soldier left Mexico February 5th and no Yanqui invading force has ever come across the border since—although there have been moments when commanders-in-chief have seriously considered the move.

But, even as the U.S. troops were exiting Mexico for the foreseeable future, the next chapter in the eternal war between these two irreconcilable neighbors was brewing. Precisely on the day the withdrawal was completed, Carranza's rewrite of Juárez's 1857 *magna carta* was signed, with great revolutionary flourish, in Querétaro. The new constitution contained a number of clauses that U.S. investors would not find at all copacetic. For one matter, Article 27, which incorporated much of Zapata's "Plan of Ayala" agrarian program, restricted the rights of foreigners to buy and own land in strategic areas of the nation. Article 33 postulated that troublesome foreigners could summarily be removed from Mexico and the new constitution removed the diplomatic protection afforded U.S. businessmen before Mexican courts. Article 123 promised the most progressive labor code ever promulgated in the Americas (but never put into practice in Mexico) which troubled U.S. manufacturing interests. But it was constitutional restrictions under Article 27, limiting the rights of foreigners to the subsoil, and questioning the prerevolutionary concessions Díaz had granted the oil barons that would be the most abiding preoccupation of U.S. presidents for the rest of the century.

Aside from this new "Bolshevik" constitution, Venustiano Carranza had raised the hackles of the petroleum companies by upping taxes in 1915 and 1918. In 1919, the First Chief would compound the mischief by proclaiming the nationalization of the subsoil, based on his interpretation of the newly-promulgated Article 27. The First Chief called upon the companies to turn their deeds in in exchange for limited concessions, but the barons, led by Doheny, Rockefeller and the British-Dutch interests, refused, arguing this was tantamount to confiscation.

Woodrow Wilson rolled his eyes in appropriate horror at Carranza's constitution. He regarded Mexico's new constitution as being a frontal attack "on democracy and civilization itself,"[62] but would wait until the European hostilities calmed before settling Carranza's hash. The revolutionary constitution converted Mexico into the Great Satan in the eyes of international capitalism. But, fortuitously, the Russian Revolution, just nine months later, soon eclipsed Red Mexico as Public Enemy Número Uno.

"After 1917, U.S. activities in Mexico were largely directed at ameliorating the impact of the revolutionary reforms upon foreign interests" (Lorenzo Meyer).[63] Carranza's radical constitution and his resistance to Yanqui invasion reduced the U.S. annexation of Mexico to an uphill, inch-by-inch battle to return to the privileges Washington had enjoyed under Porfirio Díaz. Viewed from the end of the 20th century, this campaign has not been unsuccessful.

THE REVOLUTION EATS ITSELF

Carranza consolidated his command of the nation with the assassination of Zapata on April 10th, 1919, a day that some historians consider the death day of the Mexican Revolution. The First Chief had always considered Emiliano Zapata little more than an illiterate peon to be eliminated when he had the time, but the Liberator of the South had evaded Carranza's ambushes for years before he was finally suckered to the Chinameca hacienda to pick up a load of ammunition and was swisscheesed by the Federales. The following year, the revolution would eat Venustiano Carranza too.

The First Chief's fall came as hard and as swiftly as Díaz's and Huerta's. Like Juárez, who had framed the first constitution which barred reelection, and then violated the clause by running in the election of 1872, Carranza—whose document contained the same prohibition—refused to cede the presidency to his designated successor, Alvaro Obregón, and instead, once again, loaded his government, treasury and all, on a 21-car train bound for Veracruz. Forced by his pursuers to abandon the route in the Sierra of Puebla, he sought refuge in Nahua Indian villages until he was run to ground and executed at Tlaxcalantongo by soldiers under the command of Manuel Palaez, a general in the employ of the oil companies, from whom he received $15,000 USD every month to protect their enclaves.[64]

Pancho Villa, who retired on a handsome government pension, was ambushed in Parral by Obregón hit men three years later—Katz has found a letter that suggests the U.S. ordered the hit (La Jornada, April 15th, 1997) The First Chief and the crafty guerrillero, two northerners who knew their U.S. neighbors up close and tormented them for a decade, disappeared into the revolutionary ether. The parade of generals moved on, the revolution eating itself year after year. Woodrow Wilson, exasperated by "the Mexican Problem," suffered a crippling stroke in 1919 and finally expired in 1923. In his last days, he expressed only bitterness for his neighbors to the south and the trouble they had caused him.

One final note on Mexico's fitful revolution. Despite a war that killed a million Mexicans, most of them poor and dark, and drove perhaps a million more into exile, a toll as great as that of Tenochtitlán and the struggle for Independence taken together; despite a conflict that wrecked the nation's industrial plant, generated widespread famine and plague (the influenza epidemic of '17 killed hundreds of thousands) and left the country a $750 million foreign debt, pitted brother against brother in fratricidal bloodshed that so scarred national memory that Mexicans still wince at the word "revolution," the U.S. presence in that wounded land grew by leaps and bounds between 1910 and 1920. At the beginning of the revolution, U.S. and British oil producers were exporting 12 million barrels yearly—by 1918, the export platform was 63.8 million and the part of "Mexico" the companies had annexed was now the most powerful producer of petroleum on the planet. Land controlled by the oil moguls now totaled over 5,000,000 acres.[65] By 1920, U.S. investors, who had sunk $645 million into the Díaz regime, now owned over a $900 million stake in Mexico's uncertain future.[66]

Chapter 6

From Invasion to Investment

Co-opting the Revolution

Uncle Sam emerged from the First World War as a global military and commercial giant. Vital to maintaining and augmenting this preeminence were the resources embedded beneath the subsoil of its Monroe indoctrinated "backdoor" neighbors. The continued annexation of Mexican oil lands was seen by statesmen, tycoons and generals as a crucial piece in the U.S. consolidation of its global powers.

"So long as the major portion of oil properties in Mexico are controlled by Americans, then American commerce with foreign nations is assured," the veteran Latin diplomat Boaz Long argued,[1] as the revolution south of the border mellowed into sporadic gunfire. Seen through this prism of U.S. global priorities, the continued annexation of the oil enclaves now became a question of "national security" for the gringos, one that could be settled either by an amicable surrender to North American hegemony—or by the usual arrogant display of force.

The State Department official opted for the former—military "annexation from the Río Grande to Panama" was no longer necessary because United States commercial influence was now so pervasive in the region.[2] Long was quite correct—by the mid-1920s, U.S. investments in Mexico totaled over a billion dollars and no new military adventure had actually been consummated (although several were threatened) to guarantee and protect the growth of that investment. Yanqui pragmatism had to concede that, for good or for ill, the Mexican revolution was a fact. Rather, now Washington sought to co-opt— and corrupt—the "Revolutionary Family" who were the immediate heirs to this monumental social upheaval, so that the U.S. Founding Fathers' historic mission of annexation might continue apace.

"THE BEST RULER SINCE DÍAZ"

Alvaro Obregón, the one-armed "Caudillo of Caudillos," a Sonora landowner with a Madero-like inclination for private property and an immense disdain for the impoverished masses who had "won" (and would soon "lose") the Mexican Revolution, was to be Washington's first vehicle for re-conquest. After Carranza's fierce, Fidel Castro-like rejection of the United States' divine mandate to rule the Americas, a smiling Obregón was welcomed to Washington, when he breezed through Washington in a 1920 pre-inaugural stop-in. The stricken Wilson's Republican successor, Warren Harding, a shady Ohio politician who was in bed with the oil companies, now nailed down the White House.

The *quid pro quo* was diplomatic recognition of the Obregón regime in exchange for unbreakable assurances that no U.S. oil properties would ever be expropriated. Obregón, pledged to the reconstruction of his damaged, bankrupt nation, needed U.S. diplomatic recognition in order to borrow new monies from the international banking "community." To this end, the Caudillo of Caudillos wooed Washington like an ardent suitor. Foreign minister Iglesias journeyed to the U.S. capital to ballyhoo the "exquisite considerations" foreigners were suddenly receiving in Mexico.[3] When an international banking delegation, headed by Thomas Lamont of J.P. Morgan, ventured to Mexico City, a gregarious Obregón announced that now "they were in a free country" and offered them jeroboams of champagne and magnums of Scotch that Prohibition had whisked from U.S. shelves.[4] The bankers' rail car was stocked with expensive liquors and high-class prostitutes strolled the aisles. Similarly, when Secretary of Finance Adolfo de la Huerta traveled to Washington, he invited Harding aboard his own private rail car to sample prohibited fermented beverages.

Enthused by all of this pump priming, A.B. Farquhar, a midwestern farm machinery manufacturer who was eager to trade with his diplomatically unrecognizable southern neighbor, wrote Harding that Obregón was "the best ruler of Mexico since Díaz."[5]

RED SCARES, BAD DEBTS, & DIPLOMATIC RECOGNITION

Recognition was opposed by all the usual suspects. World War I had reconfigured the petroleum interests: Royal Dutch now dominated Cowdry's Aguila empire but played second fiddle to the U.S. companies. Doheny was still a fixture in the Caribbean oil enclaves, doing business as the Huasteca and the Pan American petroleum corporations but Gulf, Texaco, Sinclair and Standard of New Jersey were equal players. Together, the U.S. oil barons convened the "National Association For the Protection of American Rights in Mexico" to fight diplomatic recognition until their éternal, God-given right to Mexico's oil was signed in stone.

As always, their legislative spokesperson was Senator Albert Bacon Fall of New Mexico, soon to be first Harding's Secretary of the Interior, and then a state convict for his management of the Teapot Dome Naval oil reserve swindle. Fall and Senator Walker (Pennsylvania) introduced the usual invasion measure—Walker, apparently deeply religious when it came to petroleum issues, considered that the U.S. had the right to exploit Mexican oil "for the greater glory of God."[6] Fall bandied lists of 550 Americans killed in Mexico between 1910 and 1920 and called down vengeance—the list began with Lane Wilson's 17 dubiously dead Yanquis. As Robert Freeman Smith points out in his deeply researched "The U.S. and Revolutionary Nationalism in Mexico," this toll was balanced by at least 541 Mexicans killed—on their own soil—during the 1914 and 1916 incursions.[7]

No matter. Fall's call for retribution was supported by such flag-waving enterprises as the American Legion and the Patriotic Sons of America, as well as the National Committee to Protect American Rights in Mexico. The Red Scare of 1919 extended its tentacles below the border—Mexican revolutionaries were alleged to be fomenting insurrection in the heartland of the U.S. One agitator fingered by Secretary of State Lansing: black heavyweight champ Jack Johnson, hounded out of the U.S. by racism, whom Lansing accused of "spreading social equity propaganda to Mexican blacks and endeavoring to incite the colored elements in this country."[8] Ricardo Flores Magón, the ideologue of Madero's challenge to the Díaz oligarchy, was another suspect—Flores Magón was murdered in Leavenworth federal penitentiary on November 21st, 1922.[9] U.S. oilman William F. Buckley Sr. boasted that he was financing armed counterrevolution in Baja California, and Lansing himself confessed that war with Mexico might not be a bad idea if it would unify what had become a deeply divided United States, its cities torn apart by race rioting and the crackdown on radical labor.[10]

But by the early 1920s, the economic equation had been transfigured. The oil companies no longer packed the wallop they once had in U.S. ruling circles. The post-World War oil glut, a product of their own avarice, dampened prices, and Mexican production began to decline after 1921. Bankers and traders increasingly gained the upper hand with a Harding administration that had been elected behind the long-winded slogan of "Less Government In Business & More Business in Government." A coalition of manufacturers, not unlike the USA-NAFTA amalgam assembled to boost the North American Free Trade Agreement through Congress in 1992, pointed to the healthy U.S. trade surplus with Mexico ($267 million to $112 million) and pushed for diplomatic recognition.

The bankers were more focused on collecting their now more than half- billion-dollar U.S. piece of the Mexican foreign debt. Lamont, rejecting past bullying debt collection techniques, advised patience and offered negotiations: "Mexican are peculiar people…you can't change them into Anglo-Saxons overnight."[11] With the Morgan man captaining the ship, the 1922 conference between the Obregón government and the International Bankers Committee produced an agreement that was to serve as model for Mexico's future shabby treatment by its U.S. creditors—the revolutionary government would shell out $30 million annually against the standing debt, one-quarter of its yearly income in a nation devastated by war and endemic poverty. To sweeten the pot, Obregón was permitted to raise taxes on export petroleum production, with the new revenues being put aside to pay off the interest on the renegotiated debt.

Then, as now, the foreign debt excited Mexican nationalists. "While the government pays its foreign creditors, it leaves unpaid its national creditors and reduces its public employees to the point of starvation," editorialized *El Universal* in 1924.[12]

Although the conditions imposed by the bankers were so harsh that payments quickly trailed off to zero, the signing of the agreement presaged the government-to-government Bucareli conference in the spring of 1923.

The negotiations were convened at the Interior Secretary (*Gobernación*) Palace on Mexico City's Bucareli Street, but the siting did not give the local negotiators much of a hometown advantage. Diplomatic recognition had now become increasingly crucial to the survival of the Obregón regime which was prepared to cede whatever it took to achieve same. "Obregón's problem was that he could not seem to cave in to U.S. demands and make the revolution into a farce [in which] Mexico would appear to become a protectorate of the U.S.," notes Lorenzo Meyer.[13]

The Obregón loophole to justify surrender was a 1921 Mexican Supreme Court decision on a Texas Oil claim which exempted properties acquired before 1917 from Constitutional Article 27's long reach. Behind locked doors on Bucareli, a formula was devised to effectively prohibit expropriation of properties larger than 1,700 hectares, thereby protecting the oil barons' enclaves. Although no agreement was ever ratified by the congress of either country, Harding got what he wanted: an iron-clad pledge of protection for the U.S. companies. In return, diplomatic relations, broken off when Huerta sent Ambassador O'Shaughnessy packing in 1914, were renewed. For more than a decade, the United States had failed to recognize its most immediate neighbor to the south as one of the earth's nations, a case of diplomatic myopia comparable to the Cold War-inspired omission of the People's Republic of China from the State Department's roster of real countries for more than 30 years.

"A VIOLENT AND SEVERE REFORMER"

The resumption of diplomatic relations did not calm the waters north or south of the Río Bravo. Buckley Sr., the oil mogul, for one, could not understand how patriotic Americans could support the recognition of a government "that places Americans in Mexico in the same category as Japanese in California."[14]

Recognition by Washington led to almost immediate instability on the other side of the river with two names. De la Huerta, an army general, charging that the Bucareli agreement had "humiliated" Mexico, raced back to Sonora and rose up in arms—his ulterior motive was the 1924 presidential nomination for which Obregón had already fingered his old lieutenant, Plutarco Elías Calles (all three generals were Sonorans). 7,000 more Mexican deaths and the congruent leaching of the national treasury later, Calles succeeded Obregón.

"A violent and severe reformer,"[15] Calles, with his drill-like gaze and ponderous silences engendered an atmosphere of menace about his bulky personage. Like Madero, he was a committed spiritualist, but his virulent anti-clericalism drove him towards the Reds, rather than the milksop middle classes. Turning his back on Obregón's Bucareli agreement, he sought, instead, to monumentalize the revolution. Diego Rivera daubed the walls of the capital's public buildings with gargantuan murals that depicted the revolutionary wrath of the working class, the pitiable plight of the nation's campesinos, and idyllic scenes from the mythical Indian past of the still-downtrodden citizenry. To cool down the masses, Calles capitalized on the talented goons of the official labor movement, acronymed as the CROM, under the very corruptible Luis Morones. In public harangues, Morones threatened to bring about the Dictatorship of the Proletariat, but was tasked instead with keeping the workers in line. Calles' hatred for the Church led to the promulgation of "The Socialist Catechism": "Hail Socialism…great shall be the fruits of your doctrinal womb."[16]

Oil was as much of a flashpoint as ever. In 1925, Calles pushed the U.S. envelope to the wall with the issuance of long-awaited laws implementing Article 27 of Carranza's 1917 Constitution, laws that finally, absolutely, decreed all prerevolutionary land concessions null and void. The oil companies were instructed to turn in the deeds granted them in perpetuity by Díaz. 50-year concessions would be granted if the oil giants could demonstrate that they had "improved" their properties.

The Calles initiative provoked swift retaliation from the White House, now under the command of Calvin Coolidge. The vice-president had been called in soon after Harding succumbed to "food poisoning" (purportedly bad crab) at San Francisco's Sheraton-Palace Hotel—suggestions that the 29th president took his own life just as revelations that his Secretary of the Interior, Albert

Bacon Fall, had sold off U.S. naval oil reserves to Doheny and Sinclair Oil for great personal profit, have never been adequately probed. Another theory of Harding's demise is that he was poisoned by his wife.[17]

BOOLAH BOOLAH

Coolidge's revenge for Calles' unfriendly act was the appointment of James Rockwell Sheffield as the new U.S. ambassador in Mexico City. Sheffield "apparently felt it was the obligation of Anglo-Saxons to teach non-white Mexicans their true interests which could not differ from those of the United States" (Lorenzo Meyer).[18] The ambassador, who, like outgoing U.S. envoy Jim Jones, spoke no Spanish, was both an arrogant racist and an insufferable Yalee. "There is very little white blood in Calles' cabinet," he posted his State Department superiors, ticking off the racial impurities ("Calles is Indian and Armenian...Sáinz is a Jew and an Indian").[19] Only Yale could save Mexico from itself: "Somewhere within us all, dear Mother Yale has planted that spirit of struggle against odds shown in the last half of the Pennsylvania game, and the Army game..." he wrote his old professor. "I hope I have accumulated enough of it to carry me through down here." [20]

A member of the Skull & Bones secret society like George Bush (Ernesto Zedillo, also a Yalee, was not invited to pledge), Sheffield instilled in his staff an admiration for Eli's gridiron achievements. In 1929, Embassy undersecretary Arthur Bliss Lane sought to organize an American football team at the National Autonomous University of Mexico (UNAM). U.S.-style football (*futbol* or soccer is the national sport),[21] "would teach the high idols of American sportsmanship to Mexican youth" and would have "incalculable benefits," he appealed to the Yale Alumni Association, sweet-talking the Old Blues out of the funds to hire a coach. [22]

Sheffield's game plan was to hold the line in Mexico. Noting that 44% of all U.S. investments were concentrated in Latin America, he emphasized that "any weakness in Mexico" would put the United States' commercial interests throughout the hemisphere at risk. The Calles law could not be allowed to prevail. Force was a viable option—Sheffield, misreading his foe with gringo flair, was convinced that Calles would back down before Yanqui might. Once again, the revolution and the White House were on a collision course.

MEXICAN SADDAM

Although Senator Fall, the first U.S. cabinet member ever to be indicted on a felony charge, was, by now, battling long prison time (he wound up doing a year in the New Mexico state pen), agitation for intervention surged in Washington. "Mexico is being judged in the eyes of the world" the State Department warned.[23] The National Committee to Protect American Rights in Mexico revived the Red Scare, picturing American industry paralyzed by Mexico's Bolshevik pigheadedness. U.S. marines were dispatched to keep a liberal-minded government from taking office in Nicaragua and Calles' support of Juan B. Sacasa, backed up by César Augusto Sandino, the Nicaraguan Zapata, and a former Huasteca Oil worker,[24] added more kindling to the brush fire the National Committee was bent on igniting—the Nicaraguan dispute is eerily reminiscent of the Bill Casey CIA's attack on the de la Madrid government for selling oil to a new wave of Nicaraguan Sandinistas, a half-century later.

Coolidge upped the ante by ordering troop maneuvers on the border in February 1927. Anti-U.S. sentiment in Mexican cities crescendoed once again. Sheffield petitioned the State Department for a case of revolvers—they were buried in the embassy's basement, anticipating mob attack. Then, in an apocalyptical, Saddam-like pronouncement in April, Calles ordered Obregón to set fire to the Caribbean oil fields and "make a light they will see all the way to New Orleans" when and if the U.S. attacked.[25]

But "the business of America is business," as Calvin Coolidge never failed to remind his countrymen and women. By 1927, 72% of all Mexico's imports flowed south from the U.S. and, traders argued, it would be foolhardy to wreck such a flourishing market. Besides, the bleating of the oil companies lacked conviction. In 1925, Standard of New Jersey (operating under the Trans-continental label) packed up its pipeline and oil rigs and relocated in Venezuela. Other U.S. drillers followed suit.

Ultimately, Dwight Morrow, a J.P. Morgan operative and Lamont protégé, was sped to Mexico City to replace the hapless Sheffield as ambassador and to defuse this volatile confrontation. Like his mentor, Morrow opposed invasion because such incursions did not tend to encourage swift debt repayment. The Morgan man's appointment was conceived of by Coolidge, his old Amherst roommate, as possibly having a salubriously civilizing impact upon the savages who lived below the Río Grande.

MEXICAN JIHAD

By 1927, actualities were appropriately savage south of the border. In July 1926, utilizing the mendacious pretext that the Church was supporting the oil companies in the approaching showdown with the gringos, the Catholic-baiting Calles enforced Articles 3 and 130 of the Constitution, seizing all Church property, closing down Church-run schools and throwing foreign priests and nuns out of the country. Throughout Mexico, Calles' henchmen outdid each other in acts of repression against the Church. In Tabasco, the "Red" governor, Tomás Garrido Canabal prohibited the saying of Mass by any priest who was unmarried. Calles himself invented his own "Mexican Catholic Church" in an effort to displace the Pope's priests from Mexico City houses of worship.

The Vatican retaliated by ordering its priests to go on strike. The rebellion spread like a grass fire in the central Mexican countryside where, fanned by *campesino* frustration at the revolution's stalled agrarian reform program, it burst into a full-blown guerrilla war, with perhaps 50,000 combatants in the field. The cruelties were routinely barbaric: generals shot their own troops for wearing crucifixes into battle and priests failed to intervene when government soldiers were dismembered by unruly Christian mobs, save to perform last rites. 25,000 Mexican died, according to historian Jean Meyer's count, and the countryside was devastated—Mexican agricultural production declined 38% between 1926 and 1929.[26] At least 200,000 citizens fled across the border in terror.[27]

The *"Cristiada"* crossed the border with them. The U.S. Catholic Bishops Conference and the Knights of Columbus demanded that Coolidge teach the Red Ogre Calles a lesson. The Ku Klux Klan, on the other hand, "felt protective warmth" for the uncuddly caudillo because the general was so rough on the papists.[28]

On the ground in Mexico City, Morrow became the conciliator, arranging a meeting between the strongman and the U.S. Bishops' envoy, Father John J. Burke, whom the Vatican had designated as interlocutor. Morrow himself penned portions of the 1929 treaty that ultimately ended the bloodletting.

THE SIMPÁTICO AMBASSADOR

Dwight Morrow cultivated the "severe and violent" Calles. The Ambassador initiated cultural interchange by flying in Charles Lindbergh (the first nonstop flight between Washington and Mexico City). The political satirist, Will Rogers, came to Mexico City. He professed deep admiration for Rivera's increasingly anti-Yanqui murals and the paternalistic mythification of indigenous culture (*"Indigenismo"*) that was then sweeping Mexican intellectual circles. He won assurances from Calles that the new Ford Motor Car plant just north of Mexico City in Cuautitlán would have no labor problems and even had a private hot line installed between the White House and the National Palace—although it is difficult to imagine what Silent Cal and the equally silent Calles ever talked about.

Morrow, like his predecessor Sheffield, did not speak Spanish, and stubbornly refused to learn the language, often committing such social gaffes as addressing society matrons as "Sonora" (Calles' home state) rather than "Señora."[29]

In December, 1927, not three months after his arrival in country, Morrow engineered his *coup de grace*, convincing Calles that Article 27 should not be interpreted retroactively, and that oil company concessions granted by Díaz should be held in perpetuity The subsequent supreme court decision, dictated by Calles, was a bit anticlimatic: the big companies had mostly moved south to Colombia and Venezuela and east to fabled Arabia. 125 out of 147 U.S. drillers still in Mexico were already in compliance with Calles' 1925 decree and many had never stopped punching new holes while their fates pingponged between Washington and Mexico City.[30] Nonetheless, Morrow crowed to Coolidge that Calles "was the best president of Mexico since Díaz."[31]

After the revolution, notes Meyer, "Americans involved in negotiations in Mexico were always on the lookout for another Díaz."[32]

A MURKY CAPER

1928 signaled the final year of Plutarco Elías Calles' four-year presidency, and, like all his predecessors in this fractious chain of succession, he was reluctant to leave office, an attitude that soured relations with the rest of the revolutionary family. For years, Obregón had waged a campaign to alter the Constitution so that he might be returned to the presidency for a second term, a goal to which Calles offered unconvincing lip service. An oblique attempt on Obregón's life was made in November 1927 when bombs were tossed at the one-armed candidate's limousine. Although Calles pinned the blame on a priestly conspiracy and had a number of clerics fusilladed (including Father Miguel Pro, now a certified martyr of the Roman Catholic Church), there were some who considered that the president's own ruthless labor czar, Luis Morones, had ordered the hit.

Then, on July 17th, a few days after Obregón's victory in the presidential balloting, the Caudillo of Caudillos was gunned down by a devout Catholic cartoonist. José de Leon Toral had been asked to sketch his portrait during an election victory party at the La Bombilla nightclub in southern Mexico City. Like the contemporary assassin Mario Aburto, the self-confessed triggerman in the March 1994 murder of the ruling PRI's presidential candidate, Luis Donaldo Colosio, Toral was savagely beaten by a mob of the president-elect's cronies and tortured by authorities before confessing his culpability. Public suspicion that Calles had himself orchestrated the hit erupted when the *"Jefe Máximo"* ("Maximum Chief"—as he had taken to calling himself) arrived at Obregón's funeral and was angrily confronted by the dead man's supporters. Colosio's rival, Manuel Camacho Solís was similarly attacked when he sought to attend the PRI candidate's funeral. Calles' complicity remains conjectural, but Obregón's murder doubly served the Maximum Leader's purposes: it demonized the Catholic Church (and pushed the Vatican into signing a peace treaty rather than be further stigmatized by the fanatic *Cristeros* and their war) and it excluded the Caudillo of Caudillos from further political participation.

WASHINGTON'S PARTY

During Calles' four years as president and the four more during which he would control that office, lasting institutions were created that survive today. Under Calles, José Vasconcelos, a crusader for "humanist" education, built thousands of schools and the National Autonomous University (UNAM) was expanded into a mass higher education system. The Bank of Mexico was established as a central bank and the Bank of Credit began operations (although it was almost immediately bankrupted by extravagant loans to deadbeat generals). Auto plants were installed and infrastructure blossomed. Highways were constructed from the border, bringing the first wave of U.S. tourists to Mexico.

Among the visitors were photographer Edward Weston and his lover, Tina Modotti, who helped spread the word of the nation's exotic cultural revolution far beyond the cactus curtain. Sergei Eisenstein arrived to film "*Que Viva México!*" the unfinished odyssey shot between 1930 and '32, with Upton Sinclair's backing—Eisenstein's epic was eventually turned over to *Tarzan* director Saul Lester and cut up for travelogues.[33]

The Maximum Chief also built monuments. The Monument to the Revolution, the massive dome at the end of Juárez Avenue in central Mexico City, was erected to contain the remains of Carranza and Obregón and, some critics suggest,[34] to inter the Mexican Revolution itself. Another monument designed to enshrine—and embalm—the revolution was the Party of the National Revolution.

The PNR was constructed to contain all of Mexico's increasingly contentious political currents under one big tent. With 8,000 separate parties (Krauze's estimate)[35] gerrymandering the land, many of them led by revolutionary caudillos run amuck, Calles had two options to achieve national cohesion: kill off the generals one by one (he was only partially successful on this score) and/or encourage them to join the PNR. The latter project was endorsed by Ambassador Morrow from its conception,

On September 1st, just scant weeks after Obregón's assassination, El Jefe Máximo fulfilled his constitutional duty by delivering to Congress his final State of the Nation address (the "*Informe*"). In the course of the hours-long speech, Calles unveiled his plans to establish a system of institutions led by a state party that would both unite the nation and insure future peaceful transition of power from one president to the next. At the *Informe*'s conclusion, the ritual ovation for the Supreme Chief was led by Dwight Morrow, an embarrassing violation of protocol[36] that was noticed by the newspapers of the day and "an explicit signal that Washington would totally support Mexican authoritarianism," as social analyst Sergio Aguayo recently noted in the daily *La Jornada*: "Thus began an understanding [between Washington and the Mexican state party] that is still maintained."[37]

The PNR was officially constituted in Querétaro in March, 1928. The party was initiated "not so much to win elections but to hold in check interest groups" such as farmers, workers, bureaucrats and the military, notes Meyer.[38] Every elected officer in the land was obligated to join the PNR and pay dues to it.[39] The establishment of a state party, opines Cosio Villegas, was a mechanism "for controlling the real contradictions in Mexican society."[40]

A decade later, the Party of the National Revolution became the Party of the Mexican Revolution (PRM) and eight years after that, the Party of the Institutionalized Revolution (PRI) which still holds power, even as you read these words—although more tentatively than ever—the longest-running political dynasty in the known universe and one which, from its very first breath, has drawn Washington's applause.

THE MAXIMATO

El Jefe Máximo inserted his proxies as president between 1928 and 1932, regularly stepping in to take back the reigns of power whenever his appointees deviated from the company line. Mexican history labels this period the "*Maximato*." The first "*minimato*" was presided over by interim president Emilio Portes Gil, a puppet who aped Calles' increasingly fascist tendencies. Never a great fan of agrarian reform, the general halted all land distribution, an endeavor encouraged by Morrow who, on the other hand, was buying up so much land in the Zapatista state of Morelos that wags wagged that the entity should be called "Morrow-los."[41] Calles also muzzled Morones' labor movement, and, increasingly suspicious of the Reds he had once embraced, the general ordered Portes Gil to break relations with the Soviet Union in 1929 and set about to liquidate the Bolshevik menace at home. Cuban socialist Julio Antonio Mella was assassinated and his lover, Tina Modotti, driven from the country.

The U.S. ambassador once again came to Calles' rescue in the winter of 1929 after half the army, under General Gonzalo Escobar, rose up against the imposition of Portes Gil. Rushing in U.S. military aid, some of it fresh from U.S. army arsenals, including 32 planes used to bomb Escobar positions (Lindbergh was signed on to train the pilots), the revolt was squashed flat—45 generals were hauled before firing squads.[42]

Pascual Ortiz Rubio, a former governor of Michoacán, was imposed on the PNR as its presidential candidate in the 1930 election. José Vasconcelos, veering wildly rightwards himself, threw his hat into the ring in opposition. What happened to the Vasconcelos campaign proved a blueprint for what would happen to every opposition candidate that challenged the PNR, the PRM, or the PRI in future Mexican elections. The press either ignored the educator's campaign or attacked him relentlessly as the reactionary he had become.

Vasconcelos' campaign propaganda was destroyed and meetings were systematically broken up—in March 1930, Calles' "Gold Shirts" opened fire at a Mexico City rally, killing several supporters. And when, despite the violence and the vilification, Vasconcelos actually won the balloting (or so Krauze insists),[43] the election was just stolen from him— "in (the Vasconcelos) contest, the PNR made its bones in electoral technology, a science in which it has, since then, specialized..."[44]

The PNR had one hidden hand in stealing the election from Vaconcelos: Dwight Morrow's. The ambassador worked ceaselessly behind the scenes to promote the fortunes of Calles' puppet and the party which he represented.[45]

But despite Morrow's support, the PNR candidate's ascendancy to high office did not begin easily. Ortiz Rubio was shot and severely wounded upon leaving his own inauguration. Although he eventually recovered, his stay as chief of state was soon curtailed. Inheriting the presidency as the Great Depression settled in over the land, he had the audacity to suggest a suspension of debt payments after U.S. creditor banks advised him to slash education and military budgets in order to finance repayment. Ortiz Rubio's threatened suspension did not at all please the Jefe Máximo and his associate at the U.S. embassy, who, after all, had been dispatched to Mexico by J.P. Morgan to resolve the debt question once and for all. Ex-President Ortiz Rubio read about his removal in the morning *El Universal*.

Dwight Morrow, having democratized Mexico for J.P. Morgan, now grew weary of the place and returned to New Jersey where he ran for, and won, a senate seat in 1930. He dropped dead the following year.

Abelardo Rodríguez, a Baja California entrepreneur who made his fortune rum-running during U.S. Prohibition[46]—he is also reputed to have been the only Mexican president to have actually been born in the United States—took over for Ortiz Rubio and lasted through the scheduled 1934 elections. Calles' next stooge would also be an ex-governor of Michoacán, who had fought alongside him against Villa and Zapata and the *Cristeros* and collaborated in his extermination campaign against the Yaquis, Lázaro Cárdenas Del Río.

Chapter 7

"GENERAL, PRESIDENT OF THE AMERICAS"

The Revolution's Last Gasp

Don Saturnino straddled the silver counter-stool at the Café La Blanca on Cinco de Mayo Street in the old quarter of Mexico City and noticed that I was leafing through the Lázaro Cárdenas volume of Enrique Krauze's series, "Biographies of Power."

" *'Ta Bien, 'ta bien*," the tiny Aztec-featured man remarked: "That's good. That's good."

Like many Mexicans his age, Don Saturnino loves to chat away history. Cárdenas is a favorite topic. Saturnino is a great admirer of the man who served as Mexico's president during his youth—but he is profoundly distrustful of Lázaro's son, Cuauhtémoc, who left the ruling PRI in 1987 to found the left-center opposition Party of the Democratic Revolution. In order to justify his own—I think—delusional PRI tendencies, Saturnino draws fanciful distinctions between the father and the son.

We have had this discussion several times in the decade I've hunkered down at La Blanca's for evening tamales and *café con leche*.

"Cuauhtémoc talks too big—that's why they will never let him become president," Saturnino admonished, an odd assertion, given the parsimony of the younger Cárdenas's speech patterns.

"Saturnino, they will never let him be president because he says the right things," I corrected. Cuauhtémoc Cárdenas has since become the first opposition mayor of Mexico City and an odds-on choice for the presidency in the year 2000.

Manuel, the courteous, white-tunicked waiter, served up *oaxaqueños* and *cafés con leche*.

"*Pues*, Cuauhtémoc should have learned from his father to keep his mouth shut until he had enough firepower to back him up," the old man pounded lightly on the counter, "That's precisely how Lázaro Cárdenas *chingo á* Plutarco Elías Calles."

DEPRESSION PRESIDENTS

Like Franklin Delano Roosevelt, his counterpart across the border, Lázaro Cárdenas was a Depression president, and the destinies of both men were shaped by that tumultuous epoch of proletarian agitation and heightened class warfare. By 1932, Mexico had hit rock bottom. Half the workforce was not working, and a half-million more unemployed Mexicans were being shipped home by U.S. authorities—scapegoats for the failures of the U.S. economy, then as now. Mexico's industrial output, including petroleum production, had plummeted to an all-time low and the nation lost two-thirds of its export trade—65% of Mexico's commercial transactions were with the United States,[1] an early warning of the dangers of tying national fortunes to the economic salubrity of the Colossus to the north. Payments on the foreign debt, now shaved to $237 million by Morrow-inspired renegotiations, were once again suspended, and U.S. and British capital flight had dried up all investment.[2]

Lázaro Cárdenas learned just how deep the depression cut during his eight-month-long election campaign tour of the remotest corners of the nation. Standing in the middle of scorched cornfields or squatting over smoky hearths in the Indian sierras, Cárdenas paused and listened up. The complaints and the dreams of the nation's rural masses filtered through his enormous ears and what he heard told him that, as painful as the Depression was, for too many Mexicans, there was no difference between the economic nosedive and what had come before. Propelled by the empty promises of the revolution, desperation stalked the land.

An apocryphal tale, with which the Communist Party USA used to regale converts, had Franklin Delano Roosevelt marching into the National Association of Manufacturers and ordering the tycoons to regulate the excesses of capitalism. "You either get me—or the revolution," he is supposed to have snorted. Similarly, Cárdenas committed his presidency to cutting the cards in favor of those who needed the most help—so long as the Revolutionary family held onto the deck.

The aspirations of the great majority of Mexicans, who had suffered, without recompense, two decades and more of the social turmoil historically clumped together as the Mexican Revolution, had to be rescued—or else the revolution was lost. Beholden as he still was to the Maximum Chief, Lázaro Cárdenas moved cautiously, consolidating a base for change that would not force Calles' hand before the younger man was ready to deal him out.

Pivotal to Cárdenas's political survival—and that of the revolution with which he identified his presidency—was the creation of a nationalistic popular front of workers and farmers, bolstered by the nascent middle class, a quiescent military and a neutralized Catholic Church. Such a convergence could only be built on deeds, and throughout his presidency, Lázaro Cárdenas traveled incessantly, spending a third of his six years in office out of the capital, listening to his impoverished subjects rather than spouting the hollow rhetoric of the revolution, expropriating land from the land rich and passing it on to those who had none, inaugurating schools and dams and paved highways. The president's option for the poor was as sure as that of any liberation priest, but the sermon he preached was one of revolutionary nationalism.

During the *sexenio* (1934-40) of Lázaro Cárdenas, the revolution stopped mocking itself, rolled up its sleeves, and handed out 45 million acres to the landless in the form of *ejidos* (rural community production units), communities (indigenous communal land holdings) and "small properties" (*pequeñas propiedades*—100 hectares or less.)[3] By the time Lázaro Cárdenas was done, a third of all Mexican citizens had access to a piece of land—less than 3% of the population had owned land when the revolution commenced.[4] From the Yucatán *heniquen* plantations to the private Caribbean oil enclaves, and throughout the great expanses of the north, the wellspring of the revolution, Cárdenas challenged the gringos' rights to annex huge slices of productive Mexican land. In the Laguna region of Coahuila-Durango, the president confiscated 220,000 hectares from foreign owners and returned them to the communities[5]—his portrait still hangs in revered niches in many Laguna households. Cárdenas confiscated Yanqui spreads in the Yaqui Valley of Sonora and Baja California's Mexicali Valley where the Colorado River Land Corporation and the Anderson-Clayton agribusiness conglomerate had laid claim to a cotton empire, founded on Imperial Valley water and coolie and Mexican labor. Although U.S. ambassador Joséphus Daniels fretted at the expropriations, he was mollified by assurances that confiscation of U.S. oil company holdings was not in the cards.

Lázaro Cárdenas's overtures to urban workers exhibited a similar vocation for the underclass. Rather than curtailing and controlling a restless labor movement, as Calles had demanded of his jewel-encrusted labor boss, Luis Morones, Cárdenas permitted a thousand flowers to bloom and blaze. 642 strikes broke out during his first year in office—only seven had been permitted during Calles' final year as president.[6]

A parallel strike wave gripped Roosevelt's first term. When CIO autoworkers in Flint, Michigan seized the means of production (Fisher Body #2), the National Association of Manufacturers prevailed upon Roosevelt to "condemn trespass" but the president "remained silent."[7] Lamentably, Roosevelt also remained silent after the Republic Steel massacre on Memorial Day, 1937, during which police and strikebreakers gunned down a dozen workers.[8]

South of the border, Cárdenas never allowed the force of the state to crush Mexican labor democracy. Audaciously declaring that workers had every right to seek to narrow the distances between management and labor, the president refused to intervene on behalf of irritated industrialists and foreign factory owners.[9] Lázaro Cárdenas's understanding of the role of his government was that it should serve as the rector between social forces, always striving to nullify the inequities implicit in Mexico's glacial class structure.

MEIN KAMPF

As Don Saturnino quite correctly appreciates, the young president (at 39, he was the youngest ever to assume the job—Carlos Salinas subsequently jumped that claim by being several months his junior) Lázaro Cárdenas did not reveal his cards for a full year. But his constant forays to dispense *ejido* lands and his non-interventionist blessing of striking workers nettled the Jefe Máximo, who still fancied himself a kingmaker. The ultimate straw was said to be a telephone workers' walkout that tied up service in the capital for months—Calles reportedly owned a chunk of Mexican Telephone Company (an AT&T subsidiary) stock.[10] Cordial relations between the Maximum Chief and his one-time protégé sagged precipitously and the president staged a series of preemptive strikes, first kicking Calles out of the party he had founded and then out of the country of which he had been maximum chief. On April 10th, 1936, the soon-to-be-ex-strongman was routed from bed by federal agents and put on a plane for Texas, a copy of *Mein Kampf* wedged under his arm, and Luis Morones covering his right side.[11] "I was expelled from Mexico for fighting communism," Calles told reporters when he touched down in Dallas.[12] Mexico's most oedipal political drama was finally over.

THE CHAIRMAN OF THE BOARD

Lázaro Cárdenas now was free to consolidate his dominion. The Mexican Workers Confederation (CTM) was created, pulling together 1,200 unions and 200,000 workers under the firebrand leadership of Vicente Lombardo Tolédano. While never a member of the Mexican Communist Party, Tolédano swallowed the Soviet line hook, line, and sickle. The CNC or National Campesino Confederation incorporated newly-formed ejido associations and agrarian leagues from throughout the nation—Cárdenas proposed to arm its members to protect their newly-acquired lands, but the military balked at the idea. The president took control of the shell of the state party and molded it into his own model for control.

In April, 1938, 12 days after expropriating the holdings of the foreign oil companies, a decree that captured his country's heart and soul and made

Lázaro Cárdenas "the president with the most personal power in the history of Mexico,"[13] Cárdenas decreed the transformation of the PNR into the Party of the Mexican Revolution (PRM). In place of the vertical structure through which Calles had imposed his dictates, the PRM would be built horizontally, composed of corporate sectors, each with an equal voice—farmers, workers, and "popular" (loose enough to include lumpen and middle class, bureaucrats and businesspeople). The military was the fourth horseman of the corporatization of the ruling party. Although he would have to personally suppress one last uprising two months later in San Luis Potosí, Cárdenas had tamed the military's ambition to take state power. Despite the investiture of the four sectors, the president clearly remained the Chairman of the Board—"inclusive but authoritarian" is how Meyer[14] describes the new party.

The creation of a modern state party is Lázaro Cárdenas's most enduring—and most damning—contribution to Mexico's tortured political drama. For 68 years, the party, which eventually Cárdenas came to rue, has monopolized the public life of the nation, stealing elections with impunity, co-opting and coercing opposition parties into submission, and all but extinguishing the spark of democracy which millions of Mexicans crave. From the day of its birth, it has been welcomed into the world by its overseers in Washington—first as the PNR by Dwight Morrow, then as the PRM by Daniels and Roosevelt, and, finally, as the PRI, by U.S. presidents from Harry Truman to Bill Clinton—as the best guarantee for stability in Mexico and, thus, U.S. national security—which, as we have learned repeatedly in this volume, is roughly equivalent to the security of U.S. investments and investors in Mexico. Today, U.S. interests continue to be served—at the cost of Mexican democracy.

The PRM got its first workout in the 1940 election to choose Cárdenas's successor. The outgoing president selected Manuel Avila Camacho, a moderate general, utilizing the identical undemocratic mechanism that Calles had used to select him—a ritual still quite the rage among PRI heads of state (the only kind there have been around here up until now), known, variously, as the "*dedazo*" ("the big fingerpoint"), or the "*destape*" ("the unveiling'), in which, without benefit of pre-candidate conventions or primaries, the outgoing president simply designates his heir.

In its debut performance, the PRM behaved as might be expected. Avila Camacho's self-anointed opponent was another general, the flamboyant flyboy Juan Andrew Almazán, who ran as the right-wing antidote to Cárdenas's "Bolshevik collectivism" by pulling together a hodgepodge of dissident trade unionists and discredited intellectuals, ominous Cristero-descended "*Sinarquistas*," and even prominent Reds like Diego Rivera who claimed he saw "the fascist face beneath Cárdenas's socialist masque."[15]

Like Vasconcelos a decade before, Almazán weathered vicious attacks and may well have won the election, but we'll never know—the highly dubious official count was 2.76 million for Avila, 15,000 for the right-winger.[16] Fists flew. Street fighting broke out in downtown Mexico City and military rebellion was hinted further south. In the end, the beaten candidate did what most out-of-favor Mexican politicians have always had to do—he fled north across the border and appealed to U.S. President Franklin Roosevelt, who refused to see him (although he did get as far as lunch with Roosevelt's son, Elliot). The U.S. blueprint for the re-annexation of Mexico required the dictatorship of the state party.

Ironically, nearly a half-century later the next Cárdenas found himself on the other side of the money. After he won a conflictive election at the polls from Carlos Salinas in 1988, computerized vote manipulation snatched victory for the PRI from Cuauhtémoc's lanky jaws, setting off months of political turmoil. Even before the "official" vote count had been issued in the July 6th election, Ronald Reagan became the first foreign head of state to extend his congratulations to the ambitious Salinas.[17] Blinded by habit and purposeful delusion, U.S. presidents continue to believe that U.S. interests in Mexico are best served by reflexively welcoming the election of still another PRI president.

THUNDER FROM A BLUE SKY

The week beginning March 11th, 1938 started on a wretched note. Hitler marched into Austria. Further south, after resisting months of siege from Franco's black legions, General Vicente Rojo ordered the evacuation of Teruel, a retreat that sealed the fate of Republican Spain. Later in the week, the Luftwaffe strafed Barcelona, killing 1,300 in a single night, a bombing of a civilian population that sowed the terrible seeds of Dresden and Hiroshima. On the eastern front, Stalin's executioners slaved around the clock to purge the Motherland of dissidents. This writer saw first light in New York City, born to Jewish communist parents. Fascism was on the horizon.

In Mexico City that week, labor militancy continued to stir up the stew. Over 500 strikes occurred in 1938. In the upper class Condesa colony, servants laid down their mops and hung the red and black flags that are the symbols of strikes here from the balconies of the town houses where they toiled.[18]

But a longer-lived and infinitely more troubling labor conflict was the one between the foreign petroleum companies and the oil workers, amalgamated, under Cárdenas, from various company unions into the Mexican Revolutionary Oil workers (STPRM). In late 1936, the *petroleros* had demanded a 66-million-peso package in wages and benefits and the companies offered 14 million. The issue was ultimately submitted to the Mexican Supreme Court for arbitration. During the first week in March 1938, the justices decided, at long last, that 26 million was an appropriate compromise. The companies were given seven days to comply. "We can't pay and we won't pay," retorted a Standard Oil executive[19], thereby risking contempt of the court and daring Cárdenas to have the *cojones* to spit in the face of the International Capitalist Conspiracy by expropriating foreign holdings.

When, on Friday, March 18th at 10:30 in the evening, Lázaro Cárdenas went on Mexican radio direct from the Palacio Nacional to announce the end of the Anglo-American annexation of the *Patria's* oil lands, both the companies and the Roosevelt administration were dumbfounded. Expropriation "struck like thunder from a blue sky," Daniels later noted unhappily.[20] But the president's defiance thrilled the Mexican people every bit as much as had Pancho Villa's raid on Columbus. Cárdenas had "returned to the humiliated and those denigrated for centuries, their lost dignity," pens the poet José Emilio Pacheco. News of the expropriation vibrated an entire continent. "General, President of the Americas," Pablo Neruda eulogized.[21]

On the pages of his ever-faithful diary, Lázaro Cárdenas remembered how, on his very first day as a young soldier serving under Calles in the Huasteca region, an oil company executive had offered him a bribe. "The companies, with their great estates on our coasts and in the heart of our national territory, insult and hurt us…"[22]

200,000 jubilant Mexicans, as flushed with victory as if the national selection had won the World Cup, jammed the Zócalo on March 20th. Women shook piggybanks on street corners and lined up to hock their excess jewelry outside the Belles Artes Institute to raise the compensation Cárdenas promised the oil companies he would pay in ten years time. Campesinos came from the countryside, offering their turkeys.

In one decisive stroke, Lázaro Cárdenas had united the nation by giving it what it most needed to sustain the revolution—a sense of sovereignty in this cursed geography "so close to the United States and so far from God." Over the years, the Expropriation has acquired a sort of sacred, nationalist aura on "the altar of the *Patria*" and is still celebrated with grand fanfare each March 18th by Mexico's presidents, even in this age of neo-liberal privatization, while they hypocritically plot to sell the nation's petroleum resources to the highest foreign bidder.

Cárdenas's nationalization of the oil holdings and the creation of Petroleos Mexicanos (PEMEX) was designed to vault Mexico into the modern world—the new, expropriated reserves would be the engine of industrial development. But the net impact of channeling the nation's petroleum into internal consumption all but drove Mexico out of the international oil market by the mid-'40s and limited foreign investments.[23] Nonetheless, what Mexico lost in international revenues was well worth its weight in national pride.

WAR CLOUDS MASSING

In another age, Lázaro Cárdenas's audacity would have automatically activated a U.S. Naval blockade of its Caribbean ports and the landing of the marines at Veracruz—bellicose antics that both Roosevelt and Daniels had once collaborated upon in 1914. In his biography, Daniels continued to argue that he had done so to help "liberty-loving Mexicans" throw off Huerta's tyranny.[24]

But times were decidedly more dicey now than in the days when U.S. gunboats ruled the southern sea. Indeed, in his diary entry on the eve of expropriation, Cárdenas wrote that the moment was propitious because a new World War was knocking on the door: "Let us see if democracy-loving U.S. and Britain will respect Mexican sovereignty now…"[25]

By 1938, the oil producers no longer exhibited the enthusiasm for Mexico as in those first ebullient days of discovery—production had slipped to a mere 47 million-barrel drop in the bucket by 1937, and most of the majors were serenading dictators in other latitudes. Still, the "Mexican Problem" had cost them abundant grief down the years and the companies were not going to let Cárdenas off the hook without a fight. A boycott on Mexican oil and silver was organized and oil production equipment needed for the survival of the fledgling PEMEX was denied by U.S. vendors. Standard Oil of New Jersey issued a steamy pamphlet, "Legal Robbery in Mexico," and there were persistent rumors that the companies were fingering Calles for a comeback from his San Diego exile. Royal Dutch, which now owned Aguila, was particularly incensed—it had hit important strikes in its Poza Rica field in 1938, and actually owned 60% of the total confiscated resource. The multinational was able to prod Great Britain into breaking off diplomatic relations with Cárdenas.

But the companies had little juice with Roosevelt, who had put down cousin Teddy's Big Stick when U.S. troops finally abandoned Nicaragua and Haiti in '33-'34. The Roosevelt braintrust had another, more pressing agenda now: the consolidation of the so-called "Good Neighbor" policy, a strategic alliance to immunize Western Hemisphere markets from Axis competition. Memories of the Zimmerman telegram, with its Teutonic pledge of restoring to Mexico its mutilated other half, had more scratch than the companies' indignation.

Yet, as president of the world capital of Capitalism, Roosevelt had to save face: expropriation without immediate compensation was confiscation and a violation of international law. Secretary of State Cordell Hull argued that Mexico should be taught a lesson[26] but, in the end, the notion of a Nazi beachhead south of the border cooled reflexive urges to intervene. The fascistoid Sinarquistas had been tramping through central Mexico for several seasons and residual anti-Semitism was prodded to life by Vasconcelos's paranoiac ravings and the drawings of the once-visionary artist Dr. Atl, in *Jews Over America*, which gleefully depicts the Chosen People being dragged off to the gas chambers.[27] Calles had not bought the only copy of *Mein Kampf*, which sold briskly all over Mexico.

While a staunch anti-fascist, Cárdenas got around the oil boycott by selling on the spot market, a significant source for the Nazis, Mussolini's Italy and Imperial Japan—some scholars suggest that the availability of Mexican oil fueled Hitler's invasion of France and the Low Countries.[28] Cárdenas also hinted that if he could not acquire a tanker fleet from the allies, he would turn to the Third Reich. The Mexican air force bought a number of German airplanes at discount.[29]

Yet even as Lázaro Cárdenas played high stakes poker around the oil table, Mexico grew closer to the Roosevelt administration on just about every other front. By November 1941, the two sides reached agreement on the general terms of a compensation package. Although the U.S. was temporarily out of the Mexican oil business, eight years later Miguel Alemán would ease them back in.

"The entrance of the United States into World War II put an end to the conflict".[30] As is the rule of thumb in their complicated waltz, whenever the U.S. is threatened by global conflict, it cajoles Mexico into becoming its good neighbor.

And when, scant weeks after the preliminary compensation agreement was inked, the United States declared war upon Japan and Germany, it had a firm ally on its southern border. Mexico responded to the bombing of Pearl Harbor by recalling its ambassadors from the axis capitals and, taking a cue from Roosevelt, rounded up its own Japanese residents, foreclosed on their bank accounts, and concentrated them in the capital of the country. Some were deported to serve time in United States "relocation" camps, and one group was incarcerated on a government official's ranch near Chihuahua, where they performed slave labor for the duration of the war.[31]

Despite Lázaro Cárdenas's defiant heroics against U.S. annexation schemes, geopolitical tumult had converted these ancient enemies into new allies in a series of global conflicts that would "integrate" Mexico into North American defense mechanisms. Now, with a pliable state party at the helm and common foes on both horizons, the co-optation of the revolution appeared to be complete.

PART TWO

ENEMIES INTO AMIGOS

The Military Annexation

Chapter 8

FIGHTING U.S. WARS

Soon after a tour of the Persian Gulf in the wake of the 1991 U.S.-directed blitzkrieg of Iraq, I returned to Santa Cruz Tanaco, a Purépecha Indian village high in the Meseta Tarasca of Michoacán state, just in time for the spring planting. It was the day of the Holy Cross and brass bands and weirdly-garbed dancers were pumping away all over town.

I first visited Tanaco 37 years ago on a similar spring day, liked what I saw, built a house on the edge of town, and dug in for what I thought would be the duration. Now I return on important feast days to visit my godchildren, my compadres and comadres, always bringing with me the baggage of the urban orbit in which being a globe-trotting foreign correspondent forces me to spin.

I sometimes refer to Tanaco as my social laboratory, a place to probe how deeply the issues of bad government, economic crisis, and incipient rebellion cut in a remote indigenous community whose rhythms are dictated by the stations of the agrarian year. But Tanaco is much more than an interview for me. I have a child buried in the cluttered cemetery here and I have grown gray with my old friends in this oasis of bracingly fresh mountain air and disappearing pine forests. When I return to Tanaco for my too-brief visits now, I always feel like I'm coming home.

Geography has long been a thread of interchange with my insular sierra-bound *compañeros*. They teach me the Purépecha names of the nooks of the mountains and the wild flowers that grow on their furry flanks, and I offer them exotic tales of what life is like out in the world beyond Tanaco. Just a few years ago, Nicaragua was a new concept around here.

Now, armed with snapshots, maps, and even a leaf from an Iraqi ammunition log that I had discovered embedded in the sand between two unexploded land mines just outside Kuwait City on the "Highway to Hell," where, in violation of international strictures against firing on retreating troops, 26,000 are said to have perished under U.S. attack on February 25th, 1991, I came home to report to my old comrades the aberrant cruelties that are inflicted upon commonfolks such as they by geopolitical posturing over petroleum.

We stood under the bare light bulb and I spread the map out for the *compas* to study. "This is Baghdad right here," I instructed.

"And this must be Kuwait down here," Don Santiago whispered to Miguel Baltazar. Miguel peered at the tattered map and wanted to know where the bombs had come from. "Out here, see, the blue part, where the ships were anchored," Santiago responded with authority.

I was impressed by my old friend's knowledge of this strange terrain. As in the boy Clinton's hometown of La Realidad, the agent was the mass media. In Tanaco now, there are television antennas poking through the shingled roofs of the peculiar wooden cabins the Purépechas call *trojes* and even a satellite dish or two. During the Top Gun days of American slaughter in the Persian Gulf, the Televisa network had hooked into CNN, and Mexicans, among them the Purépechas of Santa Cruz Tanaco had gotten a prolonged eyeful of the Middle East, complete with TV military experts pointing out the hot spots with their professorial pool cues. Santiago Bravo had been a good student.

Not only are Mexicans naming their babies after profligate U.S. presidents but they are also fighting, if only vicariously, America's wars. During the Persian Gulf spectacular they had gathered around the family screens just like their neighbors to the north, rooting for the USA Dream Team as if it were Saturday morning cartoon time. The Salinas government had been dissing Uncle Saddam and cheering on Uncle Sam too, upping its oil production to cover possible U.S. shortages and voting with the U.S. at the United Nations to bomb Iraq back to the Stone Age. A *maquiladora* in Monterrey had turned out cluster bomb parts of the sort dumped on the Highway to Hell, on contract with a U.S. defense manufacturer.[1]

This syndrome of affection for the modern day anti-infidel crusades of Mexico's old adversary has a history here in Tanaco...

The holiday afternoon wore on and Miguel invited me down to his homestead for a ritual meal of *choripo* chile stew and *corundas* (leaden Purépecha tamales). As luck would have it, his brother-in-law, Marcelino, was in town for the fiesta—Don Marsa is usually tramping Jalisco, hawking his homemade brooms and brushes.

During the Second World War, Marcelino had been a volunteer *bracero*, working railroad track all over the western United States—200,000 Mexicans traveled north to help the U.S. fight Hirohito and Hitler on the domestic front. Don Marsa has always been enamored of that period in his life, often regaling us with hilarious adventures in Montana or Oakland. "You know, Juanito," the old *bracero* is fond of reminding me, "we won that *pinche* war for the gringos..."

A TURNING POINT

During the final two-thirds of the 20th century, the integration of Mexico into three U.S. wars—World War II, the Cold War, and the War on Drugs— has been the North Americans' most useful mechanism for pursuing the annexation of their southern neighbors.

The entrance of Mexico into World War II was a turning point in the valiant resistance of rank and file Mexicans to U.S. domination. Just four years after Lázaro Cárdenas defied the Norteamericanos by nationalizing the oil enclaves the barons had so long annexed, Mexico became a slavish subsidiary of the U.S. wartime economy, even providing cannon fodder for the Yanqui war machine. Despite residual rage at the 1847 invasion, Mexico quite willingly volunteered for World War II, and, overnight, transformed itself from an implacable foe, always vigilant for fresh incursions from the north, into an eager ally of the eternally despised gringos.

Although Avila Camacho broke off diplomatic relations with the axis powers, diligently rounded up the Japanese on the heels of Pearl Harbor and cut commercial ties to businesses listed in the U.S. "black book" as Nazi agents, Mexico did not actually declare war on anyone until May 1942. First there were outstanding accounts to settle with Washington—the dollar price of compensation for the oil expropriation had to be agreed upon before Mexico and the U.S. could fight a war together—on the same side.

Moreover, domestic opposition to this odd twist of allegiances had first to be overcome. "Isn't it a violation of your sovereignty to permit the United States government to tell you who you can do business with?" the German ambassador pointedly asked a Mexican diplomat.[2]

Even without an arrangement on compensation, the instruments for strategic alliance rapidly fell into place. In January 1942, the Mexican-North American Defense Commission was established to coordinate joint operations and President Avila appointed Lázaro Cárdenas to direct Pacific Coast defenses against Japanese attack. General Cárdenas's appointment underscored "the limits of cooperation" between these two former adversaries, reasons Lorenzo Meyer.[3] Cárdenas patiently explained to his new comrades-in-arms that, while Mexico and the U.S. shared "a common cause," the North Americans should not consider his countrymen and women to be "inferiors."[4] When the United States sought to install radar stations on the Baja California peninsula, Cárdenas would only okay emplacement if they were operated by Mexicans, and despite repeated U.S. requests to build landing fields on Mexico's Pacific coast, permission was never granted.

But as vital to Washington's war effort as the physical defense of the American Pacific rim, was the conversion of Mexico into an enthusiastic supplier of raw materials for the U.S. arsenal. The Mexican-North American Commission on Economic Cooperation, a primitive forerunner of the North American Free Trade Agreement, committed Mexico to supply vast quantities of lead, nickel, mercury, graphite and antimony for U.S. munitions stockpiles. By late 1942, Mexico was literally arming its old foe and U.S. domination of the Mexican economy was so complete that fully 90% of the nation's trade was with its new boss to the north.[5]

¡GUERRA MUNDIAL!

Oil was, of course, the critical ingredient—the U.S. boycott, imposed at the companies' behest after expropriation, was frittered away to symbolic pretense by 1942. Oil was also the fluid that finally prodded Mexico into declaring world war. On the 14th and 22nd of May in that year, German U-boats operating in the Caribbean (a sea described by naval historian Samuel Eliot Morrison as the Nazis' "happiest hunting grounds"[6]), sank Mexican tankers heading for the U.S.—causing a combined loss of 12 lives. Even after the lethal attacks, Mexican disdain for its northern neighbor was so intense in some quarters that many still opposed taking sides. Long before the Tonkin Gulf perfidy, U.S. complicity in the tanker sinkings was suspected—some nationalists considered the events had been contrived to push Mexico into the war.[7]

Curiously, although the Sinarquista Right, which dreamed of a Nazi Mexico, resisted a declaration of war with all the nationalist fervor it could muster, the Communist Left, spearheaded by Lombardo Tolédano, who was furious at Hitler's tearing up of the non-aggression pact with Moscow, pushed for an immediate Mexican plunge into the gringos' war. On May 28th, President Avila formally declared Mexico at war with Germany, Italy and Japan and was granted emergency war powers by his Congress to suspend constitutional guarantees if he sensed that the nation's security was at stake.

Proclaiming his as a government of "National Unity," the nation's six ex-presidents—including both Cárdenas and Calles—were lined up to stand with Avila Camacho on a Palacio Nacional balcony for a photo op that would graphically demonstrate their common commitment to winning the gringos' war. Cosio Villegas was not convinced by the display: "National unity silenced social demands and favored the resurgence of factors and powers that had been weakened" during Cárdenas's rule."[8] Under "National Unity" policies, land distribution was paralyzed and the class struggle put on indefinite hold so that Mexico might more effectively fight the North Americans' battles. Howard Cline, whose histories of the era are vigorously skewed towards U.S. State Department views, crows at this capitulation: "It came as a shock for most Mexicans to find themselves fighting with, rather than against, the Colossus of the North. This surprise was…made palatable by the Left, which had been so recently flaying 'Yanqui Imperialism.' "[9]

Mexico's entrance into World War II under Washington's wing marked the nation's emergence as a member of the global community. For the first time, Mexico would take sides in an international conflict. But such alliance did not do much to solve the nation's historical geopolitical quandary—which has always been one defined by south-north contradictions. Now the Aztec nation was fighting for the "West" against the "East" in a dogfight over markets in which Mexico had only the most minimal share.

TÍO SAM WANTS YOU!

Although compliance with U.S. economic demands was Mexico's most strategic contribution to the West's victory, Mexicans fought and died alongside their Yanqui brothers and sisters on World War II battlefields. Mexican troops were ultimately placed under the United States Western regional command directed by General John De Witt Jr.[10] Entrusted with safeguarding the southern California coast from another Pearl Harbor, Mexican submarines patrolled Pacific waters. Cárdenas's fleet was integral to U.S. defenses until the Japanese threat diminished after 1942. It had never been much of one anyway—the only enemy attacks on the U.S. West Coast were the shelling of a Santa Barbara refinery and the September 8th, 1942 bombing eight miles north of Brookings, Oregon, when an Imperial Japanese sub launched a custom-made Zero over the mainland. The incendiary attack, designed to ignite coastal forests, fizzled out in an unseasonable rainstorm.[11]

But Mexico's most celebrated exploits on World War II battlefronts were in the Far Pacific. Squadron 201, 300 air force volunteers trained in the U.S. to fly P-47 "Thunderbolts," were ordered to the Philippines under the command of Douglas MacArthur in June 1945, a largely ceremonial appearance dedicated to mopping up Japanese positions around Luzon and Formosa. The Aztecs flew 50 missions and lost eight men.[12] Despite their late arrival in the Asian skies, the Mexican pilots showed up just in time to be tainted by the mega-war crimes committed by their U.S. commanders at Hiroshima and Nagasaki that August.

300,000 Mexicans, like my old pal Marcelino, put down their hoes and their sledgehammers and marched off to the U.S. to fight the war on the gringos' home front, leaving Mexico's agribusiness bosses wondering who would harvest their crops and get them to market. The bracero effort was actually a reincarnation of a World War I program that brought tens of thousands of Mexicans to the U.S. each year between 1917 and 1920. Many of the braceros who now returned to the U.S. had been booted out during the Depression-era mass deportations. Now Washington welcomed them back, "to win the *pinche* war…" Others who went north had more specialized tasks: Atomic physicist Rafael Bejarmo worked on the first bomb.[13]

On the U.S. side of the dividing line, Mexican nationals living in the U.S. were recruited into the military in exchange for promises of citizenship. A quarter of a million Mexicans and Mexican-Americans joined up. Of those who eventually saw action, almost a thousand were killed. 1,500 survivors received Purple Heart citations, and 17 Mexicans, more than any other minority ethnic group, were awarded the Congressional Medal of Honor.[14] Returning vets formed their own version of the American Legion after a Mexican-American war hero, Félix Langoria, was denied a funeral service at a Texas burial chapel—the American G.I. Forum.[15]

Despite Mexican heroics overseas, the conflict did not prove much of a race equalizer in California. Mexicans suffered discrimination within the Armed

Forces and the June 1943 Los Angeles riots followed repeated racist assaults against Mexican *pachucos* on the east side of that city by drunken off-duty sailors. The so-called "Zoot Suiters" were accused of being unpatriotic because their "drapes" used up cloth that, presumably, otherwise could have been dedicated to wartime pursuits.[16]

THE PROFITS OF WAR

While Mexican raw materials armed the U.S., the U.S. armed the Mexican military. Under the lend-lease program, Mexico accumulated $40 million USD worth of military equipment at a 67% discount,[17] a donation that re-equipped and reshaped the Mexican army's tactical capacity—the Mexican air force is, in fact, a war baby. Mexican officers were sent north to train under their former enemies, an unthinkable turn-around from ten years previous. Meanwhile, Avila Camacho, a general himself, dissolved the military bloc in his Congress (an elected faction of retired officers has returned in the 1990s). His successor, Miguel Alemán, cut the military budget to 10% of what it had been before the war and eliminated the military as a sector of the PRI. In return, the generals were compensated with their own small arms, munitions and uniforms industries and given total autonomy over their own internal affairs. Whereas the military had once been an overtly political player, it now became sphinx-like in its relations with civilian power.

War was also highly profitable for the Mexican economy. The shortage of U.S. goods had forced Avila Camacho to institute an import substitution program that spurred private manufacturing. Protectionist tariffs, handsome subsidies and deferred taxes oiled the skids for the new industrialists, who were often the direct descendants of the revolutionary family—such as Alemán, the nation's first civilian president since Madero, but the son of a revolutionary general.

Foreign investment recovered dramatically, reaching almost a half-billion by 1945—but it had been twice that in 1921.[18] In 1944, the investment statutes were revised to allow for 100% foreign ownership of Mexican enterprises—if the government considered it in "the national interest" to do so—and the debt burden was finally discharged at 10 cents on the dollar. The settlement once again allowed Mexico to borrow on the international market. Such preferential treatment sent an unmistakable message to Mexico's rulers: fighting U.S. wars can shower blessings upon national economic health.

Fortunately for the PRI politicos that now ran the revolution, Washington was already plotting a new war from which they would profit handsomely. Even as skeletal POWs were being liberated from the Nazi concentration camps and the mushroom clouds dissipated into invincible venoms over Japan, the U.S. was revving up its war machine to mow down the Commies. Adjusting nicely to its new vassal state status, Mexico would be a firm Cold War partner.

Chapter 9

COLD WARRIORS

From the Truman Doctrine to Tlatelolco to the Teheran Next Door

The campaign to vaccinate the Western Hemisphere against the Red Virus was first unveiled at the U.S.-convened Inter-American Conference on War & Peace, celebrated in the Spring of 1945 at Chapultepec Castle in Mexico City, the site of the purported suicide plunge of the Heroic Children almost a century previous. The conference set the parameters for Latin American participation in the soon-to-be-formed United Nations, but its subtext was hemispheric security and continued economic "cooperation"—Assistant Secretary of State William Clayton did not win kudos from his "Good Neighbors" when he proposed that Latin American nations continue to funnel cheap, raw materials to power U.S. postwar industry at the expense of their own.[1]

The Inter-American Reciprocal Assistance Treaty, signed in Río in 1947, reinforced the Monroe Doctrine and pledged signatories to safeguard the continent from "foreign ideologies." The Río conference also chartered the Organization of American States as a rampart against communism. The OAS was formally constituted the following year, in Bogotá, coincident with the assassination of the liberal Jorge Eliécer Gaitán. The "*Bogotazo*," which commenced minutes after Gaitán's slaying April 9th, 1948, and culminated in the burning of hundreds of offices and churches and the loss of at least 3,000 lives (Fidel Castro was a witness), set off years of bloodcurdling violence between Colombian Liberals and Conservatives. Such an inauspicious beginning did not augur well for democracy in Latin America.

At the conclusion of World War II, popular labor-backed governments held power in many Latin nations: Perón ruled in Argentina, Gertulio Vargas in Brazil, Juan José Arévalo led a liberal civilian government in Guatemala, Haya de la Torre's APRA party was a rising force in Peru, and Gaitán came to power in Colombia.[2] But after U.S. President Harry Truman declared the Cold War in 1947, the phantom of Communist infiltration became justification for Washington's support of conservative civilian presidents and military dictatorships that could more ruthlessly sanitize Latin America's wedge of the so-called "Free World" of the Red Threat.

WASHINGTON'S MAN IN MEXICO

Miguel Alemán was Washington's Man in Mexico. The son of an Obregónista general who had committed suicide after the Caudillo's assassination rather than submit to four more years of Calles' rule, Alemán was the first non-military heir to the Revolutionary throne. As governor of Veracruz, he had first captured Cárdenas's attention for his patriotic support of the oil expropriations in that state. From Avila Camacho's campaign manager, he had gone on to become the youngest and most ambitious member of the General's wartime cabinet. As Interior Secretary (*Gobernación*), he was charged with insuring internal security and, armed with dictatorial powers granted the Avila government when the president declared war in 1942, he tormented subversives mostly on the left side of the political spectrum. Lombardo Tolédano was hounded from the CTM by Alemán's unprincipled red-baiting and replaced by a Mexico state milkman. 56 years later, the mummified Fidel Velázquez was still leading that moribund labor confederation when he passed on at the ripe age of 97. "Miguel Alemán knew more about the Red underground" than anyone else in Mexico, gushes State Department apologist Howard Cline.[3]

Miguel Alemán assumed the presidency in 1946 without the difficulties that marred the investitures of his predecessors. He entertained virtually no opposition to his candidacy, save for Máximo Avila Camacho, the outgoing president's brutish brother, who inexplicably passed away just on the eve of the PRM-PRI's nomination of Alemán. The six years that Miguel Alemán ruled Mexico stand in cruel contrast to the Cárdenas *sexenio*. "Alemán reappraised the Mexican revolutionary process and found it absurd."[4] His guiding thesis was that wealth had to be created before it could be distributed to the masses, a non-functional concept in no-trickle-down Mexico.

The new president dismantled Cárdenas's social revolution, introducing *amparos* (exemptions) that allowed big landowners to retain and augment their holdings. The process permitted the consolidation of the very *latifundias* that Cárdenas-inspired agrarian reform had sought to dismantle. Not a decade after the oil expropriation, Alemán allowed the oil companies access to Mexican petroleum under the scam of "risk contracts" that permitted drillers a hefty share of any resource they brought in.[5] To guarantee the success of his pals in the booming industrial sector, Alemán threw up a wall of tariffs against the U.S. imports Mexican manufacturers were trying to imitate for domestic consumption. Despite this stinging slap at free market economics, U.S. investments in Mexico rose to $752 million in 1952, Alemán's final year in office.[6]

ALEMÁN'S MEXICAN MIRACLE

Miguel Alemán also recast Cárdenas's party as the Party of the Institutional Revolution: "The official party was reorganized to eliminate from its program any dangerous elements of social reform," affirms Daniel Cosio Villegas.[7] Although the military was sent back to barracks, the sectorial structure was retained. Alemán, like Cárdenas, remained the supreme chief, favoring party fortunes with state resources and designating candidates for every office in the land. The PRI won its first election in 1946 by a crushing margin that would be repeated year after year for generations of Mexico's legislative life—147 seats in the Chamber of Deputies to seven for the right- and the left-wing opposition The PRI obtained a "*carro completo*" ("full car"—every seat filled by a PRIista) in the Senate—to which no opposition member would be admitted for the next four decades.

"The only real political party in Mexico is the PRI, which is run by Mexicans for Mexicans," wrote Cline in one of several volumes of then-current history that are still prominently featured on the shelves of the U.S. embassy's Ben Franklin Library in Mexico City.[8] Cline celebrates Alemán's "driving desire to democratize Mexico," gullibly swallowing such Orwellian New Speak as the PRI's long-standing commitment to "perfecting democracy" (by seeking to obliterate those opposed to its rule, I suppose).[9]

In order to rationalize its Cold War bias, the State Department purposefully hoodwinks the citizenry for which it is said to be working by affirming that the PRI is a paragon of democratic intent. This same sort of perverted argument has led Washington to tout the perfection of democracy by such model democrats as Papa Doc Duvalier, Generals Pinochet and Videla, Admiral Bordaberry, Rafael Trujillo, Alfredo Stroessner, the various Somozas, and Efren Ríos Montt, the first evangelical Christian practitioner of genocide in Latin America.

Those golden years of growth and optimism inaugurated by Miguel Alemán and exalted as the "Mexican Miracle" were also ripe with nepotism and corruption. Alemán himself bought up half of Acapulco and sold it to the government he ran, which then sank millions into infrastructure and tourist promotion for luxury hotels at which the president controlled the action.[10] Having granted radio mogul Emilio "*El Tigre*" Azcarraga Mexico's first television license, the president was made a major stockholder in what has become Televisa, the largest entertainment conglomerate in Latin America.

A RED UNDER EVERY BED

If Roosevelt and Cárdenas shared destinies shaped by the Depression, Truman and Alemán grounded their authority in the Cold War. Harry Truman's celebrated visit to Mexico City on March 3rd, 1947, the first-ever U.S. president to set foot in the Mexican capital despite four centuries of political and geographic contiguity, came just nine days before "Give-'em-Hell Harry" delineated the "Truman Doctrine" to the U.S. Congress, an address agreed upon by historians as the declaration of the Cold War between the "free world" and the Evil Red Slave Empire. The 1847 battle flags of the defeated Mexican army that Truman returned to Alemán by way of healing up old wounds were one more depressing reminder that Mexico had indeed lost the war for political independence—as well as half its national territory. From now on, Alemán's Mexico would be the perfect Cold War ally.

To reciprocate for amigo Miguel's effusive hospitality, Truman sent the presidential airbus, jocularly dubbed the "Sacred Cow," to Mexico City to fly the Mexican president to Washington where, in April 1947, the suave Alemán became the first of his race to address a joint session of the U.S. Congress—the honor has subsequently been bestowed upon Mexican presidents through Carlos Salinas (Ernesto Zedillo has yet to be asked). Alemán's speech dutifully endorsed both Truman's and Monroe's Doctrine. A ticker-tape parade was arranged by New York City Mayor William O'Dwyer, soon to be appointed ambassador to Mexico—O'Dwyer fled the Big Apple just as a congressional committee began probing his ties to Frank Costello and other influential Mafiosi.[11] Miguel Alemán came home from North America with two $50 million USD loans and the "Plan Alemán" under his wing, his own version of the Truman Doctrine that spoke to keeping "foreign influences" (a code word for Communism) out of Mexico.[12]

One clause in Alemán's Cold War pact with the Gringo Devil allowed U.S. security agencies to operate in Mexico. Both the FBI and the CIA were given *carte blanche* to ferret out nests of suspected Reds. Mexico was the only country in Latin America where the FBI continued operations against the local Left after the CIA took over in 1947, as rogue agent Philip Agee notes in his highly-revealing diary.[13]

According to the late Manuel Buendía, CIA offices were established at Melchor Ocampo #252 in Mexico City in 1948, the year after the agency was birthed from the World War II Office of Strategic Service.[14] Buendía, whose *CIA In Mexico* remains a popular guide here, was himself assassinated on orders from the chief of the Federal Security Direction (DFS), the CIA's longstanding Mexican government contact agency. [15]

One focus of FBI-CIA vigilance: the Mexico City-based "American Communist Group" or ACGMC—expatriates driven out of the U.S. by the draconian anti-Communist purges then boiling on the other side of the Río Bravo. Because passports were being denied prospective subversives, many U.S. Reds fled to Mexico, where such documents not required—and ran right into Alemán's U.S.-sponsored anti-Communist security apparatus. Morton Sobell, escaping the witch hunt that would lead to the burning at the stake of his comrades, Julius and Ethel Rosenberg, came to sunny Mexico in 1950 and was immediately handed over to the FBI, who hauled him off to Alcatraz to serve a 30-year sentence. The next year, perennial Communist Party U.S.A. presidential candidate Gus Hall jumped bail on his Smith Act indictment and swam the Río Grande south. Hall woke up in a Mexico City motel room surrounded by a combined team of Mexican and U.S. agents who escorted him back across the border.[16] But not every political soul in Mexico had joined the Cold War zombie legions. 10,000 Communist sympathizers marched to the *zócalo* to protest Hall's summary deportation.[17]

With the approval of Alemán and his Secretary of the Interior and successor Adolfo Ruiz Cortines, Mexican authorities encouraged FBI and CIA agents to make mail stops and tap telephones of U.S. Communists.[18] As late as 1958, American Reds were still being rounded up and charged with promoting a student strike at the UNAM.[19]

Mexico's Cold War assignment was to support U.S. anti-Communist standards on the international front and suppress domestic Communism at home, which, you will recall, is only a stone's throw away from U.S. soil. Anti-Communism was not an alien philosophy in Mexico—it had been one of the few principals that Calles and the Church eventually came to agree upon. "*¡Cristianismo Sí! ¡Comunismo No!*" signs dotted Mexican roadways in the '50s. Middle class Mexicans seemed particularly susceptible to the Red Under Every Bed theory of subversion, gobbling up the lurid tales they were fed daily by the Mexican yellow press. The U.S. propaganda operation in Mexico, which had been installed to convince the Mexican people that Nazism was not in their best interests, was converted overnight to Cold War attack, hand-delivering regular dispatches to Mexico City newspapers where red-baiting editors and columnists parroted them in print. E. Howard Hunt, that lean and hungry spook, boasts of perpetrating such dirty tricks against Mexican leftists. [20] The CIA's Pan-American News Agency, housed at Río Plata #48 in the Cuauhtémoc Colony, near the embassy, was one source of misinformation, the murdered Manuel Buendía informs us. [21]

Diplomatic relations between Mexico and the Soviet Union had been restored in 1942 to facilitate the common front against fascism and ambassador Constantino Ousmanski "wasted no time in building up a suspiciously large embassy staff."[22] For the next half-century, the FBI and the CIA and their Mexican proxies would expend countless numbers of man and woman hours spooking that staff. Despite the surveillance, issues of *Soviet Life* were distributed freely throughout the country, even in Santa Cruz Tanaco, where Santiago Bravo and I browsed through them with interest every month. Another source of local Soviet life in Michoacán in the late '50s was the Stalingrado barber shop, a gathering spot just behind the bus station in Uruápan—the proprietor sported a faithful replica of Stalin's bristling mustache.

Alemán and Ruiz Cortines waged a relentless war on Communism, expunging leftists from their governments in McCarthyesque purges, hiring labor goons to break up the Communist-led railroad workers union, imposing their own "Charro" leadership upon the workers and red-baiting left opposition candidates wherever the left dared to raise its head. "Only careful unraveling could distinguish between homegrown ideology and the general Russian conspiracy to subvert worldwide and local order," Howard Cline reassured his readers.[23]

PAVLOVIAN SERVILITY

Beyond its border, Mexico performed in lockstep with the U.S., backing Washington at the United Nations in every confrontation with the Soviet Union. Mexico voted the U.S. line on U.N. participation in the Korean War, but unlike other Third World stooges, sent no token troops. Instead, old wartime economic cooperation treaties were reinstated and Mexico stepped up production to supply U.S. G.I.s in the Far East with such strategic goods as sisal rope and bananas.[24] Alemán's Pavlovian servility to his Cold War Masters was played out upon a backdrop of wholesale human rights abuse being committed against his countrymen and -women by the United States Immigration and Naturalization Service—in 1950, 600,000 Mexicans were deported by the U.S. Border Patrol during "Operation Wetback" and another 700,000 are estimated to have left on their own.[25]

Alemán's appointment of Ruiz Cortines, a fellow Veracruzano, as the PRI nominee in 1952 laid to rest rumors that he would seek reelection. The Interior Secretary's run for the roses was not as smooth a one as his predecessor's. The colorless Cortines was challenged by General Miguel Henríquez Guzmán, a populist who proposed to rescue the revolution that Alemán had hijacked. Henríquez appealed to the Left to support his cause and received Cárdenas's blessing in the early stages of his campaign. But government repression soon scared off followers—a few dozen Henríquezites were killed in the weeks leading up to the July 6th balloting, and on election night Mexico City police descended upon a rally, killing six and jailing 561 Henríquez supporters .[26] Ruiz Cortines was awarded the presidency with 75% of the vote and the PRI held Congress 170 to 15. Washington breathed easier.

THE FRUITS OF ANTI-COMMUNISM

Accused by Henríquez of having collaborated with the Yanquis during Wilson's infamous 1914 invasion of Veracruz, Ruiz Cortines assumed an anti-U.S. posture on stage but, behind the scenes, proved to be a noble Cold Warrior.[27] One of the first tests of his anti-communist mettle was next door in Guatemala. General Jacobo Arbenz had confiscated unused United Fruit land in a 1952 agrarian reform campaign and General Eisenhower's secretary of state, John Foster Dulles, hit the ceiling—Dulles had long represented the company's interests in Latin American.[28] The Secretary of State warned that Arbenz was introducing a "foreign ideology" into the Americas' bloodstream and pressured U.S. OAS allies for backup. Cortines timidly pleaded with Washington not to confuse domestic reform with Communism but when Dulles put the screws on and demanded that Arbenz rid his administration of known Communists (Ernesto Che Guevara was a low-level health official), the Mexican president clammed up. Purportedly committed to a foreign policy of non-intervention in the internal affairs of other Latin nations, a lesson it had bitterly learned itself, Mexico was "discreetly silent" after the CIA overthrow of Arbenz forced the general into exile, in his underwear.[29] The coup condemned Guatemala to a 40-year-long nightmare of murderous dictatorships under which 300,000 mostly indigenous people were massacred.

Cold War compliance was good for business—U.S. investment in Mexico rose from a half-billion to $806 million by 1956 and bank loans were easily available—the nation's foreign debt rose from $156 million in 1950 to $603 million by the end of Ruiz Cortines's administration.[30] Still, high protective tariffs—and Mexico's quixotic application of the principle of non-intervention—were stones in the shoes of this otherwise chummy relationship.

The hard hand displayed by Ruiz Cortines against the Marxist Menace notwithstanding, the Mexican security apparatus let one pair of soon-to-be-dangerous subversives slip right through its fingers. After a year-long residence in Mexico City, plotting to liberate Cuba from Batista's iron claw, Fidel Castro and Che Guevara were detained by Mexican authorities and tortured "until the wax ran out of their ears" (Arturo Durazo).[31] The two were rescued by another hard-nosed DFS official, Fernando Gutiérrez Barrio, also a Veracruz native, and on November 26th, 1956, they and 80 other Cuban patriots sailed off from Tuxpán (Veracruz) on the leaky 62-foot fishing trawler, the *Granma*. The rest, one must concede, is history.

SOCIAL DISSOLUTION

Two consecutive conservative presidents signaled a shift to the left and Ruiz Cortines elevated his labor secretary, Adolfo López Mateos, to the presidency in the 1958 "*dedazo*." A dashing figure after his predecessor's pallid political personality, López Mateos enjoyed unconditional support from labor during his campaign, but on the eve of the election, railroad workers—the Communists had regained the leadership—staged a nationwide strike, signaling months of fitful work stoppages that dragged on through Holy Week 1959, the most traveled season of the year. Finally, López Mateos responded with military force, sending the army onto the trains and jailing 2,600 militants, among them leaders Demetrio Vallejo and Valentín Campa.

With his newly designated Secretary of the Interior, Gustavo Díaz Ordaz, at the controls of the engine of repression, Communists and fellow travelers were pursued for the felony crime of "Social Dissolution." One prominent victim of this crackdown was the Stalin-loving muralist David Alfaro Siqueiros, imprisoned with Campa and Vallejo and the journalist Filomino Mata at the Lecumberri Black Palace, where political prisoners became the star tenants. The drab Cold War routine of censorship, coercion, imprisonment and capitulation dampened the spirits of social activists. Nothing short of a revolution, instigated by two former travelers on Mexican shores, would snap the Left out of the doldrums.

¡CUBA SÍ! ¡YANQUI NO!

The eruption of Fidel Castro's revolutionary army into Havana on New Year's Day 1959 put a serious crimp in the Cold War alliance between Washington and Mexico. The U.S. panicked that "this beachhead for International Communism threatened to spread everywhere in the Western Hemisphere"[32] but many Mexicans were looking in another direction and saw Fidel's triumph as a victory of the south over the north, rather than a setback for the west. Ever since the 12 survivors of the *Granma* had fought their way into the Sierra Maestra, the vicissitudes of the Cuban revolution had been tracked in many Mexican homes and there was genuine jubilation in Mexico City that New Year's season.

Lázaro Cárdenas was an early booster of the "*Barbudos*" and on July 26th, 1960, before a mammoth Havana throng, he pledged the Mexican people's defense of Fidel's triumph, until "the ultimate consequence." Like Mexico, the annexation of Cuba had been coveted by the Yanqui Founding Fathers, and, as in the Mexican Revolution, the Cubans had overthrown a corrupt U.S. puppet regime, instituted land reform and expropriated U.S. oil installations.

Washington's consternation at the outpouring of pro-Cuban sentiment in the heartland of its southern "good neighbor" and Cold War accomplice was poignant. The *Saturday Evening Post*, that paragon of capitalist virtue, sent a reporter to Mexico to find out "Will Mexico Go Castro?"[33] Both Eisenhower and Kennedy energetically set about to reverse this appalling trend. The OAS was convened time and again to read the Cuban commies out of the Inter-American system. The initial conclave was finally sited in San José, Costa Rica, after one OAS member nation after another, fearful that Fidel's Latin legions would ignite a new "*Bogatazo*"-like social explosion, balked at volunteering their capitals for the conclave.

The 1960 Declaration of San José was a curious document. On one hand, the U.S. managed to impose reaffirmation of the Monroe Doctrine, which condemned the presence of "extra-continental powers" in the Western Hemisphere.[34] On the other, López Mateos' foreign minister, Manuel Tello refused his signature unless this exclusionary clause was balanced by one condemning the intervention of one American state in the internal affairs of another. The two theses canceled each other out and rendered the declaration worthless, and, at any rate, Fidel Castro tore the document up before 300,000 chanting fans in Havana, defiantly tweaking Washington by announcing that he had established diplomatic relations with Mao's China.

The U.S. tried again to oust Cuba from the OAS at Punta del Este, Uruguay in 1962. Because it had reflexively broken off diplomatic relations with Castro, following the expropriation of one-time U.S. firms, Washington felt it was now the duty of all other law-abiding American states to follow suit, an argument Mexico again rejected. The OAS was summoned into session a third time the next year, in Caracas, where Venezuelan President Rómulo Betancourt, greased up by easy Alliance for Progress cash, charged that Cuba had sent its guerrillas into his hills in order to overthrow the prevailing Oil-ocracy. Mexico found the evidence weak and refused to join the stampede to blockade and boycott into which Washington herded all other member states—recent revelations by Cuban generals suggest that the charges were not so trumped up after all.[35]

What the U.S. could never get into its arrogant skull was that the more it kicked Cuba, the more the Mexican people obligated their government to defend the revolution. López Mateos caught a taste of this bitter reality in April 1961 when CIA-hired-and-trained anti-Castro *gusanos* (worms) sailed into the Bay of Pigs on Cuba's southwestern coast and were captured, one by one, by revolutionary forces as they stumbled onto the beach at Playa Girón. The failed Yanqui-sponsored invasion stirred Lázaro Cárdenas to fly off to Havana to make good on his promise to defend Cuban socialism "until the ultimate consequence," but López Mateos sent troops to the Mexico City International airport to prevent the flight from lifting off.[36]

The next evening, a frustrated Cárdenas climbed atop a truck in a *zócalo* jammed with more than 100,000 Mexican Fidelistas and reiterated his commitment. The cries of "*¡Patria o Muerte! ¡Venceremos!*" and "*¡Cuba Sí! ¡Yanqui No!*" reverberated in the plazas of the nation's major cities. The Stars & Bars were charred with Bolivarian rancor and the mood was unmistakably anti-*Norteamericano* as I huddled cautiously in the shadows of downtown Uruápan, Michoacán where a mob was gleefully torching the North American Institute.

Rather than risk the domestic repercussions that voting Washington's anti-Castro ticket would bring down upon his "Leftist" image, the Mexican president steered a middle course and recommitted his nation to non-intervention, the ostensible bedrock of Mexican foreign policy. Despite Washington's admonitions, López Mateos continued to maintain diplomatic relations with the pariah revolution across the Caribbean.

KING KENNEDY'S KOLD WAR

Adolfo López Mateos was a crypto Cold War operator and his support of the three U.S. presidents—Eisenhower, Kennedy and Johnson—who served during his own six-year term was forged on shared anti-Communist sympathies.

John Fitzgerald Kennedy's June 1962 visit to Mexico was a high point in López Mateos's Cold War partnership. Young, movie-star handsome, and, above all, a professional Catholic, Kennedy came bearing gifts: the return of El Chamizal, an island in the middle of the Río Grande-Bravo that had reverted to the U.S. when the river changed course in the 19th century. The aforementioned Alliance for Progress, a high-gloss counterinsurgency effort designed to dim the glamour of Cuban social reforms, was imposed upon Mexico. The soon-to-be-assassinated U.S. president sweetened the pot by dealing López Mateos a piece of the former Cuban sugar quota.[37] A million Mexicans lined the capital's avenues to greet the U.S. royal couple, the first presidential pairing ever to set foot on Mexican soil. Jackie, in a shimmering pink suit, spoke in the Mexicans' native tongue. JFK stood on the sidelines and cheered "Viva to Mexico!" [sic].[38]

Mexican intellectuals who did not go along with the Kennedy program soon found themselves excluded from the (North) American Dream. During Kennedy's missile crisis "quarantine" of Cuba in October, 1962, Carlos Fuentes opined, in the weekly Siempre, that the U.S. blockade demonstrated the failure of JFK's Alliance for Progress. For years after, Mexico's premier novelist was barred from visiting the country where he had grown up, the son of Lázaro Cárdenas's consul in Washington. "Fuentes is a dedicated, dues-paying member of the Mexican Communist Party," reads the visa turndown, a document signed by one Saxton Bradford and recently made available through the U.S. Freedom of Information Act to the critical weekly Proceso.[39]

SCREWING THE CUBANS

Adolfo López Mateos spouted lefty rhetoric ("I am an extreme leftist within the Constitution")[40] for the home crowd even while he jailed and executed leftists. "To restore law and order, the government rounded up the more flagrant agitators" was how Cline saw it.[41] Vallejo and Campa and 23 other railroad union leaders were sentenced to 16-year jail terms and two Soviet diplomats were thrown out of Mexico for supposedly fomenting their strike. Teachers' Union leader Othón Salazar, who had marched tens of thousands of maestros up from Oaxaca to lay siege to Mexico City, was jailed dozens of times and removed from office. Rubén Jaramillo, the heir to Zapata's popular movement in Morelos, and his entire family were executed by government thugs in May, 1962. When push came to shove on the Cuban issue, López Mateos showed his true colors and they were not red, white, and green: Mexico backed up Kennedy against Soviet anti-Monroe Doctrine mischief in the Americas during the 1962 Cuban missile crisis.

To insure continuity in the anti-Communist alliance with Washington, López Mateos designated his Red-baiting Interior Secretary, Gustavo Díaz Ordaz, as his successor. The presidente-elect met with Lyndon Johnson at the LBJ ranch in November 1964 and affirmed that, despite his country's ongoing diplomatic relations with Cuba ("we can be a bridge to Cuba's eventual liberty"),[42] Mexico "stood shoulder to shoulder" with the U.S. in the defense of the Free World.

In time, Washington came to accept and even appreciate Mexico's "special relationship" with Fidel Castro. The Cubana day-flight from Mexico City to Havana provided U.S. spooks with a window through which they could crawl in and out of that besieged island. The CIA arrogantly infiltrated the staff of Mexico's Havana embassy[43] and every traveler bound for that socialist paradise was photographed, fingerprinted, and otherwise intimidated by Mexican police. Returnees were brutally interrogated—the former Cuban ambassador to Nicaragua, Julian López, still bears the scars of one encounter[44]—their souvenirs confiscated, and their names placed on a blacklist for U.S. embassy consumption.

Other aspects of the Cuban-Mexican relationship were equally prejudicial to that Beacon of Socialism in the Americas: trade was virtually nonexistent and Mexico refused to send PEMEX technicians to assist Cuba in maintaining the recently expropriated petroleum installations.

"Mexico did develop a disguised blockade," affirms Lorenzo Meyer.[45] The arrangement eventually pleased Washington and the investors for which it stands—U.S. investments in Mexico soared to $1.3 billion, an all-time high, by 1964, López Mateos's final season as president.[46]

THE SPOOK AT THE DOOR

Both Adolfo López Mateos and Gustavo Díaz Ordaz had another "special relationship"—with one Winston Scott, CIA station chief in Mexico City from 1956 through 1969, a lengthy and tumultuous stretch. Despite the unfortunate similarity in names to the despoiler of Mexico in 1847, Scott and López Mateos grew so thick that the Mexican president was the official witness to the chief spook's second wedding.[47] Under Scott's direction, the Agency performed a rainbow of services for the Mexican presidency. Agents kept close tabs on comings and goings at the Cuban and Soviet embassies, whose phones were also scrupulously bugged. Just how close the surveillance was is evidenced by Lee Harvey Oswald's September 26th-October 2nd, 1963 visit to Mexico City when agents snapped his photo ten times at both diplomatic outposts, and recorded half as many phone calls from the presumed assassin—but apparently failed to detect his deadly mission.[47]

Scott's boys also trained their binoculars on the Mexican Left, building up more extensive files than local intelligence—the dossiers were then shared with the DFS and federal police. A CIA-prepared summary of Leftist plans and activities was placed on Díaz Ordaz's desk every morning. "The station also prepares a daily intelligence summary for Díaz Ordaz with a section on activities of Mexican revolutionary organizations," according to one of Scott's aces, the fast-becoming-disillusioned Philip Agee.[48]

By the mid-1960s, anti-Communism had become so ingrained in local security agencies here that the CIA could just sit back, feed data to the government, and watch the Mexican cops go to work. "Mexican security services were so effective in keeping the left down that we didn't have to worry about it," Agee confessed. Instead, the Agency provided guidance: "the station is of great assistance in planning for raids, arrests, and other repressive action."[49]

But, despite the Company's best efforts to defuse the forces of revolution, the Mexican time bomb was ticking towards explosion.

TICK TOCK

In 1964, Díaz Ordaz was forced to use the military to crush a strike of doctors and nurses. "¡Cuba Sí! ¡Yanqui No!" signs proliferated on the picket lines. A singular incident in 1965 ought to have sent chills running down the spooks' spines. On September 23rd, a group of 13 armed guerilleros, led by a normal school teacher, Arturo Gamiz, attacked an army barracks in the Chihuahua hills at Ciudad Madero, not 150 miles from the U.S. border. Although most of the rebels were killed, the assault paralleled the one staged a dozen years previous by Fidel Castro at the Moncada Barracks outside Santiago. Mexican police spread throughout Chihuahua, showing campesinos pictures of Che Guevara and interrogating them about his whereabouts—Che was then missing on the world scene:[50]

By the early 1970s, 15 distinct guerrilla "focos" were active in Mexico robbing banks, bombing foreign corporations, kidnapping prominent governors, businessmen, and even U.S. consuls in Guadalajara and Hermosillo. The most prolific of these focos honored Gamiz by calling itself "The 23rd of September Communist League."

One space where radical temperatures grew particularly feverish was the Autonomous University in southern Mexico City. A 1966 strike there had forced the rector to resign and now Maoists and Castroites, Sovietchiks, Trots, New Lefties, Anarchos and Social Democrats battled for leadership of the burgeoning student movement. The CIA and its Mexican colleagues kept Díaz Ordaz apprised of the developing situation.[51]

COLD WAR OLYMPICS

But the Mexican President's attentions were distracted. By 1968, Díaz Ordaz was obsessed by the prospect of the 17th modern Olympic Games to be held in Mexico City in mid-October, the first ever to be staged in a developing nation. Although López Mateos had snagged the Games for Mexico, bringing them off was to be Díaz Ordaz's crowning achievement, showcasing the Mexican Miracle for the whole world to witness. $200 million USD, a princely sum in those days, was abstracted from social budgets to spruce up Mexico City for the magnum event—which critics compared to Porfirio Díaz's 100-year birthday party for Mexico's Independence in 1910, a spectacular whose lavishness had contributed to his downfall.

The Olympics have always been much more than sporting events. With scads of chiefs of states and their security teams popping up to urge on their nation's athletes, the Games are always ripe with intrigue. While onstage hi-jinks steal the spotlight, what goes on backstage can determine global advantage. The finishing touches to Franco's fascist putsch were applied at the 1936 Berlin Games while Hitler flacked his Master Race. The postwar anti-communist conspiracy was active at London and Helsinki, Melbourne, Rome and Tokyo, in infiltrating Soviet-bloc delegations, planting spies, and scoring "defections." Mexico City would be no exception.

The Company shipped Philip Agee to Mexico City to set up the intelligence operation inside the Olympic organizing committee. Ostensibly, he was arranging poetry festivals and science exhibits, but his subterranean duties included infiltrating the Red enemy's ranks and cultivating potential conduits inside the PRI.[52]

Agee arrived with the usual Cold War illusions: "In Mexico, the government keeps our common enemy rather well-controlled—with our help. And what the government can't do, the station can usually handle by itself. The operational environment is friendly, even though the enemy is considerable in size and danger."[53] For Agee, the enemy were the Communists, radical students, and their Soviet bosses. But by the time the super snoop left Mexico City after the student massacre, in late 1968, he was an altered and embittered soul, about to resign from the CIA: "What happened at the Plaza of Three Cultures is happening all over the world to people trying to change the system."[54]

TLATELOLCO: COLD WAR MASSACRE

From east to west and pole to pole, Mother Earth was on fire in 1968. In February, the forces of Vietnamese National Liberation blasted the Yanqui invaders during the Tet offensive, knocking Lyndon B. Johnson off the presidential throne. Red Guards rampaged through Chinese cities and tens of thousands took to the streets in conformist Japan to prevent the docking of a U.S.

nuclear missile-carrying vessel. In May, workers and students came within a hairsbreadth of toppling the De Gaulle government and the Prague Spring signaled the beginning of the end for Soviet hegemony in eastern Europe. Martyrdom was much in mode: the previous October, the Agency had taken out Che in the Bolivian outback, creating an instant logo for the revolution. In April, Dr. King was gunned down in Memphis, and in May, Bobby Kennedy caught a dose of lead from a PLO supporter in L.A. In Chicago, the whole world was watching. But few North Americans, outside of Agee and his associates, were watching Mexico City that summer.

The fuse was ignited by a street brawl between high school gangs, during which police invaded a UNAM preparatory school, violating the university's treasured autonomy, guaranteed in 1929 by Vasconcelos. On July 26th, the 15th anniversary of Fidel's suicidal assault on Moncada, students merged with a Mexican Communist Party (PCM) march to the zócalo that quickly disintegrated into a running street battle. Buses were overturned and burnt. Communist party headquarters were raided, and by dawn, eight were reported dead and hundreds of protesters were under arrest. The great student strike of '68 was declared the next day and by July 29th the Army was firing bazooka shells through the massive wooden doors of an historic UNAM school a block away from the National Palace.

The CIA was quick to intervene. "In the station, the Op section is very busy, getting information on planning by the strike committee and positions taken by the Communists and other Left groups," Agee wrote in his diary in early August. "Highlights of this intelligence are being passed to Díaz Ordaz and Echeverría, for use by security forces..."[55]

Fed by CIA reports, Díaz Ordaz and the PRI lynch mob majority in Congress went on the offensive: "riot coaches" had been imported from France, the students were "subversives," "professional agitators," "Pro-Castroites" and believers in "exotic ideologies."[56] The last allegation could not be denied: the music of the Doors and Dylan resounded on campus and one Cassius Clay, having refused induction into the U.S. military because "the Vietnamese ain't my enemies," became an unlikely icon of the Mexican student movement.

The most damaging charge leveled at the students was that they were "anti-Mexican," hell-bent on derailing the Olympics and blackening the eye of the nation before the whole world that soon would be watching. In spite of the government attacks, the strike spread from the UNAM to the much more working class National Polytechnic Institute (IPN) and grew precipitously from week to week—by the end of August, 400,000 mostly young people, one of the largest gatherings in the nation's stormy history of protest, were tramping towards the zócalo—among their not-very-radical demands were freedom for the all-but-forgotten Vallejo and Campa.

With the Olympics now less than a month away, Díaz Ordaz, alarmed by intelligence obtained from inside the National Student Strike Council, took off the gloves. The PRI-controlled Congress invested the president with extraordinary powers to deploy the army in order to guarantee internal security and, on September 18th, soldiers occupied first the UNAM and then the IPN, arresting virtually the entire front-line leadership of the strike council. Several students were shot in subsequent downtown street demonstrations and the turbulence forced Agee to dismantle a Jupiter missile exhibition at the UNAM. A visiting astronaut was sent home for his own protection. Washington's concerns that the conflict was getting out of hand was manifested when CIA bigwigs Allen Dulles and Richard Helms flew into Mexico City on September 27th-28th to consort with Win Scott.[57]

But the backbone of the movement had been broken by Díaz Ordaz's hard hand and on October 2nd, just ten days before the torch would come streaming into the spanking new Olympic stadium, students could only assemble 10,000 supporters, many of them mothers and siblings, for a rally on the Plaza of Three Cultures in the labyrinthine Tlatelolco housing complex—the site of Cuauhtémoc's final battle with Cortez.

The gathering was on the verge of dispersing when a military helicopter dropped two green flares over the plaza. Suddenly, a heavy volley of gunfire erupted on the plaza floor. Jonathan Kendell, in his excellent volume La Capital, describes the carnage: "While soldiers shot their way into the plaza, other troops and police, dressed in civilian clothes but identifiable by the white gloves on their left hands, began firing on the crowd from within the square. Students, parents and children were indiscriminately gunned down. With armored vehicles and security forces blocking escape routes, the panic-stricken crowd dashed back and forth from one end of the plaza to the other, unable to avoid the murderous barrage. Attempts to surrender were met with gunfire and even those who prostrated themselves on the ground were raked with bullets."[58]

By the next morning, city workers had scrubbed the plaza clean of shoes and brains and bloodstains. What had happened here? Nothing really, if you read the newspapers the next morning. A rally had gotten out of hand. Professional snipers had opened fire on the police. A few agitators, no more than 26 or 32 or 49 had been killed—the numbers vacillated from edition to edition.

Out at Military Camp #1 on the western edge of the city, soldiers burnt the corpses of the murdered students. 1,400 prisoners taken at Tlatelolco retched on the stench of their incinerated comrades. No one has ever definitively quantified the number of those executed at Tlatelolco—a Reuters reporter's count of 337 is accepted by many as accurate. New York Times correspondent Alan Riding reports between 2 and 300.[59] Whatever the real number, the dead were all ultimately victims of Mexico's Cold War complicity with

Washington, an alliance which had cost the nation dearly, as it was just beginning to realize.

Ironically, CIA documents unearthed through *Proceso* FOI requests reveal the agency's true understanding that the student movement crushed at Tlatelolco was hardly the creature of Communist Conspiracy and had, in fact, been fomented by homegrown social tensions and the worldwide youth rebellion.[60] Agee himself knew this all along: the student rebellion had been "a spontaneous popular demonstration against political violence and the PRI's power monopoly."[61] On the other hand, *Readers' Digest* and the discredited right-wing commentator Luis Pazos insisted that the student movement was the work of the KGB. J. Edgar Hoover, whose FBI continued to infiltrate the Mexican Left, fingered "Spartacists" and "Fourth International" sharpshooters for having instigated the massacre.[62]

The shocking killings had not gone unnoticed by the Olympic organizing committee. Chairman Avery Brundage called a secret emergency meeting on the morning after the slaughter. The committee came up one vote short of canceling the Games.[63]

And on October 12th, 1968, the 476th anniversary of the White Man's conquest of America, the 17th modern Olympic Games were inaugurated by Gustavo Díaz Ordaz and now the whole world was really watching. Despite the tensions that continued to convulse the capital, the spectacle came off almost without a hitch. Only the black power salutes of U.S. sprinters John Carlos and Tommy Smith disrupted the decorum of those who had resorted to wholesale butchery so that their games could begin. As thousands of white doves swarmed against the increasingly particulate-laced Mexico City sky, the peace of the grave reigned imperviously.

GUERRILLA DAYS

"*Dos de Octubre, ¡No Se Olivide!*"—"October 2nd! Never Forget It!" Mexico never has. I write these lines as another October 2nd passes. There are 85,000 people in the zócalo, 99% of them too young to remember those months of hope and blood. Tlatelolco has become a part of their history now, handed down from one generation to the next and honored as the place where the waters parted and the resistance of the Mexican people to the tyranny of the PRI Government and their North American superiors was incubated.

The air went out of the Mexican Miracle as soon as the Olympics ended. Díaz Ordaz was rarely seen in public for the two remaining years on his contract. Deeming that the *mano duro* (hard hand) was required to keep the Red barbarians under control, Interior Secretary Luis Echeverría, a stern, balding man who affected sinister tinted shades, was appointed president in the 1970 election (although not without Díaz Ordaz's last-minute misgivings).[64] As Interior Secretary, Echeverría had received frequent CIA briefings[65] and was the most senior civilian to sign off on the massacre of the students, a mass killing repeated in miniature on June 10th, 1971 when 11 students were cut down by Mexico City plainclothes police at the first march since '68, welcoming home exiled leaders of the National Strike Committee.

Outside of the capital, Echeverría's security apparatus was less discreet in suppressing the rural and urban guerrilla *focos* whose ranks were swelled by the survivors of the student movement. During his six years in office, hundreds of farmers and family members were "disappeared" along Guerrero's "Costa Grande" north of Acapulco, their tortured bodies dismembered and fed to the sea in an attempt to crush the rebellion of rural schoolteacher Lucio Cabañas and his Party of the Poor. Despite 25,000 troops and the reported presence of U.S. military and CIA advisers, it took seven years to run Lucio to ground.[65] The flame of that uprising has never quite been extinguished, as testified to by the emergence of the guerrilla Popular Revolutionary Army a generation later, in June 1996, in that same Pacific region.[66]

VEERING LEFT

Despite Echeverría's long-time association with Mexico's Cold War masters, exploding internal tensions soon drove him Leftwards. The president's expulsion of four Soviet diplomats in 1971 pleased U.S. embassy officials (no U.S. spies were ever similarly tossed), but his revival of a Cárdenas-like revolutionary nationalism as his governing ideology did not. Like Cárdenas, Echeverría traveled the country, decked out in smart leather jackets or tropical *guayaberas* depending upon the climate, handing out land to the landless (much of it waterless, worthless tracts) and, like his role model, he flew to Cuba to embrace Fidel Castro. His six years in office, which paralleled the U.S.'s stunning defeat in Vietnam and the ignominious downfall of Richard Nixon, were marked by often cosmetic paroxysms of Third World solidarity. Even while mowing down the Mexican Left at home, Echeverría roamed the south, adopting revolutions like they were collectibles—his solidarity with Salvador Allende's popular unity government did not much endear the Mexican president to his northern neighbor. After the U.S. had engineered that martyr's obliteration, Echeverría welcomed Chilean Leftists to Mexico and even took them into his administration. Indeed, Echeverría was a master at coopting his own homegrown non-armed leftists, welcoming them into the bureaucracy where their militancy was reduced to Institutional Party cant. Nonetheless, the Mexican president appeared to be a dangerous revolutionary to some U.S. congressional representatives and in 1976, 76 of them introduced a House resolution condemning Echeverría as a communist.[67]

But the United States was a divided house by the mid-'70s and the Cold War had lost a lot of its savor as a political elixir. And besides, Luis Echeverría was borrowing an enormous amount of money from U.S. banks in order to finance his version of revolutionary nationalism—the Mexican foreign debt grew to a record-busting $20 billion USD during his stint in Los Pinos, a sum that we shall soon see would help to annex Mexico's economy to Washington for the foreseeable future.

In the end, it all came tumbling down for Don Luis—economic chaos led to the first devaluation of the peso in 22 years and he left office under a darkening cloud amid rumors of military coup probably spread by the CIA which, if Manuel Buendía is to be believed, had infiltrated the campaign of Echeverría's hand-picked successor, José López Portillo.[68]

Despite the rough and tumble economic and political life that had marked Luis Echeverría's reign, U.S. investors were not frightened off. Direct investment in Mexico topped out at a whopping $4.1 billion in 1976.[69]

THE IRAN NEXT DOOR

Washington perceived López Portillo, the conservative finance minister and partisan of such free market conundrums as the General Agreement on Tariffs and Trade (GATT), as the light at the end of the Mexican tunnel. The U.S. needed a steady Cold War partner because the Central American volcano was about to blow sky high and JLP was their new Great Latin Hope. Such optimism was dashed early on, when, in 1977, Mexico confirmed the discovery of enormous oil fields in the Caribbean Sound of Campeche—a revelation that the CIA soon shared. By 1978, López Portillo was borrowing even more wildly than Echeverría had ever dreamed of doing, and informing his people that Mexico's job, from now on, was "to prepare to administrate the abundance."

The oil boom made Mexico even more strategically vital to U.S. designs on world domination, but it also gave López Portillo a lot of room in which to chart a course independent of Washington. No Mexican president since Cárdenas had such leverage.

The tall, stoop-shouldered president invited Fidel to Cozumel island in 1978, the first time the Cuban premier had touched down on Mexican soil since he sailed off on the *Granma*. That same year, working through the PRI, López Portillo took up the banner of Nicaragua's rebel Sandinistas, proclaiming their revolution, like the Cuban revolution, an extension of the Mexican one[70]—to this day, FSLN leaders like Tomás Borges and Daniel Ortega remain admirers of the PRI, which became the model for their political party. Sandinista efforts to create a similar monolithic institution was one cause of their devastating loss in the 1990 elections.

Breaking diplomatic relations with the sinking Somoza, López Portillo sent his presidential jet to Costa Rica on July 19th, 1979, to ferry the Sandinista leaders into Managua for the victory party. The following year, López Portillo joined with the freshly-elected François Mitterrand to urge the government of El Salvador to negotiate with the insurgent Farabundo Martí National

Liberation Front (FMLN), and encouraged the FMLN to set up Mexico City offices, a diplomatic gesture that other OAS nations considered shocking intervention in the internal affairs of that tiny, restless "flea" of Latin America.

López Portillo's behavior seemed calculated to outrage Washington. Revolution in Central America had revitalized Cold War phobias. Ronald Reagan had captured the White House and instructed Secretary of State Al Haig to lance the boil of Red revolution festering on America's behind. At the CIA, senior Cold Warrior Bill Casey cranked up the covert action organ. Constantine Mengis, an ideologue who "assumed total evil everywhere,"[71] was brought in to concoct the plot. Mexico was Mengis's curse. He saw it as the main strategic target for a "destabilizing coalition" that included Cuba, the Soviet Union, regional guerrilla groups like the Sandinistas, even Palestinian "terrorists" and Libyans.[72] Before moving on to the National Security Council, Mengis impressed upon Casey that Mexico was the next Iran from which a Red Ayatollah would soon arise[73]—the U.S. intelligence gaffe re the Ayatollah's rise had made "Iran" an explosive buzzword around the CIA and Mengis had written a *New York Times* op ed in which he spoke of Mexico as "the Iran Next Door."[74]

In 1981-82, with perhaps 200,000 Guatemalan Mayans fleeing across Mexico's southern border to escape the genocidal campaign of Latin America's first Hallelujah Hitler, Efren Ríos Montt, Casey became pathologically convinced that the Guatemalan Army of the Poor would soon be encamped on the White House lawn. Jeanne Kirkpatrick, Reagan's caustic-tongued United Nations *repre*sentative, considered Mexico "the next domino," a theory the lesson of Vietnam had not yet trashed around the Heritage Foundation.[75] By now, the commies were only two days' drive from Harlingen, Texas and Hollywood was wrapping up "Red Dawn," an epic that predicted Red invasion from the south. It was all very neo-Cold War.

CUTTING OFF THE SANDINISTAS

The collapse of world oil prices in 1981 pulled the rug out from under López Portillo's philanthropy and by August 1982, Mexico was so deep in foreign debt that foreclosure was threatened. Humungous capital flight depleted what margin was left and López Portillo retaliated by nationalizing the banking system to stanch the tidal wave of exiting greenbacks. We shall talk about all this in a few pages. In 1982, the president left office a few months after pledging to defend the peso "like a dog" and then ordering a brutal devaluation. When the old man appears in public these days, people still are wont to bark at him.

The debt crisis finished Mexico's flirtation with Cold War non-alignment. Under López Portillo's substitute, Miguel de la Madrid, also the ex-finance minister and the first Harvard-educated president of Mexico, the pendulum swung back to the U.S. side of the time clock. Still dabbling in Central

America, Mexico sponsored the Contadora peace process, but Reagan and Casey could not allow the Sandinistas to stay in power and soon killed that peace pact, employing Costa Rican president Oscar Arias to wreck it.

Mexican oil shipments to the Sandinistas under the San José Pact, which provides Caribbean nations with high discount petroleum, accounted for 75% of Nicaragua's oil. The spigot was turned off in 1985 after a Mexican tanker was threatened in the port of Corinto by CIA-provided Contra speed boats. "Our intention is to severely disrupt the flow of shipping essential to Nicaraguan trade...in this case, our objective is to further impair the already critical fuel capacity..." Oliver North wrote to Robert McFarland March 2nd, 1984 after four Contra "barracuda" speed boats emplaced magnetic mines in the Corinto harbor.[76] The Mexican cut-off was soon forthcoming. It was applauded by no less a Red-baiter than Elliot Abrams, the reviled U.S. Undersecretary of State for Latin American Affairs, at a senate hearing conducted by the equally unappreciated Jesse Helms.[77] By 1986, U.S. military helicopters were making fuel stops in Mexico on their way south to Palma Sola, where the Contras were being prepared to invade Nicaragua.

Much of this re-conversion to Washington's point of view was presided over by Reagan's ambassador to Mexico, John Gavin, a patronizing, Poinsett-like personality whose acting skills were known locally because of the Bacardi commercials in which he starred before taking up diplomatic cudgels. Fluent in Spanish—his mother was a Sonoran—Gavin berated Mexicans for their lack of anti-Communist enthusiasm, even browbeating the English-language *The News* into becoming a mouthpiece for the Reagan administration's Central American tricks.[78] But the Red Dread wasn't playing the way it had back in the glory days of the Cold War. With the Berlin Wall about to fall, Washington needed a new war to convince Mexicans that their national security was identical to the national security of their eternal nemesis across the Río Bravo. The War on Drugs was declared.

Chapter 10

WAR ON DRUGS

Whose National Security?

President Bill Clinton proclaims that "protecting our people, our territory, our way of life" are the objectives of U.S. national security policy, goals that are to be advanced "through engagement and enlargement"—NAFTA and drug control are listed as two key elements of such "engagement and enlargement."[1]

"U.S. National Security is a global strategic doctrine, relative to maintaining economic, political and military supremacy in its zone of influence" is how Mexican politilogue Adolfo Aguilar Zinser defines these same policies.[2]

U.S. "National Security" is a Cold War concept codified in the 1947 National Security Act, which also created the National Security Council, to combat Communist penetration of U.S. spheres of influence.[3] In the name of its hallowed "national security," the United States has mounted military invasions and suppressed internal dissent in Latin America, encouraged political assassination, civil wars and military coups, winked at torture, applauded fraudulent elections and ignored genocide. In the process, the U.S. has also transformed itself into what Daniel Yergin labels "a national security state—a nation in which external and national security concerns become dominant and domestic concerns are subordinated..."[4]

As the U.S.'s Latin American "sphere of influence" has deepened, every challenge to U.S. hegemony—from guerrilla movements to a moratorium on foreign debt payments to a reluctance to privatize a national petroleum corporation to drug money laundered in Latin political campaigns—is evaluated by Washington as a possible threat to its own "national security." Mexico, by the sheer weight of propinquity, presents the greatest threat to the "national security" of its northern neighbor. Oil, drugs, immigration, and subversion are all issues that heighten U.S. paranoia.

CASPAR WEINBERGER INVADES MEXICO

To protect its "national security" against the Mexican threat, the U.S. prepares for war. Ever since Pershing crossed back into New Mexico, the contingency plans have been on the books. From 1920 through 1940, the plan was called "The General Mexican War Plan," which mapped out the sealing of the border, blockading ports, seizing the Tampico oil fields and disconnecting rail service from the south. The General Mexican War Plan was replaced by the "Rainbow War Plan" during World War II, which color-coded Latin nations and pinpointed scenarios for intervention and cooperation—Mexico was designated green.[5]

Under former Reagan defense secretary Caspar Weinberger's contingency plans, the designated color is also green—as in dollar bills. Weinberger's scenario is detailed in his hot-selling compilation of seven scripts for U.S. global conquest, *The Next War* (with a foreward by Lady Margaret Thatcher). The year is 1999. President Lázaro Paz, a U.S.-trained economist, is assassinated and a charismatic Jesuit-trained populist, Eduardo Ruiz, takes over, nationalizing the banks (again!) and the insurance companies and "forcibly" distributing farmland to the people. The DEA establishes that the new president is in debt to the narco-lords. His repressive regime and failed economic policies drive 7,000,000 Mexicans across the border. Cocaine prices hit an all-time low on U.S. streets. When a terrorist bomb rips through San Diego's swank Horton Plaza mall (237 innocent shoppers dead), the White House is ready to move.

On April 14th, 2003, not quite 156 years to the day that Polk sent Scott across the border at Matamoros, the 24th mechanized division from Fort Steward, Georgia pushes across the Gateway Bridge and takes that same city. The 7th infantry (Fort Lewis, Washington) smashes through Reynosa and the 2nd Marine division out of Camp Lejeune stages an amphibious landing north of Tampico. When the three units hook up, "Operation Aztec" is set in motion. B-2 bombers and F-15 Strike Eagles, based in Texas and Louisiana, flush out the Mexican air force while it is still on the ground. Psy-ops planes drift over Mexico City, jammng radio and television signals, to announce the gringos' good intentions. Ruiz spews out an anti-American harangue in front of the Museum of Interventions and flees to a Zacatecas base camp, vowing to carry out a Juárez-like guerrilla war "from the Yaqui river to Oaxaca." Months later, a fleet of Apache helicopters, loaded with laser-guided missiles, finally flush out his stronghold. The former president (he has been replaced by a U.S. stooge) is pursued by the 10th Mountain division (Fort Drumm, New York), led by a black officer named James Monroe. At scenario's end, Ruiz is still on the loose but Weinberger has lost interest and moved on to script four, "Russia: 2006."

Weinberger's fantasy is backed up by firepower. To emphasize the defense of its "national security," the U.S. lines up, on its southern border, tens of thousands of Marines, Army troops, Air Force and Navy personnel, National Guardsmen and women, Border Patrol, Drug, Customs and Firearms agents, civilian and military intelligence officers, local, state and federal police forces and joint task forces of every size and shape. A solid line of 52 military installations extending from Camp Pendleton on the Pacific to the Corpus Christi Naval Station and Army Depot on the Gulf, and including 14 air bases, 15 naval air and weapons stations, four infantry forts, six marine bases, two missile testing ranges, and one submarine center,[7] back up front-line "national security" defenses. An unknown number of "defense" installations located within 100 miles of the southern border are equipped with nuclear weapons—which are manufactured in proximity to that border, at Pantex in Abilene, Texas, and tested under White Sands, New Mexico, so close to Ciudad Juárez that when simulations or actual blasts are detonated, it sets that whole city to trembling.

NATIONAL INSECURITY

One nation's "national security" is another's "national insecurity." Mexico has too often been the victim of quixotic U.S. applications of the term to much trust it. Time and again, Mexico has been cursed and incursed, intervened with, penetrated, invaded, amputated and annexed by U.S. "national security" exigencies. Without any defenses at all—although the Heroic War College does teach a military scenario that prepares for invasion from the north,[8] there is little that Mexico could do to defend its national territory if U.S. troops came rushing across the border, 1847-style.

But even if the U.S. never invades Mexico again, there are grave dangers to Mexico's own "national security" just from having the U.S. gorilla encamped on its northern border. A nuclear attack by one of the United States' many enemies on any one of its military installations in the U.S. southwest would kill thousands in Mexico's north on contact. Mexico's partnership with the U.S. in World War II was not founded on some mutual gripe with Japan, but rather the result of dangers presented to Mexican "national security" by the U.S.-Japanese conflict—contiguity with the U.S. insured that an attack on San Diego would also be an attack on Baja California.

The success of the U.S. annexation of Mexico rests upon convincing Mexicans that their "national security" is equivalent to that of the North Americans. This is not an easy sell for the Pentagon. Mexico does not even have a hard and fast definition of what constitutes "national security." Vigilant defense of national sovereignty might be a more accurate description of the Mexican "national security" equation.

In the early 1970s, Echeverría asked security planners to draw up the nation's first "national security" policy—one shudders to imagine what the infamous Federal Security Direction (DFS) considered to be "national security" priorities. After the mammoth oil discoveries of the late 1970s, these parameters were re-focused on protection of the southern oil fields. With the dissolution of the DFS, the national security mechanism was shifted to the super secret Center for the Investigation of National Security (CISEN), which signed up many former DFS agents. But social analyst Sergio Aguayo, editor of the volume *In Search of National Security*, suggests that "national security" does not have to be the bailiwick of coercive agencies—for Mexico, argues Aguayo, real national security is associated with sustainable development, repudiation of hunger and better health care.[9] Such pacifist lollygagging does not exactly fit into U.S. priorities.

CREATING THE PROBLEM

Although many battles had already been fought and lost, U.S. Commander-in-chief Ronald Reagan officially proclaimed the War on Drugs on September 14th, 1985, during a poignant nationally televised address to the American People. With his wife by his side, the elderly, orange-haired president announced he was sending on to Congress what would become the National Drug Enforcement, Education and Control Act of 1986, a bill that elevated drug enforcement to national security status. That's when Nancy stepped before the cameras to urge America's youth to "just say no."

"When the chapter of how America won the War on Drugs is written, [this speech] will be the turning point," a White House press release exulted. To prove Reagan's commitment to the drug war, his flacks pumped, the president would submit to a urine test.[10]

A defense decision directive, issued under Vice President George Bush's name that year, associated drug trafficking with Latin guerrilla groups like Colombia's M-19 and urged that steps be taken to convince supplier nations that narco-subversion be addressed as a matter of their own "national security."[11] Thus, it became the U.S. government's permanent mission to persuade Mexico that "Colombianization" and the addiction of Mexican youth loomed, if President Miguel de la Madrid, and all subsequent Mexican presidents, did not immediately commit their governments to such goals.

Mexican national security was threatened by narco-trafficking because "its judiciary is intimidated, its political system will become compromised, corruption will spread, there will be assassinations of government officials, and the sovereign powers of the state eroded," warned Robert Pastor, Jimmy Carter's "national security" advisor for Latin America, describing pretty much what has happened here in the ten years since he co-authored *Limits of Friendship* with Jorge G. Castañeda.[12]

Convincing Miguel de la Madrid that narcotics trafficking was a "national security" issue for Mexico was made easier because of the economic choke-hold Washington already had on the Mexican president as a result of 1982 and 1986 downturns.[13] De la Madrid's appointed heir, Carlos Salinas de Gortari, actually campaigned on the issue, which impressed his pal and parallel president

George Bush—it was ex-CIA chief Bush's defense directive that had, two years earlier, called for Mexico to give drugs the "national security" imprimatur.

The War on Drugs is not logo'd a war merely for propaganda purposes. The Pentagon mindset is that, in the words of the Joint Chiefs of Staff, North America is under "air, sea, and land attack"[14] from criminal Latin cartels who are trying to seduce and destroy American youth. "It's like we are the U.S. troops sitting on the Yalu river during the Korean war—we're well-trained, well-disciplined, and well-equipped, but we face an enemy with unlimited resource and safe bases," is how former Customs Commissioner Willy Von Raab encapsulated this sense of siege to *Time* magazine reporter Elaine Shannon.[15]

The urgency is a bit distinct on the other side of the Wall. Although drug traffic is criminalized one is punished here for "crimes against health" and use is not epidemic. Polls conducted by the National Psychiatric Institute since 1989 demonstrate only a slight rise in drug use—only 3% of the sample admits to having tried drugs and, for 75%, that drug was marijuana. Although Mexico is a major heroin producer (25 to 30% of the U.S. supply), only .09% of those surveyed had ever tried it.[16] The popularity and availability of cocaine, which has actually been a Mexican import since the 1950s, is, however, spreading among "juniors" (the offspring of the affluent), and its use is pandemic in drug police circles.

According to Ernesto Zedillo's health minister, the ratio of U.S. and Mexican users is about 70 to one. Secretary Juan de la Fuente asserts that 72 million North Americans have admitted to using an illegal substance at least once in their lives—as opposed to 1.5 million Mexicans.[17] But even if the drug problem is exponentially smaller in Mexico, these figures are surely cooked. Hard drug consumption is escalating along the northern border where heroin, cocaine and methamphetamines are freely hawked in Tijuana and Juárez often the result of "leakage" onto the Mexican market. The longer drugs that are on their way north are held up in-country due to increased border restraints, the more apt they are to leak onto the street.[18]

One ominous sign of rising use is the marketing of "crack" in Mexico City and Monterrey slums—the U.S. "crack" plague was the result of a new processing technique that opened up mass markets in minority neighborhood and, effectively, "democratized" a formerly exclusive drug. If U.S. security planners wanted to deliberately addict Mexican youth in order to inflict a real drug problem on the country, one that would heighten Mexican adherence to the War on Drugs, neighborhoods like the grimy Vallejo colony in northern Mexico City would be the place to begin. Such a scenario is not out of the realm of the credible, given CIA-Contra precedents.[19] Although present Mexican drug use does not seem a threat to "national security," unleashing the crack scourge upon the urban poor would certainly convert it into one.

The most seriously abused drug among the poor is alcohol, which takes a catastrophic toll in violent deaths, vehicular slaughter and the destruction of families—the social security health system calculates that 16 million citizens abuse alcohol, about a fifth of the population, and five million Mexicans are permanently damaged by this pernicious drug.[20] Industrial solvents, many of them manufactured on U.S. licenses, such as Sherwin Williams paint thinner and the ever-popular "Resistol," once part of the Dupont empire, are a crucial problem among working class urban youth. A case can be made that Mexico's most serious addiction problem is sustained by transnational corporations headquartered north of the Rio Bravo.

A BLESSING IN DISGUISE?

Convincing Mexico that drug abuse is destroying the fabric of society when so many other social cancers are involved has been a hard sell for the national security apologists. Rather than a curse, the U.S. appetite for drugs has been a blessing for many Mexicans. At one end of the social spectrum, marijuana and opium poppy cropping means that impoverished farming communities with little access to national and international markets suddenly find themselves with a new source of subsidy. At the other, Mexico's banking system, which has been teetering on the brink of disaster since the bottom fell out of the peso in late 1994, would probably be bellyup if not for the liquidity $25 billion (DEA estimate) in laundered drug money has lent it.[21] Whole economic sectors are maintained by laundered drug money—the construction industry might have succumbed to the Great 1994-96 recession if not for the narco-dollars washed through it.

Mexico's drug industry conforms to the prevailing export-oriented economic model, with just about 100% of the product being shipped north to Mexico's NAFTA trading partner. Every kilo of cocaine that gets through to Los Angeles is just further proof of the integration of the North American market, notes Jorge G. Castañeda.[22]

Like Mexico's participation in the North American Free Trade Agreement, the decision to enlist in the U.S. War on Drugs was not determined by popular referendum, but was rather a matter of political and economic expediency imposed upon the nation by the last three of its presidents. These arrangements have exposed Mexico to grave violations of its "national security"— often from yahoo gringo law enforcement agents who seem to think the War on Drugs erases the border. Mexico's participation in the U.S. Drug War has cost the lives of hundreds of members of its security forces, deepened the poisoning of the police and the military, sustained a culture of violence and impunity, and, most of all, is doomed to failure because it is really not in Mexico's "national security" interest or inclination to keep the gringos from burning out their neurons with self-designated "illegal" drugs.

Cultural resistance is an underestimated factor in this reluctance to comply with U.S. exigencies. Mexico's drug world is quirky, folkloric, touched with evil, full of bad hoodoo. It does not accommodate the computerized U.S. war machine very well. All one has to do to comprehend the incongruities is spend a morning at the shrine of Jesús Malverde down by the railroad tracks in Culiacán, Sinaloa.

BAD GREEN

History first. Jesús Malverde ("Bad Green") is reported to have been a turn-of-the-century Robin Hood who, wrapped in banana leaves, would leap from the Sinaloa underbrush to fleece wealthy travelers. When finally he was betrayed and hanged at the crossroads leading out of Culiacán to the valley beyond, the governor general, a great friend of Don Porfirio's, ordained that his body rot there to remind the campesinos what fate befell those who dared to question authority. But the farmers defied General Cañedo and each would deposit a stone to cover old Bad Green's bones as they traveled out to their fields. The first to put his stone found a lost cow. That was the first Miracle of Malverde.[23]

Now Malverde has his own shrine, near the Culiacán railroad terminal, a block from that same crossroads. The chapel is a spired Plexiglas structure, whose makeshift walls are plastered with crutches and trusses and shaved hair, artificial flowers and thousands of notes giving thanks for a new pick-up, a reduced jail sentence, a saved marriage. Malverde's head, or a ceramic facsimile of same, is balanced in a glass box. You light a candle, touch his head, throw a stone, and your dream of winning the lottery or getting a load of marijuana across to the Other Side comes true.

In addition to being the lay saint of hookers, one-legged men and migrant workers, Jesús Malverde is also the patron of Culiacán's *narcotraficantes*. It is said that when the federal government sought to build new administrative offices across the street from the burial mound that houses the bones of Malverde, a saint whose cult includes some of the most powerful men in the country, the construction machinery just stopped dead.

The Culiacán valley is the birthplace of the modern Mexican drug industry. Here, in 1943, with the blessing of the wartime Mexico-North American Economic Cooperation Commission, U.S. pharmaceutical companies were licensed to grow poppies for morphine production—traditional U.S. opium sources being cut off because of the war in the Far East.[24] Legal poppy production lasted until the end of the war when the Yanquis went home, leaving a well-trained corps of *gomeros* to score and bleed the poppies and the technological skills to process their precious gum. Mexican brown heroin poured into Texas and California in the 1950s but has been replaced by more lethal "Black Tar" in the '80s and '90s, as heroin use has revived in the U.S.

Particularly attached to its *gomero* roots is the Tierra Blanca colony where many of the region's narcos learned the trade. Jesús Malverde is a revered icon in the Tierra Blanca.

A FOOT IN THE DOOR

Mexicans plied the drug lanes long before Merck made it to Culiacán. The Aztecs utilized cannabis in their medicinal preparations and the weed survived the centuries all the way to Pancho Villa whose troops couldn't *caminar* (travel on) without it. The "muggles" that "Mezz" Mezzrow pushed on the streets of Harlem in the 1920s were grown in Mexico, most probably Michoacán.[25] Like bootleg tequila, the "contrabandistas" moved the mota across the big river as recorded in such popular *corridos* of the '20s and '30s, as "Maríano Resendez" who "killed 60 officers and carried their names on a list."[26] By the Great Depression, U.S. authorities were trying to control Mexican marijuana smuggling—deportees were often accused of being users and, in congressional testimony, the evils of Mexican reefer were so sinisterly drawn that the U.S. Congress felt impelled to pass the Marijuana Tax Act in 1938.[27] Mexico itself began eradicating drug crops in the 1940s under the military-run Operation Canador, re-baptized Operation Condor in the 1970s, when it was captained by General José Hernández Toledo, a veteran of Tlatelolco. On the other side of the ledger: during wartime, the U.S. also subsidized Mexican hemp production.[28]

U.S. Bureau of Narcotics agents, under Harry Anslinger, J. Edgar Hoover's doppelganger on the dope front, sent trainers to Mexico in the 1950s, initiating an unbroken chain of U.S. drug enforcement agents on the ground, with license to act ugly in Mexico. Nonetheless, the flow north of Culiacán heroin and Golden Triangle marijuana (Sinaloa, Durango, Chihuahua) thickened as the U.S. market exploded in the 1960s. Richard Nixon's perfidious "Operation Intercept" which created chaos along the border for three weeks between September 21st and October 10th, 1969, infuriated Díaz Ordaz and his subaltern Echeverría no end. All cars heading north were stopped and 4,000,000 travelers were searched by U.S. customs agents, hopelessly snarling traffic and commerce.[29] The escapade was designed to punish Mexico for not accepting U.S. Paraquat eradication plans quickly enough. "Operation Intercept was an exercise in international extortion," chortled G. Gordon Liddy, its operational officer.[30]

"Intercept" got the U.S. boot further inside the door. Mexico agreed to Paraquat the Golden Triangle, a contributing factor to the boom in the U.S. domestic marijuana-growing industry, particularly in northern California.[31] Mexico also received spray planes and helicopters to be flown by DEA pilots—by 1975, the agency boasted to Shannon that the U.S. was flying "every inch" of Mexico.[32] The aircraft would always need spare parts—to this day, what remains of that original fleet is still being serviced by the Texas-based E-Systems. The war being fought against drugs is being fought by defense contractors as well. The business of war is always business.

In retaliation for Operation Intercept, Díaz Ordaz and Echeverría stepped up persecution of North American hippies traveling blithely through Mexico and hundreds of young gringos suddenly found themselves at the mercy of Mexico's not very merciful justice system. Meanwhile, successful U.S. eradication programs in Turkey had dried up that important heroin source and Mexican production soared to 75% of the U.S. market (DEA stats)[33] in 1975 and '76—Golden Crescent production, after the war in Afghanistan revived production there, reduced Mexico's share of U.S. sales to 25% by 1981.

A CORRIDO FOR CARO QUINTERO

Ronald Reagan's proclamation of the War on Drugs was really the story of another U.S.-engineered drug displacement. With Veep George Bush's Navy on the high seas in the early 1980s, the all-powerful Colombian cartels began transferring Caribbean routes to Mexico which, as we are all painfully aware, shares 1,962 miles of porous border with a potential 22-million-member drug buying club.

The cocaine blizzard that was pounding Mexico by 1984 turned U.S. drug strategies topsy-turvy. Instead of a producer country in which eradication programs were prescribed, Mexico was now the world's largest trampoline for Colombian cocaine, and stopping the blow before it got out of Mexico's air and land space became the name of the game.

The Colombians were pragmatic business folks. The cartels contracted the Sinaloa heroin and marijuana capos to guide their product north—the Sinaloa boys knew the routes, knew the marketing networks, and, once more, they knew the vulnerabilities of the Mexican police. At first they asked a flat fee for each kilo unloaded at private airstrips strategically pinpointed around the country. This was not unrewarding. Rafael Caro Quintero, a farm boy from Badiragueto in the hills above Culiacán, and the brashest of these original gangsters, once boasted that he could pay Mexico's then-$100 billion USD foreign debt. Caro, who was said to finance the *tambor* or Sinaloa brass band that tootles outside of Malverde's shrine, became a hot commodity in the mid-1980s. Popular corridos sang of his love life, and a purported interview was a best-selling comedy tape in the winter of 1986. "For a hundred years the gringos have made our people slaves, have stolen our oil and left our bones in the middle of the desert," the Caro character intones in NBC's docudrama "Drug Wars: The Camarena Story": "now we will return the favor by sending them the *chiva, the sinsemilla*, the cocaine..."[34]

The saga of Caro's flame-out captured attentions on both sides of the border and taught U.S. national security proponents a hard lesson. In the autumn of

1984, Caro Quintero and associate Ernesto Fonseca ("*Don Neto*") were the kingpins of a spectacular marijuana operation at El Búfalo in the Chihuahua hills near Delicias—7,000 peons were said to be harvesting 10,000 tons of herb[35] when DEA agent Enrique "Kiki" Camarena and his pilot, Alberto Zavela floated over the fabled fields—another version has Camarena conspiring with Caro to concentrate production at Búfalo. Embarrassed Army troops were promptly ordered by Secretary of Defense Juan Arévalo Godarqui to occupy Búfalo, a vast sea of green that Arévalo's officers had somehow failed to detect until the gringos pointed it out to them. Búfalo reportedly had been in production for several growing seasons and *Time* magazine described the haul, a new world's record, as "the bust of a century."[36]

Much grass was said to have been salvaged for sale, but the mercurial Caro Quintero was pissed. On February 7th, 1985, he had Kiki Camarena and Zavela kidnapped in Guadalajara, taken to a home on Lope de Vega street in an upscale neighborhood, and, under the supervision of a doctor, tortured unceasingly for three days. The Camarena snatch aggravated international relations. Reagan ambassador John Gavin went ballistic at the news and the *New York Times* blasted "the distressingly casual search for the kidnappers" on the part of the de la Madrid government.[37]

The decomposing bodies turned up on a Michoacán ranch in March (police hit the wrong ranch first, killing the owner and his entire family). Meanwhile, Caro Quintero had paid off Guadalajara's top cop and flown off to Costa Rica. Judicial Police commander Guillermo González Calderoni was dispatched to bring Caro Quintero back alive and the kingpin was subsequently lodged in a sumptuous suite in Mexico City's northern penitentiary, where he reportedly installed his own discotheque. "Our level of tolerance has been exceeded," Secretary of State Schultz warned as U.S.-Mexican relations soured from day to day.[38] Defense Secretary Weinberger drew up contingency plans.

In the end, though, the woofing was deliberately quelled on orders from the chief. Reagan needed de la Madrid's help in pacifying Central America. Mexico was about to enter GATT, a long time U.S. objective. Caro Quintero or no, default on the Mexican debt would take a bunch of U.S. banks with it.

The Camarena killing still poisons the air between Washington and Mexico City. DEA administrator after administrator vows never to rest until their comrade's murderers are brought to justice and the scenes have sometimes gotten out of hand. DEA agent Victor Cortez, steering a carful of guns through downtown Guadalajara, was rousted and generically tortured by local police in 1986, while de la Madrid was on an awkward reconciliation trip to Washington. René Verdugo, a Caro Quintero associate, was kidnapped by DEA bounty hunters for $32,000, and transported to Los Angeles where he was sentenced to heavy time on a trafficking beef. Mexico's attorney general was forced to turn over to U.S. authorities recorded tapes of the Camarena torture sessions, an embarrassing moment for Mexican justice. In 1990, bounty hunters put the snatch on Dr. Humberto Alvarez Machain, a thickly set, alleged former DFS medic and abortionist, stuffed him into the trunk of a car in Guadalajara, and delivered the load to Texas for $100,000 USD, drawn down from PIPE ("Police Informers, Police Enforcement") monies.[39] Charges against Machain for supervising the Camarena torture sessions were annulled and he was deported to Mexico in 1992, but the incident seriously disrupted U.S. drug programs south of the border.

To further curdle relations, Elaine Shannon's *Desperados*, a whitewash of the DEA's role in the Camarena killing, that unrelentingly depicts the Mexicans as bad guys, hit the best-seller lists and "Miami Vice"'s Michael Mann produced "Drug Wars" from it, a pseudo-documentary in which Tom Brokaw called for avenging Camarena, dubbed Mexican officials "little Noriegas" and identified prominent political leaders thought to be complicit in the murder, including former Interior Secretary Manuel Bartlett, General Arévalo, and de la Madrid himself.[40]

Mexico lashed back, insinuating that Kiki Camarena worked for the "Mafia" and had once been arrested on trafficking charges. Ex-Interpol chieftain Miguel Aldana (later imprisoned on trafficking charges himself) claimed Camarena had received $11 million USD for protecting Búfalo and was presently working on his tan in La Jolla, California.[41]

Further revenge for the Camarena killing was extracted by the certification procedure. Each year, since 1987, as a provision of the Drug Enforcement, Education and Control Act, the sitting president of the United States has been legally obligated to certify the allegiance of 32 drug producing and running countries to the White House-declared War on Drugs. Since the process was first drawn into legislation, Mexico has been in the center ring of the certification circus—after all, the legislation, which dictates certification, sailed through the U.S. Congress on the back of Camarena's corpse (the cocaine overdose death of basketball pheenom Len Bias also contributed to the mood of Congress).

The annual March 1st star chamber proceedings ushers in a season of Mexico-bashing, leaks to the *New York Times* that speak of complicity between high-ranking Mexican officials and the cartels, and genuine resentment on the part of the average Mexican in the street, who does not appreciate being judged by his or her drug-crazed northern neighbor. Inevitably disparaged for the poor job it is perceived to do in fighting the U.S. Drug War, the certification rigmarole has "turned Mexico into a whipping boy for American legislators, self-righteously indignant law enforcement agents, and conservative ideologues."[42]

The Camarena affair taught advocates of the "drug enforcement-as-National Security" school that strengthening corrupt police agencies, which have little public support anyway, does not stop the drug flow. Mexican police do not guarantee Mexican "national security." Indeed, a 1990 Americas Watch report on police abuses cautions that Mexico's police are the nation's "greatest threat to national security."[43] After Camarena, Washington set its sights on contracting the presumably better-disciplined military, to wage the War on Drugs on behalf of the American people.

THE THIRD LINK

It is argued that the October 23rd, 1995 appearance of U.S. Secretary of Defense William Perry before the top brass of Mexico's armed forces at an elite Mexico City military installation signaled the melding of U.S. and Mexican security forces, "the third link" as author Carlos Fazio dubs it. The event certainly had all the appearances of a turning point. No United States defense secretary had ever touched down in Mexico before, let alone been invited to address the nation's military commanders during an unprecedented state ceremony at the highly insular Military Camp #1 on the western edge of the capital.

Perry had been personally invited to Mexico by Defense Secretary Enrique Cervantes, a former military attaché in Washington, during a White House ceremony the previous June, marking the retirement of the commander of the U.S. presidential guard. Now, the bookish darling of U.S. defense contractors stood at stiff attention as 10,000 crack troops and convoys of surplus U.S. military hardware rolled out on the parade grounds before him. A civilian defense secretary (in pointed contrast to General Barry McCaffery, the White House drug czar, who accompanied him on this historic junket), William Perry spoke of "a new era of political, economic, and *military cooperation*"—the "third link." He also heartily plugged Bill Clinton's $20 billion USD bail-out of the Zedillo government following the peso collapse in December 1994 and boosted the concept of a multilateral military force to defend the Americas. Scrupulously careful not to tramp on Mexican sovereignty on its own soil, Perry repeatedly stressed that the U.S. and Mexico's futures "are indissolubly linked."[44]

The Perry visit did not play well with diehard nationalists, who suspected that the U.S. Defense Secretary and McCaffery, the architect of the militarization of the drug war in Latin America, had come to Mexico to enlist the Patria in a war, under Pentagon command, that would violate Mexican sovereignty and the autonomy of the Mexican military. Carlos Fazio, ironically a Uruguayan, writes that Perry's mission "was to enlist the Mexican army in the scheme of inter-American defense, designed by the Pentagon, as a Trojan horse for U.S. expansionist interests in the era of globalization."[45]

HOUSE OF PAIN

William Perry's brief visit to Military Camp #1, the site of the most notorious political prison in Mexico, where dissidents have been tortured and "disappeared" for decades, is a fresh example of the Pentagon's penchant for backing the bad guys in Latin America. In fact, Perry just missed a golden opportunity to witness a typical Military Camp #1 "interrogation" of suspected dissidents. 48 hours before the Secretary of Defense showed up, on October 21st, Fernando Yañez, aka (purportedly) "Comandante Germán," whom the Zedillo government designates as the founder of the Zapatista Army of National Liberation, paid a forced visit to the military camp. Bound and blindfolded, he was questioned for 14 hours by a "General Diego," complained Yañez to *Proceso*.[46] Yañez had been arrested despite the suspension of warrants for his apprehension as a condition of the ongoing peace talks between the Zapatistas and the Zedillo government. The suspected Zapatista was hustled off to a civilian prison on the eve of Perry's visit to Military Camp #1.

Because President Zedillo was out of the country—in New York, celebrating the 50th anniversary of the United Nations—"Germán's" capture by the military suggested to some political analysts, like *La Jornada*'s Ricardo Alemán, that a coup was in the works.[47] Perry's blanket endorsement of the Mexican military the following day did not contradict this appraisal.

"Germán" emerged relatively unscathed from this brush with Military Camp #1. He was fortunate. Since Tlatelolco, *Campo Militar Número Uno* has achieved a grisly reputation. Many of those who were taken into custody during the guerrilla uprisings of the Echeverría years disappeared into prison cells here and were never found again. Between 1979 and 1981, former Mexican paratrooper Zacarias Osorio claims that he escorted as many as 140 prisoners to military bases in Hidalgo and Mexico states where they were executed by a team of sharpshooters—the bodies were then burnt at nearby incinerators.[48] This reporter visited those bases soon after Osorio confessed to a Canadian attorney in 1988 that he had participated in Mexican military death squad activity, and found the physical details to be true to the ex-soldier's testimony. At the time, the Salinas government refused to comment on Zacarias Osorio's charges, which had arisen out of his Canadian political asylum claim.[49]

Zacarias Osorio's military career casts a light on the darkest recesses of this Sphinx-like institution. Born in the Poza Rica region of Veracruz, Osorio is a Totonaco Indian whose ancestors had joined forces with Hernán Cortez against the Aztec empire. One indigenous ritual that impressed the ex-soldier as a child were the *voladores* (flyers) of nearby Papantla whose precarious spinnings, suspended ten meters above the earth, celebrate the perambulations of the sun. As a young adult, Osorio was equally impressed when he visited an air base in Mexico state, witnessed the paratroopers gliding from the heavens, and signed up.[50]

The boy soon caught the eye of superiors because of his eagle-eye marksmanship. Osorio was selected to serve at Military Camp #1 as part of an execution squad, sworn to secrecy by military discipline. Ultimately, unable to continue killing, Zacarias deserted and fled, first to the United States, and then to Canada, where he has led a violent, alcohol-plagued life in exile.

A WOUNDED INSTITUTION

There is more than one Zacarias Osorio in Mexico's soon-to-be-200,000 strong military—150,000 army troops, 35,000 in the Navy, 10,000 in the Air Force.[51] The military is organized into 38 regions, one for each state—states with high guerrilla potential (Guerrero, Chiapas, Tabasco, Veracruz) rate two regions worth of troops. 40,000 troops are stationed in the capital and troops are moved from region to region as contingencies arise. At this writing (1997), 60,000 troops are thought to be mobilized to counter guerrilla threats in Guerrero, Oaxaca, Chiapas, and the Huasteca mountains. At the pinnacle of the chain of command are the Secretary of Defense and the Secretary of the Navy, who are always chosen from and by the military, and rubber-stamped by the president.

Historically, the generals and the admirals lead young armed forces—with ancient roots. Aztec commanders could raise 16,000- to 18,000-man armies on an hour's notice—the Aztec Eagle Warrior is today displayed as the emblem of modern Mexico's Heroic Military College. The royal army that supplanted the Aztecs was largely composed of creoles and, after Independence, was beset by brigands like Santa Anna, whose barefoot troops were rounded up by local caciques and, more often than not, led off to battle with nooses around their necks. Benito Juárez sought to conform an army from the guerrilla bands that had sent the French bolting back to their ships in 1867. Under Díaz, military funding absorbed a quarter of the federal budget.[52] But 34 years of dictatorship corroded the federales' capabilities and Díaz's military finally fell apart under Huerta after Villa routed federal troops at Zacatecas.

Its reincarnation was the revolutionary army. Born of the amalgam of Carranza's Constitutionalists, the Sonoran legions and their mutual allies, and weaned on the Yanqui invasions at Veracruz and Chihuahua, the Mexican army was created to battle no outside enemy other than that fielded by its northern neighbor. In spite of the peculiar hiatus of cooperation during World War II, and the admonishments of U.S. diplomats to grow up and put revolutionary nationalism behind them, the generals have never quite been able to abandon their burden of history.

The Mexican military is charged with defending national territory, safeguarding internal security and performing an array of "civic action" duties that range from tree-planting to the eradication of drug crops to cutting hair and fixing household appliances in rural communities. Class distinctions within the military are sharply drawn—largely white officers, increasingly trained in the United States, and a largely Indian (often urbanized Indian) and mestizo fighting force. Young recruits, like Zacarias Osorio, are drawn to the military by the action and promise of steady advancement that such a life guarantees. Indian troops are deployed against Indian rebels in the jungles of Chiapas and the sierra of Oaxaca. The use of rural Indian troops against middle class students at Tlatelolco is one explanation for the disgraceful military rampage that took place October 2nd, 1968.

The military has been a wounded institution since Tlatelolco. Although Díaz Ordaz took full responsibility for the massacre, the dimensions of which he never conceded, the directors of the operation—then-Secretary of Defense Marcelino Barragán and General José Hernández Toledo—were never held to account. 30 years later, to charge the Mexican army with murder at Tlatelolco invites counter-charges of disloyalty and treason. The military's impunity remains as sacred as that of the Virgin of Guadalupe.

Just how sensitive the brass remains to public perceptions of the army's role in the killing of hundreds of unarmed students was succinctly illustrated by the famous textbook controversy of 1991, in which millions of freshly-revised fourth, fifth, and sixth grade history books were removed from circulation by then-Education Secretary Ernesto Zedillo just before the school year opened, because the military objected to being mention as a possible participant in the Tlatelolco killings.[53] The books, which had cost the state a tidy sum, still languish in a Mexico City warehouse. In the latest edition of the textbooks, Mexican history now ends in 1964.

A COMPLICATED DANCE

Much is made of the obedience of the military to Mexico's civilian rulers— the nation enjoys the longest military coup-less skein in the Americas. The army has kept to its barracks for 50 years—ever since General Saturnino Hernández's 1938 uprising in San Luis Potosí, (although both Almazán and Henríquez made veiled threats of military rebellion). The last general to serve as president left office in 1946, but the PRI had a general at the helm as late as 1964. Despite its vaunted reputation for foreswearing coups d'état, the military's proximity to power is much closer than is casually perceived.

The textbook controversy was an illuminating step in the complicated dance between civilian and military authority in Mexico, where the operating thesis is that the loyalty of the president to the armed forces is at least as important as the loyalty of the military to the president.

The military's reward for keeping its nose out of politics is an impenetrable bubble of impunity that exempts the armed forces from all accountability. Even as its heroic revolutionary legacy is mytholigized by state apologists, troops are mobilized to crush popular movements by brute force. Members of the military are sworn to a Sicilian-like code of "*omertá*," rarely breaking their institutional silence. They are never subject to civilian justice and never held responsible for accusations of human rights abuses committed against civilians who are often of the soldiers' own race and class.

Such impunity is matched by healthy, if covert, military budgets. Mexico is lauded for having the lowest military budget in Latin America—just 0.9% of the gross domestic product (PIB) is allocated to the military, about 2.2% of all federal expenditures.[54] Starvation funding supposedly demonstrates the dominance of civilian authority over the generals—but like much of the trappings of the Mexican state, the figures are ornamental. The president has access to billions of dollars in discretionary funding each year, a good piece of which goes to the military in the form of bonuses and new equipment outlays. In fiscal 1982, for example, López Portillo, still flush with petro-pesos, purchased 55 Swiss Pilatus fighter-trainers (still in use against the Zapatistas in 1994) and 10 U.S. F-5Es jet fighters (the last of which crashed during a 1995 Independence Day flyover) for a price that was never listed in the budget.[55]

The dance between civilian and military authority has a lot of tricky moves to it. Military influence in civilian decision-making has been greatly enhanced by the commitment of the last three Mexican presidents to consider the war on drugs a matter of "national security," worthy of the competence of the armed forces. Also boosting civilian power's indebtedness to the military is the army's willingness to be used as an instrument of presidential authority. López Mateos's call-up of the army against the railroad workers in 1959 was matched 30 years later by Carlos Salinas's dispatch of troops to break a strike at the Cananea copper pit in northern Sonora, the birthplace of the Mexican labor movement. Soon after, Salinas privatized the mine, the eighth largest in the world, suggesting future use of the military to uphold such neo-liberal strokes, thinks Lorenzo Meyer.[56] In one of his first acts as president, Salinas deployed troops to capture oil worker union boss Joaquín "*La Quina*" Hernández Galicia. He also used the military to intimidate supporters of Cuauhtemoc Cárdenas's PRD in Michoacán and Guerrero state elections.

Salinas's reluctant successor, Ernesto Zedillo (1994-2000) has not been reluctant to send the military into battle to quell civil rebellion. The army was unleashed against the Zapatistas in February 1995 to back up judicial police attempting to serve arrest warrants on the EZLN leadership. The army also joined forces with Tabasco state police in self-designated BOM squads to break blockades thrown up by thousands of Chontal Indians at 60 state oil wells in February 1996.[57] When the president appointed General Enrique Salgado, a former army commander in guerrilla-riddled Guerrero, Mexico City police chief in 1996, he brought 11 generals and nine colonels along with him. Now all 35 top command posts are filled by high-ranking military officers and nearly 3,000 troops have replaced beat cops on the streets of Iztapalapa, one of the capital's toughest districts. Such involvement in internal policing gives the military a greatly increased voice in forging civilian security policy.

A REPORTED COUP

The emergence of guerrilla challenges in southern Mexico has been as crucial to the strengthening of the military's hand in the Zedillo presidency as it was during the Díaz Ordaz and Echeverría sexenios. Secretary of Defense Cervantes won his spurs in the campaign against Lucio Cabañas in Guerrero in the 1970s and General Mario Acosta Chaparro, a military intelligence expert, ran the homicidal police-military counterinsurgency effort in that state. The torrent of Guatemalan refugees who washed across the southern border in 1981-82, a sea in which many *guerrilleros* were thought to be swimming, gave Miguel de la Madrid the opportunity to select the hard-handed General, Absalón Castellanos, as governor of Chiapas. The 1994 Zapatista rebellion in that southern state has raised the military profile even higher. Zedillo's February 9th, 1995 army offensive was reportedly instigated by a military ultimatum to retake control of national territory or face a coup.[58] Zedillo's frequent ceremonial appearances with Cervantes during that period lends credence to this interpretation.

When he first came to power, Ernesto Zedillo was a weak and bloodless president, mysteriously elevated to the PRI nomination by the assassination of candidate Luis Donaldo Colosio. He arrived in the presidency having never been elected to public office before and, as a hard-boiled technocrat, has no real constituency in the Institutional Revolutionary Party other than considerable presidential authority. Confronted by rebel defiance and the collapse of the peso in the first weeks of his administration, the military, given to long-winded professions of institutional loyalty, has became his most consistent supporter.

But it is a very conditional loyalty, one that appears to include an increased role in the affairs of state. When, in late 1995, Zedillo, for the first time in political memory here, submitted his economic plan for national recovery to the generals for their approbation, coup rumors flew through the capital. On November 3rd, a Dow Jones stringer in Mexico City reported that Zedillo was negotiating his abdication with the military. The peso promptly dropped 31 centavos on the dollar and financial turbulence loomed.[59] The headline-grabbing coup was symptomatic of "a power vacuum" in civilian authority which a lot of people think can only be filled by the military, wrote *Reforma* columnist Raymundo Riva Palacios,[60] who worried that participation in civil law enforcement could only expose the military to the veniality that has poisoned the police.

Two years after the rumored coup, blockbuster revelations of corruption inside the military and its increasingly conflictive role in public life confirm Riva Palacios' preoccupations.

NAFTA FOR THE MILITARY

In order to militarize Mexico's drug war, the U.S. had first to militarize its own. Reagan-ordered revision of the Civil War-era *Posse Comitatus* statutes in 1981 gave the Commander-in-Chief the green light to order the military to move into civilian drug law enforcement. The first operations were against California marijuana farmers, with the Defense Department providing helicopters and satellite tracking of sinsemilla cropping. Both Reagan and Bush sponsored "joint" military operations in Bolivia and Peru in the 1980s. General McCaffery, Bush's southern zone commander, was instrumental in convincing Peru's Fujimori to deploy his country's military against guerrilla-protected coca growers in the upper Huallaga valley, where U.S. drug enforcers even built a Wild West-like fort to protect their operatives. McCaffrey's determination to militarize the drug war made him the perfect choice as Bill Clinton's "civilian" drug czar. Now the czar seeks to construct a multilateral Latin force to take on this very North American problem.

Mexico's aloofness to the multilateral drug war blueprint was on pointed display at the Hemispheric Summit of defense secretaries (excluding Cuba) in July,1995, held at the historic preservation site of Williamsburg, Virginia. With 32 out of 34 (acceptable) American defense chiefs on hand, the Hemispheric Summit was a sort of military free trade treaty-in-the works. Indeed, this junta had grown from Bill Clinton's heavily-flacked December 1993 Miami "Summit of the Americas," at which all of Latin America was invited to join an expanded North American Free Trade Agreement.

"We must redefine the role of the military in the Americas," Perry urged, before rushing off to an urgent National Security Council meeting on Bosnia-Herzegovina.[61] Al Gore took up the baton: by "redefine," the U.S. meant to "redirect" military attentions to "the plague" of demon drugs flooding across U.S. borders. Gore's speech was curiously splattered with patriotic name-dropping—Patrick Henry, Jefferson, Washington, Madison (but no James Monroe). Brass bands in colonial outfits tootled "Yankie Doodle Dandy" to the Latin generals.[62]

Mexico sent only its Washington ambassador to "observe" the martial proceedings—although General Cervantes was kept closely informed in Mexico City. Despite its perceived aloofness, Mexico was dealing behind the scenes for 90 new helicopters, including several S-170 Blackhawks[63]—the deal fell through when the U.S. insisted on supplying its own pilots. Mexico subsequently purchased three sets of Blackhawks directly from Sikorsky, the manufacturer, recalls Kate Doyle, who watchdogs Mexican military-Pentagon transactions at the National Security Archives.

SPARE PARTS

Despite the Blackhawk controversy, the Mexican military's natural reluctance to join forces with an old adversary is being worn thin by a deluge of equipment transfers and the expanded training of Mexican officers in the U.S. The Pentagon can well afford to wine and dine its southern amigos—U.S. defense expenditures are equal to Mexico's entire Gross Domestic Product .[64]

In addition to hardware, the Pentagon woos the Aztec generals and their commander-in-chief with doses of flowery flattery. Witness the DOD's 1992 congressional budget request for military "assistance" to Mexico: "Since he became president, Carlos Salinas has committed his government in terms of human rights and political reform. He has also privatized state enterprises and has increased the role of the private sector in the economy." The 1992 Pentagon presentation also lauded Salinas for helping the Desert Storm coalition by making Mexican oil available to the allies. Military aid, the request stressed, would "strengthen the relations between the armed forces of both countries—and promote the sales of U.S. military equipment."[65]

Both sales, and more importantly, grants, are accelerating. Mexico picked up nearly a half-billion dollars worth of U.S. military equipment and services from 1990 to 1992—about what it received in the previous seven years (1982-89).[66] Mexico obtains U.S. military equipment through two channels: straight-out grants of surplus stocks and over-the-counter commercial sales of everything from jet fighters to Meals-Ready-To-Eat. 1997 Pentagon to Mexico outlays totaled $37 million worth of helicopters, troop transport planes and spare parts; $10 million in night vision equipment has already been programmed for 1998.[67] Virtually all transfers are justified by the exigencies of the drug war.

The most proffered item is the helicopter—which has become a sort of fetish of this one-way interchange, with ritualized deliveries of Hueys and Bells every few years, always under the rubric of the War on Drugs—nonetheless the choppers have been used for fighting rebels and, purportedly, delivering cocaine shipments to judicial police command posts.[68] Although, in theory, the DOD keeps tabs on "final use:"—i.e. how or where the equipment is used, embassy vigilance is not very persistent and Mexican human rights groups continually complain that such equipment is being used against Zapatista and Popular Revolutionary Army rebels in Chiapas, Oaxaca, and Guerrero.

The last transfer of helicopters, at this writing, involves 73 helicopters, 43 for 1996-7 delivery. From 1989 through 1994, at least 60 helicopters were apparently transferred to Mexico's military and police. Such commerce more closely obeys the permutation of the free market than any national security contingency—the Defense Department recently retired 1,500 Hueys and wants to unload them where they will do the most damage. Although DOD would like auditors to believe that it is merely getting rid of flying junkers, Hueys, built for Vietnam's rugged terrain, are sturdy machines, "perfect for counterinsurgency," reflects Doyle.

Helicopters are not the only bellicose commodities being transferred. Riot control gear, water cannons, bulletproof vests, rockets, grenades and machine guns go south. So may high-tech aircraft like Cobra helicopters and F-16 and F-18 fighter-bombers, if, as speculated, the Pentagon abandons its ban on selling such sophisticated systems in Latin America. In 1993-94, Mexico tripled armed vehicles purchases from the U.S., accumulating a fleet of 5,000 "Hummers" that now see service in counterinsurgency campaigns in Chiapas and Guerrero.[69] Since 1980, the U.S. State Department, which controls licensing of private sales, has granted 99 Mexico-directed licenses for "civil disturbance control" equipment, including 33 electric shock units, a transfer denounced by Amnesty International.[70]

Although Mexico's Defense Secretary seeks to diversify sources by buying French tanks and German HK machine guns and even Soviet MI8 helicopters (from countries, which, unlike the U.S., do not care what their equipment is being used for), the problem is that such machinery breaks down and, unlike U.S.-supplied equipment, spare parts are hard to find. For the U.S. defense industry, spare parts are what it's all about. The U.S. sells $12 billion worth of weaponry a year worldwide (four times that of Germany, its closest competitor)[71] and all of this equipment, sooner or later, is going to need replacement parts. In terms of U.S. strategic planning, it is the spare parts that most tangibly will link up the two militaries.

A Few Good Men

The second bridge being built between the two armed forces is the IMET (International Military Education Training) program. Although Mexicans trained in the U.S. in World War II—training extends as far back as the Calles-Morrow period—the IMET program has built a foundation for long-term contact between militaries. High-ranking Mexican officers generally are in positions of influence for a generation, 20 years, during which time contact made through IMET can be crucial in national security decision-making.

From 1982 through 1992, IMET trained 512 Mexican officers, and another 700 positions were promised by Perry. Mexican officers attend U.S. military training sessions at Fort Benning, Georgia's notorious School of the Americas, a vocational academy for Latin torturers, as well as such exotic learning establishments as the U.S. Army's public relations school in Indianapolis, Indiana. They go on tours of U.S. bases, fly U.S. planes, and learn U.S. English, presumably so they can take orders in that language, when the time comes. "IMET is our best access to the Mexican military," Elliot Abrams thought.[72] "I need not dwell upon the value of having in positions of leadership men who have first-hand knowledge of how Americans do things and how they think," declares Robert McNamara, the remorse-ridden butcher of Vietnam.[73]

INTERVENTION IN CHIAPAS

The presence of U.S.-trained officers in the Chiapas conflict zone, some of them School of America graduates, has been tracked by researcher Darren Wood.[74] Subcomandante Marcos claims that U.S. military advisors are present in the conflict zone, but none have yet appeared in public—other than two U.S. Army "photographers" who, several days after the February 9th army offensive, rolled up to the Nuevo Momón roadblock on the way to the former Zapatista stronghold of Guadalupe Tepeyac, and were turned back by Mexican troops.[75] Although the U.S. repeatedly denies that it has intervened in Chiapas, embassy military attachés were on the ground in San Cristóbal de las Casas in the first days of the rebellion (January 5th-13th 1994)[76] and the U.S. military shares responsibility for an early warning radar tower on the Hill of Strangers outside that highland city.

U.S. equipment is deployed in the conflict zone. State Department licenses record the transfer of gear designated for "south-east units" to be used "under jungle conditions."[77] U.S. C-130 Hercules transport planes flew paratroopers into Guadalupe Tepeyac, the Zapatista headquarters, on the first morning of the February 9th, 1995 offensive.[78] Yet when U.S. and Mexican defense chiefs huddle, as they have several times since the Zapatista rebellion, they deny ever mentioning that word, "Chiapas."

But in other guerrilla zones, the U.S. has been less reticent to offer aid and advice. Soon after the Popular Revolutionary Army (EPR) appeared in Guerrero in June 1996, ambassador Jim Jones volunteered U.S. expertise in tracking down the rebels. U.S.-supplied helicopters and Hummers now back up tens of thousands of Mexican army troops in Guerrero.[79]

CONTAMINATING THE MILITARY

The Pentagon's romancing of Mexico's military brass has borne early fruit. The simple acceptance of U.S. military grants is an astonishing sea change for a Mexican military that still rehearses invasion scenarios from the north. As the result of Perry's "Third Link" visit, a bilateral working group was created to focus drug war efforts, the first joint U.S.-Mexican strategic planning group since the halcyon days of the World War II joint defense command. The high-level commission now meets regularly and joint exercises have at least been discussed, provoking nationalist horror on the Mexican side of this equation— President Zedillo was obligated to swear that "no U.S. soldier will ever operate on Mexican soil."[80]

In addition, Mexico has opened its air space to U.S. drug war overflights— permission for 66 such flights was granted by September 1996, according to a

La Jornada investigation,[81] and U.S. radar planes beam down Caribbean and Pacific flyways that overlap Mexican skies. Despite Mexican Navy negatives on joint maneuvers with U.S. ships, Mexico has conducted parallel operations with the U.S. Coast Guard.[82] Mexico's Northern Border Rapid Response Team and U.S. Drug enforcement tactical units at least plan combined operations, even if they don't carry them out just yet. Although hot pursuit across the border remains as much of a sore point as it was in Pancho Villa's day, Bill Clinton's May 1997 visit to Mexico City apparently softened Mexican opposition to U.S. aerial penetration.

But collaboration has not always yielded the desired results. November 7th, 1991 was a bad day for this developing alliance. On that morning, U.S. military-controlled radar picked up a suspected drug plane winging across the Guatemala border. For reasons that will soon become clear, U.S. military intelligence asked Mexican federal judicial police to tail the plane through to its destination—but distrust of the "*judiciales*" led to the dispatch of a DEA craft to track the cops tracking the drug plane. When the latter finally put down on the Plain of Snakes, near Tlaxicoyan in southern Veracruz, the police went in after the narcos. As they bailed out of their craft, they were cut down by army troops stationed on the ground to unload the cocaine—seven federal cops were killed by the soldiers. Hovering above, the DEA filmed the massacre.

The contamination of the Mexican military through its drug enforcement operations could not have been made more explicit than it was February 19th, 1997, with the detention of General Jesús Gutiérrez Rebollo, the commander of Mexico's War on Drugs. As the director of the National Institute for Drug Control (INCD), the shaved-headed, neckless brigadier general had been welcomed to the White House just three weeks previous by General McCaffery, who commended his counterpart for his "firmness and incorruptibility."[83] General Gutiérrez, who was apparently in the employ of the nation's late Número Uno narco-lord, Amado Carrillo, having accepted luxury automobiles and lavishly furnished apartments in the interchange, took at least two other generals with him.

The downfall of the nation's first military drug czar should not have dismayed the Pentagon. Even as U.S. security planners were militarizing the Mexican drug war, the Mexican military's taint was evident. In 1988, three years before the shoot-out on the Plain of Snakes, General Juan Poblano Silva was indicted by a federal court in San Diego but never tried for his role in a Bolivia to Mexico City to California cocaine operation. General Arévalo, de la Madrid's defense secretary, was charged with complicity in the Camarena killing, during the Machain trial. A drug scandal involving 50 Naval officers resulted in the resignation of Salinas's Secretary of Navy, Mauricio Schleske. In 1993, Mexican troops in the Tarahumara sierra of Chihuahua were accused of protecting drug plantations—commanding officers were shifted. Testimony taken during the 1996 Houston trial of narco king Juan García Abrego implicates Naval units in Tamaulipas state in transporting drug shipments north. [84]

The detention of General Gutiérrez is emblematic of the institutional rot that has been stimulated by Pentagon schemes to convince the Mexican military to fight the U.S.'s War on Drugs. Most efforts to collude with corrupt, authoritarian institutions cause similar disappointment.

The Mexican brass is quick to accept gifts of hardware, even solicits them. But history has a long reach south of the Río Bravo. Like most Mexicans, the generals really do not trust the gringos and the Pentagon knows this only too well. An early 1994 DOD document, code-numbered SCG 90-01 and described by *La Jornada*'s Blanche Petrich, articulates the Defense Department's acceptance of the prickly status quo between these two old enemies: "it's conceivable that an eventual display of U.S. troops would be received favorably if the Mexican government was threatened with overthrow from general social and economic chaos, but given the history of the U.S.-Mexican relationship, it's not very probable."[85]

Chapter 11

WAR ON DRUGS

Of Cops, Capos, Big Fish, Madrinas and the Lord of the Skies

The so-called "Colombianization" of Mexico, with its attending pathology of epidemic corruption, political assassination and absolute impunity, is a coordinate of the "Americanization" of the drug war. The U.S. invented the War on Drugs to deal with its own drug tragedy, then created the conditions that drove the Colombian cartels to set up in Mexico, and now seeks to convict Mexico in the court of world opinion for having succumbed to the siren song of the Cocaine Kings.

But the dynamic is not quite so simplistic. In Mexico, the virus found a cordial host: a political and judicial system already contaminated beyond repair, managed as it is by a dying state party for which everything is on sale—personal principles, political office, state enterprises, impunity from prosecution, the resources and the sovereignty of the nation. Winked at and nourished for seven decades by its pals in Washington, the PRI embraced the new capital flows that cocaine brought to Mexico. Under the PRI's investment rules, refusal to offer a bribe could be injurious to one's health. The credo of *plata o plomo* (lit. silver or lead) must have made the Colombians feel very much at home—but "Colombianization" is a misnomer: the PRI's lucre-ocracy is strictly Mexican. "Colombia has less problems than Mexico because Mexico has a PRI to foment corruption," writes Bogotá columnist (*El Espectador*) María Jiménez Duzan.[1]

During the six years that Carlos Salinas ruled Mexico (1988-94), the bargains were as abundant as they were back in the golden days of the Porfiriato. The nationalized banks were returned to their oligarchical owners, with a few Salinas-era sharpies sprinkled in. The telephone company was sold at a pittance to one campaign backer, the airlines to another and Cananea to still another. The fire sale also put the nation's "national security" on the block, hocked to George Bush as a down payment on the North American Free Trade Agreement.

THE IRON D.A.

Carlos Salinas and George Bush entertained one of those "special relationships" that have sometimes smiled on Mexican presidents. Both were elected to lead their countries in 1988—although Salinas's victory was a lot murkier—a coincidence of terms that last cursed López Portillo and Jimmy Carter in 1976. Days before his December 1st inauguration, Salinas flew into Houston to meet with President-elect Bush at the Lyndon B. Johnson Space Center. The two noshed on digestible gold leaf-wrapped bonbons.[2] and discussed priorities. Bush made it clear that his were drugs. The astute Salinas had already scored points by listing narco-trafficking as a national security priority while out on the campaign trail. Now it was time to translate words into deeds. If there were advancements in the drug war, there could be advancements in other areas trade for example. Salinas's Porfirio-esque scheme of springboarding Mexico into the First World on the back of a free trade pact with Washington could soon become a reality. The rangy U.S. president stooped to shake hands with the diminutive Carlos, whose father he had once dealt with when Raúl Salinas, Sr. was Commerce Secretary and George Bush the main man at the Zapata Off-Shore Oil Corporation.[3] Now it looked like he had a deal with the son.

There would be many potholes in the road to NAFTA. "The Spirit of Houston" had first to weather the decertification threat that Jesse Helms and his gang presented every spring up on the Hill. Salinas jumped to the crack of the whip. He appointed his own drug czar: the 300-pound "Iron D.A.," Javier Coello Trejo, a jowly G. Gordon Liddy type who did interviews with a .357 Magnum prominently displayed on his desktop.[4] There were massive incinerations of presumed drugs at Military Camp #1, the bales and boxes ritually stacked up and set ablaze by foot soldiers, to the polite applause of invited officials and the blank stares of the international press. Seizures were made to seem even larger when the number of joints that could be rolled from the confiscated weed was micro-calculated—correspondents were faxed bulletins from the Attorney General's office that boasted a recent seizure had yielded one marijuana cigarette for every man, woman, and child in Latin America.

But Bush wanted one more token of Carlos Salinas's fidelity to the New World Order: the head of Miguel Angel Félix Gallardo, Caro Quintero's cousin, an old heroin runner who had become the brains of the Sinaloa syndicate. It was Félix Gallardo who reputedly had made the first connection to Pablo Escobar's Medellín Cartel. He had been on the lam since the Camarena killing, never sleeping in the same place two nights running. Coello Trejo and his longtime crony, Guillermo González Calderoni, the cops' cop who had brought back Caro Quintero in Costa Rica, pinned down Félix Gallardo in March 1989 at one of his many safe houses in the Guadalajara area, on a street named

Arcos, where so many drug dealers dwelt, that popular wit and wisdom had re-dubbed the thoroughfare "Narcos."

"Why do you want us to get him now when you didn't want to get him before?" González Calderoni says he asked the Iron D.A. "Certification is coming up," he was told.[5] One distinguishing feature of the Félix Gallardo operation: army troops replaced police as backup. There were to be no slip-ups tonight, no tip-offs. Washington was watching. The Bush administration praise was effusive. Mexico survived the certification process, despite the Helmslings' howlings. NAFTA negotiations would be announced within the year.

NORIEGA'S UNDERWEAR

1989 was a watershed year for the U.S. War on Drugs. There had been many skirmishes on foreign soil, but there had never been a full-scale invasion. Now, in December, Bush pulled the pin on the first post-communist invasion of a Latin American nation, with the object of corraling General Manuel Noriega and bringing him to U.S. Drug War justice. 24,000 Yanqui troops fell on Panama City. B-52s blasted the capital's Chorillo and San Miguel slums, where Noriega had a loyal social base. The U.S. military claimed only 314 Panamanians (202 of them civilians) had died—23 GIs were also downed during Bush's Christmas-time extravaganza.[6] Conversely, an investigation headed by former U.S. Attorney General Ramsey Clark calculated 2,000 dead, an additional 1,400 missing, and 20,000 left homeless in the first-ever drug war carpet bombing of a civilian population.[7]

Noriega took refuge in the local papal nuncio's hideaway. His cocaine stash turned out to be corn flour to make Mexican tamales. GIs rifled through his underwear drawer and blasted the Pope's outpost with classic rock and roll—"I Fought the Law and the Law Won" was one selection. Noriega surrendered. It was a supremely undignified episode in the lurid history of Yanqui interventionism. In Mexico City, where the fragrance of burning polyester U.S. flags wafted over the U.S. embassy, Salinas gently chided his pal George for the flagrant intervention in another nation's underwear drawer—but reaffirmed his wholehearted commitment to the U.S. War on Drugs.[8]

Months earlier, during an address to a joint session of the U.S. Congress that considerably brightened the climate for a free trade treaty, Salinas had lashed out at Noriega for both his ethical imperfections and the general's stealing of the May 1989 elections—that the Mexican president himself had achieved high office through identical electoral flimflam less than one year earlier was an irony lost on snoozing members of the House and Senate.[9]

PLAYING FAVORITES

In the New World Order, much as in the old, one man's misfortune can make another's fortune. After Félix Gallardo went down, the Sinaloa syndicate split into several factions, one led by Héctor "*Guero*" ("Paleface") Palma, and another by the four Arellano Félix brothers. Both bands murdered each other so assiduously that even the Colombians got nervous and shifted routes to the Caribbean coast, a shorter, safer flight up the gulf anyway. The designated capo on the ground was Juan García Abrego, scion of a legendary Matamoros con-trabandista family, who made his rep running Oaxaca grass into Texas and dri-ving stolen cars south for re-sale in Mexico. García Abrego, who is implicated in an even hundred homicides by Mexican authorities, consolidated his hold on the Brownsville-Matamoros corridor by twice gunning down his principal rival: when the first hit failed, his *pistoleros* invaded the local hospital and fin-ished the job.[10]

"The Baron" did his first deals with the Gonzalo Gacha wing of the Medellín Drug Exchange. After Gacha, aka "*El Mexicano*" (because he loved all things Mexican), was terminated by Colombian narcotics police in 1989, García Abrego went shopping in Cali. In the late 1980s and early '90s, a time frame paralleling the Salinas years, the Baron moved at least 930 tons of Orejuela brothers' alkaloid into eight U.S. states—according to the indictment that led to the imposition of 11 life sentences upon García Abrego by a Texas federal court in 1997.[11]

García Abrego also became the first Mexican narco-lord to make the U.S. Post Office walls when he was included in the FBI's Ten Most Wanted list, an honor bestowed with much fanfare by U.S. Attorney General Janet Reno in a pointed prodding of President Ernesto Zedillo to pounce on the Baron.

According to published reports, Juan García Abrego amassed a personal for-tune of nearly $7 billion USD in two decades of trafficking along the east Texas border—which would put him ahead of tycoon Carlos Slim, the man who got the phone company from Salinas, and the wealthiest man in Mexico on the *Forbes* magazine's annual super-rich rankings.[12] The Baron's success can be attributed to his astuteness and memory for detail, his readiness to waste rivals without compunction and his friends in high places. According to Eduardo Valle, "*El Buho*" ("The Owl"), a former Mexican government drug advisor (and Tlatelolco survivor), who claims he was once about to arrest García but was pulled off the case by superiors, the Baron distributed $10 mil-lion a month to police in order to stay in business.[13] The preferred target of his bribes: the Secretary of Communication and Transportation (SCT) which monitors private airstrip travel and whose Federal Highway patrol supervises ground transportation.

Also on the payroll ($1.5 million USD a month, according to testimony at García Abrego's 1996 Houston trial) was Javier Coello Trejo, Salinas's iron-fisted drug czar.[14] Suspected of aiding and abetting the Gulf Cartel in its ambi-tious endeavor to fly hundreds of small drug planes into Nuevo León and Tamaulipas states in Mexico's northeast was Coello's confederate, Memo

González Calderoni, then chief of air interception for the Federal Judicial Police,[15] and now a presumed DEA informant living under U.S. government protection in McAllen, Texas.[16]

The Baron's protection is thought to have reached into the highest spheres of Mexican government—the Salinas family itself. Black sheep big brother Raúl Salinas, jailed at this writing and charged with masterminding the murder of the PRI's Secretary General José Francisco Ruiz Massieu, was a guest at private horse races at the Baron's many haciendas in the Monterrey area, according to what one former associate, now in the Federal Witness Protection Program, has told U.S. authorities.[17] It has been repeatedly suggested—although unproven—that at least some of the $124 million USD that Raúl stashed away in secret foreign bank accounts during his brother's reign was laundered Gulf Cartel money. "Every administration has its favorite drug trafficker," Peter Lupsha, a professor of such things at the University of New Mexico told the *New York Times*, following the Baron's fall: "García Abrego was the favorite of the last administration. This administration has a new favorite."[18]

"BRING ME THE HEAD OF GARCÍA ABREGO"

García Abrego's come-uppance complied with Lupsha's rule: the Salinases were either in jail or in exile and Zedillo had other priorities—certification was, as usual, one of them. The scenario was a virtual Félix Gallardo re-run. The president needed a "big fish"—"*pez gordo*"—to reciprocate for Clinton White House salvation from the bankruptcy that free-fall peso collapse and massive capital flight had crafted. García Abrego, ill and no long number one in his own cartel, had agreed to surrender months before in exchange for a Mexican trial. But, in January 1996, Zedillo pulled a double-cross. Instead of hauling the Baron off to Almoloya, the maximum federal lock-up where the biggest fish (Caro Quintero, Félix Gallardo) are kept, the Mexican president shipped García to the U.S. of A., pretending that he was really an American citizen. Under Constitutional article 33, the president can exclude any foreigner whom he considers to be "inconvenient."

Although García Abrego had once tried to obtain U.S. citizenship with a phony baptismal certificate, Cameron County, Texas had long ago voided the claim and there is little question that the Baron was born on the Solesino *ejido* near Matamoros in December 1943, as is recorded in that city's registrar's office. Such niceties of birth did not ruffle Ernesto Zedillo's decision-making process. "This was a question of national security," he told the Spanish daily *ABC* in an exclusive morning-after interview.[19] National security? asked an incredulous Sergio Aguayo on the pages of *La Jornada*, "we just handed over our national identity!" "We are now errand boys for U.S. justice," an anonymous member of the Mexican Supreme Court sighed to the same paper.[20]

Pushing the head of Juan García Abrego before it, the Clinton White House was able to navigate around the shark-like Helms. Colombia, however, was sacrificed, a decision that provoked the city of Medellín to decertify the United States for promoting widespread drug use.[21] Ernesto Zedillo, overjoyed at evading the disgrace of decertification, rang up Bill Clinton to offer his heartfelt gratitude.

By 1997, Zedillo was even more indebted than ever to Clinton for his drug war mercies. The arrest of General Gutiérrez just a month before the March 1st certification deadline once again jeopardized Mexico's good standing, and perhaps its recovering macro-economic health. Once again, Zedillo went to the Gulf Cartel for a head, delivering García Abrego's second-in-command, Oscar Malherbe, to Secretary of State Madeleine Albright just hours before her recommendation was to be sent on to Clinton. Once the U.S. president's John Hancock was indelibly affixed, the Zedillo government sheepishly let it be known that, although Malherbe was in captivity, García Abrego's money-laundering brother had "escaped" from the National Institute for Drug Control. Actually, Humberto had just walked out the front door.[22]

NAFTA BOOSTERS

The annual certification test continues to torture Mexican-U.S. relations— but it is a hollow threat. No American president could afford to have his fourth most important trading partner stigmatized as an international pariah. Decertification would gravely endanger NAFTA's survival.

Ironically, the drug traffickers are big NAFTA boosters. Drugs are an export item and fit neatly into Mexico's booming export economy. The infrastructure that allows freer transit of goods between the two countries also enhances business opportunities for the narco-lords.

The hundreds of truckloads of Culiacán tomatoes that line up at the Nogales crossing each winter are traditional cover for Golden Triangle marijuana and heroin. One U.S. embassy intelligence document, pried loose by the National Security Archive, reveals the White House knew, long before the trade treaty kicked in, that Colombian cartel frontmen had bought up a battery factory and were assembling a truck fleet in the Ciudad Juárez area to facilitate drug deliveries. NAFTA ideologue Gary Huffbaur, a major flogger of the initiative, called the cartels' enhanced access to U.S markets "a painfully obvious problem."[23]

Not to be outdone by their Ciudad Juárez rivals, the Tijuana cartel "is acquiring counsel on how to take advantage of NAFTA to move their product," DEA spokesperson Craig Cretien admitted to the *Los Angeles Times*.[24] The admission is a rare one for the DEA, whose agents were forbidden to talk about the smuggling opportunities NAFTA affords during the run-up to passage of the free trade pact.

WHO'S WHO IN THE NARCO WORLD

With García Abrego exorcised from the battlefield, Amado Carrillo, chairman of the board of the Juárez Cartel, appeared to be the most influential of the Zedillo-era narco kings—it was Carrillo who enlisted General Gutiérrez and his associates in the war against the War on Drugs.

The Juárez family has achieved legendary status for smuggling mountainous shipments of cocaine into the U.S.—in 1989, the DEA picked off 21 tons of Juárez blow in a Sylmar, California storage locker that the group is alleged to have moved into the U.S., packed in piñatas and other hollowed-out trinkets.[25] Amado Carrillo, a Sinaloa boy who assumed directorship of the Chihuahua or "Juárez" Cartel in a hostile 1993 takeover (the former CEO, a police comandante, was bumped off in Cancún), kept the big shipment tradition alive by flying 727s and French-made Caravels, stuffed to the gunnels with alkaloid, into northern Mexico—for which he has earned the title "the Lord of the Skies." "*El Señor de los Cielos*" was rumored to have landing strips under his control from the Peruvian jungle to the Sonoran desert. The first Mexican capo to go 50-50 with the Colombian cartels,[26] Carrillo no longer waited around for shipments, but sent his own planes to Colombia to pick up drug shipments, according to former Colombian Justice Minister Gonzalo de Grieff.[27] He was also contracting his own production fields in Ecuador and Bolivia—an agricultural enterpriese that elevated Carrillo to world-class drug dealership status.

Such standing was quite a step up for this Sinaloa farm boy, a native of El Guamuchilito and nephew of Ernesto "*Don Neto*" Fonseca, Caro's close associate, now doing long time with him in Almoloya. Carrillo's top dog position returned domination of the Mexican drug trade from the gulf to the Sinaloa boys.

In July 1997, the Lord of the Skies expired in a swank Mexico City gynecological hospital after undergoing eight hours of plastic surgery and liposcution. How the most wanted man in the Americas could rent out a private hospital in the midst of the capital's uppercrust Polanco district sheds light on the current state of impunity in Mexico.

After much hesitation, three autopsies and extensive DNA testing Carrillos's blackening corpse was returned to his native Guamuchilito for a funeral that featured a ton of roses.

The Lord of the Skies' seven surviving brothers, who inherit the Juarez cartel, are sure to be challenged by another set of siblings, the four Arrellano Felix brothers, also Sinaloa natives but now doing business as the Tijuana cartel.

The Arellano Félixes are, arguably, the most trigger-happy of Mexico's frontline drug mafias. With control of the Tijuana pipeline into California at stake, the Arellanos defend their turf from both rival drug gangs and the police of two nations, with equal dedication to mayhem. Seven high-level Tijuana justice officials were gunned down in the first nine months of 1996 alone, for apparently coming too close to the keys to the kingdom.[28] A typical hit: Tijuana police chief Ernesto Ibarra, rubbed out along with three bodyguards September 14th, 1996, as he drove away from the Mexico City airport—Ibarra had 50,000 unexplained U.S. dollars in his pocket, which rules out robbery as a motive, but begs a lot of other questions. The week before the killings, Ibarra had led fruitless raids on abandoned Arellano Félix safehouses.[29]

To expedite the violence, the Arellanos have developed working relations with San Diego youth gangs like the Barrio Logan "Crazy 30s."[30] The Arellanos also enjoy protection from the military, as manifested by the March 1997 arrest of General Gutiérrez's crony, General Alfredo Navarro, for tendering a million dollar bribe to a fellow officer on the Sinaloa boys' behalf.[31]

The Tijuana cartel's most spectacular accomplishment to date was the assassination of Guadalajara Cardinal Juan Jesús Posadas at that city's airport in May 1993—Mexican authorities continue to insist that the hit was a case of mistaken identity, although the Cardinal was clad in full regalia and wearing a large pectoral cross. Immediately following the gunplay, an Arellano brother and a host of hitmen hopped an Aeroméxico flight to Tijuana that appears to have been held for them, and melted into that border city's bustling underground.

Although their pictures have been displayed on wanted posters that once lined the walls of the country, no one ever actually sees the Arellano Félixes in person. Except, that is, now-retired Papal Nuncio Giralamo Prigione, who twice met with brothers Ramón and Benjamín in December 1994 and January 1995, to hear out their professions of innocence.

Other syndicates that have a piece of the narco sector include the Sinaloa or "Pacific" Cartel, an offshoot of Félix Gallardo's old group, which has been much diminished by the imprisonment of its two top leaders: Joaquín "*Chapo*" Guzmán, purportedly the true target of the Arellano Félixes at the Guadalajara airport, and "*Guero*" Palma, who crashed his executive jet into a Nayarit mountainside in 1995, and, when arrested, was recuperating at a palatial Guadalajara mansion, his security guaranteed by the Guadalajara branch of the Federal Judicial Police.[32]

In their salad days, "*Chapo*" and "*Guero*" were noted for such engineering feats as the burrowing of "narco-tunnels" under the border between Agua Prieta, Sonora and Douglas, Arizona (discovered in 1989) and under the Otay Mesa, between a point just around the bend from Tijuana international airport and unincorporated San Diego County (1994).

The "Paleface" was personally arrested by General Gutiérrez, his most ardent pursuer—the War on Drugs commander selectively cleaned up the Pacific Cartel, but let Carrillo, his benefactor, alone. Mexican drug enforcement has often been directed at eliminating rivals.

Also still on the scene are Miguel Caro Quintero, Rafael's brother and a Caborca, Sonora feedlot king whom the DEA identifies as the capo of the Sonora Cartel, and the veteran Juan "El Azul" Esparragoza, reputedly a conciliator between the cartels, who is also mentioned as a possible successor to Carrillo.

Such figures as Amado Carrillo and Guero Palma have achieved instant name recognition in Mexico, folk heroes if you will, who cultivate Robin Hood images and have corridos written in their honor. While Mexicans know the names and their exploits of their narco-lords, the U.S. public—the source of these reputations and fortunes—does not have a clue as to the names of their own regional kingpins and *capos di tutti capi*. In fact, Washington's outgoing ambassador Jim Jones insists there are no North American *capos*, that, up in the USA, the drug trade is all retail.[33]

COPS AND CAPOS

Arrayed against this all-star lineup of bad guys are both the military and a bewildering potpourri of civilian police agencies ranging from the elite CISEN (Center for the Investigation of National Security), to the lowliest "*Preventivo*" walking a Mexico City beat. Both the CISEN and the Federal Judicial Police (PJF) inherit the dubious mantle of the old Direction of Federal Security and many of that blighted outfit's agents. According to the Secretary of the Interior, the agency responsible for internal security, 400,000 police agents— 300,000 of them armed—are employed by some 2,000 separate public agencies.[34]

"*Judiciales*," both federal and state, are the investigative arm of local justice ministries, and are celebrated for such torture techniques as the "Tehuacanazo" (chili-laced mineral water forced up the victim's nose), and the "*pozo*" (repeated dunkings in feces-filled toilets), to extract confessions from unwilling suspects—torture remains the judicials' surest investigative tool. Despite much-heralded laws against the practice, torture by Mexican security forces continues unabated and is the object of constant international condemnation. In May, 1997, the United Nations Committee Against Torture flatly told the Mexican government to stop making speeches and start reining in torturers.[35]

The PJF is constantly being sifted for bad apples. On one August day in 1996, then-Attorney General Antonio Lozano Gracia fired 737 agents on charges of corruption. Included among the dismissed: the cop who had bagged García Abrego just months before.[36] Lozano himself was later fired by Zedillo for incompetence. In the 19 months ending in September 1996, the federal district (Mexico City) prosecutor had terminated 1,679 employees for similar crimes.[37] According to one federal informant, as told to *La Jornada*'s Juan Manuel Venegas, profitable PJF command posts along the border can be bought beginning at $500,000 USD.[38] The sale of such positions under

Lozano's aegis was denounced by ex-INCD commander Ricardo Cordero in July 1996. Cordero threatened to take his evidence to a U.S. House drug oversight committee hearing in September—but Attorney General Lozano had him jailed and held incommunicado before he could make the trip.[39]

Unemployed cops are probably a more lethal threat to law and order than employed ones—they are not even obligated to share their booty with their superiors anymore. Many just keep their badge (*placa* or *concha*) and their gun and become freelance kidnappers and bank robbers, or join the drug gangs they were once sworn to combat. Some sign on with other police agencies because no national registry of bad cops is kept or become members of shadowy elite units like the "*Brigadas Blancas*" ("White Brigades") that have operated sub rosa since the dirty war of the 1970s. Others, of a more rural bent, join the private White Guard armies of large landowners. Many, however, are reduced to becoming "*madrinas*" ("godmothers") who serve as informants and bounty hunters for the state and federal judiciales.

YANQUI SHERIFFS

The U.S., of course, has funded a great deal of this mischief through its infernal drug war. Historically, Mexico has been awarded the lion's share of U.S. State Department foreign drug control funds, receiving $150 million between 1978 and 1990.[40] Contributions took off in the '90s, reaching $26 million in 1992, when Salinas abruptly canceled the aid program because of fall-out from the Machain kidnapping—the precipitating factor was a U.S. Supreme Court decision that ok'd the snatch, ruling that it did not matter how or where drug criminals were captured.

Declaring that Mexico would refuse all U.S. drug funding until such time as "our national sovereignty is respected,"[41] Carlos Salinas committed his government to go it alone in the drug war, even suspending all DEA activity in Mexico—for exactly 24 hours—and refusing to accept any new anti-narcotics monetary allocations from Washington. Of course, all sorts of deviousness has been encouraged in order to keep the funds flowing to Mexican police agencies, under other civilian and military programs.

U.S. police agencies continue to build bridges to their Mexican counterparts even if, as DEA administrator Thomas Constantine recently affirmed during 1997 certification hearings, "there is not one Mexican security agency in which we have confidence."[42] U.S. cops who come in daily contact with Mexican police seem to want to do something, anything, to clean up this swamp of corruption. Collaboration is thought to be a moralizing influence and FBI and DEA agents are encouraged to establish close personal contacts.

The FBI provided police training in 12 Mexican states in 1996, according to a U.S. embassy spokesperson, and conducts special seminars on kidnapping and hostage negotiations throughout the country. Much as Hoover tracked

U.S. Reds here in the 1950s, the FBI pursues investigations of North American citizens living in Mexico—as well as investigating Mexicans. The Feds were instrumental in identifying Subcomandante Marcos as "Rafael Guillén" in February 1995[43] and investigated alleged second gunman Othón Cortez's role in the Colosio assassination,[44] both at the request of Mexican authorities.

Just how civilizing the contact has been is questioned by a singular incident in November, 1996, when two Zapotec Indians, suspected of being members of the Popular Revolutionary Army guerrilla front, were tortured near San Augustín Loxicha in the Oaxaca coastal sierra under the direction of a pair of light-skinned and light-eyed men wearing FBI caps. The Oaxaca state prosecutor explains that his police may have exchanged caps with their FBI trainers during 1996 capacitation sessions in that state.

U.S. intelligence agencies have operated on Mexican soil from the 1846-8 invasion onwards—Ethan Alan Hitchcock, the son of the Green Mountain boy, was a notable spook. Pershing's doomed expedition was a gold mine for the burgeoning U.S. intelligence apparatus.[45] Today, the CIA, FBI, DEA, INS, BATF, Customs Service, Defense Intelligence Agency, National Security Agency and the DOD's National Imaging and Mapping Agency (NIMA) all spy on Mexico. The practices of U.S. agencies operating on Mexican turf are often open to question. The DEA, for example, probably utilizing National Defense Agency assets, taps phones at Los Pinos, the Mexican White House.[46] One leaked tape features a compromising phone call between Salinas's chief of staff, José María Cordoba, and Marcela Bodenstadt, a blonde bombshell and ex-judicial, said by "El Buho" to be the public relations liaison for the Gulf Cartel.[47]

Further mischief: in 1994, the DEA smuggled 5.4 tons of cocaine into and out of Mexico as part of a sting on the Cali cartel, without ever notifying Mexican authorities.[48] With 39 agents and 12 administrators, plus a sophisticated network of informants covering the country, the DEA operates circumspectly, encouraging Mexican authorities to make arrests on cases its agents have worked.[49]

Customs, immigration and firearms agents also track alleged bad guys within Mexico's border. "A country that allows others to defend its territorial integrity begins to lose one of the first attributes of nationhood," notes Jorge Castañeda.[50]

THE PRICE OF ADMISSION

The use of drugs in the United States is not a Mexican problem, and, indeed, if drugs were legalized and the profit motive stripped from trafficking in them, they would probably not be a problem north of the Río Grande either.

But, as it stands, because the U.S. government cannot jail 12 million American users (3.2 million addicts)[51]

without serious objections from its citizenry, it beats up on Mexico to take care of business and then gets huffy when Mexico doesn't do a very good job. It really doesn't matter what the drug of choice is—today, it is cocaine, but there are signs that Washington wants to hit its southern neighbor over the head for not cracking down hard enough on methamphetamine ("crystal," "crank," "ice," "meth") production—of course, U.S. drug enforcement drove the meth labs into Mexico in the first place.[52]

The use of drugs and the war on it are an expression of great unhappiness amongst the population of North America. But whether alienation, boredom, frustration, fear or loathing drives so many North Americans to use drugs in such impressive numbers is not really the concern of Mexicans. They have plenty of problems of their own. Nonetheless, Mexico has been threatened and condemned for not doing more to defend its best trading partner from this self-inflicted scourge. I suspect it is the price of admission that is being paid for here—being annexed by the American dream also means being annexed by the American nightmare.

PART THREE

WELCOME TO THE FIRST WORLD

The Annexation
of the Mexican Economy

VAMPIRES AND GUSHERS

Mexico's Open Veins

The plasma centers are on the U.S. side of the border, running east from Chula Vista and San Diego to all the way to Brownsville on the gulf—at least 17 of them, according to one plasma industry spokesperson. At Calexico's Alpha Therapeutics Plasma Center, not 50 feet from the high border fence, just about every potential vendor approached by an undercover reporter in the packed waiting room readily concedes that they live across the line. At Alpha, vendors can sell their blood every 48 hours, according to the house rules, and the most prolific "donors" receive raffle tickets on items like Christmas turkeys.

"Our donors are healthy," explains Dr. Lenore Elmore, of the Los Angeles-based plasma spinner, a subsidiary of the Japanese Green Cross pharmaceutical conglomerate. "People can increase their incomes here. They eat better because they have more money for food."

Green Cross, which runs three border plasma centers, is a harried transnational these days. Founded by Ryoichi Naiti, "an officer in the notorious Unit 731 of the Imperial Army which conducted germ warfare experiments on civilians and prisoners in China,"[1] the pharmaceutical powerhouse has been hit hard by billion-yen suits from hemophiliacs who contracted the HIV virus from the company's plasma.

Further east along the border, *maquiladora* workers in Ciudad Juárez sell their sweat by day and their plasma in the off-hours. José Luis, who assembles auto seats on the Mexican side, agrees with the Green Cross doctor. He eats meat twice a week now—Wednesday and Saturday—so that when he crosses the river to sell his body fluids at the El Paso Plasma Collection Center his protein levels will be up to snuff. Other plasma centers promise free rides across the border and distribute coupons to potential donors in the squares of Mexican border towns.

Indocumentados who want to vend their plasma risk the wrath of the U.S. Border Patrol when they swim the Río Bravo-Grande, hoist themselves up on the levee, cut through the chain-link fence that was the original "Tortilla Curtain," and dash across six lines of freeway to El Paso Biologicals. "It's harder to get at them there," commented Border Patrol supervisor Gary Runyan, while observing the action one afternoon "they run right in the door and the nurses get them down on the couches with all the needles sticking into them before we can even run a check."[2]

The metaphor of the Border "Draculas," as Mexican newspapers label these dubious institutions, is an apt one for the economic vampirism that the U.S. inflicts upon Mexico in the name of free trade and North American "integration." The bloodletting has drained a vital resource from Mexico, transforming a once insular, nationalist state into a net exporter of capital its anemic economy can ill afford to spare, assembled goods for First World consumers, and not for sale to Mexicans, the cheapest labor in industrialized Latin America and nearly two billion barrels of petroleum every day of the year.

"Integration" is a euphemism for annexation, dreamt up by free trade fanatics and their public relations reps to better sell their products to the victim state. When the proverbial ten-ton North American gorilla "integrates" with the much-abused Mexican burro, someone is going to get screwed and the smart money says it won't be the gorilla.

"Integration" implies three mechanisms for forced penetration—investment, trade and debt. The gorilla's handlers stand to make a bundle no matter which way the Great American Ape defiles the donkey. The burro's owners share in the reward too, by simply casting a blind eye while their animal is abused. Of all the abuses the poor donkey endures, debt must be the most torturous ordeal.

THE MIRACLE OF INDEBTEDNESS

Debt "has made Mexico an object of international humiliation," writes historian Enrique Semo.[3] Mexico has been in debt to the nations of the north since it drew its first breath as a nation. The republic was baptized in such humiliation. British loans, tendered in 1823-24, under extremely onerous conditions, prodded the infant nation's first international debt crisis in 1828. Since then, Mexico has been dunned, shunned, threatened, throttled, invaded, conquered, and annexed under the pretext of the collection of a foreign debt, the principle of which has often been repaid, if only in the currency of sweat and blood, ten times over. In 176 years of perpetual bankruptcy, Mexico has been forced to suspend debt payments 14 times,[4] a decision that automatically cuts off the country's access to international largess. When it has been able to pay, Mexico often pays through the nose—of its poor, who are the first to suffer the brunt of depleted government treasuries. Cutbacks in social services translate to such outrages as an absence of syringes in public hospitals and the curtailment of school breakfast programs in a nation where millions of children go to school hungry. Mexicans suffer the general malaise of a debtor nation whose economic life blood is siphoned off minute by minute ($30,000 USD in debt payments every minute of 1994)[5] by the vampires of the north.

Mexico's history is crafted by indebtedness. Even the so-called "Miracle Years" (1940-70), when "stabilized development" and "import substitution" policies supposedly satisfied the needs of the nation, the vaunted 6% annual growth was driven by debt. These growth rates, which made Mexico the beacon of Latin America capitalism, were sustained by U.S. loans that were then used to mask yearly budget deficits.

Under Adolfo Ruiz Cortines (1952-8), a Miracle Years president, the foreign debt ballooned 500%, to over a half-billion USD. One such loan that helped bind Mexico to Washington's mandate followed the June 1954 devaluation of the peso—the $75 million jolt pried loose from the U.S. Federal Reserve carried a laundry list of anti-protectionist suggestions, reveal U.S. State Department documents.[6] Such indebtedness augmented Mexican subservience to U.S. political and economic projects and solidified Cold War partnership. This lopsided relationship was institutionalized in 1967, the last year of import substitution success, when Mexico was invited to join the Fed's institutional open markets committee. To cement Mexico's new junior partner-in-the-free market status, Díaz Ordaz was granted a $130 million USD bone to further the project of "integration"[7]—much of which found its way into preparations for the ill-fated 1968 Olympics.

By the end of the 1960s, the Mexican Miracle was in tatters. To many, it had never been much more than a myth anyway. In Tanaco, there was little that was miraculous about the "miracle" years except that the community survived at all—a third of the babies born did not, dying before they reached their first year. The closest doctor was two towns away in Paracho and there were no vehicles to get there over a rough-hewn mountain track. My neighbors ate meat twice a year, during the spring planting and fall harvest fiestas. "*Coyotes*" (or middlemen) bought up the corn harvest for a pittance and resold it in the cities at great profit. The forests from which the Purépechas drew their one salable product—pine resin—were cut down by timber barons from the big cities. The golden years of growth and stability never dawned in Tanaco and not much has changed since. Indeed, what is usually defined as growth by the development industry is measured less by the plight of the poor than it is by what the elites and the middle classes, who are its exclusive beneficiaries, can glean from it.

LETTER OF INTENTION

Whether it is the anger of the Gods or historical catharsis, catastrophes tend to converge in Mexico and the 1968 Tlatelolco holocaust was a watershed of this coalescence, a process often described in political diction here as a "*coyuntura*" (coming together). Urban migration had created deep pockets of poverty within the cities and serious imbalances in the agricultural sector. Suddenly Mexico, which had been able to feed itself for centuries, could not, and millions of tons of grains and other foodstuffs had to be imported. Although the nation was producing more oil than at any other time since 1921, it was burning off more than it could pump, and President Luis Echeverría was forced to import 100,000 barrels a day from Venezuela between 1971 and 1974, an unprecedented hiatus in the history of Mexican energy development. Consumer prices that had barely fluctuated in years suddenly soared and double-digit inflation became the rule. Budgets that once were balanced now ran 600% deficit increases.[8]

Echeverría's manic neo-Cardenist vision spawned grandiose projects on the drawing board that, once inaugurated by the president, ultimately littered the landscape with unfinished structures. When finance minister Hugo Margain finally summoned up the courage to tell Echeverría that his government was running out of funds for such monuments, El Presidente fired him and got one who knew where to find the scratch.

José López Portillo and Willie Sutton, the slick '50s New York City bank robber, shared an understanding. They both turned to the banking community because "that's where the money was." Mexico immediately borrowed $6 billion, mostly from U.S. banks, doubling the nation's indebtedness to $11 billion. Such profligacy, combined with fiscal lethargy (big business was virtually exempt from taxation), precipitated economic disaster. Echeverría was forced to devalue the peso for the first time since Ruiz Cortines did 22 years previous, a rude blow to the average Joséfina's already battered pocketbook.

Despite his Third World pretensions, El Presidente called upon the Lords of International Finance to rescue his sinking ship of state. The International Monetary Fund heard the drowning man's cries and threw Echeverría a $1.5 billion lifeline in 1976, three months before he left office. In return, the Mexican president signed the first of eight letters of intention with the IMF that, over the next generation, would serve to annex Mexico's economy to the policies dictated by the Fund, the World Bank and the White House.

MALPRACTICE

The IMF prescription for salvation involves the equivalent of the application of leeches to bleed and suck out the evil that festers within the victim's life systems. Such quackery includes axing the public sector, privatizing state enterprises no matter what may be their social benefit and trade liberalization, i.e. handing over the nation's economic development to the free traders and their magic wand of export-driven commerce. The going theory is that exports generate enough income to pay off the lenders. Whatever crumbs might be left over are supposed to cover the deluge of imports that free trade dumps upon the domestic market.

Conversely, because such voodoo economics tends to be inflationary, the IMF advocates driving interest rates beyond the reach of mere mortals and savaging the buying power of the working masses so as to remove money from circulation. Whether the patient lives or dies as the result of such malpractice is more a question of constitution and culture than the effectiveness of the treatment. Although multiple letters of intention have bolted Mexico's economic structures to the IMF's global hacienda, the foundation is not a sturdy one. Cyclical turbulence forces periodic postponement and rescheduling of payments. Moreover, centuries of abuse by their creditors make the resistance of the Mexican people to foreign usury a hurdle as tall as the 12-foot-tall Border Wall on the road to permanent "integration."

In his first year in office (1977), López Portillo obeyed the IMF's instructions and initiated an austerity program that slowed growth to 3%—after tumbling into negative numbers in 1970, Echeverría's growth rates, artificially inflated by massive borrowing, had averaged 5%. At last, it seemed, the feverish ups and downs of the Echeverría years had settled down to manageable proportions. But a sudden surge in Mexico's oil reserves in 1978 torpedoed this prognosis. From now on, the president told the nation, that "administration" of the newly discovered oil "abundance" would be the central theme of his governance

BOOM!

Mexican reserves had actually been surging for several years. The discovery of vast fields around Reforma on the Chiapas-Tabasco border in 1974 had become public knowledge, but Echeverría, savvy that oil brought friction and pressure from the U.S., had been reluctant to disclose the extent of the find. An unsigned memorandum making the rounds in Washington in 1974 (apparently leaked by a disgruntled PEMEX subcontractor) spoke of a 20 billion barrel increase in Mexican reserves.[9] López Portillo partially acknowledged the increased volume when he doubled announced reserves to 11 billion barrels shortly after taking office.

But the real story was not on land at all. In the mid-1970s, so the legend goes, Carmen Island fishermen had told PEMEX of the black *chapopote* gushing up from the Caribbean floor, about 50 miles north of their sleepy Campeche village. Akal 1 came in in 1979, soon platforms in the Campeche Sound were pumping 1.5 million barrels a day and Mexico had upped its estimated total reserves to 66 billion barrels, the fifth grandest on the planet.[10] The first pipeline was completed to Dos Bocas, Tabasco in June 1979, and the crude began to spill onto international markets soon after. Days later, a second Caribbean well, Ixtoc 1, blew sky-high, spewing 30,000 barrels a day into the sea for the next nine months, the most momentous spill on the oil record books (you could look it up), and one which befouled beaches and habitat all the way to Texas.[11]

The out-of-control Ixtoc blow-out was a graphic emblem of what oil did to the economy and the environment, splattering everything with black gold, fueling phenomenal 8.2% growth and igniting massive corruption inside the enterprise—kickbacks and bribes were part of the PEMEX operating manual. On the books, PEMEX did more business than the next six Mexican industries combined, but record-keeping was not a strong suit. Millions of barrels were sold off on the European spot market with no records kept of the transactions.[12] López Portillo's director of the state monopoly, Jorge Díaz Serrano, went to prison for an oil tanker flimflam.

"The oil boom hypnotized the country with the illusion of greatness," Alan Riding wrote in his valuable *Distant Neighbors*.[13] Following the model of oleogarchies like Iran under the Shah and Nigeria under the generals, the boom spawned social discontent, environmental havoc and rampant greed. 20 years after the first great finds in his native Tabasco state, Andrés Manuel López Obrador, national leader of the social democrat PRD party, wrote in his political memoir *Between History and Hope*, of the destruction that the oil boom inflicted upon the Mexican southeast: "Petroleum has contaminated everything: the earth, the water, the air, the public morals, customs and traditions, the ways of work, and social development."[14]

López Portillo's tastes tended towards the pharaonic. One example: the "Otomí Ceremonial Center" in Temoaya, Mexico state, an enormous UFO landing pad-like complex that boasts shocking pink pyramids and has been featured in James Bond films. Other expenditures were more socially grounded—such as the "Mexican Food System" or SAM program, which subsidized farmers to grow for the cities, and briefly restored Mexican sovereignty over its own food supply.

It goes without saying that the discoveries generated enormous interest in U.S. ruling circles. The CIA had been in on the ground floor, feeding the estimates to a salivating Washington.[15] Petroleum prices then hovered around $35 a barrel, the result of the 1973 OPEC boycott. Strategic planners, thoroughly soured on the "crazy Arabs," wanted to move the U.S.'s primary energy suppliers a lot closer to home. For the next half decade, Venezuela, Canada and Mexico would provide the basic U.S. import platform. To accommodate its northern neighbor, Mexico pushed production up past two million barrels daily by 1980, about half going north—oil now accounted for 75% of all exports (it had been 10% in 1972).[16]

BUSTED!

The boom was driven by mounting debt. The more money Mexico borrowed, the more resource it was forced to pump to pay it back. Flush with petrodollars reaped from vastly inflated oil prices in the Middle East, the bankers jammed Diez Serrano's waiting rooms, briefcases stuffed with greenbacks they were only too pleased to unload at extravagant early 1980s interest rates. In 1981, the López Portillo government borrowed $24 billion USD, $5 billion alone in the month of September—the latter sum represented what the nation had owed from Independence through 1970 when Echeverría took office.[17] The foreign debt itself now exceeded $40 billion (it would climb to $80 billion by López Portillo's 1982 departure from Los Pinos) and interest payments equaled half of Mexico's exports. Much of the bundle was lent short term at 15% plus rates to cover short term debt, a Ponzi scheme that spelled disaster. Nonetheless, the president did not yet understand that the fiesta, she was over.

An ominous June 1981 $4 slip in the price of the product failed to snap López Portillo from his oily reverie. As prices staggered, confidence in the president wobbled. In 1981, capital flight, palpitated by Mexican billionaires like Carlos Hank González, reached a meaningful $8 billion USD.[18] López Portillo began 1982 by devaluating the peso he had sworn to defend like a canine. By mid-1982, it suddenly dawned on the president's inner circle that with $10 billion in short-term debt about to come due, they no longer had a snow goddess's chance in Chiapas of meeting their obligations. On the evening of August 12th, López Portillo shut down the foreign exchange houses and closed all dollar bank accounts, dangerously disaffecting the Mexican middle classes. Later that night, Finance Minister Jesús Silva Herzog rang up U.S. Secretary of the Treasury Donald Regan. He had "this little problem" he needed to talk to him about—in person.[19]

WEIRD BLUE LIGHTS IN WASHINGTON

Silva Herzog and his entourage were on the ground in Washington the next morning. Regan took him over to talk with the IMF. The IMF sent the Mexican to the Federal Reserve. Paul Volker understood the "little problem" quite clearly: Mexico was about to default, threatening U.S. financial stability and perhaps the world banking system. 13 U.S. banks had $16 billion sunk in Mexico, 48% of their combined capital.[20] A Mexican default would domino throughout Latin America where exposure was even more indecent. Volker, who, for his efforts would be awarded the "Aztec Eagle," the highest honor Mexico can bestow upon a foreigner, got on the phone, buttonholing European bankers through the wonders of fiber optics. The sessions lasted into the dawns. One early morning, Silva Herzog's aide, Angel Gurria (at this writing, foreign minister under whom Silva serves as Mexican ambassador to Washington), found himself hallucinating that the U.S. Department of the Treasury was radiating an extraterrestrial blue light.[21] Had the UFOs landed?

Finally, on August 17th, with his panicked compatriots glued to the tube, Silva Herzog went on Mexican national television to explain the denouement: the nation was not really bankrupt—it just had this little cash flow problem. The Reagan Administration would lend Mexico an emergency billion bucks in exchange for oil shipments to the U.S. Strategic Reserve (the nearly 20% interest on this charitable bail-out was never communicated).[22] Negotiations with the IMF were on-going—they would soon blossom into $6.64 billion in total loans. But it was not so much what their finance minister told them but rather from where he spoke that signaled to Mexicans the shape of the future: the news was beamed in from the capital of the United States of North America.

Mexico's near default left high finance feeling queasy. A former Citibank president described the mood at the IMF-World Bank yearly get-together a few weeks later in Toronto: "150 odd finance ministers, 50-odd central bankers, 1,000 journalists, 1,000 commercial bankers, a large supply of whiskey, and a reasonably small city. This produced an enormous head of steam driving an engine called 'the end-of-the-world is coming.'"[23] The Latin American debt crisis was on full boil.

López Portillo was already a lame duck during these dark days, Miguel de la Madrid having been elected in July. But the outgoing president had one more wild card up his sleeve. During his September 1st 1982 state of the nation address, López Portillo pounded the podium in fury and, in a futile gesture to staunch hemorrhaging capital flight that the *sacadolares* (literally, "the dollar-pullers") were inflicting upon the republic, declared the nationalization of the banking system. The nationalization, which López Portillo vainly hoped would cast him in a Cárdenas-like light, drove a wedge between government and what is tagged "the Private Initiative" here, that took two presidents to heal.

THE DEBTORS' CLUB

15 years later, the cost of the debt crisis to Mexico's national sovereignty is still being sorted out. A new letter of intention, finally signed in August 1983, locked the IMF program into place and committed Mexico to shell out between $10 and $12 billion USD yearly for the next six years, to its creditors—an extraction that when combined with flagging investment, converted the country into a net exporter of capital, a crippling burden that, like the border "vampires," bled the economy dry, kicked inflation up to record levels and drove an estimated two million Mexicans north to the U.S. One early prize for

the new neo-liberal bosses of Mexico: a 1983 investment law that opened up 34 sectors of the Mexican economy to 100% foreign ownership.

Volker's appraisal that the Mexican near-default would trigger similar travesties was accurate. Between 1983 and '84, the dominoes tumbled as 15 Third World nations threatened default and then renegotiated their debts.[24] Brazil (1983), Argentina (1984), and Peru (1985) all partially suspended payments, inspiring dire lamentations on Wall Street and in Washington. The air over Latin America crackled with talk of moratorium and the creation of a debtors' cartel. But, by signing the letter of intention with the IMF, Mexico abstracted itself from its Latin neighbors, and incoming President de la Madrid actively sought to dissuade his Latin counterparts from forming such a club. The 1982 debt crisis not only placed the Mexican economy under the hegemonic rectorship of the IMF and the U.S. but also undermined the Bolivarian ideology that had historically been one leg of Mexico's foreign policy.

DE LA MADRID: AGENT-IN-CHARGE

Harvard Yard-trained Miguel de la Madrid was a committed technocrat, an updated version of one of Don Porfirio's "*Científicos*," and his gray presence seemed color-coordinated to the years over which he presided. When de la Madrid took office, wrote Riding, "his political options were defined by his economic options and these were now being decided outside of the country."[25] Mexico was not governed by de la Madrid, but rather by the debt crisis—he was merely the IMF's agent on the ground. Ordered by his Washington managers to institute severe austerity measures, he complied with slavish dedication.

A 1984 letter of intention that brought in a few billion committed Mexico to divest itself of 1,200 state enterprises and reduce public sector participation in the gross domestic product (PIB) from 18 to 8%.[26] That same year, Mexico borrowed $14 billion from a smorgasbord of international sources to cover $12 billion in interest payments on its swelling foreign debt.[27] Meanwhile, de la Madrid was pumping record quantities of oil—3,000,000 barrels a day in a world of falling prices. From 1982 through 1986, Mexico replaced Saudi Arabia as the U.S.'s number one supplier. But extraction was an increasingly losing proposition as oil prices bottomed out. The 1985 nose dive cost Mexico $6 billion in 1986, and provoked a crisis within what had become known universally as "*La Crisis*"—which, in turn, was countered with new IMF loans and still another letter of intention with even more severe conditions.[28] By the time de la Madrid retired from office, the foreign debt topped $100 billion, about $1,222 per capita for each Mexican man, woman, and child. Each time interest rates jumped one point, the country owed $700 million more.[29]

Despite the IMF-White House ministrations, the patient got no better. 98% inflation in 1982 was topped by negative 4.7% growth in 1983. Between 1982 and 1986, Mexican workers lost 40% of their buying power and, by 1987, inflation was topping 159%.[30] Ironically, the nation ran a $13 billion trade surplus in 1983, mostly spurred by massive oil shipments and *maquiladora* production, which had discovered that *La Crisis* made Mexican workers the cheapest in industrial Latin America. Despite IMF conventional wisdom, Mexican trade surpluses are usually a sign of deep recession, in which wage depreciations and internal consumption cutbacks make Mexico competitive in a dog-eat-dog commercial world.

A MODEL DEBTOR

Disregarding the social and economic devastation over which he presided, Miguel de la Madrid was a model debtor, never missing a payment no matter what sort of pain it caused those he ruled. In fact, such pain bailed him out of the 1985-86 plunge. Just as suspension of payments loomed, a massive Mexico City earthquake in September 1985 leveled whole neighborhoods in the capital, killing between 10,000 (government estimates) and 30,000 citizens (non-governmental estimates). The tragedy tugged at the world's heartstrings and stirred fresh World Bank infusions. "They disappeared right into de la Madrid's pocket," sneers Lalo Miranda, an activist in the *damnificado* (earthquake victim) movement that evolved from the tragedy and became a force for social change in the late 1980s.

The litmus test for free marketeers is what is called, in the IMF hymnal, "trade liberalization"—the greatest possible reliance on the world market and international competition to dictate economic activity. De la Madrid marched lockstep into the General Agreement on Tariffs and Trade (GATT) in 1986, for which he was warmly applauded by the Reagan White House. At the zenith of the oil boom in '79, Mexico had been about to join up but López Portillo pulled back, even with his negotiators in Geneva, because he thought he might wheedle a better deal from Washington outside of the agreement—de la Madrid, his finance minister, argued forcefully at the time in favor of taking the GATT plunge.

Similarly, de la Madrid's hand-picked successor, Carlos Salinas, then budget director, was a vocal booster of the GATT strategy. Trade would be a vital concern of Salinas's presidency, which would seal IMF neo-liberal impositions so deep in concrete that one would have to wreck the nation's economic foundations to get at them. Indeed, Salinas's enthusiasm for free trade would literally turn Mexico's geopolitical position upside down, from the northernmost nation in Latin America to the southernmost component of North America, permanently annexing Mexico's economy to that of the U.S.

Chapter 13

CARLOS'S HOUSE OF CARDS

The New Year's Day dawn broke over the frigid Sonora desert, bathing the Sahuaro and the mesquite in the golden light of the New World Order. January 1st, 1994 was the first day of the North American Free Trade Agreement (*"El Tratado de Libre Comercio"* or "Tay-Elay-Say" in Mexican) and out there in the NAFTA Industrial Park, just beyond San Luis Río Colorado, a wedge of border that corners upper and lower Californias, Arizona and Sonora, the prospects seemed as endless as the desolate desert horizon.

The land upon which the NAFTA Industrial Park is sited had been recently sold by the San Luis ejido under terms dictated by the revised Mexican Constitution—Article 27 of which governs agrarian reform, Emiliano Zapata's contribution to Mexico's magna carta. Now Article 27 had been mutilated, under President Carlos Salinas's auspices, to allow foreign investors to buy, sell and lease Mexican ejido land. For the past year, NAFTA Industrial Park pitchman Enrique Orozco had been subdividing the desert into lots and dealing it to Canadian and U.S. corporations for maquiladora construction. Orozco couldn't tell me the corporate names of his clients "just yet" but confided that Raúl Salinas Lozano, father of the then-president of Mexico, was an enthusiastic supporter of the project. One U.S. electronics outfit, Bose Speakers—the lucrative brainchild of an MIT professor—was already operating, but the NAFTA Industrial Park was otherwise still a dream, terminating abruptly in the hardscrabble, rattlesnake-infested desert just beyond the last paved street.

Taxista #55, who had brought me out to the park, was a voting member of the ejido—the land had been given to the farmers of San Luis Río Colorado by Lázaro Cárdenas himself back in the 1930s. Still Enrique Ayala had voted to sell the tract at the ejido assembly. The governor had come to urge their vote. This morning, he was not so sure.

"We can't lose," ejido president Rafael Meza had told me earlier, in an interview. "We already lost," said Ayala now. "We lost control of our land and we did not get one peso for it.

"We went into this project because we thought this would bring good jobs for our kids but I have two sons working at Bose. They make 140 pesos a week [a little less than $40 USD at the time]. I make more money in the cab."[1]

Back at the dilapidated hotel on the main drag in San Luis, Televisa was already reporting the takeover of an undetermined number of towns, far away in the highlands of Chiapas at the other end of the country, by a mysterious ski-masked army of Mayan Indian rebels who invoked the name of Emiliano Zapata. The fact that they had chosen the first day of the NAFTA-TLC on which to move did not escape Washington's attention.

FREE TRADE = ECONOMIC ANNEXATION

"Free Trade" is related less to freedom and trade than it is to power. Free trade is a formula for aggrandizement imposed upon the weak by the strong, the Crown upon the colony, the hegemonic state upon its satellites, with little room for choice by the designated trading "partner." When the recipient of such magnanimity dares to rebel and defend itself by erecting protectionist barriers, the fall-out can lead to military invasion in the name of keeping the "free" market open. Because of such bitter experience, "Free Trade" has never left a good taste on the Mexican tongue.

Joel Poinsett came proffering "Free Trade" as an opening gambit in U.S. designs to annex Texas. The French sought to impose preferred trade status on Mexico in the absurd Pastry War of 1838. 10 years later, Trist dangled his vision of "Free Trade" before the despoiled Mexicans at Guadalupe Hidalgo. The foiled sale of the Tehuantepec Isthmus contained "Free Trade" clauses. Porfirio Díaz imposed 34 years of "Free Trade" upon Mexico that cost the Mexican people their own freedom. Ever since, U.S. policy towards Mexico has been held captive by the "Free Traders"—Lane Wilson fought to save Porfirian free trade privileges, Sheffield and Morrow sought to reestablish them. World War II was a window of opportunity for the "Free Trade" zealots, a creed that was subsequently made incarnate in July 1944, at the Mount Washington Hotel in Bretton Woods, New Hampshire, when the International Monetary and Finance Conference convened to give birth to the World Bank and the IMF. John Gavin and John Negroponte, among other U.S. ambassadors, took up the "Free Trade" cudgels as a bulwark against Communism. The "North American Free Trade Agreement" (or "Treaty of Free Trade" in its Spanish equivalent) that kicked in January 1st, 1994 was just the post-Berlin Wall version of this antique scam.

"Free Trade" is hardly trade or free at all—at least not the way real free trade is practiced down in the thieves' kitchen Tepito neighborhood of Mexico City's old quarter, where the *fayuca*—smuggled goods from El Norte—changes hands relentlessly, with little regard for tariffs, taxes or bills of sales. In Tepito, the traditional home of the toughest boxers in Mexico, invading armies of fiscal police are stoned when they try to collect for their government.

On the other hand, the "free trade" that NAFTA promised was more directed at opening up Mexican money markets for freewheeling speculation, land and oil for transnational exploitation, and a giant pool of cheap labor to assemble goods designed to maintain First World USA in the style to which it has become accustomed—in addition to dumping tons of excess junk in the Mexican marketplace. For the Masters of the Universe, it had been a long hike from Bretton Woods to the NAFTA Industrial Park, but on January 1st, 1994, the annexation of the Mexican economy seemed finally in sight.

A BAD BEGINNING

The July 6th, 1988 Mexican presidential election had loosened a slagheap of resentment against the ruling PRI. Beaten down by six years of La Crisis that culminated in 1987 in runaway, triple-digit inflation, PRIistas abandoned their party like lemmings leaping into the fjords. To many, it seemed de la Madrid was hellbent on giving the country away to the gringos and the feral, balding successor he had chosen, former budget minister Carlos Salinas de Gortari, pledged more of the same. On the other hand, Cuauhtémoc Cárdenas, the tall, taciturn son of Lázaro, appeared an antidote to La Crisis and the gringo-ization of the Patria and the revolution for which it stands.

Cárdenas's stormy exit from the PRI—he had been the PRI governor of Michoacán from 1980 through 1986—attracted popular attention to his left coalition candidacy and his critique of a corrupt, corporate political system that his own father had played a definitive role in shaping, struck a chord. This reporter barnstormed the countryside with Cárdenas from 1987 to 1989 and never failed to be moved by the groundswell of democratic aspirations that his crusade excited throughout grassroots Mexico. The Cárdenas candidacy was an expression of hope and no matter how strenuously the PRI has labored to make the nation forget the debacle of 1988, it has never quite been able to re-imprison the genie of democratic aspiration (he repeated this sweep in 1997) that escaped from the bottle that fateful July 6th. Indeed, nine years later, on another July 6th, Cárdenas won an election—as Mexico City's governor, and the Zocalo filled quickly with tens of thousands of wildly dancing supporters that had stood with him every inch of his lengthy sojourn.

1988 surprised the pants off the PRI. As expected, Cárdenas won his home state of Michoacán by a landslide, but he also took Baja California on the northern border, Morelos and Mexico state and Guerrero in the center of the country and probably Oaxaca too. Lázaro's son also swept 37 out of 40 Mexico City voting districts, where a sixth of the nation's electorate resides. The impressive turnout caused the Institutionals extreme consternation. Three hours after the polls closed, when opposition observers sat down at the computer consoles, Federal Election Commission's screens went blank—the "system" was said to have "crashed." Eight days later, Carlos Salinas was declared the winner with a smidgen over 50% of the votes cast. Cárdenas's tally showed him edging Salinas 39% to 37% with about 40,000 of the electoral commission's 56,000 polling places accounted for—results from thousands of precincts were never posted in final commission tallies. When the electoral college convened in early September to confirm Salinas's "victory," the leftists seized the rostrum and dumped burlap sacks of partially burnt ballots, marked for Cárdenas, onto the floor of the Congress.

Cárdenas supporters began to disappear. Xavier Ovando, Cuauhtémoc's electoral pointman, was gunned down three nights before the elections—reporters speculated that he had obtained the secret PRI-held password to election commission computers. The son of a Cárdenas organizer, who had borrowed a decal-decorated campaign car for an outing, and three companions were murdered by Mexico City cops, their blood-soaked bodies discovered, under an urban freeway on the eve of the convening of the electoral college. Two weeks after Salinas's December 1st inauguration, José Ramón García, the Cárdenas leader up in Cuautla, Zapata's homeland, was taken—the new president's first *desaparecido*—and has never been found since.

Despite the multiple violations of civil and human rights that accompanied his election, the Reagan administration embraced Carlos Salinas as the new liberator of his people, extending early congratulations for his dubious triumph even before he had been confirmed in office. Reporters for major U.S. newspapers did their best to convey the fraudulent birth of the Salinas presidency,[2] but their editors were unconvinced. Citing State Department sources, the *New York Times*' ace Johnny Apple hyped Salinas as "a member of the reform wing of the PRI."[3] The Mexican election, which was thoroughly obscured by the impending Democratic Party convention, was not of prime concern to the U.S. press—or even the U.S. government. According to the *Times*' Larry Rohter, North American officials, who appeared to be pulling for Salinas, "seemed unconcerned about voting irregularities."[4] The *Times* editorial board demonstrated its true allegiance when it expressed trepidation at Salinas's possible defeat because the PRI candidate was "widely recognized as a capable and committed free market exponent."[5] The efforts of the U.S. directorship to sanitize the foul stench of the July 6th chicanery had Cold War context—even then, in the final days of of the Evil Empire, Cuauhtémoc

Cárdenas loomed large as the Red Ayatollah that Bill Casey had once conjured up as leading Mexico into an ultimate anti-U.S. jihad. The blind, blanket approval accorded Carlos Salinas by both Reagan and his own hand-picked successor, George Bush, legitimized the balding little man's stolen presidency. The price was, of course, the onrushing economic annexation of Mexico.

THE TABLE IS SET

On November 22nd, 1988, the 25th anniversary of the assassination of John F. Kennedy one Texas city away, the presidents-elect of the United States of Mexico and the United States of North America, George Bush and Carlos Salinas, sat down in Houston at the Lyndon B. Johnson space center to plot the course towards the free trade future of the two nations they would, within a matter of days, rule. The NAFTA clock was wound and ticking. The concept of economic integration had already been mapped out in a 1987 "framework" agreement, following de la Madrid's plunge into GATT. From Houston onwards, Salinas, an obsessive jogger nicknamed "the Atomic Ant" because of both his size and maniacal peppiness, would always be racing to get the job done before his six years in office ran out on him. To the former budget minister's odd way of thinking, locking Mexico into the neo-liberal world order would earn him history's laurels.

From the outset of this venture, Carlos Salinas categorically denied that Mexico would ever enter into a North American common market relationship with the U.S. and Canada.[6] Nonetheless, he behaved like he had already entered into certain understandings with Bush. In January 1989, one month after his inauguration, Salinas sent army troops to arrest "*La Quina*," Joaquín Hernández Galicia, the corrupt king of the oilworkers' union. The bust appears to be a classic frame-up—the shipment of arms found in the old man's bunker had been imported during the 1970s by Mexican police and planted on the compound rather than, as the government charged, smuggled into the country by *La Quina* to foment revolution. Moreover, the cadaver of a judicial police agent, purportedly killed in the raid, was said to have been imported from Ciudad Juárez for the occasion.[7] La Quina was sent up the river for 35 years, and the US press hailed the frame-up as a bold blow against corruption, a sign that Salinas would not let the union stand in the way of PEMEX privatization. "The action removes a powerful obstacle to reform [read, the privatization of PEMEX] and shows that [Salinas's] reform program is not up for barter."[8]

The truth was more revealing of the appallingly vindictive nature of the Salinas sexenio: La Quina, panicked by the shadow of privatization, had told oil workers to cast their ballot for the son of the man who had nationalized the oil industry, Cuauhtémoc Cárdenas. In addition to this heinous crime against a PRI he had always embraced, Hernández Galicia was accused of financing publication of a sensationalist volume, *A Killer In Los Pinos*, which detailed how Carlos and his older brother, Raúl, had killed a young Indian servant during a childhood game of Cowboys and *Indígenas*. The author of the book has since received political asylum in the U.S.[9]

In March, 1989, Salinas further warmed the cockles of Washington's heart by capturing drug kingpin Félix Gallardo, Caro Quintero's brainier cousin, in Guadalajara, and Mexico survived congressional certification—a peevish Senate had withheld certification the year previous. In June, the president ordered troops into Cananea to break a miners' strike in anticipation of privatization, another blow against the public sector that brightened Salinas's star in Washington.

But debt reduction, not free trade, was *número uno* on the Salinas economic agenda. By 1988, foreign debt had zoomed to 60% of the GDP and six out of the top 10 lenders were U.S. banks (Citicorp, Bank of America, Manufacturers Hanover, Chase, Chemical Bank, Morgan Guaranty).[10] In February 1989, Finance Minister Pedro Aspe and Bank of Mexico director Miguel Mancera flew to Washington to huddle with Bush Treasury Secretary Nicholas Brady.[11] Complicated international haggling followed. The Mexicans took to the skies, barnstorming European capitals to stage their dog-and-burro shows. The Brady Plan cobbled together some 300 banks to back up to $7.4 billion USD in credits, in what my colleague Duncan Green describes as the sort of "jiggery-pokery" much beloved by the international banking community.[12] When finally all the i's were dotted (Spring 1990), Mexico had realized a 10% reduction in its $100 billion external debt and payments had been rescheduled to balloon only after Salinas left office, but the nation was still shelling out 20% of its export income to service international loans.[13] Between 1986 and 1996, according to both Banamex, the leading private bank, and the Secretary of Energy, Mexico paid out 51.2% of its oil production and income to service the foreign debt[14]—both before and after Brady.

Brady Plan relief was barely perceptible in Mexico, but this latest "final solution" defused, once and for all, the phantom of a debtors' cartel. Subsequent "special" Brady Plan deals were worked out with Brazil, Argentina, and even IMF Bad Boy Alan García's Peru.

Thus, the table was set for NAFTA. In February of 1990, a year after the Brady Plan had first been proposed, Salinas dispatched his Svengali-like chief of staff José Marie Córdoba Montoya, a Spaniard born in France, and the vigorous, Yale-educated Commerce Secretary, Jaime Serra Puche, to Washington for hush-hush huddles with Brady and Secretary of State James Baker.[15] Negotiations towards a North American Free Trade Agreement were announced after Bush and Salinas met in the U.S. capital in June—Salinas had flown in for a "Business Roundtable" seance. The U.S. president magnanimously tabbed the forthcoming free trade treaty as an "Initiative to the Americas."

What changed Salinas's approach to a free trade accord with Washington and Canada has not been adequately explored. Certainly, the fall of the Berlin Wall was a motivator—no longer could Mexico Mao-Mao Washington by flirting with the Reds. It was the end of history, Mexican and otherwise, Francis Fukayama postulated.[16] Salinas said as much: "the Cold War ended and only one of the super powers survived and it was our neighbor."[17]

BIG MAQ

NAFTA negotiations kicked off in Toronto the next month. Canada was chosen for the initiation of talks because of the free trade treaty it had forged with Washington in 1988-89, a pact Reagan had dubbed "the new constitution of North America."[18] According to Canadian unionists, the new North American magna carta had done little for Canadian workers and industry, costing substantial manufacturing job loss and permitting U.S.-based transnationals to dominate national industry with little reciprocity from the U.S.[19] One poll conducted during the NAFTA run-up listed 63% of the Canadian public as being opposed to "free trade" with the U.S.[20]

Such negative appraisals did not much ruffle the Great Communicator's belief in free trade. Although George Bush and Bill Clinton are prone to pass themselves off as the papas of NAFTA, Ronald Reagan is the real father. As far back as his successful 1980 campaign, the old huckster was selling a free trade pact that would open up a 360 million-customer consumer market from "the Yukon to the Yucatán." Now, with the Wall crumbling and George Bush piloting the American Airship, Carlos Salinas ran it up on his flagpole and figured red, white, and blue was the best deal he going to get. The post-Communist world was rapidly subdividing into trade blocs and Mexico needed to assert its newly revised geopolitical status and take its rightful place at the North American trough.

Mexico's assignment in the New World Order would be as a maquiladora, a giant assembly plant that would play helpmate to the global aspirations of the Fortune 500. The model was already in place and had been booming from 1982 upwards, when López Portillo's devaluation made Mexican workers the worst paid in Latin America (Argentina, Uruguay, Brazil, Colombia, Chile, Venezuela and Costa Rica all did better by their proletarians).[21] Where the maquiladoras had produced but 3% of all exports in 1980, in post-NAFTA 1996, they accounted for 38%.[22] Since NAFTA was first postulated, the number of "maqs," mostly strung along the northern border, has topped 2,500, producing everything from bikinis to missile components.

No matter how rank the economic climate has been in Mexico, the maquiladoras have done well. Now, with the installation of dozens of Japanese and Korean *maqs* (Sony, Sanyo, Hyundai, Mitsubishi, Matsushita, Daewoo, Samsung and Gold Star, among others) seeking to crash the NAFTA party, the western border from El Paso-Juárez to Tijuana-San Diego has become a gold mine and although the origin of parts assembled for finished products is monopolized by the three North American nations, it hasn't slowed down the inscrutables from the Orient. Mexico shipped 14 million television sets to the U.S. in 1996, most of them assembled by Japanese- and Korean-based maquiladoras.[23]

Regardless of its owner's national origins, the maquiladora industry is 100% U.S.-dominated and directed and constitutes an extension of U.S. commerce into Mexico, de facto annexation of Mexican soil by the kings of U.S. corporate capitalism.

"SOLIDARITY"—WITH THE WEALTHY

As Washington saw it, Carlos Salinas could do no wrong. He privatized the telephone company and the banks. The latter decree was "a profoundly patriotic act" cheered his finance minister, Gustavo Petrocelli—59 veteran PRI legislators, who had voted to nationalize the banks in 1982 for "patriotic" reasons, reversed themselves, robot-like, when the privatization measure hit the floor of Congress.[24] Salinas privatized the airlines and the highways, paper production, the sugar mills, the movie theaters, and the television dial (he sold off government channels), in a frenzy of crony capitalism unseen since Don Porfirio's heyday.

Having inherited some 700 state enterprises, he auctioned off 400 of them to the most profitable bidders, brother Raúl picking up so many commissions that the transnationals were soon referring to him as "Mister 10%." The wave of privatizations was confirmation of the Americanization of an economy that had been mostly public ever since the silver mines of Zacatecas were blasted open by the Crown, back in the 1540s. "The only thing that is not negotiable is the virginity of the Virgin of Guadalupe," bubbled David Goldman of Polyeconomics, a New Jersey p.r. firm subcontracted to stimulate interest in Salinas-era giveaways.[25]

In the eyes of his White House beholders, Salinas's accomplishments heralded a new Mexican Miracle. He claimed to have reduced the public deficit to zero, at least cosmetically—but, of course, he really did not: his bookkeepers simply neglected to factor in interest payments on public sector debt.[26] In reality, by 1990, internal debt was roughly where it had been when de la Madrid took office a decade earlier, and was now almost equal to the government's external debt obligations.

To further underscore his class allegiances, Salinas broke strikes for transnational auto makers at the sprawling Volkswagen plant up in Puebla and turned a blind eye when the hoary Fidel Velázquez sent his thugs to beat and kill striking workers at Ford's Cuautitlán facility in late 1990.

Salinas also kept a lid on the anti-neo-liberal thrust represented by Cárdenas, beating down and buying off his supporters in traditional PRI fashion. Those who were bad and reluctant to return to the Institutional fold were punished by police violence (over 340 members of the PRD were killed during the Salinas sexenio, according to the party's human rights commission) and PRD communities were blackballed from government services and seed moneys. The Solidarity program was invented to piece off the more obedient masses and enable the PRI to rebuild an electoral clientele. Solidarity paid off big when the PRI scored a sweep in 1991 mid-term federal elections.

Monies accrued from fire sale privatizations would, in theory, be used to foment development among Mexico's extreme poor—*los que menos tienen* (those who have the least), a popular Salinas refrain. Salinas's 1988 campaign manager, Luis Donaldo Colosio, was put in charge to incubate in the *bao publico* (literally "public bath" or mob scene) where he would eventually be killed—he was assassinated after a pro-Solidarity rally in the Tijuana slum colony of Lomas Taurinas, while in the heat of the 1994 election campaign. Once a week, Salinas and Colosio would fly out to the countryside to be serenaded by starving Indians caroling the "Solidarity Hymn." Solidarity soon had its own institute and its own week—the only time, it seemed, that brown people appeared on Mexican television.

The Solidarity style is, perhaps, best typified by the program's birthplace, Chalco, a million-vote misery belt squatter settlement of dusty, unpaved streets and cinder-block hovels just east of the capital. Today, several years after Colosio's assassination, Chalco and its surrounding shantytowns feature multiple shells of abandoned public works projects and an enormous billboard, towering above the plaza, that flashes the red, white, and green Solidarity logo—the colors of both the flag and the PRI.

BUSHWA

The Solidarity hoopla was the way Salinas did business. During the NAFTA run-up, Mexico maintained a larger public relations presence in Washington than any of the U.S.'s 15 top trading partners. To burnish his image, Salinas signed on with Burson-Marsteller, flacksters for such democratic stalwarts as the Nigerian generals, the Salvadoran government, Saudi Arabia and Suharto's Indonesia (but not East Timor), Jonas Savimbi, the Republic of Korea, Phillip Morris and the anti-environmental Wise Use Movement.[27] Ex-Republican

National Chairman Bill Brock was brought on board to replace the disgraced Reagan insider Michael Deaver as chief congressional lobbyist.

The p.r. paid off in spades: *Business Week* glowingly referred to Salinista Mexico as "the young jaguar" (you know, like the Asian Pacific Tigers)[28] and the Atomic Ant made the front cover of *Newsweek*, although only in the latter's Latin American edition (he was replaced by Roger Rabbit stateside). Carlos was a "Modern Hero for a Modern Nation," headlined the Canadian *McClean's* magazine[29] and *Forbes* ballyhooed "forget about Eastern Europe— here's a revolution you can really invest in."[30]

The television lights blazed whenever Salinas arrived in Washington, which he often did, visiting the Bush White House six times in six years—he also met with Bush in Paris and the American president visited Salinas once in northern Mexico where he attended a private rodeo at the Salinas family hacienda at Aguasleguas, Nuevo León. Bush's Mexican journey came just weeks before the Persian Gulf bombing began, an effort to which Salinas pledged 100,000 daily barrels of Mexican petroleum production.

Salinas's obsequious lobbying of both George Bush and the U.S. Congress, on behalf of NAFTA, bothered many Mexicans. "We are treated to the spectacle of our president courting the U.S. Congress while he treats his own congress with complete indifference," wrote star columnist Raymundo Riva Palacios in *El Financiero*.[31] Nonetheless, the public relations push paved the path with gold for Salinas, now the darling of the neo-liberal set. Between 1988 and 1993, Mexico received 27 loans totaling $8 billion USD from the World Bank (letters of intention were signed for each) to become that institution's most favored borrower.[32]

During the long march towards NAFTA, Salinas's hyperbolic press notices and his glad-handing of the world's financial elite brought more than $50 billion in mostly U.S. investment to Mexico, $38 billion of which was hot money, looking to make a killing in the Mexican Bolsa de Valores, then the most profitable emerging market in the Third World. To give you some understanding of just how such market growth relates to the impoverishment of the populace, in 1995, the Mexican stock market was knocked out of first place on the emerging markets hit parade—by Bangladesh.

FAST TRACK

The first hurdle for NAFTA was Fast Track. "Fast Track" meant the treaty or agreement or whatever would be wrought was going to be voted up as a package and not picked apart by special interests clause by clause, like buzzards on a dead buffalo. Fast Track was the key to the project's success and Salinas played his p.r. card like he was in the pits at Vegas. Commuting between the three would-be NAFTA nations, the diminutive president touted the cheapness of Mexican labor and Burson-Marsteller painted a portrait of hard-working, happy, modern Mexico, eager to team up with its old amigo, Tío Sam.

"I want to export goods, not Mexicans," Salinas told the *Wall Street Journal* on the eve of one Washington junket.[33] Salinas's Washington jaunts also included an overnight with the Bushes at Camp David. Such veiled threats that immigration would skyrocket if Fast Track was rejected sprinkled his speeches. In private sessions with U.S. congresspeople, the Mexican President affirmed that rejection would only aid his left-wing rival, Cuauhtémoc Cárdenas, the Red Ayatollah, a sworn enemy of this historic U.S.-Mexico rapprochement.[34]

George Bush pushed for Fast Track as if it were a commercial Desert Storm. He spoke endearingly of his "little brown ones," his Mexican-American grandchildren and the offspring of son Jeb (reportedly a "special" friend of Raúl's)[35] and Columba, a native of Mexico's shoe manufacturing capital, León, Guanajuato.[36] President Bush suggested that for Congress to turn back Fast Track would be a display of crass racism which would drive Mexico away forever. "It felt like you were a traitor if you spoke against Fast Track," North Dakota Senator Byron Dorgan remembers.[37]

When in June 1991, the 231-192 vote in favor was finally secure, the champagne corks popped at the Mexican embassy on Pennsylvania Avenue just down the street from the Casa Blanca. Out in Las Vegas, the newly-crowned Miss Universe, Lupita Jones of Guadalajara, toasted the victory and became the instant emblem of Mexico's growing stature in the New World Order. Back in Washington, an old critic of Mexico's Central American policy was similarly elated—but Elliot Abrams offered Salinas one caution: "Latin America is going to be convinced that Mexico has resigned from the continent and now belongs to the U.S."[38]

DIRTY LAUNDRY

All this joy was not shared south of the Bravo River. On May Day that year, Ricardo Barco, leader of the militant Mexico City bus drivers' union SUTAUR-100 (dissolved when the bus system was privatized in 1995), planted himself in front of the U.S. embassy on Reforma Boulevard and declared NAFTA "the new big stick of U.S. Imperialism." Then he and 35,000 workers and their families intoned the old Marxian anthem, "The Internationale," a melody that probably gave ambassador John Negroponte heartburn.

Further up the avenue, at a second May Day rally, white-haired Evangelina Corona, then head of the September 19th Garment Workers Union, railed against the trade treaty: UPS was bringing its "Mailboxes Etc." franchises to Mexico and had already obtained contracts from the Mexican post office. "Just imagine! Now the gringos are going to be delivering our mail," she indignantly complained.

"Cheap labor, cheap energy, raw materials and lax environmental enforcement should not be the basis of partnership," Salinas nemesis Cárdenas told a tri-national anti-NAFTA gathering in Berkeley in the spring of 1991. The PRD leader was repeatedly chastised by the Mexican press for such a negative assessment of Mexico's impending elevation to the First World. Debate in Mexico was muted by PRI control of both the legislature and most of the press. A vigorous campaign, waged by dissidents grouped in the anti-TLC Mexican Network (RMALC), was ignored by the media. Fed an unceasing torrent of optimistic puff pieces through a p.r. machine cranked up by Mexican industrialists and the American Chamber of Commerce ("Amcham"—cited by Philip Agee as a CIA conduit),[39] most Mexicans just surrendered to geopolitical inevitability. Mexico would finally shed its Bolivarian pretensions and go the way of Texas and California 145 years earlier.

Jorge Castañeda was another to warn of annexation. "In the case of two nations so disparate in size and power and wealth, the weight of economic superiority can be crushing and can lead to a significant loss of sovereignty and cultural identity."[40] For washing Mexico's dirty laundry outside of the country, as the old political saw goes, Castañeda, like Cárdenas, was savaged in the government press, branded a traitor and a snitch, and threatened with death by what appear to be Mexico City judicial police.

Despite Salinas's nefarious campaign to quash criticism of NAFTA on the home front, in the end he was sandbagged by the usual Yanqui interventionism.

PRO CONSUL

John Negroponte was George Bush's first gift to Mexico. A protégé of Al Haig, Negroponte has a curriculum vita that reads like a road map of international conspiracy. He served in Saigon from 1964 through 1968 and as a Kissinger aide during the shape-of-the-table peace talks with the Vietnamese in Paris from 1970-72. Turned over to Tom Enders at State, Negroponte worked the Quito outpost before becoming "pro consul" in Honduras in 1981, where he ran the CIA-Oliver North Contra operation across the border, through 1985—the Contras knew Negroponte as "El Jefe."[41] After a stint under Colin Powell at the National Security Council, Bush, a former head of the CIA, appointed Negroponte to succeed tire manufacturer Charles Pilliod as U.S. ambassador to Mexico. His mission was to smooth the road to NAFTA.

"Transnationals are not agents of imperialism, but agents of change," Negroponte told the Mexican press by way of introduction.[42] Change, mostly of the monetary type, was in the air.

"Mexico's foreign policy is replacing Third World demagoguery with responsible internationalism," the ambassador wrote Under-Secretary for Latin American Affairs Bernard Aronson, Elliot Abrams' successor, December 10th, 1990: "a free trade agreement will institutionalize acceptance of a North American orientation to Mexico's foreign policy. Just think how this contrasts with past behavior—if you listened to Mexico debating at the U.N., you would have thought they were our enemies."

The briefing document, obtained by *Proceso*,[43] reveals that Negroponte's ulterior mission was not all that different from his predecessors': "Mexico is in the process of dramatically changing the substance and image of its foreign policy from a nationalist and protectionist ideology to a more pragmatic vision of world problems—I think it is reasonable to suppose that free trade negotiations will also be a useful lever in prying open the Mexican economy even further [read PEMEX]."

Not even Negroponte would deny the authenticity of this incriminating document. The ambassador's statements only confirmed what many Mexicans already knew. Behind the fortress-like facade of the U.S. embassy, as always, the annexation of Mexico was being plotted.

CLINTON MAKES MISCHIEF

If U.S. Mexico-watchers perennially grouse about that neighbor nation's spectacularly undemocratic political system, Mexico's U.S.-watchers are equally critical of the U.S. for what is considered an excess of electoral democracy. The short periods between presidential elections effectively limit a U.S. chief executive's term to three years (the fourth is spent campaigning for reelection), a stretch which corresponds to half the Mexican non-electable sexenio, and an abbreviation of administration that is disruptive to the pursuit of consistent bilateral policies.

Upon occasion, the electoral calendars of the two countries are congruent—such as in 1988 when both nations elected presidents within months of each other; 1976, when Carter and López Portillo were simultaneously elevated to high office; and 2000 AD, an upcoming example of political synchronicity. George Bush and Carlos Salinas were elected together, saw eye-to-eye for three years (although, given their disparity in height, their eyelines were on distinct vertical planes), and expected to work together through the end of Salinas's six-year presidency. But a funny thing happened on the way to Bush's 1992 reelection.

Despite having engineered three highly-suspect Christmastime military incursions against once-upon-a-time Third World allies (Panama, Iraq, Somalia) to entertain the North American voting public during the holiday season, the president was ambushed by a pervasive recession and his campaign floundered as badly as the economy.

The summer of '92 was critical. Salinas and Bush strained mightily to achieve agreement before the Republican National Convention was called into session. For ten days and nights in August, negotiators locked themselves in at Washington's ill-famed Watergate Hotel. The intrigues echoed the Watergate motif: under the code name "Operation Cornflower," Canadian intelligence bugged Mexican telephones, according to one former wire woman,[44] and Washington is thought to have illicitly eavesdropped on both its future NAFTA partners. Finally, on August 13th, a puff of white smoke went up from this citadel of conspiracy.

In a gesture of masculine gallantry, Carla Hill, chief U.S. negotiator, and the "Doña" of NAFTA, was chosen to announce agreement: "Today marks the beginning of a new era on our continent, the continent of North America [sic]."[45] The deal was done. Mexico had at last moved into North America. Whoopie!

The two presidents celebrated this continental shift before 59,000 fans in San Diego where the Republicans would soon convene, attending four-and-a-half innings of the major league all-star game (just to make the game—and the pact—official, I suppose). "The past shall be history," Salinas pronounced at a subsequent appearance, significantly just blocks from the Alamo in San Antonio, apparently referring to centuries of unpleasantries between the two cultures.[46] The date itself was dipped in portentous irony—10 years earlier to the day, a harried Jesús Silva Herzog had put down in Washington with a Mexican default just hours away.

With Salinas and daughter-in-law Colu (she gave up her Mexican citizenship to vote for George) as his chief Hispanic cheerleaders, Bush campaigned on the Free Trade ticket. The portly Arkansas governor, Bill Clinton, a longshot Democrat nominee and designated political flash in the pan à la Dukakis in '88, waffled on NAFTA until the closing weeks of the campaign. Badgered by the AFL-CIO into neutrality on the pact, Clinton at last gave guarded support to the trade treaty in a Carolina college speech in October—but attached a caveat: the negotiation of three side agreements dealing with labor, the environment and import surges. South of the border, Salinas winced. His application for a cherished place in the Mexican pantheon was about to get complicated.

The Clinton victory was advertised as "a slap in Mexico's face" by the Salinas regime.[47] Issues like labor rights and the destruction of the environment were internal ones and any attempt to impose trilateral regulation would be a violation of the nation's sovereignty. But Bush's defeat had signaled a downturn in Salinas's fortunes, and despite copious grumbling, the Mexican president was prevailed upon to send his negotiators back to Washington to fashion side accords that would do minimum damage. The side agreements were on the page by mid-summer, 1993.

THE NAFTA SWEEPSTAKES

November was the target month. Because NAFTA was a trade treaty, the House got first crack at ratifying it. NAFTA would hit the House floor before the Thanksgiving recess and the battle for the hearts and minds of its 435 members was deafening. The stakes kept getting ratcheted up. For the Clinton administration, NAFTA would be a test of its political credibility—the White House had won a budget battle the previous August by just two votes in the House and Vice President Al Gore's presence in the Senate, and the president's controversial universal health care coverage plan would be next on the post-NAFTA agenda.

For the Free Traders of USA-NAFTA—more or less North America's 400 top manufacturers and exporters—domination of the Mexican market of 21 million middle class consumers and a bottomless supply of low wage labor was crucial to expanding profit margins. For the unions and the ecologists, leftists, rightists and populists who opposed the trade treaty because it proposed to wreck the environment and impoverish the American working class, November 17th was an Armageddon which would determine the future of the planet and the race.

As interest escalated, media workers were deluged with requests to explain Mexico to the Yanqui masses: what would NAFTA mean at the Mexican grassroots? Editors did not want to hear the bad news. Reputations were minted as experts mushroomed from the woodwork. Jorge Castañeda was a mandatory "anti" sound bite. Wayne Cornelius and John Womack, Salinas's mentors, extolled their one-time student's new Mexican Miracle. MIT's Rudy Dornbush supported NAFTA as fiercely as he had the Pinochet regime in Chile. An original "Chicago Boy," having schooled at the University of Chicago under Milton Friedman, and both the finance minister Pedro Aspe's and upcoming technocrat Luis Tellez's (now Zedillo's chief of staff) mentor at MIT, Dornbush lauded the agreement as "immunization against a return to populism." On the other side of the money, his MIT colleague Noam Chomsky penned jeremiads for La Jornada, warning of the dire consequences of economic "integration."

The television sweeps were high stakes. Both camps invested small fortunes in primetime pitches. Badly outgunned by USA-NAFTA's corporate coffers, Big Labor ran spots that featured shuttered factories and voice-overs of doom and depression. Lee Iacocca lit up the screen for the pro-NAFTAs. "We will raise up their living standards. They are a great market for our products," he confidently told the viewers. "Salinas wants to be part of the First World and be part of the U.S. and Canada." The hogwash ran thick. "Salinas is the first president to have brought democracy to Mexico," the former Chrysler CEO lied, even as dozens of Cárdenas supporters were being pistol-whipped and gunned down by PRIistas following conflictive Michoacán and Guerrero state elections.[48] For Iacocca and other captains of U.S. industry and commerce, Carlos Salinas was the new Porfirio Díaz for whom they had long been searching.

A CLASS NERVE

Surprisingly, the battle for and against NAFTA found an audience. The debate on the trade treaty had touched a class nerve just below the U.S. epidermis. Labor asserted that NAFTA would cost U.S. unions a half-million jobs in factory flight, and flood U.S. markets with cheap goods American workers once made a living wage producing. The question of who ran North America and for what purpose was asked repeatedly. Perhaps for this reason, when two of the most inept debaters on the North American mainland stepped into the ring to slug out NAFTA on the U.S. tube, the audience numbered in the millions. H. Ross Perot, a living parody of heartland populism, was designated to denigrate the trade treaty. Clinton selected his slow-talking veep, Al Gore, to defend the NAFTA crown. Talk show wizard Larry King would ref.

Perot swarmed all over Gore from the opening bell, telling it pretty much as it really is, and earning the enduring enmity of the Mexican people in the process by washing their soiled undergarments on international television—the debate was cabled into Mexico, attracting large audiences even though it was broadcast entirely in English. Perot fulminated about murdered journalists, police violence, dead workers, child labor, maquiladora workers who lived in cardboard shacks with no plumbing, the 36 people who owned Mexico, the great sucking sound to the south...[49]

Gore lackadaisically conceded that Mexico was not perfect but NAFTA and the free market would convert its people into decent, law-abiding, rights-respecting citizens. In fact, the treaty agreement presented opportunities unparalleled since the "Louisiana Purchase," that Jeffersonian paragon of U.S. expansionism that set the stage for the annexation of half of Mexico. The vice-president's unfortunate inference that Mexico was about to be similarly purchased would dog the NAFTA-TLC's footsteps south of the river for a long time to come.[50]

THE MAIN EVENT

The Main Event was set for November 17th. Mexicans were already more than a little edgy at the spectacle of watching gringo politicians determine their nation's fate on television beamed in from Washington. One popular art store in the fashionable Zona Rosa district of the capital did a brisk business in miniature boxes labeled the *"Tratado de Libre Comercio"* that featured the corpse of a Mexican, spread under the crossed flags of the U.S. and Mexico.

With the vote in the U.S. Congress too close to call, Clinton backslapped and buttonholed his way through the congressional directory, dispensing whatever the House members might need to enhance their political careers back in their home districts, in exchange for their vote up on NAFTA: protection for tomatoes and brooms and corn sugar and oranges and pickles (Rep. Jake Pickle got a guarantee for the construction of a "Center for Free Trade" in his Texas district),[51] even the arrest of an accused baby raper—Iacocca got on the horn himself with Salinas to request the capture of a Mexican national alleged to have raped the infant niece of the secretary of Rep. Clay Shaw. Salinas's assurances that the man would be arrested and extradited locked up the Florida republican's vote (Serapio Zuñiga was never extradited, according to Shaw legislative assistant Scott Spear).[52]

While the deals were cut, the floor debate raged. Mexico was portrayed as "a model democracy," "a brutal dictatorship" and "an investor's paradise"[53]—not really contradictory characterizations, given what passes for "democracy" in Washington's vision. Half-truths, outright lies and racist epithets poisoned the airwaves. After 13 hours of seesaw name-calling, NAFTA carried by a scant 34 votes, five less than Fast Track had carried the House with 16 months before. The obligatory champagne corks were loosened from their moorings. "NAFTA insures our leadership, economic power, and global influence," cheered Robert Zoelick, the former Reagan trade advisor who had framed the issue for Bush's 1988 campaign.

AN UNWHOLESOME MARRIAGE

The conventional argument for North American Free Trade agreement is that whatever the document actually said, it only codified a silent integration of the two economies, one that has been fermenting since Díaz sold the railroad concessions to the Bostonians. But NAFTA also sanctified the unwholesome union of a painfully thin burro with a gorilla approximately 25 times its size, whose huge bulk would dictate the terms of the marital contact. Whereas the U.S. accounts for 85% of all Mexican trade (if the *fayuca* is factored in), Mexico notches only 5.7% of U.S. commerce. The two economies are vastly disproportionate—$5.4 trillion to $237 billion in GDP.[54] Mexico's four top dollar earners—oil, maquiladoras, tourism, and income from Mexicans working in the U.S. ($4.6 billion annually),[55] are totally U.S.-dependent. Yet, despite the inequities, Washington insisted upon reciprocity, as if the two trading partners were actually equals. The NAFTA-TLC language barely acknowledges the most dramatic disparities between the U.S., Canada, and Mexico—and institutionalizes them.

NAFTA trespasses into Mexico's soul far deeper than other foreign invasions have dared to penetrate. The revision of Article 27 is a case in point. Long before the treaty was inked, Mexico's Secretary of Agriculture and Hydraulic Resources, then under the command of the notoriously venal Carlos Hank González ("a poor politician is a bad politician") took a look at the consequences unrestricted corn imports might bring. According to UCLA professor Raúl Hinojosa, who was contracted to do the study, as many as 670,000 farm families could be forced from the land and into the immigration steam by the rubble-ization of the internal corn market through cheap, petroleum-driven Canadian and U.S. grain imports.[56] One tale making the reportorial rounds at the time had Finance minister Pedro Aspe cracking that 13 million Mexican farmers were "redundant."

Despite such dreadful prognostications, Salinas pushed unflinchingly ahead with the revision of Article 27, ending the *reparto* (the distribution of land), and granting land title to the campesinos who worked the plots as their own— a process that freed dirt-poor ejidos to rent or sell off their farm or forestland to national and trans-national speculators, much as San Luis Río Colorado had done, to accommodate the NAFTA Industrial Park.

The Salinas-Hank revision of the Mexican Constitution emulated explicit World Bank guidelines, as published in a March 1990 outline issued by its Regional Office of Rural and Agrarian Development, and signed off by one John Richard Heath. The memorandum recommended government policies that encouraged farmers to sell or rent their land, and an end to limitations on plot sizes. The same conditions were attached to a $400 million USD World Bank loan, tendered in May 1991.[57] Such were NAFTA's precursors.

Even as Mexico's mostly Indian corn farmers were being stripped of the reasonable protections that Emiliano Zapata had instilled in the Mexican constitution, the Zapatista Army of National Liberation was forming in the Lacandón jungle of southeastern Chiapas—Subcomandante Marcos describes the revision of Article 27 as the detonating blow to the Mayan Indian rebels' fortunes. Now there were no options. The Zapatistas would have to go to war.[58]

But the new trade treaty did not only wreak havoc with the corn market. Banking services would soon be made competitive, truck transport would become contiguous, the composition of cars on all North American highways would be reformulated, movie ticket prices would go up in all three NAFTA nations, cable television transmission would be transformed, how to copyright a book would change, so would advertising norms and investment rules. Under the provisions of NAFTA's Chapters Six and Seven, Mexico was enticed to open up its energy sector to private U.S. and Canadian investment and supply the US. with increased petroleum shipments during emergency periods, such as world wars.[59]

The 2,000-page document gradually abolishes tariffs and taxes on a cornucopia of goods and services that move both ways across the border, but it makes no mention of the servers and the servicers. Early on, Salinas dropped the free movement of migrant labor as an issue, fearing it would put the kibosh on the outcome of the negotiations and his contemplated place in history. In fact, NAFTA, unlike the European Economic Community, incorporates no social charter that defines norms for such items as immigration rights, democratic elections, and compliance with human rights guarantees as a condition of membership.

FIRST WORLD? HA! HA! HA!

"MEXICO! PARTNER OF THE CHOSEN PEOPLE AT LAST!" *Proceso* cynically slugged the coming of the Age of NAFTA.[60] The hangover south of the NAFTA Industrial Park set in before the ink blotted. "This is not integration, but the absorption of Mexico," wrote revolutionary nationalist John Saxe Fernández in *Excelsior*.[61] The radicals wove dark visions of life under the NAFTA-TLC as the McDonald's and the Kentucky Fried Chickens spread out across the landscape. "500 years after the destruction of the pre-Cortez culture, we are threatened by the danger of a new conquest," the old Marxist, Heberto Castillo, warned.[62] Mexico would soon be a nation of motel maids, hod carriers, farm laborers, itinerant dishwashers and fast food franchise servers. Already the Ninja turtles and the Kitkat candy bars were flooding across the border, demolishing Mexico City toy and candy manufacturing. Whole sectors of national industry, such as textile production, were faced with bankruptcy—though more from GATT-lowered tariffs than NAFTA attack. After all the hullabaloo, the increased paperwork and the free trade treaty's initial failure to produce handsome profits for all but a handful of assemblers and exporters even the big business confederations were complaining.

But one product NAFTA was cranking out during its first year in operation was negative numbers, quietly breeding a $12 billion USD trade deficit in its first year (Mexico had run surpluses through 1990) that proved a contributing nail in Mexico's coffin when Salinas's caca finally hit the fan in December 1994.

The Salinas years gave birth to 22 Mexican billionaires, as listed by *Forbes* magazine in its 1994 super-rich rankings[63] (only Televisa's Azcárraga had ever appeared on the list prior to Salinas' stay in Los Pinos). One explanation for the sudden jump: privatizations had further concentrated wealth in this no-trickle-down country, empowering a few select tycoons to increase their already obscene fortunes. The numbers of Mexico's super-ricos were only exceeded by the super-rich of the United States, Germany and Japan. At the top of the list was Carlos Slim, the fourth richest man in the world and the wealthiest man in Latin America. The son of a Lebanese immigrant and a gen-erous PRI benefactor, Salinas had sold TELMEX, the phone monopoly, to Slim in 1991 to add to his monopoly on cigarette manufacturing, his chains of Sanborn's and Denny's, investment houses and holding companies.

Meanwhile, "*los que menos tienen*," Mexico's extremely poor, grew in number from 14 to 18 to 21 million, depending on whose database you hold account-able, during Salinas's six years at the helm of the nation.[64] Yet, on January 1st, 1994, despite the brewing economic and political troubles, out there at dawn in the Sonora desert, the land of giant Sahuaros, Don Juan's visions, and the NAFTA Industrial Park, it was hard to imagine that Salinas's House of Cards would not last the year.

The Zapatistas were the first chickens to come home to roost. Their rising, just a half-hour after the trade treaty kicked in, put the lie to Mexico's newly-conferred First World status. They demonstrated that the culture of resistance that has always shaped Mexican history was still a formidable challenge to the New World Order. They proved that Mexico was still Mexico, still part of the Third World south. The de facto annexation that passage of NAFTA implied stalled when the Clinton White House woke up and smelled the coffee.

For months, Salinas had successfully squelched intelligence reports of the imminent rebellion, so as not to queer his NAFTA chances in the U.S. Congress.[65] Now, he could no longer hold back the dawn. The revolution that could never come again was here and happening and it knocked the legs out from under the stock market. Investment tailed off precipitously. When marchers took to the streets, they mocked Carlos's aspirations with chants of "First World? Ha! Ha! Ha!" The new Mexican Miracle had begun to disinte-grate like a poorly stacked house of cards.

THE ROCK

The still-murky assassination of Luis Donaldo Colosio that March further tore the mask off Salinas's presidency, revealing a brutal power struggle at the highest echelons of a PRI that was not done with the killing yet. A hemor-rhage of capital flight was averted when Salinas shut down the stock market in mourning and negotiated an emergency line of credit from Bill Clinton total-ing $6.2 billion, exceeding even U.S. loans to its former ideological adversary, now known simply as Russia—a harbinger of hand-outs to come.[66] Though badly damaged, Carlos Salinas showed a flash of his old talent for bullshitting his First World masters when he parlayed the Colosio assassination into

Mexico's admission to the prestigious Organization for Commerce and Development, the so-called "rich nations" club, just two days after the hit.[67]

By the third quarter of 1994, economic growth—which had gone as high as 7.2% at the end of 1990—shuddered to a stop. An unsuspecting public went to the polls in August and overwhelmingly selected the PRI's obscure substitute candidate, former budget minister Ernesto Zedillo, as Mexico's new president. By November, the indicators were growing more bothersome. The peso was overvalued by at least a quarter and Salinas refused to devalue, leaving the difficult task to his hapless successor. Moreover, $33 billion USD in short-term bonds would come due in 1995 and reserves were falling from week to week. All of these factors coalesced three weeks after Carlos Salinas stepped down on December 1st.

By February of 1995, brother Raúl was behind bars, charged with masterminding the murder of his ex-brother-in-law José Francisco Ruiz Massieu, Zedillo's designated legislative leader and secretary general of the PRI, and, by March, Carlos Salinas himself was conducting a short-lived hunger strike in a Monterrey Solidarity slum and loudly proclaiming his innocence. Soon after, the former president was flown into self-exile—he is currently holed up in a well-guarded Dublin residence. Although his questionable reputation was irrevocably sullied by the economic debacle to which his new Mexican Miracle had been reduced, Salinas bequeathed the NAFTA-TLC to the nation, a rock out from under which Mexico would not wriggle any time soon.

In the agitated U.S.-Mexico dynamic, "free trade" is code for penetration and assimilation. Much as the railroad routes to the northern border, which Don Porfirio gave away to the Yanquis a century before were the first mechanism for Mexico's subordination to the United States economy, NAFTA was a great leap forward in completing the process of economic annexation.

Chapter 14

THE MEXICAN MELTDOWN

Jump to another winter dawn, nearly a year after the Zapatistas had welcomed in NAFTA.

Early on Mexico City winter mornings, before the dread thermal inversions set in sealing tens of thousands of tons of industrial and automobile effluvia into the immediate atmosphere and making life a living hell for millions of *capitalinos*, the snowcapped scarps of Popocatépetl glisten on the southern horizon, a majestic edifice of ice and granite whose frequent eruptions and proximity to the capital and the evils that lurk therein have given the volcano the aura of an angry god.

Popo, which lies 35 miles south of the city, where Puebla, Morelos and Mexico states come together, had been smoking for several years. Just after the Zapatista uprising in the winter of 1994, Popo's *fumerola* (smoke plume) grew considerably thicker. My call to the authorities elicited lethargic response: there was no danger to the public. Then, in the last days of the year, just as the peso devaluation plummeted Mexico into renewed financial crisis, the mountain began to rumble ominously, as if seriously outraged that its portentous warnings had so long been ignored. Molten rock and ash and noxious gases vomited from its throat and showered the villages that lay on the volcano's skirts. Panic-stricken refugees were evacuated to Huejotzingo and Cholula. The eruptions brought respiratory ailments and pustules broke out on the skin. For many traditional Mexicans, Popo's tantrum felt like ancient prophecy being fulfilled. The Aztec-Mexicas had also looked to the volcano for council.

WHAT DID THE WHITE HOUSE KNOW AND WHEN?

In his six years in Los Pinos, Carlos Salinas had contributed more to the annexation of Mexico than any Mexican president since Santa Anna. But by December 1994, the house of cards had collapsed and Mexico was once again spinning into the abyss. Still another chapter had been written in the annexation of Mexico by its northern neighbor.

Ernesto Zedillo, Salinas's hand-picked second choice (after Colosio was slain), easily won the August 21st 1994 election with 48% of the vote by scapegoating the Zapatistas for the ills that menaced the nation. His election campaign had been conducted behind thinly-veiled reminders of the public insecurity and social destabilization that the rebel threat posed: "I'm scared," one kid told another in a Zedillo-for-president radio spot. "Why are you scared?" his pal asks. "Because my daddy is scared," he is told. Now, in December, not three weeks into his presidency, Zedillo was forced by economic circumstance to go to this well of recrimination again.

On December 19th, the newly-appointed Finance Minister Jaime Serra Puche, the hero of the NAFTA negotiations, was selected to inform the nation and its foreign creditors that, due to pressures put upon the peso by an EZLN offensive at dawn that day, the Mexican government had decided to widen the band in which the currency was allowed to fluctuate against the dollar by 15%. The pretext for this sudden devaluation was the surprise appearance of ski-masked Zapatistas in 38 of Chiapas state's 112 municipalities. In most cases, the rebels simply marched around the town plazas and then melted into the surrounding mountains. The full force of the military was quickly mobilized for counter-attack, screwing up tensions throughout the region. Although Subcomandante Marcos triumphantly proclaimed that the Zapatistas had finally broken through the encirclement of their communities by tens of thousands of Mexican army troops, it is more probable that supporters outside of the conflict zone simply slipped on their ski-masks and kerchiefs and picked up their rusty .22s for a pre-dawn stroll around the plaza.

Like the Zapatista surprise attacks the previous January, the occupation of the towns coincided with a stunning drop on the Bolsa (stock exchange)— over 4% of total equity value. Most market-watchers now agree that investors were reacting more to the rumors of devaluation than to the rebels' ragtag attacks.

Blaming the Zapatistas for the abrupt devaluation of the peso did not wash very well in international financial circles. "This is pure shit," sputtered NAFTA guru Rudy Dornbush, the Pinochet fan[1] who now advises the Mexicans that they should substitute the dollar for their weak peso currency. Wall Street investors seethed: had not Serra Puche just pledged to both the *Financial Times* and their own bible, the *Wall Street Journal* (Craig Torres' piece ran December 16th), that there would be no peso devaluation? About the only financial "expert" to buy the Zedillo conspiracy line was the right-wing economist Luis Pazos, who drew up arcane flow charts and graphs to "prove" the Zapatista destabilization theory.[2]

Although Zedillo was intimately familiar with the necessity for devaluation, he feigned astonishment at the turn of events. But on November 20th, ten days before taking office, the new president had been summoned to Salinas's Tlalpan mansion and told by Aspe and the about-to-be ex-king Carlos that, unlike Echeverría and López Portillo before them, they were not about to cede their slot in history by devaluating before they left office—Zedillo was known to have argued for such a devaluation ever since the Colosio assassination in March, suggesting that one crisis could conveniently cover the other and lessen the impact on Salinas's prestige.[3]

Despite Zedillo's advocacy of floating the peso, he apparently failed to advise Bill Clinton of this scenario when he met with him in Washington in a get-to-know-the White House session the day after the dressing down at Salinas's home. Similarly, Zedillo failed to mention the necessity for devaluation of the peso during his December 1st inaugural address. Nor was Mexico's economic malaise a subject when Clinton addressed the Summit of the Americas in Miami, a week before the devaluation, touting his new NAFTA partner as "the prototype of successful economic development" to the assembled nations of Latin America.[4] One might beg that age-old Nixonian question: what did the White House know and when?

CHICKENS, AT ROOST

Pinning the blame on the EZLN for the pain that devaluation inflicts upon the populace almost certainly took its cue from a December 16th report issued by the U.S. financial whizkids, Félix Boni and Gray Newman, over at Interacciones. The bank and investment house is owned by Carlos Hank Rhon, the son of the billionaire with the same first two names. Regarded as the godfather of the PRI's dinosaur wing, Carlos Hank Sr. plays hardball. Urging the new president to put on his *pantalones* and tackle the Zapatista problem head-on before it wrecked the economy, Boni and Newman critiqued "the *fracaso* of Zedillo to demonstrate that he has the political capacity to control a situation that is increasingly turbulent."[5]

The Interacciones memorandum stimulated a tidal wave of capital flight—about $1.5 billion USD a day between the 17th and the 21st.[6] In 1981-82, the Hanks (the elder Hank was then the unelected mayor of Mexico City) had led the charge of "dollar-pullers"—Mexican businessmen who sent billions out of the country, depleted financial reserves, and provoked López Portillo into nationalizing the banks. Such graphic lack of confidence displayed by Mexico's own investors in the future of their nation invariably leads to stampede by their non-Mexican brethren.

1995 was 1982 redux. Not only the Hanks made out like bandits with their newly-acquired greenbacks. The late Televisa mogul, Emilio Azcárraga, appears to have had inside intelligence that devaluation was in the cards, converting bushels of pesos into dead American presidents on the eve of Serra Puche's "surprise" announcement, according to one *Proceso* account.[7] But other members of Mexico's ruling clique were apparently left out of the loop. "Idiot!" barked Alfonso Romo of the Monterrey-based Pulsar group to a nosy reporter: "How do you think it feels to drop 35 million dollars in an hour?"[8]

By December 21st, the band of fluctuation in which Serra Puche had encased the peso could no longer contain it. From the northern border to the capital's Angel of Independence monument, the lines outside the banks and change houses were long and restless. Security guards would post the new exchange rates as the dollar shot up from hour to hour. By the middle of the day, the currency was up to 6.50 to the dollar, 40% higher than the 3.70 pesos it had cost just 48 hours before, and the Bolsa was off a whopping 12% of its total value.[9] Again Serra Puche was pushed before the TV cameras to communicate the fledgling administration's latest change of heart: the peso would be floated freely until it had found its true level against the Yanqui dollar. But this latest Zedillo flipflop did not much assuage public panic.

In truth, a number of chickens were flocking to the roost beside an overpriced peso: a $28 billion current accounts deficit ($12 billion in trade, $16 in foreign debt payments), the approaching pay-out of nearly $18 out of $33 billion in foreign-owned short term bonds (*"Tesobonos"*) that the Salinas people had hawked to keep hope fleetingly alive, and, most chillingly, a drop in foreign reserves from $29 billion on January 1st to $17 billion on November 1st to $11 billion and sinking on December 21st[10]—much of which had been either gobbled up bolstering the viability of the peso, or been pumped into the stock market to cover hot money siphoned off by upped interest rates decreed by that ultimate saboteur of international finance, Alan Greenspan of the U.S. Federal Reserve. The wolf was at the door.

UNHAPPY NEW YEAR

With a crisis as treacherous as '82 on his hands, Serra Puche journeyed forth into the jaws of the dragon three days before Christmas, to meet with a not very joyous mob of Wall street overlords. Overnight, U.S. investors holding Mexican paper had lost half their bundle to Zedillo's fumbling devaluation. The Wisconsin Investment Board dropped $95 million, Chemical Bank $70 million[11]—the *Wall Street Journal* calculated a total loss of $6.5 billion worth of paper for the street for which it was christened.[12]

Serra Puche's flow charts convinced no one up in New York. Angry investors, burnt by the Zedillo finance minister's promises to the international financial press, reportedly hurled racist epithets.[13] Emerging from behind locked doors, John F. H. Purcell, director of emerging markets for Brown

Brothers, bitterly told reporters "I am not convinced."[14] Serra Puche's sudden loss of credibility signaled his public demise—the former "Rey de Washington" deserted the sinking ship for a Princeton sinecure.

His replacement, Guillermo Ortiz, had been, like Zedillo, one of Salinas economic dream team. A close associate of chief-of-staff José Córdoba, Ortiz had been responsible for the privatization of the banking system, selling government financial institutions to such questionable sharpies as Tabasco tycoon Carlos Cabal Peniche, (the Union Bank, and later the Cremi Bank, which Cabal picked up for a song from a failed investor)—Cabal eventually flew the coop to Monte Carlo, along with $700 million USD in depositors' money, and remains an international fugitive.[15] Such were the cards with which Salinas—and now, Zedillo—built their houses

By the New Year, the peso was plummeting to seven to the dollar, interest rates had multiplied 280 times, and the stock market was in the toilet. Celebrating the Zapatistas' first anniversary deep in the Lacandón jungle near Guadalupe Tepeyac, a supremely defiant Marcos and his comrades marked their initial year on public display by firing a volley into the moonlit night sky, an ominous sign for Zedillo's rudderless presidency.

BUBBAH—SAVIOR OF MEXICO

The Mexican president's anguished cries for help did not elicit immediate White House alarm. The meltdown had caught Clinton with his own pants down. Just as in the year previous, when the White House, still throbbing with a New Year's hangover, had seemed dazed by the Zapatista rebellion, reaction was excruciatingly slow in formulation. In truth, Bill Clinton was particularly indisposed this Holiday season—the Republicans, having won smashing midterm victories in November, now controlled both houses of Congress and it was a whole new ball game up on Capitol Hill. Bailing out Zedillo could have high political costs down the road in '96. As he done on NAFTA, the U.S. president waffled right up to the final out.

Finally, after a particularly desperate phone call from Los Pinos on January 10th,[16] Clinton was moved to save Mexico for NAFTA and the Free Market. Announcing a $40 billion rescue package—the initiative was sent over to an opposition Congress the next day—Bubbah went on the offensive at last. The bail-out would not only be Clinton's first test in handling a hostile majority on the Hill, but also an initial shakedown in dealing with the nasty new Speaker Newt Gingrich and Senate majority leader and soon-to-be Republican presidential nominee Robert Dole. The 1996 presidential race put its prints in this doleful experience very early in the Mexican meltdown.

For Gingrich and Dole, their own talent for controlling vengeance-bent veteran conservatives and incandescent Christian Coalition-elected freshmen was on the line, and both stumbled badly. On the Senate side, New York's belligerent Alfonso D'Amato all but demanded that diplomatic relations with Mexico be severed because of "the falsification of financial information."[17] Republican colleague Arlen Spector, an outsider candidate for the GOP presidential nomination, suggested that NAFTA be declared null and void because Washington had been so baldfacedly lied to. Confronted by a rabid right-wing crop of neophytes in the House heatedly opposed to the Mexican bail-out, Gingrich suddenly seemed lame and in the way.

House members began tacking all sorts of outrageous conditions to the bail-out package: Mexico had to break diplomatic relations with Cuba, PEMEX had to be privatized, Zedillo had to control out-migration, capture his ten top narco-lords, raise the minimum wage, find a peaceful solution in Chiapas. Although many liberals contributed to these interventionist demands, to her credit, New York Democrat Nydia Valázquez refused to vote on such measures because she considered them to be "a violation of Mexican sovereignty."[18] The congressional debate "unleashed the demons of intervention, disdain, paternalism, commiseration, and racism," wrote *Proceso*'s Pascal del Beltrán. Mexico's fate had once again been placed in the hands of 435 U.S. representatives and 100 senators, the correspondent noted.[19]

While Congress spent much of January stewing and spewing, Mexican reserves were hemorrhaging—a billion dollars worth of *Tesobonos* were coming due each day and no one was rolling over. In late January, reports Andrés Oppenheimer in his problematical *Mexico On The Edge of Chaos*,[20] former Salinas ambassador to Washington, Jorge Montaño, contacted Sandy Berger at the National Security Council to inform him that there was not enough cash in the vaults to carry Mexico past Tuesday (the 31st). On Monday morning, $3.7 billion in Tesobono bonds would come due and only $2.7 billion was left on hand to cover pay-outs. $4 billion in new credits already pledged by the Clinton administration in emergency loans would not be enough to bridge the shortfall, Ortiz had warned Leon Panetta earlier in the month.[21]

Thus, on the 30th, after Gingrich and Dole had confessed that they did not have the votes to pass the bail-out initiative, Clinton withdrew the rescue plan from congressional scrutiny and went it alone, utilizing a little-known currency stabilization fund under his discretionary authority, to loan Mexico $20 billion outright—the fund had never been used to support any currency other than the dollar before and Treasury Department go-fers had to scurry among world currency exchanges to sell enough marks and francs to make the nut.[22] The burden of the rescue would be split—international lenders, led by the IMF, would provide up to $32 billion more. Clinton took to the tube to explain that he had acted "to avoid a world financial crisis" and "save thousands of jobs and tens of thousands of millions of dollars in U.S. exports."[23]

The use of the fund to bypass congressional opposition to the bail-out infuriated congresspeople on both sides of the aisle. Republicans capitalized on the discontent and it transfused their phalanxes right on through the 1996 presidential election. 81% of the American public, according to a *Los Angeles Times* poll, opposed the bail-out[24]—Clinton's multibillion-dollar Mexican rescue reopened the populist artery in U.S. political life, from which the opposition to NAFTA had drawn its lifeblood. "This is a bail-out for Wall Street, not for Main Street," Rush Limbaugh, then at the apex of his bilious influence, sneered on his nightly television shoot-em-up, an episode that was shown to Mexican cable audiences, courtesy of the wonders of NAFTA.

Notwithstanding, Mexico's ruling clique licked Bill Clinton's boots for getting frazzled investors off their backs. "VIVA CLINTON!" toasted Ovaciones, the Televisa-owned afternoon paper, in foot-high black letters.[25] *Proceso* was less sanguine. "CHAINED (to the U.S.)" it shouted across a full-color photo of a grinning Bubbah.[26]

"THE FIRST CRISIS OF THE 21ST CENTURY"

At $20 billion, the Mexican rescue was the biggest bail-out ever for the U.S. government, topping the billions thrown at Israel, the ex-Soviet Union, New York City, Boeing, Iacocca's Chrysler, and the Savings & Loan mafia.[27] The gesture was hardly an altruistic one—by 1995, the economies of the U.S. and Mexico had become so enmeshed that separation would be as painful as a Caesarian section. Ever-expanding U.S. mutual funds, swollen by union and government pension moneys, totalling in the trillions, had landed in Mexico during the Salinas boom. Funds set up by Wall Street houses like Goldman Sachs and Bear Sterns had sunk the modest fortunes of U.S. retirees in the then-torrid Mexican stock market and snatched up the Tesobonos like they were so much free *ceviche* (Mexican sushi). Goldman Sachs was a particularly visible player because of the brokerage house's long association with Robert Rubin, Clinton's as-yet-unconfirmed Secretary of the Treasury. Such interlocking directorship provoked suspicion on both sides of the border. In Mexico, it is popular lore that Clinton's billions never reached these shores at all, but were, instead, paid out to angry investors in the canyons of downtown Manhattan.

The International Monetary Fund was the White House's very willing partner in this plot to complete the annexation of Mexico's economic policies, kicking in $17.7 billion, six times the spare change that venerable institution had ever rustled up for a rescue operation before. Mexico is the IMF's free market flagship and its bow could not be allowed to go down beneath the weight of the New World Order, warned IMF president Michel Camdessus, who labeled the Mexican collapse "the first major crisis of our New World of globalized financial markets,"[28] later abbreviated to "the first crisis of the 21st century."

Monsieur Camdessus knew of what he spoke. IMF-inspired globalization of money markets has made First World financial empires suddenly quite vulnerable to permutations in the third or "emerging" world. "This could cause a contagion that will spread from Brazil to Thailand," fretted Goldman Sachs honcho Robert Hormats, a key Reagan-era trade advisor. The Masters of Capital feared the Mexican Meltdown because they recognized the threat it presented to their global project. The emerging markets phenomenon, which had taken Wall Street by storm in the 1990s, was being monkey-wrenched by instruments of its own creation. Sophisticated computer transfers that moved great boodles of cash across borders and out of markets like Mexico at blinding speed could shipwreck the economies they were supposed to be globalizing. Such hot money had been a pillar of Salinas's "Miracle," sucking $38 billion into the Bolsa de Valores, but now the capital flow had turned into a gusher in reverse.

More urgently, the Mexican Meltdown invoked old domino theories—the ripple impact was felt immediately in the Brazilian stock market as the São Paolo and Río exchanges lost 16% of their worth, and the Brazilian government was forced to dump $1.5 billion USD in pesos anticipating that the currency would soon hit rock bottom.[29] Chile and Argentina suffered similar jitters from what the Latin press dubbed "the Tequila Effect," a soaking that would give investors the shakes for months to come.

Were the globalizers at the bottom of the Mexican blow-out? All of the precipitating factors appear to stem from Mexico's integration with a vastly dominant U.S. economy. One detonator was the current accounts imbalance, stoked by an unprecedented trade deficit in NAFTA's first year which, combined with foreign debt payoffs, totaled 8% of Mexico's Gross Domestic Product, not a rock-solid foundation from which to step up into the globalized future.

But Bill Clinton's decision to finally go it alone on the bail-out also turned on another globalizing syndrome: illegal immigration, which, he warned viewers on January 11th, would explode into the kind of national security crisis that Caspar Weinberger warns of in *The Next War* if the U.S. allowed Mexico to go belly up.[30]

TERMS OF ENDEARMENT

As lenders of last resort, the U.S. and the IMF (with which a letter of intention was signed February 1st) imposed a series of conditions upon Mexico that further anchored economic annexation. Perhaps the most humiliating point of "The Agreement Between the United States of Mexico and America for the

Stabilization of the Mexican Economy" was the condition that all export oil revenues be deposited in the New York City branch of the U.S. Federal Reserve, that granite fetish of U.S. world domination looming at the foot of Wall Street, as collateral on the Clinton loan. Although Mexico had bailed its way out of the '82 debacle by pledging $1 billion in future oil shipments to the U.S. Strategic Reserve, it had never before been forced "to instruct its foreign clients" to tender their checks to Wall Street.[31] The only other nation recently obligated to relinquish oil revenues to compensate for international sins? Saddam's Iraq!

But other conditions of the bail-out were as onerous as the confiscation of foreign oil revenues. As if Mexico were on parole for white collar crimes, all financial information required by the U.S. Treasury Department now had to be made available upon demand. When Mexico's foreign minister, Angel Gurria, insisted that no political conditions had been attached to the pact, Ifigenia Martínez, a UNAM economics professor and PRD loyalist who had been the mentor of several members of the Zedillo cabinet, chirped reprovingly "the foreign minister seems not to remember the history of the U.S. and Mexico."[32]

The existence of a secret list of conditions has been denied by both the White House and Los Pinos, neither of which has published the language of the "Agreement for the Stabilization of the Mexican Economy." Similarly, the conditions of the IMF letter of intention have never been made public—"a very bad sign," commented independent Mexico City economist Jonathan Heath in his weekly *Reforma* column.[33] Nonetheless, items reported to be on the closeted agenda have quietly been implemented since the agreement was inked. The schedule for the operation of U.S. financial services in Mexico, calculated far in the future by NAFTA in order to protect Mexican banks, has been advanced to this century, and a pilot program for the internal repatriation of undocumented workers has been agreed upon, wherein the U.S. will pay the freight to ship deportees far into the interior of the country, close to their homes, in an effort to slow their return to the border.[34]

IMF austerity impositions were, of course, the most dramatic immediate impact of the bail-out. Interest rates were jumped at least 20 points, the usual IMF prescription to make money more expensive, and government budgets pared 16%. Massive unemployment was factored in to drain money from circulation and curb the inflationary elements of the bail-out. The patient would hover between life and death for many months, at the mercy of the White House-IMF brand of tough love. Curiously, the U.S. Treasury made a tidy profit on this, the first crisis of the 21st century: a half-billion USD in exorbitant interest payments had been returned to Robert Rubin's vaults by January 19th when Zedillo paid off the remaining $3.5 billion drawn down on the contingency fund.[35]

Zedillo paid off the bail-out in installments. Just before the July 1996 U.S. political conventions, Mexico persuaded Japanese investors to buy enough of its paper so that Zedillo was able to advance Clinton an $8 billion balloon payment and thus defuse the loan as a 1996 election issue. "Zedillo was the biggest foreign contributor to Clinton's campaign," quipped *La Jornada* wag columnist Jaime Aviles. "Why isn't your Congress investigating?" [36]

"THE SALINAS PROJECT"

Clinton's bail-out did not halt Zedillo's stumbling performance. Typical of his presidential style, the ex-budget director sought to finger expedient targets for his maladroitness. On February 28th, Zedillo signed off on an arrest warrant for Raúl Salinas for having masterminded the execution of PRI Secretary General Ruiz Massieu. The president's new Attorney General, Antonio Lozano Gracia, the first opposition party member (National Action—the conservative PAN) ever to serve a PRI president, would execute the warrant.

The arrest successively deflected public anger from Zedillo to his predecessor. According to those hired to organize and carry out the hit by Raúl's alleged (and since disappeared) hatchet man, Manuel Muñoz Rocha, Ruiz Massieu was murdered because he knew too much about "the Salinas Project." Ultimately, it was speculated, this "Salinas Project" was aimed at reelection in 2000—after Carlos had served a four-year term as president of the brand-new World Trade Organization—the Atomic Ant had become obsessed with occupying the post.

For months after the September 28th 1994 killing, Raúl's name had been kept out of the investigation by the dead man's brother, Mario Ruiz Massieu, a drug war prosecutor appointed by Salinas to probe the assassination. Fleeing arrest orders for having covered up the author of his own brother's assassination, the surviving Ruiz Massieu was nabbed at the Newark, New Jersey airport in March 1995, and held by U.S. authorities on a series of legal pretexts. Mario's thus-far successful battle to avoid extradition to Mexico has since become a sore point in bilateral relations—as has ownership of $8 million USD found in the former prosecutor's Houston bank account and now confiscated by a U.S. federal court as laundered drug money.[37] But Ruiz Massieu's stash was peanuts compared to Raúl's—the elder Salinas brother socked at least $124 million away in Swiss and other European banks during his sibling's presidency.

Meanwhile, the root of all this evil, Carlos Salinas, was driven from his homeland and roamed the world for a year, like a jug-eared Odysseus, seeking a safe haven in Boston and Montreal, Cuba and the Bahamas, before settling in Ireland, his dream of captaining the World Trade Organization crashing in flames behind him. In late 1996, Salinas was expelled from his last legitimate sinecure—the Dow Jones board of directors—although, at this writing, he still remains a member of the PRI, whose Honor & Justice committee appears reluctant to boot him out.

In the currency of the Mexican street, the Zedillo ploy worked well. Whereas Salinas is now viewed as the wellspring of all Mexico's woes by his compatriots, Zedillo escapes history's hisses as merely bumbling and inept, an earnest fool. Among street vendors on the capital's crowded thoroughfares, Salinas's derisive latex head masks far outsell the ones of Zedillo.

INDIAN BLOOD

Zedillo's primary scapegoat for the Mexican meltdown was an old foe, the Zapatista Army of National Liberation. Isolated from his own party, with few political allies, Zedillo found his loyalist constituency in the military, which remained stung by Salinas's abrupt cease-fire order that ended the shooting war in January 1994 with the Zapatistas on the run. The military's mood was not improved by charges by international human rights groups that the Army had committed atrocities in Chiapas. One avenue to Zedillo's ear was military intelligence officers, whose influence is increasing within the hierarchy. The Intelligence component is considered the closest point of contact with the U.S. military.

Spoon-fed questionable intelligence by his military backers, Zedillo popped up on national television at the height of the peso crisis, February 9th, to announce that he had issued arrest warrants for the Zapatista leadership, including Subcomandante Marcos, who, he told viewers, was really one Rafael Sebastián Guillén Vicente, an out-of-work philosopher. The president ordered 40,000 troops into the Lacandón jungle to help police effect arrests.

U.S.-supplied C-130s began dropping paratrooper-fusiliers on Guadalupe Tepeyac at dawn on the 10th.[38] Miraculously forewarned, Marcos and his colleagues pulled out of that town only hours before and fled towards the Montes Azules biosphere reserve where United Nations-sponsored international treaties might keep the military at bay. The Army offensive panicked dozens of jungle communities where the EZLN had support and villagers trussed up their meager belongings on their backs and their heads and fled into the mountains. By mid-February, southern Chiapas looked a lot like Guatemala did in the early 1980s at the height of Ríos Montt's campaign of genocide. Some Mexican Mayans even fled across the southern border for sanctuary.

The first $7 billion installment from the IMF reached Mexican shores the day before Zedillo's February 9th TV show & tell. "This loan has been signed off in Indian blood," wrote the Subcomandante from deep cover.[39] Despite the smoldering fury of Marcos and his supporters, the Mexican president's deployment of the military was applauded in many quarters. The U.S. Department of State assured reporters that Mexico was perfectly within its sovereign rights to insure internal tranquility.[40] On Wall Street too, despite his reputation for being less than candid, Zedillo found supporters.

In a document obtained by Alexander Cockburn and Ken Silverstein and published in their collaborative weekly *Counterpunch*, Chase Manhattan Bank's Emerging Markets wizard, Ríordan Reott, echoed *Interacciones'* call for the president to put on his pants.[41] Reott urged "a military offensive to defeat the insurgency"—although he conceded that this would stimulate human rights complaints. "Although Chiapas does not constitute a fundamental threat to Mexican stability, in our opinion," read the Chase paper, "many in the investment community believe it is… the government has to eliminate the Zapatistas in order to demonstrate that it can control national territory and security policy."[42] For its chutzpah in seeking a final solution to the Zapatista question, Chase offices in Manhattan were invaded by EZLN supporters. Ski-masked Zapatistas danced on the desk tops. Reott was reportedly dismissed.[43]

The demonstrations abroad were symptomatic of the long reach the EZLN had constructed in 14 months of rebellion. The Zapatistas' message of indigenous autonomy and world struggle against neo-liberalism had stirred sympathy from Osaka to Botswana, with solidarity groups springing up like mushrooms all over western Europe. Closer to home, condemnation of Zedillo's military offensive and support for the Indian rebels was deafening. In the week following the military invasion of the Lacandón jungle, demonstrators filled the zócalo three times with over 100,000 participants on each occasion, an unprecedented display of mass support. Zedillo's supposed unmasking of Marcos had fostered a new slogan of defiance, now scrawled on walls across the land: "*Todos Somos Marcos*" ("We Are All Marcos"). Before this crisis within a crisis ignited the dry kindling that the peso collapse had set, Zedillo sued for peace.

SUICIDE TRAIN

The dimensions of the first crisis of the 21st century were bloodcurdling. The 1995 Gross Domestic Product (PIB) slipped 7% over 1994, the most frightening slide since 1932—in one quarter, the second, PIB plunged ten points and the economy would suffer six straight negative quarters of full-blown recession before Zedillo could crow about macro stats that suggested light at the end of the tunnel.[44] At the depths of the downturn, 10 million workers, a third of the workforce, were without employment[45]—two million lost formal jobs, three million youth entered the range of the economically active and obtained no employment, and at least five to six million Mexicans are endemically without a job, according to independent economists like David Márquez Ayala.[46]

The explosion of interest rates (120% on credit cards alone) forged militant debtors' unions like El Barzón which tarred and feathered bank officials who sought to foreclose on their members' properties.[47] Inflation skyrocketed from a frugal 7% in Salinas's final year to 50% in Zedillo's first. The mainstream Congress of Labor issued a report indicating that increases in the cost of the basic food basket were 100% above those in the minimum wage.[48] In Mexico, salaries are measured by multiples of the daily minimum wage. 60% of all Mexicans earn two or less minimum wages[49]—in the summer of 1996, the minimum wage was equivalent to $2.76 USD a day. The crisis reduced the daily calorie intake of half of Mexico's 92 million citizens to below nutritional standards, according to a study done by Banamex, the nation's largest banking institution. By May 1996, mobs on the outskirts of Monterrey were sacking freight cars filled with U.S. and Canadian corn in scenes reminiscent of the 1910 revolution. "At least we'll have enough for tortillas," one aproned mother from a nearby San Nicolás de las Garzas colony told La Jornada[50]—the price of tortillas, the staple of the poor, rose 100% in the first 24 months of Zedillo's crisis.

According to the Solidarity Institute, a Salinas-era legacy, the crisis drove three million more Mexicans into extreme poverty, pushing government totals up to between 20 and 22 million, more than a fifth of the population.[51] But there was little cushion for the newly extremely impoverished. The $16 billion in budget cuts ordered by the IMF gutted social programs just when they were most needed. On the aforementioned July day that Ernesto Zedillo paid Bill Clinton $8 billion of bail-out monies to take the loan out of circulation as a reelection issue for the U.S. president, Mexico City hospitals were so low on supplies that nurse Martha Perez sat down in the zócalo and drew off a syringe full of her own blood in protest. "Hunger strikes don't work anymore," she told this reporter, "the people are too hungry."

$26 billion USD is thought to have fled Mexico as the result of the crisis.[52] On the first anniversary of the peso devaluation, the currency stood at 7.76 against the dollar. Even the nation's 22 billionaires were seriously impaired by the collapse, their numbers dropping to just ten on Forbes' 1995 list of the super-rich—Carlos Slim was reduced from $6.5 billion to $3.7 and Azcárraga to a miserable $1.6 billion.[53] But Mexico's billionaires were not yet jumping out of windows. That rite was reserved for those lower down on the food chain.

Closer to the ground, the poor and the desperate inflated the suicide rate. According to SAPTEL, a suicide prevention line installed after the catastrophic 1985 earthquake, the volume of desperation calls was even greater than in the months following that tragedy. Dr. Federico Puente worried about the low self-esteem of many callers who had worked all their lives and now, suddenly, had been brusquely discarded.[54]

El Barzón reported that 300 of its members had died or committed suicide, including its leader in Coahuila state, because of pressures inflicted by the crisis[55]—Barzónistas held a wake inside a Morelia branch of Banamex for one member whose death was attributed to foreclosure. The Mexico City metro set suicide records in 1995—over 30.[56] A favorite jumping off spot was the Indios Verdes station, a stone's throw away from the Basilica. Even the Virgin of Guadalupe had abandoned the poor: religious medal vendors at the shrine were discounting the Dark Madonna's image by as much as 30% to attract customers.[57]

200,000 small businesses cashiered out in the first 18 months of the crisis. For the first time in a recorded history that stretches back to the Aztec empire, bars in the old quarter of the capital were shuttered for lack of patrons. Kidnappers, taking advantage of a popular profession during hard times here, were settling for much lower ransoms, reported *El Financiero*.[58]

ENOUGH OF NAFTA

In such a stressed-out atmosphere, sympathy for the "North American Free Trade Agreement-*Tratado de Libre Comercio*" did not flourish. In its first two years of operation, pointed out Berta Lujan, organizer of the Mexican Anti-Free Trade Network (RMALC), Mexico had suffered the most precipitous drop in employment in the 20th century.[59] On the second anniversary of the NAFTA-TLC, *La Jornada* financial writer Patricia Vega affirmed that, since the accord kicked in Mexico had broken three doubtful economic records: the biggest flight of speculation capital in its history, the largest commercial deficit ever, and the greatest volume of unemployment since such data was first gathered in the 1930s.[60]

Trade conflicts ripened under the NAFTA-TLC. A full-page ad, run in California newspapers in early 1996, depicted a menacing hangman's noose and the prominent use of the adjective "Mexican"—the ad was not paid for by some racist militia, but rather was sponsored by the California Avocado Commission,[61] demanding the protection of the health of its product from deadly Mexican plagues that even massive doses of pesticides (shipped to Mexico by U.S. agrochemical giants because they are outlawed in the U.S.) could not exterminate. Beefs over tomatoes, mangos, cement, steel, Tennessee sipping whiskey, wine coolers, bedroom furniture, UPS deliveries, and straw brooms elicited similar enmities. In one particularly ugly "trade" conflict, burly Teamsters lined up all along the border on December 18th 1995 to protest NAFTA-mandated integration of truck transportation that was about to put

Mexican freight drivers on U.S. highways. San Diego County police had to be called out up on the Otay Mesa to prevent bloodshed. When the Clinton White House, leery of labor in the '96 elections, abrogated the clause unilaterally, many saw the move as proof of the usual Yanqui treachery.

But not all union brothers and sisters were prepared to square off against their blue collar neighbors. Economic integration revealed just how closely tied transnational fortunes were to the irritation of workers in any one of the three NAFTA countries. A General Motors strike in Dayton, Ohio in mid-March 1996, over brake parts being made by a non-union subcontractor, tied up operations in Canada and Mexico (30,000 workers down)[62]—a chain reaction that was reiterated in early 1997, and a pattern for the future that surely does not escape the globalizers' attentions. Also on the agenda, if the reformers retain and rebuild the AFL-CIO into a real House of Labor: the transnationalization of unions in response to the transnationalization of capital. Already the Teamsters and the independent United Electrical Workers (UE) are organizing workers through Mexican proxies at maquiladoras run by transnationals such as Honeywell and General Electric, corporations the two unions have organized north of the Río Bravo. On the northern front, unions like the Social Service Employees (SSEIU), the Carpenters, and the United Farmworkers are signing up undocumented Mexican workers in the U.S. to refurbish their dwindling ranks and minimize scabbing from the south.

Cross-border organizing targets Mexico's most strategic economic sector: U.S.-bound exports—transnational corporations, homebased in the United States, account for a third of Mexico's manufactured exports. The export sector has been the one area of the economy that has performed in exemplary fashion for Zedillo during the agonizing months of crisis—if only because devaluation cut the cost of labor almost in half. With wages severely depressed by IMF strictures, the maquiladoras have flourished, giving credence to the notion that NAFTA's ulterior motive wass to convert Mexico into one great U.S.-owned assembly plant. The crisis of '95 has pushed this project into place.

In defense of NAFTA, Ambassador Jim Jones, once president of the American Stock Exchange, told the Am-Cham's annual 1996 luncheon that the treaty "saved Mexico from meltdown"[63]—but, traversing the *ambulante*-choked streets of Mexico City in mid-1997, one would have to be in committed denial not to think that Mexico was still in the throes of serious meltdown.

U.S. high-handedness has made NAFTA an extra-bumpy ride. In direct dissonance with his advocacy of "Free Trade," but with the Florida anti-Castro Cuban vote hanging fire, Bill Clinton signed off on the legally dubious Helms-Burton bill in the spring of 1996, a crass demonstration of political opportunism that soon had his two NAFTA trading partners in an uproar. Under

Helms-Burton's dictates, any corporate entity doing business on property in Cuba that had been confiscated by Fidel Castro from private hands three-and-a-half decades ago must either desist immediately or face U.S. sanctions, including the denial of travel visas and heavy fines. Helms-Burton impacted 200 Mexican firms with Cuban investments: CEMEX, the cement giant, pulled out before it even received a U.S. warning letter.[64] Domos, in which Salinas brother Enrique is thought to have some action, and which has bought up 50% of the Cuban phone company (once an ITT property), cashed it in in mid-1997.[65]

Although Helms-Burton won the Cuban American National Foundation's endorsement, it has also soured many on the true intentions of the "Free Trade" treaty. Facing stiff competition from AT&T and MCI after NAFTA opened up long distance service in 1997, Carlos Slim's Telmex featured a buffoon gringo phone exec in commercials designed to stir the embers of Mexican nationalism amongst its once-captive customers. The clown's name: Burton Helms.

CLOSING DOWN THE CRISIS

Street-level realities aside, the Mexican meltdown was officially declared over and done with at the annual conclave of the International Monetary Fund and the World Bank, in September 1995. The meeting was spooked from the opening gun by whatever had transpired south of the U.S. border. At one pre-junta seminar, bankers spoke from a podium draped with a banner that read "The IMF After Mexico," as if Zedillo's crisis had divided all of time.[66]

Zedillo chose the occasion for his first state visit to Washington. The *Financial Times* described the junket as more "a pilgrimage of thanksgiving" than a diplomatic gambit.[67] Treasury Secretary Robert Rubin was Zedillo's first visitor soon after his helicopter set down near the Washington monument on the evening of September 20th, presumably to pick up a pre-payment on the bail out. The next evening, Zedillo was the guest of honor at a White House state banquet (tequila ice cream, Mexican wedding cookies)[68] during which Big Bill burbled that Mexico was back on track and praised his counterpart's "bravery" in implementing "the hard measures" it took to overcome this now-momentary glitch in the globalization of practically everything.

Clinton and Zedillo had much in common, the *Washington Post* society page reported:[69] both were Yale scholarship students who had studied abroad, both their mothers were nurses, and both had "married up"—both had, in fact, honeymooned in Acapulco, to which Zedillo invited his host for a second go-round, presumably with Hillary. But Acapulco was all shook up on the evening Zedillo made his motion—a giant 7.6 earthquake had just leveled tourist infrastructure up the coast in Colima and Jalisco, putting a bruising crimp in a big dollar-producer for Mexico. Natural cataclysm dogged Zedillo throughout 1995—droughts devastated the north, a Caribbean hurricane flattened oil production for a month and a Pacific cyclone wiped out the Sinaloa shrimping fleet. Popocatépetl never stopped belching.

Zedillo's visit to Washington coincided with the IMF-World Bank's annual jubilee, but he would not be invited to address those august bodies. Nor would he be invited to address a joint session of the U.S. Congress, as is obligatory for Mexican presidents on their first state visits to Washington. The White House feared that a Zedillo appearance might re-activate Republican rancor— Alfonso D'Amato was already accusing the Clinton administration of covering up certain details of the meltdown. A leaked memorandum, directed to Assistant Treasury Secretary Larry Summers by an underling, confirmed that the Clinton administration knew the Mexican government was spending billions to support the peso months before the crisis broke.[70] What *did* the White House know and when?

Instead, a somber Zedillo met with Gingrich and Dole under the Capitol dome at a session made memorable only because Dole, his hat half in the ring, dourly complained that "NAFTA wasn't working." The *New York Times* availed itself of Zedillo's visit to condemn the lack of political change in Mexico and question the effectiveness of NAFTA (the *Times* remains an enthusiastic booster of free trade). On Pennsylvania Avenue, a handful of ski-masked Zapatista supporters circled in front of the White House to protest human rights abuses in Chiapas.

Nonetheless, the Mexican president soldiered on. This reporter caught up with him at a National Chamber of Commerce breakfast, scant blocks from the White House, where he announced, for the first time anywhere in public, the dates upon which bidding would open on Mexico's about-to-be-privatized petrochemical industry.[71] The response was heartwarming. Zedillo's ambitious privatization plans would put petrochemicals, the ports, the railroads, communication satellites, electricity generating plants and natural gas pipelines on the block in order to raise a little under $12 billion USD—but the dream has not prospered—at least initially. Nationalist opposition within his own party forced Zedillo to backtrack on petrochemical privatization, and bids on the railroads have been slow in coming in and so low that some lines were withdrawn from consideration.

Across town at the posh Sheraton Hotel, where the world's financial elite were wrapping up the globalized future, both Camdessus and James Wohlfenson, the flamboyant director of the World Bank, reiterated to the annual meeting of the two institutions' 178 members that the first crisis of the 21st century was dead and buried—although, in the unlikely event this unfortunate situation might ever repeat itself in the civilized world, members voted unanimously to raise a $50 billion USD contingency fund for any subsequent 21st century meltdowns. Furthermore, reporting nations would now have to provide new and better economic information to their Washington masters, a stinging slap at Mexico's irreverent attitude towards bookkeeping.[72]

FIRE DOWN BELOW

Despite the ministrations of the Masters of the Universe, Mexico remained throttled. As Camdessus shut down the crisis in Washington, third quarter 1995 GDP dipped 9.6%—Finance secretary Ortiz, who had bragged that recovery would begin in the third quarter, put the best spin possible on the slide: "We have finally hit rock bottom..." [73]

Discontent rattled the Zedillo regime's cage throughout 1995. The massacre of 17 dissident farmers by Guerrero state motorized police just north of Acapulco in June eclipsed Zedillo's efforts to strike a peace accord with the Zapatistas. The sudden appearance of a second guerrilla front, the Popular Revolutionary Army (EPR), on the first anniversary of the Guerrero killings sent stocks reeling and set the stage for the militarization of central and southern Mexico.

Mexico City streets were clogged with angry demonstrators throughout much of 1995 and '96. Bus drivers, resisting privatization imposed by hard-nosed Mexico City mayor Oscar Espinosa, a Carlos Hank disciple, marched daily, permanently snarling traffic. So did schoolteachers demanding higher wages, fired street-sweepers from Tabasco state (sometimes in the nude), and members of El Barzón, protesting bank foreclosures—one summer day, Barzónistas blockaded the Bank of Mexico's portals with elephants from an embargoed circus and, as if on cue, the pachyderms deposited great green turds on the front steps. Groups of oil workers and the parents of students rejected by the UNAM sat down in front of the Mexican Bolsa de Valores, delaying trading for hours. Investors did not put on a happy face. After that, hundreds of heavily armed police surrounded the bubble-topped Bolsa whenever new demonstrations threatened. By December 1995, battles between *ambulante* (street vendor) groups in the center of the city had become so violent that U.S. airlines warned travelers to stay away from the old quarter.

Another reason to keep one's distance was the soaring crime rate. Each day of 1995 and 1996, 600 to 800 automobiles were being stolen, carjacked, or stripped while stalled in traffic, and for the first time, the Mexico City murder rate topped that of New York City. Property crimes and armed robberies plagued upscale neighbors like Polanco, where the crime wave took on class war trappings.[74] Police corruption intoxicated the atmosphere—agents and ex-agents were deemed responsible for 60% of the crimes.[75] In one traffic incident, Mexico state judicial police officers tried to divest President Zedillo's son of his valuables when the youngster stopped for a red light. In light of such outrages, Zedillo's election pledge of increased public security became a sick joke.

Despite the harsh daily actualities, throughout 1996 and '97 the Mexican president never tired of proclaiming that the country was in full recovery. The chasm between the macro-economic data cranked out by Zedillo administration apologists and the depredations in the street, painted a picture so surreal that one suspected Zedillo's cheery speeches were being penned by Gabriel García Márquez. Despite vehement critiques of the neo-liberal model's propensity for impoverishing the nation issued by his own PRI party, the crumbling Valázquez's official labor movement, the Catholic Bishops Conference, and even prominent business associations like the CONCANACO,[76] Zedillo obstinately reiterated his enthusiasm for the free market in speech after speech to captive audiences of dozing accountants, bankers, and other gullible professional associations.

The president's perfumed rhapsodies of recovery were countered in the damp depths of the Lacandón rain forest by the usual suspects. The Zapatistas' August 1996, monumentally eclectic gathering of young European anarchists, aging Latin American guerrilleros, U.S. cybernauts and the indígenas of México Profundo, under the rubric of "the Intercontinental Forum In Defense of Humanity and Against Neo-Liberalism," argued that the best kind of international solidarity with the Mayan rebels was to tackle the neo-liberals where one lived.

Glimmers of Zedillo's long-prophesied rebound were first registered in mid-1996, but growth lagged far behind the 1995 nose dive, and despite the administration's hopeful forecast, the economy remained dicey. To save the banking system, for example, Zedillo and Ortiz invested twice as much cash to subsidize the banking system as the price for which the latter had sold 18 nationalized banks back in the early '90s—the rescue equaled 12% of the PIB.[77] Out in the countryside, the EPR had launched a deadly series of coordinated assaults on military and police targets throughout south central Mexico and, in Chiapas, talks between the government and the Zapatistas were broken off indefinitely and remain so at this writing. Despite Zedillo's manic gloating over macro-economic gains, the patient's prognosis remains guarded.

Down below, in Deep Mexico, one had the sensation that the fury which Hidalgo's uprising had unchained, the cataclysmic anger that had colored the revolution crimson, was, much like Popocatépetl, building for a new eruption. This first crisis of the 21st century may have consolidated the annexation of the Mexican economy into the new global order, but it does not feel like the final chapter has yet been written.

DÉJÁ VU, ALL OVER AGAIN

In the spring of 1997, precisely on Cinco de Mayo, a day set aside to celebrate victory over foreign imperialism, Bill Clinton became the first U.S. president to set foot in Mexico City since Jimmy Carter had put down 18 years
before. Things were looking up—at least from the top of the executive tower.

Clinton's visit, the first to his southern neighbor after five years of tenancy in
the White House, came at a particularly abrasive moment in bilateral relations.
The usual Mexico-bashing at certification time had been aggravated by General
Gutiérrez's detention and neophyte Secretary of State Madeleine Albright spoke
of putting Mexico "under a microscope" to see if it was performing its drug war
tasks with sufficient zeal, an unfortunate metaphor that had the folks on the
other end of the lens bristling, because they sensed they had been compared to
microbes. Then the federal version of Pete Wilson's Prop 187, "the Immigration
Responsibility Act" kicked in up north, threatening even more massive deportations. To add to this evil brew, 1997 marked the 150th anniversary of the U.S.
amputation and annexation of 51% of Mexico's national territory.

In a truly Trumanesque gesture, Clinton laid a wreath at the Monument to
the *Niños Heroes* (Heroic Children), the cadets who had elected to jump from
the ramparts of Chapultepec Castle back in '47 rather than surrender to the
Yankee Doodle Dandies. Later, the U.S. president sauntered over to the
National Auditorium to lead a pep rally for the NAFTA-TLC. 8,000 delirious,
scrupulously-selected businesspeople and a beaming Zedillo rah-rahed conge-
nially. Then the audience was hushed and Mexico's Secretary of Commerce
unveiled a new video starring hot Hollywood property Salma Hayek and Nobel
laureate Octavio Paz designed to sell the Mexican people on the successes of the
NAFTA-TLC, not an easy job considering that, in the first three years of this
treaty or agreement, unemployment had hit a record high and the economy had
plunged to the level of the Great Depression.

Down Reforma Boulevard, those who had borne the brunt of this "success"—
impoverished teachers, housewives, outraged nationalists, debtors' groups, El
Barzón, and the anti-NAFTA RMALC sought to protest the U.S. president's
intervention. Clinton's junket came just 60 days before a critical mid-term election in which the PRI stood to lose control of both the capital and the congress.
"This is an election visit on behalf of the PRI," smoldered Jorge Castañeda.[78]

But there were no demonstrations in Mexico City between May 5th and 7th
1997. Tens of thousands of police and military shoved marchers from the streets,
seized their banners and arrested their leaders. Large sections of the capital were
cordoned off and the subway system shut down without warning, in what
seemed to be a dress rehearsal for a military coup. The U.S. flag flew everywhere
in the city. It looked a lot like 1847 all over again.

Part Four

"La Lucha Sigue y Sigue"

Resistance
to the Annexation of Mexico

Chapter 15

LA MALINCHE

The old Indian woman was so tiny that the soles of her huaraches barely touched the floor of the Cristóbal Colón bus. We were winding our way towards Cuautla Morelos, Emiliano Zapata's beloved home turf. I smiled but could not catch her eye. The ancient Nahua grandmother perched on the edge of her seat, intensely focused, as if scanning the ridge line for a lost cow or inspecting a daughter's tortillas for imperfections or some such bucolic endeavor.

None of the above. The abuela's attentions were nailed to one of those tiny television screens that are now installed on virtually all Mexican buses, regardless of class distinction. Nowadays, all over Mexico, the worst Hollywood films ever made, yawp and flicker and invade one's space every kilometer of the road. I suppose it has something to do with NAFTA…

This particular video seemed tame compared to the disembowelments, rape, mayhem, and other gratuitous violence that usually fills these accursed monitors. It looked and sounded like a very U.S. White House sex comedy. In one scene, a comely reporter seemed to be heatedly flirting with a well-groomed American president but then my vision is poor and I often deliberately miss the point. I've never figured out how Mexicans follow the plot lines of these cinematic gems anyway—the films are always in English with unreadable subtitles plastered across the bottom of the screen. The bus bumps and the video system malfunctions. Watching these films requires curiosity, determination, extremely sharp eyes, and a certain level of literacy.

It seemed unlikely that the old grandmother read or spoke either Spanish or English—she addressed her granddaughter in Náhuatl. Nevertheless, her gaze never let go of the infernal little screen as the handsome U.S. president delivered press conferences, convened emergency cabinet meetings about some crisis that has escaped my memory, and made googoo eyes at the girl reporter. Even when the bus put in at the Cristóbal Colón depot up in Zapata's home town, the old woman and, indeed, most of her fellow passengers, refused to abandon the bus until the president and his sweetheart were strolling arm in arm down the aisle and the credits had begun to scroll.

Such paradoxes are abundant in the new, improved, post-NAFTA Mexico. One can live one's entire day here encapsulated by gringo-ness. A half-million North Americans do[1], ensconced in their own retirement colonies and resorts, with their own churches and schools and American Legion Posts, radio stations, newspapers, and service clubs. But for Mexicans, particularly those of the urban middle class persuasion, Gringolandia also comes home from dawn til dusk and then some.

MALINCHE'S DREAM

You stumble out of bed in the morning, brush your teeth with Crest, Gleem, or Sensodyne (the free market offers options), flip on the new shower system just purchased at Wal-Mart, rinse off with Body Shop Soap and Herbal Essence shampoo, and sit down to breakfast on Kellogg's Corn Flakes or Cap'n Crunch— both are hawked by street vendors around the Metro stops now. While your favorite breakfast food snaps, crackles, and pops, CNN Headline News unspools on your Mexican-Korean TV to keep you abreast of overnight international developments before you have to haul ass for work in your Japanese-Mexican Nissan Tsuro.

On the job, you mill around the Mr. Coffee system, punch up your e-mail on your Apple Computer, scan the *New York Times* on line, make a few calls on your Swedish Ericson phone via AT&T's new long distance service, and pretty soon, its time for comida corrida (lunch, chump.)

As advertised, NAFTA has really expanded the menu. Arby's, Roy Rogers, Subway, Carl's Jr., Burger King (stay away from "Burguer Boy"—it's Mexican), "Hamburguezas Tradicionales" (really Wendy's), and McDonald's, will satisfy your hankering for fat-saturated, red-blooded meat. Well, perhaps you should avoid the Zona Rosa McDonald's, a favorite target of anti-U.S. demonstrators— the outlet was trashed by ski-masked anarchists after California passed the infamous immigrant-bashing Proposition 187. The branch near the zócalo too gets sprayed with "Yanqui, Go Home"-type slogans whenever adolescent marchers pass its doors. Nonetheless, it's not all that black and white—even your average gringo-hating Mexican is quite capable of tossing a few eggs at the U.S. embassy on Reforma and then strolling over to the Pink Zone McDonald's to wolf down a Big Mac and a Coke Classic.

One famous franchise you won't discover on this lunch time vision quest is Taco Bell. Pepsico tried out a Taco Bell line at a popular Kentucky Fried Chicken (KTC) just off Insurgentes Sur in the first years of the NAFTA flush. The day I dined at this fast food shrine (Rufino Tamayo reproductions on the walls), there were but three customers on the Taco Bell line and two of them thought they were waiting for the Colonel's chicken. The third was running a mission of mercy for his dad, an aged bracero who liked Taco Bell nachos because they were so Americano.

Taco Bell also offered what it called a taco—dry, shredded meat in a hard anti-septic shell—for five pesos a piece. Outside, just down the street, makeshift stalls offered six tacos for the same price and you had your choice of every filler from cow's brains to squash flowers. Consumer organizations claim that dogs and cats account for 30% of the meat served in such establishments[2] and Taco Bell was counting on putting out a safe, fast, hygienic taco to get its product across. But Mexicans have been snacking on dog meat ever since the Aztecs roasted Chihuahua-like *escuincles* (it's the sauce that counts) and Taco Bell proved a bust. However, this is not to say there are no Taco Bells in Mexico today. The last time I checked up, Taco Belle #1 and Taco Belle #2, two grease-flecked rick-ety wooden stalls, stood side by side on the stretch between the border gate in Tijuana and that city's garish Revolution Avenue.

With a quick lunch out of the way, it's only 14:35 on your fake Rolex and you still have plenty of time to run errands before heading back to work. You pick up the resoled loafers at Fast Shoe, the dry cleaning at 24-Hour Martínizing, and even have a minute for a trim at the El Lay-based Unisex Sam's haircutting salon. There are a couple of Federal Express packages on your desk when you get back to the office. Your girl friend calls and wonders if you're going to the Hard Rock Cafe tonight. Your secretary is selling Amway on the weekends and bends your ear for an hour about the glories of their cleaning products. You leave the office early for a long workout at Gold's Gym. You even have an hour to squeeze in that most American of new Mexican obsessions: mall-hopping.

Most Mexican big cities have been malled in recent years. These *centros com-erciales* usually include a cavernous discount store (Gigante, Commercial Mexicana—both brimful of U.S. brands, or in more upscale locales, Sears or J.C. Penney), a triplex theater, a handful of U.S.-franchised specialty shops, and a fast food outlet. The Santa Fe spread in the west of Mexico City is a current favorite for mall-mad Chilangos (Mexico City natives). Set amidst gleaming highrises and corporate headquarters (Hewlett-Packard, Goodyear, Televisa), Santa Fe is built atop the capital's most noxious garbage dump and many garbage-pickers were left jobless and homeless by the sudden upscaling of their neighborhood. Several locals who objected to the project were "disappeared," according to Eduardo Morales, leader of the local Santa Fe defense group, the UPREZ.[3] It is not a politically correct mall.

You glide up the gleaming escalators and the high fashion salons flash by as you climb: Claudio Rocco, Dior, Nicole Miller. The Muzak is oozing soft-core soul hits from the '60s. Florsheim faces Radio Shack, the Dockers are right next door. It's confusing. What country are we in? You sit down to a falafel at a Greek Gyros stand to ground yourself and a couple of Dr Peppers later, you've recovered enough equilibrium to go shopping. You pick up a month's supply of yeast-free multi-vitamins at Nature's Fingerprints, a couple of Chicago Bulls shirts for the nephews, a Grover Washington CD. Your VISA card is maxed out but American Express will carry the load. You're still home in time for *Monday Night Football*.

You polish off a six pack of Budweiser on sale at the local 7-Eleven. Sure, Mexican beer is 100 times better than the pisswater that passes for beer up in the states, but soon the two will be indistinguishable—Anheuser-Busch is buying up Negro Modelo.[4] You contemplate a pizza—but which one: Domino's, Shakey's, or Showtime Pizza Fiesta? Then there's always Pancho's Mexican Buffet or maybe, Ouchi Sushi. The game's a blow-out and, anyway, you're ready for a hot night at the Hard Rock or better, Planet Hollywood—there are so many choices in the New Mexico...

Just to be safe, you pack your can of Mace, a "Citizens Against Crime" product—the crime rate is soaring downtown and, besides, your neighbor is selling the line.

Oh, and don't forget the lubed, extra-sensitive Trojans, just in case you score tonight...

THE CURSE

The Mexican Nightmare described above has a name here: Malinchismo, the admiration of the foreign over the native. The epithet takes its inspiration from La Malinche, Cortez's concubine—really *Malinalli*, the 12th day on the Aztec calendar, but altered by the Spanish conquerors to Malinche and, more formally, Doña Marina. La Malinche was one of 20 women given to Cortez by the Chontal elders when he landed on the coast of Tabasco in the winter of 1519. La Malinche was not Chontal at all but the daughter of Nahua aristocrats thought to be from Oluta[5], Veracruz. Although the Conqueror twice gave Malinche away to his underlings, she was always returned to him. Because she spoke both Aztec Náhuatl and Chontal Mayan, she proved invaluable as a translator. As Cortez's mistress, she bore him one son, Martín, the first mestizo born of the union of the European and the Indian. Years later, after he had risen in rebellion against the Crown, Martín was tortured and vilified on the zócalo.

Some consider that the public violence done to the first New Mexican, stamped the race for all eternity. Octavio Paz attributes the Mexican's loneliness and reserve to the trauma of Cortez's taking of La Malinche. The Mexican, the Nobel laureate opines in his once ground-breaking *Labyrinth of Solitude*, is torn apart by the contradictions of his origin.[6]

Was La Malinche the victim of brutal rape by the outsiders or was her allegiance to Cortez a consensual one? The master muralist José Clemente Orozco painted Malinche as a temptress, the Mexican Eve, a whore. Paz seems to take

Doña Marina to task for her coquetry, reducing this primal myth to a sad ranchero song: "it is true that she gave herself to him but he dropped her as soon as her usefulness was over."[7]

The Curse of La Malinche, the self-loathing that Paz discerns as being rooted in the knowledge that one was born from violence, colors Mexican history. But the Nobelist rejects the thesis that history and social circumstance—the relentless penetration by the strangers (*extranjeros*) of Mexico's borders and body, both psychically and territorially—have shaded the Mexican character. Rather, he insists, the Mexican has brought this tragedy upon himself.[8] Paz's vision is Eurocentric, misogynist, even racist—and self-revealing. The poet pokes his finger inside the wound: the Mexican's sense of inferiority in the presence of the Extranjero makes for the sort of servility so often displayed by a violated people. "Slaves, servants, and submerged races always wear a mask," Paz writes, in explaining the solitude of the Mexican.[9] But servility is a process—a defense mechanism at first, it can escalate into resentment, rebellion, and liberty in the end.

This wound radiates through every facet of what is Mexican but the pain it brings carries more than just the stock stereotype of gloomy fatalism. The real flow of Mexican history is one of epochs of slavishness, followed by violent rejection of what is imposed from the outside—Aztec imperial constraints were rejected by the many indigenous peoples of Mexico, just as bitterly as Spanish or French or U.S. Imperialism. Mexican history is not linear but goes round and round propelled forward only by its own inertia.

In defense of La Malinche, it is entirely possible that her submission to Cortez was designed to free her people from Aztec domination—just as was the complicity of the Totonaco and Tlaxcalteco kings with the European invaders. Similarly, Malinche's denunciation of Cuauhtémoc, and his execution by Cortez in Tabasco may reflect this anti-Aztec scenario. But it is the Conquerors (or in Mexico's case, the Conquerors of the Conquerors) who write history and Malinche has been stuck with a bad rap. Ironically, one of the first modern applications of the term *Malinchista* was directed at anthropologists who, after analyzing the bones discovered under the altar at Ixcateopán, decided they were not the remains of Cuauhtémoc at all.[10]

The epithet remains charged with nationalist anger—Paz equates La Malinche with another famous trollop, "La Chingada," as in "¡Viva Mexico! Fueran los hijos de la Chingada" ("Long Live Mexico. Get out of here, you sons of the Fucked One"), a traditional patriotic battle cry.

Psychosexual symbolism aside, in post-NAFTA Mexico, Malinchismo has become more a question of consumer patterns than one of punishable treason. "I don't want to seem Malinchista, but the vitamins from your country are much better than Mexican ones," Super Animal once confessed to me. Super Animal, a real-life masked wrestler and body builder, strides the streets of the capital defending wild and domestic animal life—his own pet hate is the bullfight (which really compounds his quotient of Malinchismo).

Because it now seems to be associated with product recognition and marquee value, Malinchismo is mostly a middle class affliction. But what comes first: the class or the disease?

U.S. apologists are known to argue that Mexican anti-Americanism is promulgated by a self-serving government and sycophantic intelligentsia that seek to off-load their own inadequacies upon the Norte Americanos. The love of plain, everyday Mexicans for the United States, they contend, is amply demonstrated by the great numbers who flock north and their intense desire to acquire everything that is allegedly "Made in the USA."[11] In response, Jorge G. Castañeda questions whether such consumer trends are signs of Americanization or "a similar massification of consumption, marked by their American origins..." [12]

NAFTA was, of course, Malinchismo's big moment. Sam's Club, Price Club, and Wal-Mart (96 cash registers) set up shop in Mexico City. The freezers at Gigante were stocked to the rafters with Häagen-Dazs ice creams. But political violence capped by the economic crisis that followed peso devaluation turned 21 million upwardly mobile Malinchista consumers into suddenly depressed and downwards-bound ones. Sales dipped seriously during Zedillo's Crisis—the last time I touched base at Wal-Mart only 15 registers were open and the aisles were ghostly canyons piled high with unsold plastic.

La Malinche's stock had not really plummeted though—Malinche-addicted shoppers just stepped down from the malls to the street where Alemán-era import substitution survives in underground sweat shops, cranking out cheap facsimile goods and attaching the appropriate Nike or Levi labels to insure brisk street sales in the "informal" economy. Even as Mexico's formal economy came apart at the seams in the crisis of '95-'96, the subterranean one surged.

IMAGINARY MEXICO

The Malinche syndrome takes place in a land that anthropologist Guillermo Bonfil defines as "Imaginary Mexico," a place unrooted in the daily trials and sacred rituals of its opposite pole, "Deep Mexico." Like most bourgeois syndromes, Malinche's trickle down to the underclass is minimal. The poor wear hand-me-down trinkets, Marlboro caps and San Francisco 49ers tee-shirts and, on bus rides out to Cuautla, the TV monitors become windows through which the threadbare citizens of Deep Mexico can observe the well-groomed gringo model. But México Profundo is profoundly resistant to altering the old ways, even when its sons and daughters come home from El Norte in baggy jeans, with newfangled ideas and language. My comadre, Arminda Flores, is not a traditional

Purépecha at all, but her mom was the tortilla maker in her barrio of the Lake Pátzcuaro shore town of Ihuatzio. Sitting around the wood fire one night while she was patting out the tortillas, I asked her if she ever used the new quick mix corn flour marketed by Maseca (Archer-Daniels-Midlands now owns a third of Maseca's action). Nah, she wrinkled up her nose, "my mother would never approve—and besides, Maseca tastes like chewing gum..."

Beyond the lake, up in the sierra, the Purépechas of Santa Cruz Tanaco take a long time to fashion their market goods. Pancho Merced once kept me waiting six months for a new *gaván* (serape) because he could not find the right black sheep to shear, and it takes Miguel Baltazar an eternity to build fantasy scenes inside the tequila bottles he scavenges from Tanaco's meager rubbish. The pace of production in Tanaco is dense and careful. Speaking of how the deliberateness of Mexican craftspeople is out of step with the modern Malinchized world of time clocks and efficiency experts, Paz ruminates that the outsiders "want to resolve our contradictions by annihilating them..."[13]

Assimilation is a kind of cultural genocide and, as always, the most profound resistance to it comes from those closest to the ground, the indígenas and mestizos of Deep Mexico. Bonfil juxtaposes "México Profundo" against "Mexico Imaginario," an illusion rather than a nation. "When Imaginary Mexico lives illusionary stages of expansion" and pressures increase upon the indigenous way of doing things, Deep Mexico with its "culture of resistance" "reactivates customs that seemed to be on the verge of being forgotten...there is memory and learning in all of this..."[14]

GIMME THAT OL' TIME RELIGION

The Catholic Church has cast itself as a sort of border wall against moral and cultural contamination from El Norte, a paradox of somewhat colossal proportions. Evangelization historically constitutes the most painful of northern impositions upon the Mexican character. To the Church, the U.S. is a crass consumer society mired in a cesspool of materialism, sin, pornography, and drug addiction—an analysis that does not veer wildly off the mark. With 22 million puffers (give or take 10 million), the U.S. is the world's marijuana smoker por excelencia. U.S. child pornographers prey on Mexico's street urchins, hawking their sleazy videos in pederast catalogues like "Overseas Male."[15] Opening up 800 and 900 telephone service between Mexico and the U.S. gives Mexican youngsters access to Dial-a-Porn numbers.[16] Unfettered sexual license in the U.S. beckons Mexican migrant workers who then return to their home villages in Michoacán and Jalisco dying of the shameful gringo disease SIDA (AIDS).

But Mexicans have been returning from the U.S. since the 1930s with an equally virulent plague[17], at least to the Church's reckoning: Protestantism. The "sects," as the Roman Catholic hierarchy arrogantly designates all

Protestant denominations, are anti-Mexican stalking horses of U.S. Imperialism, according to such disparate thinkers as Cuernavaca's conservative Bishop Luis Cervantes Reynoso and the Chiapas liberation theologist Don Samuel Ruiz. Bishop Martín Rebago, delegate of the Mexican Episcopado or Catholic Bishops Council, to the Vatican's Doctrinal Congregation of the Faith, critiques the free market, go-get-em energies of the sects: "They give you what you want to hear."[18]

Much like the fast food purveyors, U.S. Protestants franchised out Mexico in the post-revolution (1919) Cincinnati Plan, whereby the various sects were assigned geographical regions in which to spread their version of the Gospel.[19] Today, the northern and southern border towns are the gateways for these heretics. Anthropologist Victor Clark Alfaro counts over 30 distinct U.S.-based Protestant churches operating in Tijuana's Colonia Libertad, butt up against the California line, and, on a Friday night in la Libertad, the storefront tabernacles of the Four Square Gospels, the Witnesses and the Adventists, the Salvation Army, and Pentecostal Holy Rollers, rock with old time religion. Also whacking their tambourines up in la Libertad: *Luz del Mundo* (Light of the World), an authentic Mexican Protestant sect, dating from the Cristiada, with headquarters in Guadalajara's Beautiful Providence colony and branches in 28 nations.

Polygamy-minded Mormons, amongst them the Ervil LeBaron clan, and German-Russian Mennonites (their last stop was Canada) have held vast tracts of land in northern Chihuahua for generations. Eastern cults have a sandal in the door too: the Hare Krishnas dance in Coyoacán plaza every Sunday and Sun Myung Moon's Unification Church operates subcutaneously around the Metro stations. Mexico City archbishop Norberto Rivera rails against Transcendental Meditation, Silva Mind Control, and the Church of Scientology for doing the work of the devil. But of all the sects, perhaps the most despised are the Jehovah's Witnesses whose 100,000 members refuse to salute the Mexican flag, a nose-thumbing at patriotic virtues that guarantees social ostracism and gets their kids expelled from school.

The Evangelicals are the most single-mindedly aggressive of these interlopers, unceasingly knocking on doors in the nation's most ravished slums and jamming their storefronts to overflowing while nearby cathedrals are abandoned. Their hook is birth control (they don't object), sobriety (alcohol is a ghastly social problem), and a literal interpretation of the bible that helps make sense out of an increasingly confusing society.

One afternoon, at the height of Zedillo's peso crisis, I hopped a beat-up bus out of Anapra, Chihuahua, a desert border outpost, where I had been interviewing bedraggled migrant workers about their reasons for heading north. Two preachers, who were buttonholing potential converts out in the same wilderness, thought it their business to proselytize me. The devaluation and economic crisis did not dismay them—Jehovah had foreseen such end-of-the-world chaos. It was all there in black and white, in Revelations. The pastors pounded the pages of their bibles to emphasize this economic analysis. The Gospel's ready-made answers to the humdrum evils of this world is what keeps the poor flocking to the Hallelujah *templos*.

Perhaps the most dramatic confrontation between Catholics and Protestants has unfolded over the past quarter of a century in the highland Chiapas Tzotzil Indian municipality of San Juan Chamula. 20,000 evangelical Chamulas have been evicted from their land and exiled from their communities because they refuse to conform to ultra-traditionalist Catholic ritual that even Samuel Ruiz's diocese, in which Chamula falls, rejects—mostly because it involves the imbibing of enormous quantities of "posh" or sugar-cane "white lightning" and the intense worship of many spurious saints. But the Protestantism of so sizable a sector of the Chamula people has a curious genesis that complicates the Catholic Church's "Satanization" of the sects as being "unMexican."

Unhappy with the domination the Papists exercised over the town when he passed through Chamula during his 1933 election tour of the nation, Lázaro Cárdenas invited the Protestants to set up shop in the Chiapas highlands. One group, the Summer Institute of Linguistics, under the tutelage of William Cameron Townsend, was invited to open a school. The Institute's specialty was indigenous language. Utilizing the Wycliffe bible methodology, Summer translators began to systematize written forms of various Indian languages. Townsend took full advantage of Cárdenas's antipathy towards the Catholic Church to establish missions in Morelos and throughout the southeast, before expanding into Guatemala. By the 1960s, of course, Summer was operating in indigenous zones throughout Latin America, having translated the New Testament into 39 distinct languages, and was often accused of being the eyes and ears of the Central Intelligence Agency in the region. The Institute's alleged participation in sterilization campaigns in indigenous communities got Summer kicked out of Ecuador and Panama in 1980. In 1979, after awarding Townsend the Aztec Eagle medal for meritorious service to Mexico, López Portillo severed all government contracts with Summer and its Mexico City offices became the target for a series of presumably nationalist bombings.[20]

Cárdenas's invitation to the Protestants took a cue from Benito Juárez who opened the doors to the more established Protestants (Presbyterians, Methodists, and Baptists) during the Reform, also to combat Catholic hegemony. Although he himself was a hard-core Mason, Juárez's portrait occupies a place of honor in the temples of the sects today. Modern Mexican politicos, many of them Masons like Juárez and Cárdenas, have not been adverse to staging religious dogfights in order to strengthen secular control. Contrary to the Church's firmly held belief that Protestantism is "unMexican," it is hardly Malinchista to reject one Christian tyranny by embracing another.

SANTA CLAUS IS COMING TO TOWN

The Church has much to lose in its crusade against the gringo-instigated Protestants and secularists. Control of the calendar is one area where Malinchista subversion presents a grave threat to Mexican Catholic values.

Christmas, for example, is a Christian holiday, vital to the celebration of a nest of religious occasions that keep Catholics busy a good part of the year. In Mexico, the passage of Mary and Joseph up to Bethlehem is marked by "posadas" (the nightly fiestas asking for lodging, at which piñatas are smashed open), *pastorelas* (stylized plays in which the Devil seeks to divert the three wise men from blessing the Christ Child), and *nacimientos* or crèches. Attending Midnight Mass on *Nochebuena* (Christmas Eve) is mandatory—but Xmas day draws a blank on the religious calendar. The Miracle of the Birth is not celebrated again until January 6th, Epiphany, the day the Kings reach Bethlehem and the traditional day for giving gifts. A *rosca* or cake ring, eaten in celebration of the Kings' arrival, contains a miniature Baby Jesús and if the finder is lucky enough not to swallow it or chip a tooth, he or she is required to hold a fiesta on February 3rd, *Candelaria*, the day upon which the Madonna took the Baby Jesús to the temple to be circumcised. All over Mexico City on Candelaria, women bundle up the ivory-skinned Christ doll from their crèches and carry them to the local parish for priestly blessing. So it goes, from one Christian day of observance to the next. The calendar gives the Church coherence.

That white-bearded, pink-skinned, round-bellied old Malinchista, Santa Claus, has, of course, changed the way Mexicans make their Christmas. Each year, out on the Alameda, a rare green space in the midst of downtown Mexico City traffic, the Santas line up the kids for photos against backdrops that picture sleighs and chimneys. But Santa does not yet have a monopoly on the concession. Melchor, Gaspar, and the black-faced Baltazar host not a few of the impromptu photo studios, decorated with replica camels and desert landscapes. Gifts are now exchanged under real plastic Christmas trees December 25th and again on January 6th, National Toy Day, when the Barbies and the G.I. Joes and the Power Rangers and the Tickle-Me-Elmos that have destroyed the Mexican toy industry, sell out every year, no matter how pessimistic the economic forecast.

This truce between commerce and religious devotion is again severely tested each autumn when the Days of the Dead come up against Halloween. All Souls and All Saints are Catholic calendar days that coincide with ancient Aztec celebrations of the dead, a conjunction that finds expression in the elaborate altars families and neighborhoods lovingly assemble to remember the departed.

Traditional foods and drink, and the spirited revelry of *calaveras*, or skeletons, make Los Diás de los Muertos, perhaps, the most Mexican of fiestas.

But in NAFTA-ized 1996, the Days were decidedly under siege from Halloween. At the Sonora market, the capital's one-stop *brujería* (witchcraft) supply center, where a U.S. reporter had paused to buy *papel picado* (stenciled paper, usually with calaveras incorporated in the design) and grinning spun sugar skulls that are de rigueur when building an altar, he was almost swept from his feet by a mob of parents and children snapping up the Frankenstein and Morticia and Madonna masks for Halloween trick or treating. "This is cultural pollution," responds the poet-ecologist Homero Aridjis to such Malinchismo. "They should save their money to buy flowers and bread for their dead…"[21]

Out in the sprawling Dolores Cemetery in the west of the city on November 2nd, the little monsters scrambled amongst the tombstones, shaking plastic jack-o'-lanterns stuffed with candy corn. "This comes to us from the United States," one 15-year-old Addams Family member told the *New York Times*, "we can take culture from wherever we want"—a statement of post-modern purpose that must have fortified Aridjis's dread of contamination. Meanwhile, the monsters' elders lounged on the graves of their defunct family members, weaving garlands of *cempaxuchtl* (marigolds), chugalugging pulque, and supping on rich turkey mole—all very Aztec pastimes.[22]

HIGH ART, LOW ART, DEEP ART—WHOSE ART?

The strength of cultural identity depends upon how tenaciously a people holds onto its history, and Mexicans never let go of theirs. The so-called American people, on the other hand, are notoriously forgetful—"historyless," writes Arthur Schlesenger, succinctly summing up North American amnesia.[23] Mexican history has weight and density, it is engraved in granite four millennia deep, while the United States writes theirs on the cellophane of single-digit centuries. U.S. cultural impositions can overlay Mexico but they can never obliterate it.

Let's go back into the movies for a moment. Between 1935 and 1985, approximately 12,000 Hollywood-made movies were flashed on Mexican screens[24]—a new title opened thrice weekly for 50 years. The frames were fat with demeaning images, purportedly injurious to one's revolutionary nationalism and "Mexicanidad:" Yanqui soldiers mowed down the darker people with jingoistic bravado, cowboys massacred Indians, Pancho Villa was made out a buffoon by Wallace Beery, Zapata didn't do much better by Brando. Mexicans were bloodthirsty bandits who didn't need no stinking badges or else servile little brown ones with beatific smiles pasted across their suffering faces. The silver screen dripped with stereotypes: Cisco was noble, Pancho was a *payaso* (clown), Zorro wasn't even Mexican. When tinseltown needed a movie Mexican, it went to the

Yiddish theater (Paul Muni in *Bordertown*, 1935—Bette Davis is nearly lynched for flirting with him). Mexican performers were wild Injuns (Gilberto Roland in *Apache War Smoke*) or "spitfires" (Lupe Velez, Johnny Weismuller's consort).[25]

Perhaps the movies' most damaging blows to Mexicanness were the props: the new cars and the well-stocked refrigerators and whirring washing machines that lured so many of the nation's youth northwards to Gavacholandia in the '50s and '60s. Yet, for all this celluloid brainwashing, Mexico remained thoroughly Mexican and even developed its own flourishing film industry as a counterweight to the Yanqui Dream Machine.

Beginning in the Cárdenas administration, the Mexican government built a cinema based on national ideals that hit its peak in the post-war Alemán boom: "La Doña," María Félix, and the scrawny singing charro, Pedro Infante, were the most luminous stars in the Mexican firmament, with Emilio "El Indio" Fernández passionately directing, and Gabriel Figueroa behind the camera, framing these dramatic black-and-white epics against Mexico's unyielding sky. Juan Orol's gangsters out Cagneyed Cagney and "El Santo," a masked wrestler, heroically defended the decent people from fedora-brimmed criminal-types. But it was the little runt Mario Moreno, aka "Cantinflas," who stole the show. Moreno made over 80 Mexican black-and-whites before he gained U.S. name recognition in Mike Todd's *Around The World In 80 Days* (as Phileas Fogg's faithful, clever servant, of course). Mirroring the left populism of the Cárdenas era in which he first garnered a following, Cantinflas was the Mexican Everyman, the vagabond or waiter or beat cop or much-abused mailman or lowly country priest at the bottom of the social barrel, whose only capital was his wits.

Idols like Cantinflas or TinTan (another high-flying wise guy) or "El Santo" are icons of popular culture, low art as opposed to the High Culture that is sanctified by the Instituto Nacional de Bellas Artes y Literatura, from whose sinking, rococo palace fine painting and ballet and symphonies, poetry and opera, resonate—such highbrow events are sometimes broadcast on giant screens to the rabble assembled in the street. The Museum of Popular Culture, located, significantly, just a few blocks from the Museum of Interventions in Coyoacán, is the Bellas Artes of low art, whose exhibits showcase boxers and masked wrestlers, the Mexican circus, the thieves'-kitchen barrio of Tepito, recreations of the *carpas* or tents in which Cantinflas first wowed the public, and comic book superheroes.

Despite the vigilance of the media migra, U.S. pop culture flies easily over tall border fences and mingles in the Mexican *caldo* (soup). The Superheroes are particularly adept at such leaps of faith. Superman and Spiderman and Batman have generations of aficionados south of the border and Mexico's own most long-lived superhero, Kalimán, a Hindu-type with hypnotic eyes whose motto is "Patience and Serenity," is not much of a match on the newsstands anymore.

To counter this Malinchista trend, Mexican superheroes are rising from the comics page and going into the barrios to take on real-life bad guys and defend the masses and, well, the animals too, from the depredations of such evils as the "mal gobierno" and the venomous air quality of Mexico City—Super Barrio and Super Animal and Super Ecologista are prominent examples of this very Mexican genre. The *Chupacabras* (literally "Goat-sucker"), a mythological beast that is enjoying popularity around Latin America these days, accompanies debtors' groups when they march on the Mexico City Bankers Club. These strangely masked and caped characters who today stride the capital's streets, build their personas on the movie and comic book hero "El Santo."

By putting on the mask, every market boy navigating his *diablito* (hand truck) through the labyrinthine La Merced market can re-make himself into a champ like El Santo, the Blue Demon, *Mil Máscaras* (1,000 Masks) or "El Perro" Aguayo. The mystique of the masque is profoundly Mexican—from the Aztecs to Subcomandante Marcos, putting on the mask has given the wearer supernatural powers. One loses this power when an opponent strips you of the mask.

Is wrestling high art or low? A Malinchista burlesque or an echo of the ancients? It is eminently dangerous for a rank outsider to tread into such cultural quicksand, but on this gringo's jaundiced palate, official art tastes like Taco Bell. The Ballet Folklórico, the nation's most successful cultural export, presents "typical" Indian dances, performed by non-Indians, for international consumption. The murals of Siqueiros and Rivera and Orozco are polished propaganda pieces, monumentalizing a government-authorized view of the Mexican continuum, that are being sold to the world's culture vultures as the epitome of Modern Art. Frida-mania overshadows Kahlo's work, which is masterful, even if outrageously solipsistic, and her annexation as the pet victim of the *gavachas* (Madonna is dying to play her in the movies) has made her more a North American feminist fetish than a Mexican artist.

For this gavacho, the highest Mexican art is that which is furthest from Bellas Artes, buried deep in México Profundo, where it is insulated from contamination by government and commerce: the miraculous huipiles of the Mayas; the beaded, mystical paintings of the Huicholes; the Holy Week Matachine dances of the Raramuri, are unannexed expressions of the real Mexican soul.

PLAY BALL!

Wrestling is not at its zenith in a post-NAFTA Mexican sporting world and there are serious concerns for its future as a popular spectacle. In 1990, the nation had over 500 wrestling venues. In 1996, that number has been reduced to 50. But even as Mexico's grapplers lose constituency, an unprecedented number of their compatriots are watching and playing "U.S." sports.

Beisbol, the Great American Pastime, is also the pastime of Caribbean states like Veracruz and Tabasco—and has been so for decades. Mexican players have been moving up to the big leagues since World War II: Melo Almada, who played with the White Sox during the 1940s, was Mexico's Jackie Robinson, several years before Robinson, and the Cleveland Indians' second baseman Bobby "Beto" Avila, a Veracruzano, was the first to win a World Series ring (1948). Mexico has its own major and minor leagues, which are fine-tooth-combed by the Bigs for talent. In 1997, a record 34 Mexican players were invited to major league training camps and ten made it past opening day, with Rockies' slugger Vinnie Castillo, of Juchitán, Oaxaca, perhaps the stand-out.

Many U.S. beisboleros play in Mexico too, mostly when their careers are on the way down or up—Negro League stars like Monte Irwin, Roy Campanella, and the immortal Josh Gibson[26] played in Mexico long before the color line was broken in the majors. Willie Mays Aiken, barred from the majors after an early '80s drug scandal, became Mexico's all-time Sultan of Swat.

The World Series slows business in Mexico City, especially if one of the featured squads is the Los Angeles Dodgers, Fernando Valenzuela's former team. When an aging Valenzuela, released by both the Padres and the Cardinals but still a national hero, took the mound against the Mets in Monterrey in August 1996, 60,000 fans stood on their seats and cheered.

Is baseball a cultural imposition? Some ardent nationalists will affirm that the sport has its origins in ancient Mexican ball games. Every Sunday, Mixtecos from Oaxaca gather on the fields of the Venustiano Carranza sports complex in eastern Mexico City to play Mixtec Ball, a game that seems to combine baseball (players wear padded leather catchers'-like mitts) and Ulama or Aztec hip ball. Now, the Oaxacan game has cross-pollinated and is being played by migrating Indians who have formed leagues around Merced, in California's Central Valley.

Basketball, the World Game, also borrows from Ulama or the Mayan Pelota, in that the ball must be put through a series of hoops. In recent years, B-ball has become a Mexican passion, played from one end of the nation to the next—Zapatista teams go at each other without mercy down in the Lacandón jungle. Each year, the National Basketball Association brings the stars to Mexico City for a round-robin tournament and seven-foot-tall Horacio Llamas, a Sinaloa behemoth, became the first Mexican to sit on an NBA bench in 1997—having tried out with the Lakers and the Hawks, Llamas finally got some minutes late in the season for the Phoenix Suns. Rumors of a Monterrey franchise have circulated for several years. Monterrey is only 150 miles from Texas where the NBA has three teams, facilitating scheduling—indeed, the Dallas Mavericks and the Houston Rockets played the first regular season NBA game ever staged south of the border, in 1997-98. Should such a fait be completed, the NBA would become NAFTA's first sporting enterprise.

Football is Mexico's national sport but not the kind practiced by the Oakland Raiders. American football is a wholly-owned Malinchista imposition that radiated from James Sheffield's pugnacious stint as U.S. ambassador back in the 1920s.[27] The Ambassador would be proud of the way American football has taken root here, particularly amongst the upwardly mobile. A university league, with teams taking their names from the NFL (the Redskins are a perennial winner) has been functional since the 1930s. Annual rivalry between the Pumas of the Autonomous University (UNAM) and the Burros of the National Polytechnic Institute (IPM) generates bloodshed and mass arrests every autumn with students hijacking buses, slinging crowbars, and tossing Molotov cocktails to cheer their teams on.[28] The Aztec Bowl (*Tazón Azteca*) has been played in Mexico City each December since the 1950s—the 1996 contest pitted Mexico against Palermo, Italy (the home team won 63-7).[29] Kids as young as six are playing Mexican-American football now, in Pop Warner leagues.[30]

But Mexicans watch a lot more American football than they play—at least two games are beamed in every Sunday and *Monday Night Football* has become a Mexican institution. The Dallas "Vaqueros" became Mexico's Team in the 1970s when they signed up a pair of Mexican place-kickers, first Efren Herrera, and then national idol "Super Mex," Rafael Septien—who was forced to retire early from the NFL, after being charged with fondling a teenage baby-sitter.

"Football" and "Futbol" are distinct dimensions here. Like most Malinchista phenomena, the former's appeal is limited to the upper middle class—only affluent families can afford to invest in the expensive equipment required for this brutal, complex game. Futbol, on the other hand, a sport that does not even require a ball (tin cans and old rags can be substituted), continues to be the national past time of Deep Mexico.

SMASHING ICONS

Strapped into a wheelchair that has been customized for sound, Guillermo Goméz Peña, the Guru of Gringostroika, is engaged in a chess match with Mexico's past. The giant board that spreads before him is stocked with life-sized Mexican icons ranging from Pedro Infante to Porfirio Díaz to the passionate, poetess-nun Sor Juana to Subcomandante Marcos, all of them (save for a kinetic, laptop-tapping Marcos) frozen in place. Throughout the piece, the *Performancero* conducts a simulated gun battle with a rangy woman seated on a toilet on the opposite side of the game board. The walls are somber with giant black velvet paintings of junkies shooting up heroin and low-rider music booms throughout the old museum, once Cortez's palace. Caught up in the crossfire and the electronic babble here at the 1996 Centro Histórico Cultural Festival, in the very heart of Tenochtitlán, the assault on Mexico's cardboard totems parsed subversion.

Mexico's icons are under siege from outside and within the culture. Fine blue agave tequila and ranchero music are consecrated items on the altar of Mexicanidad but in post-Tay-Elay-Say Mexico, tequila production is no longer fine (distilling is a rush job involving too much sugar, connoisseurs complain) and, anyway, 60% of production gets exported to the U.S.[31] Mezcal, the prized nectar of the Oaxaca sierra, is now the drink of choice in North America's coolest saloons—$7 USD a shot at Chicago's fashionable Frontera Grill.[32] Back home, the Mexican thirst for cactus juice is drying up. Riding slick TV campaigns (hard liquor is a big chunk of television advertising revenues), Bacardi rums and Domecq brandies have replaced the Indian brews as the national drugs.

Lilting, sentimental *mariachi* and *ranchero* music is another staple of the Mexican Experience that is being challenged by the icon smashers. While ranchero all-stars like "Chente" Fernández and Lucha Villa continue to drive the natives wild with their time-honored swoops and yips and syrupy violins, Juan Gabriel, the prince of ranchero pop, uses an electric band and U.S. doo-wop singers as back up. Astrid Haddad, who is given to ruby red lips and hooped china poblana skirts, converts ranchero singing into a bitter critique of the Mexican penchant for suffering—Haddad herself is of Lebanese descent. But even as younger artists tweak Mexican tradition, the global circle widens: Japanese mariachis now tour Mexico.

In a splendid *New Yorker* piece describing life among mariachis in the time of NAFTA[33], Alma Guillermoprieto prowls Garibaldi plaza in the capital's old quarter where the flamboyant musicians gather to croon 100-peso ballads for the turistas. At a rehearsal of itinerant mariachis, the players saw their way through "Son del Negro" and "El Rey" and then gather around the radio and tune into Mexico City's now-defunct Rock 101. The interlude epiphanizes the global moment—but Mexican rock is not necessarily Malinche's music.

Mexican youth has been lacerating the ears of their elders with rock and roll ever since Bill Haley first rocked around the clock. The movement that died at Tlatelolco rocked out on Dylan and Creedence Clearwater and the Beatles and the Doors, still signature sounds around here. The massacre insured rock's niche as anti-authoritarian, cop-fighting music. Avandaro, the Mexican Woodstock (more accurately, an Altamont-like disaster), held in 1971 in the upscale Valley of Bravo, culminated in widespread drug use and vandalism and scandalized the neighborhood. For years, U.S. rockers were kept from performing in Mexico for fear they would incite riot—Carlos Santana, a Mexican, could not play a note in Mexico City until the NAFTA '90s. A 1989 Black Sabbath concert in San Luis Potosí ended before it began when army troops boarded trains transporting kids to the show and shipped them home to their parents, their ears thoroughly boxed. Blues festivals brought out the mounted police.

Free trade turned the prohibitions on their tin ear. By 1994, Mexico City promoters were able to showcase Madonna and Michael Jackson in the same week, and when the Rolling Stones performed their Voodoo Lounge act at the González Brothers Autodrome in early 1995, the once riot-prone audience had grown gray and fat waiting 30 years for their appearance and there was little danger from the public.

But, while the royalty of international rock and roll no longer excites revolution, Mexican homegrown still offends the government's sense of decorum. Malinchista criteria plagued Mexican rock until he came along, modestly ahems Alex Lora, whose "Tri" has long (29 years) preserved the raw, wretched sound of national rock: "Because of us, a lot of Mexican musicians stopped trying to sound like gavachos and Englishmen".[34] Today, the most earnest indigenous rock is heard in the barrios of Mexico City's Azcapatzalco delegation or out in squatter cities like Nezahualcóyotl, when the *Chavas Bandas* (youth gangs) gather "down at the corner of Concrete Pillow and Dead Buzzard streets" (the lyric belongs to "Rockdrigo, the Prophet of Nopal," who disappeared during the 1985 Mexico City earthquake), where the cop-fighting lifeblood of Mexican rock rushes to the surface.

Another setting where the music exhibits its native attitude is at the Saturday *tianguis* (Aztec for "mall") in the San Cosme sector of the capital. "Mexican rock endures because it resonates with resistance," says Jorge Pantoja, who founded the bazaar in the early 1980s[35], echoing Bonfil's commentary on the survival of Deep Mexico in the global moment.

SPEAKING THE LANGUAGE

The Tube is the most seductive source of Malinchismo. Televisa, which operates four networks and hundreds of repeater channels, and its only competitor, TV Azteca, barrage the Mexican viewing public with U.S. sports, U.S. cop shows, U.S. sit-coms, Mexican spin-offs, wanna-be Oprahs, insipid pop rock, even a main dial shopping channel, and highly fallacious news broadcasts, oriented to the PRI's point of view. About the only programming that isn't modeled on gringo pap are the telenovelas, (soap operas), an indigenous art form, Jorge G. Castañeda opines.

Mexican telenovelas have achieved global popularity—soap stars like Veronica Castro are feted as far afield as the snows of Moscow. There is no way to exaggerate the fascination that soaps like *Norte del Corazon* (North of the Heart) and *Corazón Salvaje* (Savage Heart) have for Mexicans—even Subcomandante Marcos tunes in.[36] The characters become phantom members of already extended families as they stumble through their glamorously untidy lives and torturous love affairs. Recently, Ana Colchero, the star of *Nada Personal* (Nothing Personal), a progressive tearjerker put together by a group of left writers and film people, invoked national heartbreak when she quit the show with only 15 chapters to shoot, because she felt her role had been reduced to one of a victim.

Contemporary real-life heartbreak pervades the new telenovelas—Ricardo Aldape, a Mexican released after spending 15 years on Texas's Death Row, was written into the *Norte del Corazón* script within days of his release and achieved instant stardom. Historical figures too are starring in their own tele novelas— Porfirio Díaz and Padre Hildago have been the subjects of recent series. But no one has yet filmed perhaps the most tempestuously tawdry romance of them all—that of Cortez and La Malinche.

Nonetheless, La Malinche is on the Tube, she is in the malls, on the ball field, in your pocket, and on the tip of your tongue. The Malinche knows that who controls the language controls the culture. Mexicans are speaking more English every day—it is taught in grammar schools now and migrant laborers bring home a smattering. Televisa encourages the trend. 10% of all Mexicans are bilingual, estimates the PRI's pet intellectual, Héctor Aguila Camín, the upper 10%. Internet instructions are all in English and one must speak gavacho to be computer literate. Mexicans eat hot dogs, not *perros calientes, wachar* (to watch) is a popular border amalgam, "son of a bitch" a common expletive, and "but of course" is Sub Marcos's mode of exuding irony. For a few hundred years, Mexicans have been absorbing English, contorting it, and incorporating the contortions into secret slangs like *caló*.

Mexicans speak in many tongues, some of them so insular they may as well be secret, and these insular idioms have helped them to resist invasion and imposition. The Spanish and the English and the French and the North Americans all came to annex Mexico's land and soul and lingo and all failed miserably, for a fundamental reason: Mexicans like being Mexicans, like eating Mexican, speaking Mexican. "Few components of Meso-American culture have been so systematically and brutally violated as language, yet the number of speakers of indigenous language has grown in the last 70 years,"[37] writes Bonfil of Deep Mexico's linguistic resistance.

The refusal of Mexicans to embrace U.S. culture, along with Washington's political and economic mandates, is at the nub of the friction between these two incommodious neighbors. What is certain is that the annexation of Mexico by the United States of America can never be accomplished so long as Mexicans remember who they are and what languages they speak. "With differ- ent flags and languages they came to conquer us…they came and they went and we kept being Mexicans because we only want to walk around under a flag that has an eagle devouring a snake on it…" Marcos once wrote—in a letter to his North American supporters.[38]

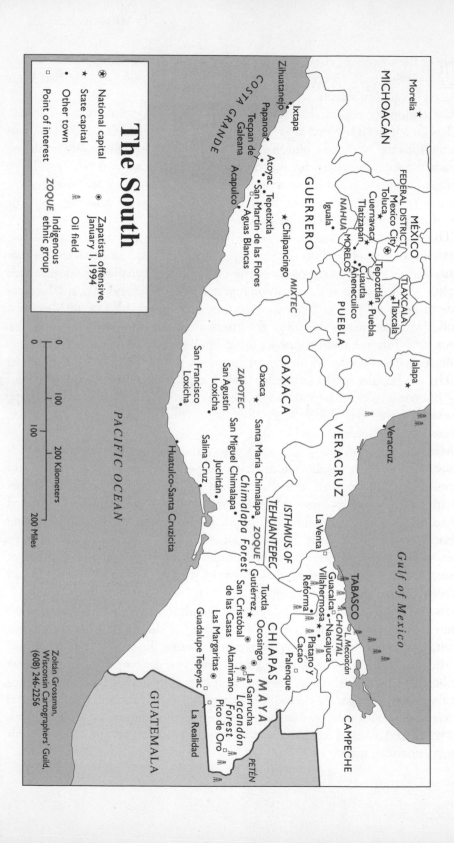

Chapter 16

LA COYUNTURA

The resistance of these diverse peoples that collectively call themselves Mexicans to the annexation of their lands and their lives by those who come from beyond their borders (*los de afuera*), runs like a bright red thread through the weave of history here. This tension between insularity and imposition from without, begins before history officially begins and extends in one unbroken band from the Chichimecas to the IMF. By the time the Aztec-Mexicas came to foist their bloody foibles upon surrounding territories, resistance was already a Mexican art form.

The Conquest itself, replete with Machiavellian treacheries, was a flawed effort to throw off one imperial yoke by substituting another. The new Lords of Anáhuac provoked an Indian uprising that they then crushed with massacre, plague, the bonfires of the Inquisition, and the images of the Virgin of Guadalupe. Down below, the irritation grew raw and painful and the suffering unified the many Mexicos—but, for centuries, little changed. Anger dripped in the subterranean chambers of the Mexican heart, buried deep beneath the rubble of the old gods and the syncretic claptrap of the new, until it blasted through to daylight in the volcanic eruption of fury behind the unlikely figure of Padre Hidalgo.

But the dream of sovereignty dissolved soon enough in pettiness and opportunism and authoritarianism. *Los de abajo* stayed there, stewing. New emperors came to feast on the carcass of this huge, enormously rich, indescribably poor nation, fighting over the scraps like the rapacious gulls up in Tijuana's grand guignol of a garbage dump. The United States inflicted the most profound wounds.

Mexican anger has a peculiar metabolism. It pulses slowly and craftily hides the accumulation of rage. It is chained up behind a wall of excessive politeness, always cause for alarm. Vengeance is plotted just beneath the imperturbable stoicism of the mask, of which Paz makes so much. "Aguantar"—to endure, is maybe the most descriptive verb on the Mexican palate. Pronounced with cynical resignation, it seems to say "we must wait for the right moment to take revenge..." But such gut-wrenching anger (Mexicans suffer from multiple stomach disorders) can only be contained for so long. The tiniest incident can lance this festering ulcer: a fender-bender in Mexico City traffic, an argument in the sweltering plaza of Acapulco, an inflection, an order, shouted in Spanish or English, directed at a taxicab driver or a railroad worker or an indocumenta-do running for his or her life on the Bordo, and the conflagration could get general very quickly. This does not happen very often, every hundred years on history's timetables if 1810 and 1910 are to be considered watersheds of upheaval, but the possibility that violence can blow up at any given moment adds a certain piquancy to life in the Mexican pressure cooker.

Don Porfirio kept the lid sealed tight for 34 years and the ferocious blood-letting that ensued when it blew, dealt those who would annex Mexico a whole new hand. Now, the North Americans sought to conquer its southern neighbor through friendship rather than frontal invasion. Washington declared war on the world and fought three of those wars with Mexico on its side. Meanwhile, the U.S. usurped the economic life of the nation. Mexicans were transformed into committed consumers with real plastic credit cards. They became Dallas Cowboys fans, and dined on Big Macs. Now they could be Just Like Them, the Outsiders, the Strangers, the Gavachos and the Gringos. Carlos Salinas invited his undernourished compatriots to sit at the First World's table.

To advance its ambition of domination, the White House never failed to authenticate any despotic ruler who could keep in check those opposed to the annexation of the Mexican nation. Huerta was installed to replace the mar-tyred Madero, Zapata was gunned down at Chinameca in 1919; his heir, Rubén Jaramillo, and his whole family, slaughtered by the state in 1962; Arturo Gamiz cut down in '65; Lucio Cabañas in '74; Genaro Vázquez and Lucio Cabañas and thousands of Indians and farmers martyred behind them. The resistance did not die under the corpse heap at Tlatelolco but flourished instead and the killing fields blossomed new flowers. Death only breathed life into this struggle. Resistance in Mexico is always built upon the premise that one must die to lib-erate the Patria—and that such a death is the only liberation because, in the end, it is the only death that won't sell you out. Mexicans always fight *hasta las últimas consequencias* (until the ultimate consequences). Subcomandante Marcos was so sure that all of the Zapatistas would die in their suicidal January 1st, 1994 attacks, that he has been breathing on borrowed time ever since.

The Zapatista struggle against the new annexation of Mexico is yet another outcropping of the endless band of resistance that is at the essence of what it takes to be Mexican. Today, the annexers are called "neo-liberals" and "global-izers" and their methodology is economic integration and free trade that turns Mexico into one gargantuan maquiladora, rips the land out from under the farmers, impoverishes the urban multitudes, and fills the bellies of a dozen Mexican billionaires.

It is appropriately Mexican that the wellspring of this resistance should come from the campesinos, who are often themselves indigenous peoples. They are, like the tiny, bird-like Zapatista comandante Ramona, "the smallest of the small," those who live closest to the earth. It is their very specific defense of place that pits them against the greed of the globalizers, a defense of what has been theirs for all the millennia it has taken to make Mexico. Such resistance is still a question of the smallest against all the rest, the weak against the all-powerful, the village against the state, the corn patch against the World Bank, the guerrilla against the U.S.-supplied military. This is a class war as much as it is a war of national liberation.

I have been covering this war for a long time, decades, and my heart still sails whenever I catch news of a wildcat strike or a sit-down in the middle of a road or the emergence of a new guerrilla in some remote sierra or jungle. I try to get there while the track is warm, hopping the next bus or the next truck ride or just hoofing it in on foot if there is no less strenuous mode of locomotion. I've slept in a lot of villages whose names never escape me or sometimes rough out in the bush, a glutton for punishment. I have grown old chasing revolution in Mexico but I haven't been bored. Although I usually get my story, most of what I write appears in alternative publications and special interest journals and not much is seen, much less demanded, by a wider public. Those who control the U.S.-Mexico sector of the global media are not interested in my message. Resistance does not lure investment. Indians are poor consumers. Rebellion is bad for business.

Nonetheless, since the Zapatista uprising and NAFTA locked in on the same New Year's night in 1994, I have been kept moving, shifting from one battleground to the next as this coming-together (*La Coyuntura*) of resistance struggles around the country, solidifies and deepens. The datelines themselves form a length of that unbroken band upon which Mexican history is written: Tepoztlán and Tabasco; in the sierra above Guerrero's Costa Grande; on the streets of Mexico City with El Barzón and the Ruta 100 bus drivers and the diehard garbage workers of Villahermosa; in the forests of the Chimilapas, and the heart of the Lacandón, where the Zapatistas, those indigenous Quixotes, fight to liberate the land from the neo-liberal curse and New World-Ordered annexation. Here, then, is history happening.

JACK NICKLAUS VS. EMILIANO ZAPATA
THE GOLF WAR
(TEPOTZLÁN, MORELOS 1910-1996)

There are 24,000 golf courses currently in operation on the face of the planet, each course covering an average of 250 acres[1], a global total of 5,000,000 acres of good, food-growing, soil dedicated to this absurd game where the affluent, sometimes in knickerbockers, whack away at a little white ball for hours on end. Most of these courses are privately owned and operated and open to only an elite clientele. Golf is the executive game. Despite Tiger Woods' exploits, Golf is a White Man's Game. Most of all, Golf is a First World Game.

"We do not play golf in Tepoztlán—it is not a part of our tradition," Lázaro Rodríguez, the Emiliano Zapata lookalike who was then the president of that unique community's "Free, Popular, and Constitutional" town council (*ayuntamiento*), dead-panned to me one day in the autumn of 1995, as if no further explanation were needed to tell how what we reporters were calling "The Golf War" had combusted.

Outside, the walls of the town hall blazed with slogans and symbols: "Tierra y Libertad," "No to Golf!," "No to Bourgeois Caprice!," and just simply "No" —the unanimous response of Tepoztecos to national and international investors, under the aegis of the Mexican KS Corporation, who were trying to site a very First World golf course on 187 hectares of community land.

BOURGEOIS CAPRICE

The KS design included 800 condominiums and "chalets" to be made available to jet-setting execs in a well-groomed, well-guarded enclave set in what the developers' handouts colored as "a natural paradise."[2] The crown jewel of this sumptuous subdivision would be an 18-hole U.S. Professional Golfers' Association-approved course to be created by multi-champion Jack Nicklaus's Florida-based Golden Bear Course Management, Inc. A golf academy was in the wings. The Tepozteco Gulf and Country Club would also feature swimming pools, tennis courts, and a full-service hotel with its own heliport. One could buy in by picking up five lots at $550,000 USD each. A minimum package of seven five-lot clusters ($3.85 million) guaranteed you a seat on the Tepozteco's board of directors. "We want to attract true leaders of opinion," KS advertised.[3]

Also on the drawing board: GTE-Data Systems' adjoining "smart" industrial park. *El Recinto* would be computerized, equipped with satellite communication devices. Technicians would work on flex time to develop fiber optic products for GTE's entrance into the NAFTA-opened Mexican long distance market. Total investment in the Tepozteco was expected to come in a bit under a half-billion Yanqui dollars, $130 million of which GTE-Data Systems would pick up.[4]

For its developers and investors, the Tepozteco represented a giant leap of faith in Mexico's new "First World" status. KS described the project as "a national and international model, demonstrating the concept of integral urban living, based on the premise of harmony and respect for nature," a high-minded notion.[5] For the then-fledgling government of Ernesto Zedillo, the Tepozteco was "a new model of development," a test case for converting agricultural lands in Morelos and Puebla, Tlaxcala, and Hidalgo into high-tech industrial parks within driving distance of the capital—a land conversion process now blessed by the revisions to Article 27 of the Constitution which allows communities and ejidos to sell their birthright to transnational corporations.

The Brave New World of NAFTA would draw software manufacturers and generate much-needed jobs (13,000 construction jobs were promised) in an area of the nation where poverty is endemic, boosted Jaime Alatorre, president of the quasi-governmental Mexican Investment Council and himself a big investor in the Tepozteco.[6] For Tim Kenny, vice-president of Golden Bear Course Management, which already operated 120 courses in 21 countries, the Tepozteco would be a first opportunity to show its stuff in the heart of Mexico (Golden Bear operates a Cabo San Lucas, Baja California club). And for GTE-Data Systems CEO Don A. Hays, well, he was "just happy to be part of Mexico's future."[7] Which Mexico Mr. Hays had in mind was clear.

What GTE failed to realize is that, although telephone communications is the most global of enterprises, there are few people who are more local than the Tepoztecos.

FOUR MILLENNIA OF RESISTANCE

The indigenous Nahua community of Tepoztlán has occupied this stony wedge of land for 4,000 years, according to local lore and carbon dating. Tepozteco warriors took on the Aztecs whenever their armies sallied forth from the Valley of Mexico and attacked from the heights of the Chichinautzín Sierra above. Tepoztlán's sheltered geographical location under the angular walls of the mountains made it a natural fortress and the rockiness of the soil did not make its lands the most appealing ones to steal from the natives—few European sugar speculators built their haciendas there during the Porfiriato, as they did next door in the Cuautla Valley. When the revolution impended, Tepoztlán's independent town council supported Madero and its members were hauled off to slave labor camps in Quintana Roo by the Dictator.[8] Emiliano

Zapata, a native of Anenecuilco, near Cuautla, controlled Tepoztlán for a decade, which guaranteed the Liberator of the South a back door down to Milpa Alta, Xochimilco, and the capital itself.

The revolution brought glory and grief to Tepoztlán—Huerta and Carranza's killer, General Pablo González, rapined with gusto and the town's population was reduced from 8,000 to 2,000 between 1910 and 1920. Despite their losses, the Tepoztecos never backed down. In the 1920s, the Bolshevik Farmers Union won 23,000 hectares of land to be held in perpetuity by the community.[9] In 1962, Tepoztecos turned back another golf course. In 1979, they banded together to beat off a ski lift that would have taken tourists to the top of the dizzying spire of rocks from which the town takes its name, an indigenous power spot that still attracts scads of shamans, swamis, boy scouts, and hippies. In 1989, townfolk nixed a ring road extending from nearby Cuernavaca, and in 1991, a scenic railroad proposal was turned back.

During his trek through Mexico in the 1930s, the U.S. writer Carleton Beals found inspiration in Tepoztlán's rugged resistance to extraneous imposition and asked of it: "Will you still be as self-sufficient and heroically independent a hundred years from now?" Although the century mark has not yet been reached, if recent history is a valid guide, the answer appears to be an unequivocal yes.[10]

A FIGHTING FLUID

The tiny state of Morelos is cursed by geography. Just south of the most congested capital on the planet, its community-held agricultural land has been relentlessly invaded by developers building second-home showcases for upwardly mobile city slickers. In the Atongo Valley, at the head of which sits Tepoztlán, U.S. developer Charles Stephens began buying up farmland in the 1950s—although it was prohibited to so transfer such lands.[11] As private residences sucked up water, irrigation systems dried up, and today, there is so little liquid that the faucets of the townspeople only function about half the time. Water is a fighting issue in Morelos.

The county seat of Tepoztlán (14,000 residents) counts with only one spring, producing just 12 liters a second, explains Anastacio Solís, who functioned as Mayor Lázaro's public works director—such a source does not even qualify for aquifer status which, says engineer Solís, requires more than 40 liters a second. In order to keep Jack Nicklaus's greens shimmering, KS would need 3,110,500 liters a day of the precious fluid, more than five times the daily allotment of the entire town.[12] Although KS insisted that it had discovered a second aquifer to water its course, Tepoztecos were profoundly suspicious that drilling would drain off what little the town spring now gurgled.

TIERRA Y LIBERTAD

KS's right to the land itself would be a first test of the revisions to Article 27. Following Stephens' model, the developers had been quietly, illegally, buying up lots here and there for years. To compound the crime, KS had sited the Tepozteco Golf and Country Club inside the borders of both the Chichinautzín Sierra environmental corridor and the Tepozteco National Park, created to the delight of Mexican rock climbers in the 1930s, by Lázaro Cárdenas.

Despite such infringements, newly-elected governor Jorge Carrillo Olea boasted, in a March 1995 letter to the developers, that he would personally guarantee the granting of state and federal permits needed for construction[13]—as former director of National Security and Salinas's drug czar, Carrillo has plenty of juice in the upper echelons of the bureaucracy. Actually, most permits were sewed up—both Carlos Salinas and his alter ego, José María Córdoba, owned property in and around the municipality of Tepoztlán. But one document that remained outstanding was permission for a change of soil use that had to be issued by the local town council. Knowing the perpetual resistance of the Tepoztecos to such projects, Carrillo imposed his own candidate, Alejandro Morales, as the PRI municipal president.

A GIFT OF GOD

The first shots in the Golf War were fired next door March 10th, 1995, at the swank El Camino Hotel over in Cuernavaca. KS director Francisco Kladt unveiled the floor plans, and the governor and a handful of investors beamed their pearly whites—Mexican investors reportedly include Ricardo Salinas Pliego, owner of Televisión Azteca (a Carlos Salinas gift), a stand-in for former president Echeverría, and Luis Slim, nephew of the richest man in Latin America.[14] Cuernavaca bishop Luis Cervantes Reynoso, an arch-conservative appointed to clean out the residue of liberation theology leftover from Red Bishop Sergio Méndez Arceo's long reign over that diocese, anointed the Tepozteco Golf and Country Club as "a gift from God that has fallen from the heavens."[15] The Bishop's car was later pelted with fruit by angry townsfolk.

3,000 unhappy Tepoztecos immediately gathered in front of their town hall to demand that Morales not grant the change of soil use permit—although the Mayor promised that he would never do such a thing, he had probably already signed off on the document.

THE SHOWDOWN

The showdown came at the end of July '95, after Secretary of Natural Resources Julia Carrabias gave the project the green light, KS claimed that all its permits were now in order, displaying the soil use document that had been signed in secret by Morales and five PRI town council members. Construction would begin immediately—heavy equipment was moved onto the site in mid-August. Aroused Tepoztecos, wielding machetes, clubs, and rusty shotguns, assembled on the steps of town hall to demand Morales's scalp—the now ex-mayor fled out of the back door and has never been back to town since.

Tepoztlán was feverish with rumor. On September 2nd, the newly formed Tepoztlán Unity Committee (CUT) broke up a highly suspicious private meeting between state officials and the president of the town's communal lands (*Bienes Comunales*), took five of Carrillo's representatives hostage, and paraded them through the steep streets with nooses around their necks. The governor grew choleric. At a September 8th town meeting, CUT militants threatened to trash and burn the equipment KS had moved onto the contested land. The next day, Secretary Carrabias reversed herself and suspended the project. Kladt showed up that night on Jacobo Zabludowsky's lie-laced *24 Hours* to whine that the environmental secretary's actions would drive foreign investors from the country, a broad hint that GTE was already re-thinking its involvement.

ZAPATA'S RETURN

The next weeks were festive ones in this peculiar community where Nahua farmers mix with prominent intellectuals and writers—Carlos Fuentes, Jorge Castañeda, and Adolfo Aguilar Zinser are all part-time residents and American anthropologist Oscar Lewis (*Five Families, The Children of Sanchez*) was a fixture for years. The Tepozteco art scene attracts bohemian elements and the scent of patchouli sometimes overwhelms the plaza.

But on the second Sunday of September, 1995, Tepoztlán returned to the root. The campesinos trooped in from the countryside to celebrate the suspension of the golf club with tamales and corridos and cries of "¡Viva Zapata, Cabrones!" According to a *La Jornada* report that day, old men had sighted the caudillo himself, up there in the sierra, atop his prize mount, "As de Oro."[16]

September 15th and 16th were days to commemorate the independence of the municipality as well as the one Hidalgo and his successors had won for the nation. On the 24th, elections were held to select Morales's successor and Rodríguez, a woodcarver and tree planter who heads a local volunteer forestry brigade, "Los Tajones" (the Badgers), was selected with nearly all of the 6,000 votes cast, a record. "Chinpi," as his neighbors know him, did not even possess a valid voting credential. He took office immediately.

LOW-INTENSITY WARFARE

Governor Carrillo was not pleased. He withdrew recognition of the town's new government, cut off its state budget, and sent a hundred police to patrol the perimeters of Tepoztlán, an exhibition of low-intensity golf warfare. Chinpi and the CUT organized to repel the coming aggression. Unpaid volunteers took over Tepoztlán's municipal functions. Barricades were thrown up on the three roads leading into town to keep police and provocateurs out, and the barrios assigned shifts to man and woman (women play a leadership role in Tepoztlán) the checkpoints. The priest, Filiberto González, was enlisted to bang the big brass bell in the churchyard as summons to self-defense when the town was attacked. "Tepoztlán has lived a history of oppression and trickery, treason and manipulation, abandonment and injustice—we are justified to rebel. The people are tired..." Padre Filiberto, a disciple of Méndez Arceo, expounded to reporters.[17]

The gunfire finally broke out December 2nd in Tepoztlán's low-slung market, a space crowded with flowers and fresh produce and embroidered fabric. Former mayor Morales's uncle, Pedro Barragán, incensed because his butcher shop had just been firebombed, stalked the aisles, brandishing pistols. Someone shot him in the back with an automatic weapon—many witnesses identify the victim's brother, Gabriel, as having tripped and fired accidentally.[18] The Free, Constitutional, and Popular Ayuntamiento's volunteer police disarmed the perpetrators and, later, turned the weapons over to the state as proof of who the real killers were. But the bloodshed had given Carrillo a pretext to enforce law and order.

The citizens of Tepoztlán began to disappear. A pair of taxi drivers and a teacher—both groups form the backbone of the CUT—were seized by state judicial police when they ventured outside of the town limits. Professor Gerardo Demesa was taken at his union headquarters in Cuernavaca and the offices ransacked by *judiciales* under the command of Jesús Miyasawa, a legendary torturer to those who follow the repression industry here. Several days later, 15,000 maestros marched through Cuernavaca to demand Demesa's release (he is still in jail at this writing), the largest protest in that provincial capital in recent memory.

Throughout the winter, tensions inside Tepoztlán climbed steadily. Small planes flew overhead and dropped unsigned leaflets that attacked CUT leader Adela Bocanegra. Carnival, celebrated in Tepoztlán since before the Conquest, with masked Chinelo dancers, was canceled because it was feared police agents would use the occasion to steal into town in disguise. The spring planting came next on the calendar year, but first it would be time to honor Zapata.

"¡PINCHE REVOLTOSOS!"

Nowhere else in Mexico is the anniversary of the betrayal and assassination of Emiliano Zapata more solemnly observed than in his home state of Morelos. Each April 10th, the martyrdom of the caudillo is marked in town squares and local churches with a fervency not distinct from that shown for another revolutionary martyr, whose own betrayal and crucifixion is remembered during Holy Week, a date never very far away from the date of Zapata's own martyrdom, under the guns of the Carranza government.

This April 10th, as is municipal tradition, an embattled Tepoztlán would reaffirm its commitment to Zapatista ideals by touring the nearby villages and cities where the Liberator had left his indelible footprints.

Chinpi and Bocanegra took the initiative and rented buses from the Ometochitl line to follow the "Route of Zapata." Under their mothers' watchful gazes, the children, costumed as 1910-style "Emilianos" and "Adelitas," sang songs as they boarded the buses. 500 Tepoztecos took the journey from their county seat to Cuautla, where Zapata's tomb stands tall in the Plaza of the Southern Revolution, to Anenecuilco, his birthplace, to Ayala where he first pronounced his agrarian program, to the Chinameca hacienda inside whose walls he was ambushed by the turncoat colonel Jesús Guajardo. At each station of this Via Cruces, the Tepoztecos laid floral wreaths and the children recited popular verses.

But when the caravan turned east towards Tlatizapán, the site of General Zapata's military headquarters, where President Ernesto Zedillo was delivering an address to a hand-picked group of PRI-affiliated farmers, the Tepoztecos were turned back by a phalanx of state police agents. An elite brigade, known as "Los Negros," blocked the two-lane highway near San Rafael. The April sun cooked tempers.

The Zapatistas of Tepoztlán were determined to continue on towards Tlatizapan and deliver a letter to Zedillo, reiterating their opposition to the infamous golf course. But when they tried to circumvent the police line on foot, they were set upon with exceptional violence. Elderly citizens, women, and children were beaten so badly they required hospitalization—one of the victims was reportedly a granddaughter of Zapata. "This will teach you to yell 'Viva Zapata,' pinche revoltosos! (you damn revolters!)" Los Negros snarled.[19]

The violence continued unabated into the evening. Vehicles were destroyed and 11 civilians wounded by police gunfire. 64-year-old CUT leader Marcos Olmedo was shot to death on the scene, his body trussed up in a burlap sack and discarded in an open field 20 kilometers away. 24 Tepoztecos, 15 of them women and their kids, were arrested and held incommunicado, and the press and local medical workers were kept from the scene by the police for eight hours. The police presence is said to have been requested by Zedillo's elite presidential guard, the Estado Mayor.

JACK NICKLAUS CRIES UNCLE

At first, Governor Carrillo denied that his officers were armed or that any deaths had occurred during the fracas. Describing the police stop as "normal procedure," Carrillo accused the CUT of inciting police repression—"they just wanted a martyr," he told *La Jornada*.[20]

The surprise appearance of a four-minute, homemade videotape that graphically illustrated police culpability, put the lie to the Governor's version. The video, one of several that have emerged, Rodney King-like, in the wake of recent police misbehavior, was shown at Olmedo's wake on the steps of town hall two nights later. Those with long memories recalled another death, 34 years previous: the maestro Esteban Flores, a local teacher who had opposed the construction of another golf course, the Monte Castillo, to have been sited on the same communal lands KS now wanted to develop. His body was found May 12th, 1962, just outside of town, perforated by 19 gunshots.[21] After Flores' death, the developers, fearful of retaliation, called off their golf course.

History has a habit of repeating itself in Tepoztlán. Now GTE-Data Systems pulled out of the Tepozteco, taking a third of the proposed investment with it—the U.S. corporation needed to get to work if it was going to win a chunk of the long distance market and the Golf War wasn't going away. A downcast Francisco Kladt went before the TV cameras to whine that what had happened April 10th was "the last straw…the project is being held hostage by these conflicts…investors don't want anarchy"—KS would take a $6 million USD bath on the Tepozteco debacle.[22]

NO END TO THIS HISTORY

Has KS really put the scheme to rest? The corporation has issued no written statement to substantiate Kladt's bitter withdrawal and Tepoztlán remains, as always, vigilant. It still says "Tierra y Libertad" and "No to Golf!" and just "No!" on the walls of the town hall. Meanwhile CUT members travel over the mountain down to Xochimilco where another golf course is threatened, to help their neighbors strategize. In March 1997, Tepoztlán felt confident enough to participate in state elections and their rebel "Free, Popular, and Constitutional" form of government was reluctantly recognized by the governor.

Tepoztlán remains a power spot of resistance against the New World ordure. Now community fury is directed at the Quinta Piedra, a 47-hectare hacienda, owned by the reviled Salinas's former brother-in-law and built on what the campesinos denounce as illegally-obtained ejido land. When local farmers reclaimed the Quinta Piedra in May 1996, they were astonished to discover that, behind the estate's six-meter-tall walls, were fountains at play, two swimming pools, and an artificial lake. The ejido itself (it is distinct from the community), has no irrigation system and the colony that borders the Quinta Piedra does not feature running water.

Squatting at a campesino checkpoint outside the hacienda—which the farmers have renamed the Casa del Pueblo (House of the People)—95-year-old Pablo García Ruiz spat into the dust on a dry September afternoon: "Without water, you can't grow corn…" Like many old men here, García claims to have ridden with Zapata. "In that time, we didn't have land. Many people died for this land. Now we have it but we can't grow anything on it because they steal our water. We are the campesinos, we have a right to our water," the veteran stammered. "If Zapata was alive, he would be with us today…"

THE GOSPEL VS. NEO-LIBERALISM
WHOSE OIL? WHOSE RIGHTS?
(TABASCO IN TURMOIL—1958-1997)

Mexican oil remains the object of U.S. annexation fixations. In a rush to pay off the Clinton administration's $12.5 billion USD bail-out of the Zedillo regime, almost 90% of the 1996 1.4 million-barrel-a-day export platform was shipped north[23], despite prohibitions on dealing any one nation more than half of export production. This frenzy to get its highly-prized Olmeca out of the ground and the ocean floor in order to satisfy U.S. hunger for Mexican cash and oil has not been salubrious for the health of many Mexicans and their land, particularly in the once-Edenesque entity of Tabasco.

With its 76 producing fields, Tabasco is the nation's oil state, bar none. Of 3,588 wells drilled in that southern state since 1958, 1,013 are still putting out petroleum[24]—540,000 barrels of it a day, the top land-based production on PEMEX's inventories.[25] Pipelines that carry the crude from well to processing plants snake through 5,044 hectares of tropical Tabasco.[26] Their ever-present danger make the farmers through whose properties they pass more than a little nervous.

PLÁTANO Y CACAO
Ernesto Martínez planted himself in the middle of the lush field of sawgrass and visualized the disaster that, in February 1995, struck the tiny farming community of Plátano y Cacao ("Bananas & Cacao beans," once the rancho's prized products): "There was a house there, right next to the gas line. When the fireball hit, six people were turned to ashes. The rest of us ran but we didn't all make it." The leathery farmer paused, remembering how the flesh of one of his neighbors came off in strips in his hands, when he rushed to help him.

"This wasn't right. Depriving people of their own life, making them suffer like that, it's a violation of their human rights..."

On February 16th, 1995, a 36-inch pipeline, one of 29 PEMEX ducts that form what locals call "a devil's knot" around this close-knit community in the swampy, oil-rich center of the state, blew sky-high, killing nine of Mr. Martínez's neighbors and gravely injuring 23 more. Months later, investigators hired by PEMEX's insurers would determine that the line that blew was worn to half its thickness by corrosion and internal pressures. The underground pipeline had not been inspected since it was laid, 27 years ago.[27]

In a precedent-setting decision, the results of which were published in October 1996, the National Human Rights Commission (CNDH) determined that PEMEX had violated the human rights of the residents of Plátano y Cacao—the first time a government-sponsored entity has dared to take the national petroleum conglomerate to task for destroying the lives and the land of Mexican citizens.[28] The CNDH recommendation was issued in response to a petition filed by the grassroots Tabasco human rights group whose initials are CODEHUTAB and whose president is Francisco Goitia, Plátano y Cacao's Jesuit priest. Mr. Martínez, a man driven by what he sees as a violation of fundamental human guarantees by the giant petroleum corporation, is the CODEHUTAB's secretary.[29]

"WHEN THE LAND IS VIOLATED, OUR RIGHTS ARE VIOLATED"

"You see how green it is now? Nature is coming back. But the ground is poisoned with heavy metals. We are farmers. When the land is violated, our rights are violated—our right to work, to feed ourselves and our children, to protect their health"—Tabasco has one of the highest child leukemia rates in Mexico. "The people here don't know when this will happen again. PEMEX has violated our right to peace and tranquility..."

CODEHUTAB is one of hundreds of independent human rights coalitions that have sprung up all over Mexico since the creation of the CNDH in 1992—at the time, the Commission was considered a Salinas gimmick to silence criticism by international human rights groups that threatened to impede NAFTA negotiations. Such groups as the Mexican Academy for Human Rights, the National Human Rights Network All for All, the Mexican League for the Defense of Human Rights, the Mexican Commission for the Defense & Promotion of Human Rights, Catholic human rights centers run by the Dominicans and the Jesuits, and Chiapas-based groups like COMPAZ and the Fray Bartolomé Center have borne witness to and become critical players in the conjunction of socioeconomic collapse, global ambitions, and the emergence of resistance groups that Mexican politilogues never tire of labeling La Coyuntura.

RAIN OF DEATH

The 1995 explosion at Plátano y Cacao was not the first to rock that rancho. On Christmas eve 1986, a similar accident injured scores and carbonized fields for half a kilometer on both sides of the blast. The Plátano y Cacao blowouts are just two on a list of 36 explosions that have killed over 200 Tabasqueños since 1976.[30]

30 kilometers east of that ill-starred community, right on the Tabasco-Chiapas line, Reforma smacks of the grit that signals a Mexican oil town. At 2 pm on a Saturday afternoon, grimy men in jumpsuits and orange hard hats tramp through the streets to wash up for a few hours of rest and relaxation. In the red-brick plaza, a fast-talking huckster sells modern electric stoves off a truck to the relatively well-paid "petroleros" and their wives. Above the central square, a huge siren tower spires into the sweltering tropical sky, to remind townsfolk of the dangers that lurk nearby.

On July 26th, 1996, the siren tower signaled big-time trouble. Two out of the five gas processing plants at PEMEX's Cactus petrochemical complex, a 300-hectare enclave on the edge of town where the arroyos run a deep yellow and the odor of gas still fills the nose, had blown up, killing six workers and injuring 33 others—Reforma's mayor at first insisted many deaths had gone unreported.[31] The blast destroyed every structure within a 500-meter radius.

The damage done to Mexico's burgeoning natural gas production was impressive too. Cactus processed a third of the nation's natural gas, virtually all of its methane (used to power industry), and a good part of southern Mexico's propane, or home gas, supply. The temporary loss of the Cactus facilities forced PEMEX to import about $130 million worth of gas from the U.S. for each day the processors were off line. Total rebuilding costs were expected to top $200 million, according to PEMEX director Adrian Lajous.[32] Consumers would bear the brunt of the disaster as home gas prices climbed 100% in just six months.[33]

But the most disastrous outfall from the Cactus blow-out was what was now drizzling from the sky. With worldwide petroleum prices zooming to $26 a barrel during the summer of 1996, PEMEX began extracting all the crude it could feasibly pump. But because it had lost Cactus processing capacity, the oil giant had to flare off massive quantities of highly sulfurous natural gas that must be separated from the crude oil before it can be pumped, sending enormous amounts of contaminants into the heavens, from which it would later return as acid rain. In the first 36 days following the explosion, according to a study conducted by the Mexican chapter of Oil Watch, an international monitoring group, 18 billion cubic feet were flared off the daily petroleum output, releasing 940,000 tons of carbon dioxide and 13,700 tons of sulfur dioxide into the atmosphere over Tabasco and Chiapas.[34]

BAD PAPAYAS

The all-powerful Article 27 places Mexico's petroleum reserves "under the dominion of the nation" but, under that dominion, PEMEX, whose expropriation by Lázaro Cárdenas still burns fiercely in the hearts of patriots, has irreparably destroyed significant areas of that nation.

The pipeline blasts only add to the appalling blight that has crept across Tabasco since PEMEX began drilling in these swampy grounds. In the 40 years since President Adolfo Ruiz Cortines inaugurated the gleaming new PEMEX City complex in 1958, the petroleum conglomerate has so thoroughly contaminated Tabasco's rivers that fish are no longer fit for human consumption. Acid rain has eaten away hundreds of thousands of acres of fruit land—a widely-quoted Chapingo Agrarian University study classifies a third of Tabasco's land area as being "gravely damaged."[35] PEMEX engineers have scooped open canals, poisoning fresh-water lagoons with 250,000 tons of salts.[36] Oil slicks strangle the coastline and the contamination touches the national food chain—Tabasco is a major meat and fish provider. Near the Caribbean coast, at Lake Mecoacán, 70% of oyster production—about 10,000 tons—have been killed off because PEMEX canal digging closed lagoons to vitally needed Gulf of Mexico seawater. "A man has a right to work," argues Melesio Pérez, who heads the Democratic Fishermen's Movement, a coalition of four cooperatives that represents 500 families, " but PEMEX has taken our jobs away…"[37]

"Before they started drilling here, the corn used to fill up our attic," recalls Don Chepe Arias, a 74-year-old campesino, who farms a few acres bordering the Samaria camp oil field. "Now the cobs are so small that it's not worth even planting a crop." At first glance, Samaria seems still to be leafily paradisiacal. A second look reveals dozens of rusting oil and gas lines winding through the underbrush. Flaring natural gas burn-offs illuminate the jungle. The streams are filmed with oil. "I used to love papayas," complains Don Chepe's wife, María de Rosario, "now they give me a stomach-ache."

"People have a right to eat too," prompts Martínez.

Ernesto Martínez remembers how PEMEX came to Plátano y Cacao in 1979: "First they drilled one hole and then another. We're all small property owners around here and they'd come and tell you we're going to drill on your property and here's what you're going to get for it. If you complained, PEMEX took you to court and said you were damaging the whole nation by not letting them perforate. My compadre Constantino Vasconcelos has an oil well right on his property but he sits there all day in his wheelchair now and he doesn't have anything to eat. I'm sure that if you have a oil well in the United States, they treat you with more respect."

OLMECAS

Olmeca, the much valued light crude that Tabasco produces in abundance, is named for Mexico's mother civilization, whose great stone heads still loom at La Venta on the coast—adjacent to a PEMEX petrochemical installation. Today, the descendants of the Olmecs, the Chontales, are not well served by the oil that bears their ancestors' name. Around the Sen complex (nine wells, 35,000 barrels a day), 15,000 hectares of indigenous land have been wrecked by PEMEX carelessness.[38] 48 hours of production from just one well in the Chontal municipality of Nacajuca is equal to that county's yearly budget.[39] 57% of Tabasco's mysteriously high child-leukemia cases occur in this municipality, according to a study done by the Benito Juárez Autonomous University.[40]

Considering environmental destruction to be an occupational hazard, PEMEX makes a point of paying indemnizations to Tabasco farmers and fishermen for what it euphemistically calls "affectations" to their property. Andrés Manuel López Obrador, now national president of the PRD and twice its candidate for governor of the state, charges such payments are used to accommodate the PRI's electoral clientele. Conversely, the PRI alleges López Obrador has built the PRD in Tabasco through the "industry of reclamation." "There is no industry of reclamation," contests CODEUTAB's Father Goitia, "the farmers are asking only for what has been taken from them."

In Tabasco, campesinos aligned with the PRD are routinely denied such compensation—Governor Roberto Madrazo is a sworn enemy of the leftists. Madrazo's 1994 election is alleged to be the result of an illicit $70 million USD in campaign contributions, according to ledgers leaked to the PRD, and now filed with Mexico's Attorney General.[41] The governor also has access to millions of USD in PEMEX yearly contributions to the state.[42]

Irritation at the petroleum consortium's failure to compensate all but 3% of the 61,000 claims filed in the Chontal heart of the state around the Sen complex[43], exploded during the first two weeks of February 1996, when 10,000 Indian farmers and fishermen, led by López Obrador and Chontal poet and actor Auldárico Hernández, blocked the entrance to 60 wells in the process of perforation (live wells were avoided). Such protests have lengthy precedent in Tabasco. In the early 1980s thousands of farmers protested PEMEX destruction of local rivers, and hundreds were arrested for refusing to yield access to the oil fields.[44]

Oil is a matter of national security and the Zedillo government viewed the blockades as a grave challenge to its authority. Legally required by the terms of the Clinton bail-out to deposit all export oil revenues with the U.S. Federal Reserve as collateral on the loan, the Chontales were impeding both the oil and the cash flow. Troops, tanks, and helicopters were mobilized. Mexican army soldiers joined forces with state police brigades (the joint forces were initialized BOM squads) to break through the milling Indians, arresting 107 peaceful resisters, many of whom were charged with sabotage although the only crime they had committed was standing tall on their own land.[45]

THE DEEP SOUTH

The February 7th clash on a bridge leading to the Sen complex at a rancho called Guacalca bloodied many heads, including that of López Obrador, who stood his ground, even as police and soldiers clubbed him to the deck. As the PRD leader went down, he kept urging his own troops to respect their pledge of nonviolence and not respond to the government's savagery.

The conflict in the Chontal zone of Tabasco a deeply southern state, drew curious parallels to the movement led by Martin Luther King in Alabama, during the mid-1960s. The actors represented an ethnic minority that has been marginalized by racism and neglect. Much as in the U.S. South, law enforcement attacked the Chontales with dogs and clubs and the local press and television never missed an opportunity to whip up a lynch-mob like hysteria against the protesters—who, like King's followers, practiced civil disobedience and vowed to fill the jails of Tabasco. Even the confrontation on the bridge in Guacalca was reminiscent of one of the U.S. civil rights movement's most dramatic moments: the battle at the Pettis Bridge in Selma, Alabama, an event which had taken place not quite 31 years before the date of the clash in Tabasco.

Seated under a shade tree in Guacalca on the day after the battle, Auldarico Hernández, his head, like López Obrador's, battered and bandaged, proclaimed, "Those who live here are Indians—everyone is united in our concern for Mother Earth. We are defending our rivers and our lakes and we only hope it is not too late." Hernández, one of two indigenous members of the Mexican senate, was threatened by the PRI with expulsion from the legislature, for instigating the blockades.

PRIVATIZING PEMEX

Like the Zapatista Mayas across the state line in Chiapas, the Chontales have declared their oil-rich region an autonomous territory, a term that triggers alarm amongst both the Zedillo inner circle and its U.S. associates. Control of these fields means control of Mexico's place in the global master plan that radiates from the north. Washington even grew so anxious about Chontal aspirations that the State Department sent two investigators to Tabasco during the blockades to find out what the Indians really wanted.[46]

U.S. concerns about Mexico's oil flows extend beyond the Zedillo government's ability to beat up on Indian protesters. Chapter 6 and 7 of the North

American Free Trade Agreement presage the opening of Mexico's energy sector to transnational investment and Zedillo seems determined to follow Salinas and De la Madrid in accommodating the gringos by privatizing PEMEX piece by piece. Natural gas distribution lines are up for sale, subcontracts with U.S. off-shore drillers have been struck, PEMEX and Shell now share a Texas refinery, and Zedillo has put the nation's petrochemical industry on the block. Once more, the 17th point in a memorandum attached to the IMF's $17 billion share of the Clinton White House-crafted bail-out dated February 1st, 1995, confirms that the Mexican government has agreed to hasten the timetable for petrochemical privatization.[47]

A FLICKER OF REVOLUTIONARY NATIONALISM

The pipelines that weave a deadly web around Plátano y Cacao run east across the state line to Coatzacoalcos, Veracruz, where four major complexes produce 88% of Mexico's petrochemical output.[48] Much as in Tabasco, the quality of life around the complexes has been irretrievably degraded. Across the highway from the rusting Pajaritos plants, the outflow runs yellow and smoking through the community of Sapo, where fruit aborts and explodes on the branch. Children suffer frequent nosebleeds and sirens wail at all hours of the day—for years, the government has promised to move the farmers out from under Pajaritos' lethal pall.[49]

Pajaritos is up for sale—although in its damaged condition, there may be few takers. First to be auctioned off, according to the schedule announced by Zedillo to the aforementioned U.S. Chamber of Commerce breakfast, was supposed to be the Cosoleaque complex, a state-of-the-art ammonia producer—back in 1962. Cosoleaque, which processes 80% of the nation's ammonia supply, is as much of a powder keg as Plátano y Cacao—in January 1996, a leak at an animal feed plant, unaptly named "Ecology & Associated Resources," killed five and poisoned 20.[50]

The possible sale of Cosoleaque presented other dangers too, explained Carlos Romero Duchamps, head of the oil workers, the STPRM a union that once was the paragon of revolutionary nationalism: ammonia is used to build fertilizers essential to feeding the nation—one ton of fertilizer equals seven tons of basic grains. Handing over the plant to transnational operators would constitute a loss of sovereignty over Mexico's food supply, he told a congressional committee that was about to rubber-stamp the privatization, in 1996.[51]

Although historically affiliated with the PRI, the STPRM stands to lose hegemony over the industry when the petrochemical plants are sold and Duchamps has sought to obstruct privatization every step of Zedillo's way. At the Institutional Revolutionary Party's 17th Congress in September 1996, the union leader successfully lobbied for a resolution condemning the sale, unprecedented defiance of a PRI president's privatization plans by a member of his own party. To keep peace within the PRI, Zedillo ordered all scheduled sales withdrawn and reformulated his privatization strategies. Under the new procedures, the government—and, presumably the nation—would retain 51% of all existing petrochemical complexes but any new plants could be 100% foreign owned.[52] Despite the lenient terms, U.S. ambassador Jim Jones bellyached about the back-tracking, warning that it threatened future U.S. investment—the PRI took out newspaper ads to tell Mister Jones to butt out.[53]

"TRAITORS" AND "COLLABORATORS"
Duchamps embraced Zedillo as a patriot equal in stature to Lázaro Cárdenas for his willingness to compromise on privatization, but the new scheme did not mollify those who keep the pot of revolutionary nationalism bubbling. "Selling off 49% of PEMEX petrochemical's capacity is like selling off 49% of the nation," commented John Saxe-Fernández, a UNAM strategic resources professor.[54] The heir to the man who nationalized Mexico's oil, Cuauhtémoc Cárdenas, brands those who are trying to sell the industry to the same interests from whom his father confiscated it, as "traitors" and "collaborators": "It's just like during the U.S. invasion when Santa Anna handed over half the country—only this time, the North Americans won't have to fire a single shot".[55]

The son of Tata Lázaro advocates an end to all crude oil exports, re-directing the resource towards revitalizing Mexico's petrochemical potential instead[56]—his father similarly sought to utilize petroleum as a building block of Mexican industrial modernization. The younger Cárdenas has even set up a fund to buy back the petrochemical plants for the nation when they are finally put up for sale—the fund resembles one established by his father to raise compensation to be paid the owners of the oil companies he dispossessed. Much like the fund launched by Lázaro, wealthy society matrons contribute their jewels to Cuauhtémoc's crusade to halt the privatization and sale of this national patrimony to multi-national conglomerates.

WHAT NEO-LIBERALISM MEANS TO PADRE PACO
The globalization of Mexico's petroleum reserves, the fifth largest on the planet, are key to the construction of neo-liberal domination of the world economy. Down on the ground in Tabasco, Father Francisco Goitia puts a more human face on this imposition. Neo-liberalism has opened the region to madcap resource exploitation while wreaking havoc on the environment and impoverishing his parishioners, Padre Paco figures. "It is cheaper for PEMEX to pay out indemnizations than it is to shut down the pipelines for inspection and

repairs, if only for a few hours a year. This is all about money," argues the white-bearded, Spanish-born priest of Plátano y Cacao.

PEMEX paid out about $800 USD to survivors of those it slew here. "This shows how much they think a human life is worth," the padre laments. "We observe with sadness that PEMEX is eager to extract as much oil as possible, as quickly as possible, without regard for human life. This is what neo-liberalism means to us."

On a weekday afternoon, Father Goitia conducts Mass at Nuestra Señora de Remedios, a church that PEMEX rebuilt after the 1986 Christmas Eve explosion. Guitars twang and a choir trills, shrilly off-key. At its conclusion, the faithful offer public prayers to open PEMEX's heart. "We ask that our deaths not be sterile ones, that they will be heard by the men in charge," prays a round woman in a faded apron. "PEMEX wants you to believe the Church has no right to intervene in these matters," Goitia challenges from the pulpit, "but the Gospel is that right."

THE MIDDLE CLASSES VS. THE BANKS
THROWING OFF THE YOKE
EL BARZÓN (1920-1997)

> *Estas tierras de la nacion*
> These lands of the nation
> *las sembré con un buey manco*
> I sowed them with a crippled ox
> *Se me reventó el barzón*
> Now the yoke strap's broke
> *y sigue la yunta andando*
> and the team just goes on walking[57]

The song came before the movement. Written by Luis Pérez Meza and popular in the aftermath of the revolution, "El Barzón" takes its name from the leather strap that held the oxen—or sometimes, the farmer himself—to the plow, on the great haciendas where the peasants were so indebted to the owners that they were virtual serfs. The song's verses read like lists of all that the poor farmer owed to the Patrón ("20 pesos for the rent of the oxen, five pesos for some maguey, six pesos for I don't know what").[58] Since the revolution, the song has become a sort of anthem of Mexican agrarian struggle. I first heard "El Barzón's" mordant lyrics when the late, lamented Amparo Ochoa would belt it out at demonstrations in the 1970s and 80s. Now, in the '90s, it is being sung again, with different words but the same bitter message. Today's "Barzón" tells of the hapless plight of a new landless class, stripped of its possessions by greedy banks that charge usurious interest rates and foreclose without mercy when one can't pay.

"El Barzón" is also the name of what became the largest and most tumultuous mass movement to have emerged from the rubble of "the First Crisis of the 21st Century," having mobilized a million Mexicans in 31 states and the Federal District since the peso collapsed in December 1994, goosing interest rates up over 100% and making repayment of bank loans a test of triage for the nation's struggling middle class. With their hopes for the future eclipsed by the avarice of the banks and the collection agencies hired at 30% commissions to squeeze debtors, small property owners (*pequeños proprietarios*), rural merchants, urban shopkeepers, self-employed salespeople, taxicab owners, truck drivers, taco stand proprietors, and other assorted Mexicans with upwardly mobile aspirations have declared class war—middle class war—on the Lords of Mexican and International Finance.

"This is a middle class revolution—we are the producers in this country and if we put our heads together, we have enough strength to bring the banks to their knees," Alfonso Ramírez Cuellar, the dark-eyed, black-bearded maven of the Metropolitan Barzón, prophesied to me during the first months of the crisis, a divination that has since been fulfilled.[59]

THE VANQUISHED WALLET

The Barzón, like Ramírez Cuellar and national director Juan José Quirino, was born in the north central breadbasket state of Zacatecas a year before the peso collapse sent the nation into its worst recession since 1932. Mexico was still basking in the artificial glow of the Salinas years but, even then, despite the unctuous optimism of the nation's leaders, interest rates were 24 to 28%— money in Mexico is always expensive in order to entice Yanqui investors. The flimflam is exquisite: Mexican banks buy cheap 6% dollars from the gringos, explains Quirino, convert them into pesos, and sell them to the Mexicans at six times the price.

In the early '90s, despite the exorbitant cost of money, Zacatecas farmers borrowed big to get in on the bonanza the about-to-be-a-fact North American Free Trade Agreement would shower upon those who still believed in Salinas's "miracle." But, by 1993, making payments had become a torturous, humiliating procedure. The *Cartera Vencida* (literally "vanquished wallet") had hit small property owners in Zacatecas hard and on October 24th, 1993, the Barzónistas jumped up on their tractors, flicked on the ignitions, and steered them slowly, very slowly, 200 miles southwards towards the capital where riot police greeted them at the city limits with truncheons and tear gas.

"The Barzón was very *bronco* (wild) in those days," laughs the fast-talking Quirino, who was dragged from his tractor, kicked around by the cops, and briefly incarcerated. "We did what we had to do to save our skins—we weren't afraid." The tractor has since become El Barzón's logo—a gleaming green and yellow John Deere is permanently parked at the doors of the group's national headquarters in Mexico City's Colonia Roma.

Small and not-so-small farmers all over central Mexico took inspiration from the Barzón broncos, running their reapers out on public highways to block toll booths or herding their animals (elephants included) into public plazas to protest the high cost of feeding them with imported grain.

AUCTIONING OFF THE NATION

El Barzón detonated in late 1994, the year that began with NAFTA and the Zapatista rebellion—of which the Barzónistas were early supporters (although more as a method of mau-mauing the government than out of class conviction). After December 21st, when the peso lost 40% of its value overnight, the Barzón was deluged by tens of thousands of dazed citizens who suddenly found themselves in serious danger of losing everything they had ever scraped together to climb up from the bottom. By February, 1995, making payments on a rate that had rocketed up to three digits was an impossibility for shell-shocked debtors. The banks tacked on late charges and compounded interest on them and now hundreds of thousands of Mexicans owed twice as much as the property or the car or the business they had financed with the loan, was worth in the first place. Hundreds of businesses were going under daily in early 1995 (200,000 in the first 18 months of the crisis) and the universal desperation transformed El Barzón from a small, angry army of farmers to a more plural and urban organization.

But, in Mexico, every city dweller is not far removed from his or her country roots and the crisis hardly shook the dirt out of the Barzón's boots. The Barzónistas behaved just as bronco as ever: Militants hurled crates of rotten tomatoes at offending lending institutions, took off all their clothes on downtown streets to illustrate how the banks had left them naked, melted their credit cards on smoky, public pyres, held bank officials hostage—on one bleak winter day in early '95, Barzónistas blocked the entrance to 894 Mexican bank branches, shutting down operations and preventing the directors from going out to lunch.[60] On another, Barzónistas dolled up like the historical figures displayed on Mexico's money and paraded in front of the Bank of Mexico (roughly equivalent to the Federal Reserve), demanding that hallowed institution apologize for the insult it had inflicted upon the heroes and martyrs who illuminate the nation's currency.

When auctions of properties seized by the banks were held, the Barzónistas disrupted the proceedings and were hauled off to jail. The auctions represented a new front in the Annexation of Mexico. The U.S.-based Lasalle Partners and the National Real Estate Clearing House proposed to auction off 600 properties upon which the banks had foreclosed (prior to the crisis). To satisfy U.S. annexation aspirations, North American real estate speculators were encouraged to bid, catalogues were distributed, and Century 21 engaged to show prospective buyers their little wedge of Mexico, but the prospect of investing in a country beset by guerrilla war, political assassination, bronco Barzónistas, and unstanchable corruption did not attract many clients and few sales were ever consummated.[61]

BEATING BACK THE BANKS

"We were all lung back then" Quirino, now a PRD senator given to button-down plaid shirts, recalls—the Barzón's multiple mobilizations were attracting attention and membership, its offices always swarming with petitioners, but there was little consolidation. Meanwhile, the pressure to pay up was driving members to suicide.

"We had to shift gears, to do something concrete to get the banks off our backs so we decided to use every legal recourse open to us and go into court in a big way. We needed lawyers and the National Bar volunteered. Pretty soon, we had a thousand lawyers working for us free of charge, to halt this terrorism of the banks."

Terrorism is a well-chosen descriptive. The banks' modus operandi was to respond to a skipped payments by hiring collection agencies like the Professional Multi-Service Group, contracted by Banco Serfín to intimidate clients. (Serfín is partially owned by General Electric.)[62] Debtors were bombarded with phone calls and dunning letters. Collection agency lawyers, accompanied by off-duty cops in full uniform, paid home visits, terrifying women and children. Despite constitutional prohibitions, those who could not or would not pay were arrested and held for 48 hours on contempt charges—at least 3,000 such detentions were recorded before a judicial truce was finally forged.[63] Ultimately, the property in question would be "embargoed" (foreclosed upon). Judges who authorized such star chamber proceedings were identified with the banks for which they worked—Barzónistas called one Judge Bancomer, another Judge Banamex, etc.[64]

El Barzón's lawyers began to win cases, block the embargoes, gain breathing space for the debtors. "This earned us confidence—people saw that the law could be used for once to defend their rights," Quirino continues. But the ace up El Barzón's sleeve was the very reason that the debtors had come together in the first place: their collective inability to pay. Operating on short margins, the newly reprivatized banks were vulnerable.

MOST DANGEROUS GROUP IN MEXICO

El Barzón is a debtors' union, not a deadbeat one. Its slogan is *Debo No Niego—¡Pago Lo Justo!* (I don't deny I owe—but I'll pay what is just.) "It's just that no one could ever catch up," Quirino muses.

With hundreds of thousands of debtors unable to pay up, El Barzón had soon imposed a moratorium on the banks that confirmed Ramírez Cuellar's prophecy that the banks would be brought to their knees. In just a few months, 40% of bank loan portfolios had became uncollectable.[65] The sum represented more than Mexico's 18 private banks had on hand, placing them in technical bankruptcy. The three top banks—Banamex, Serfín, and Bancomer—together had $6 billion USD outstanding with no way to collect and the totals kept multiplying from month to month.[66] Industry insiders whispered that without the liquidity provided by narco-money ($25-30 billion annually—DEA estimates), the vaults would have been stripped bare. Worse yet, the banks themselves were in deep hock to U.S. and European banks—$38 billion worth. With $25 billion due in 1995-1996,[67] foreign banks held their nose and swallowed the Mexicans whole. Since December 1994, 20% of the banking industry has fallen into the hands of the *extranjeros*, a situation that portends a return to the Porfirian epoch.[68]

Suddenly, in the spring of 1995, according to one *El Financiero* report out of Washington, El Barzón was being viewed by unidentified U.S. intelligence agencies as a greater threat to Mexican (and U.S.) national security than the Zapatista Army of National Liberation. "That's the only thing I've ever agreed with the gringos about," Alfonso Ramírez Cuellar growled at me during a June 1995 interview.

El Barzón's moratoriums forced the Zedillo administration to parade 11 separate re-structuring schemes before dubious debtors, each designed to save the banks at any cost (about $30 billion) and keep the victims paying something, anything.[69] With catchy acronyms like UPI and ADE, the government capped interest payments, subsidizing a third of what was owed, if only the debtor promised to stay current.[70] But anteing up 70% of a loan taken out at sharply lower interest rates in far more promising times, proved too much for about half of the nation's bank debtors, and, according to the U.S. Security Auctions Capital corporation, which tracks such numbers, 46% of the bundle remains uncollectable.[71]

"The neo-liberal model has failed. We're the proof," Ramirez gloats.[72]

MAKING LA COYUNTURA WORK

Wreaking such havoc treads on a lot of big toes. Barzón offices were broken into in Monterrey and Mexico City, crucial computer files abstracted, and bomb-like objects left behind. The governor of Nuevo León accused the Barzónistas of trying to bomb themselves.[73] At Christmas 1995, Ramirez was invited to a downtown Mexico City VIP's restaurant by an assistant district attorney to discuss charges arising out of a blockade outside an auto financing company. When the coffee was served, 40 armed-to-the-teeth plainclothes agents swiveled about from adjoining tables, flashed their badges, and carried the Barzón leader off to gaol. The hue and cry of rank and file Barzónistas and their friends in high and low places eventually won Alfonso's release but the handwriting was on the wall: "We needed to make friends quickly to head off the coming repression," Juan José Quirino narrates.

The collapse of the peso had conjured up a super-coyuntura that, during much of 1995 and '96, seemed to be drawing tighter and tighter around the Zedillo administration's neck. The Zapatistas were no longer the whole show. The proscenium was alive with darting players. The Tepoztecos and the Tabasqueños, rebellious Mexico City bus drivers whose routes had been arbitrarily privatized, and the long-suffering farmers of Guerrero, now played important roles in the Mexican drama. If the EZLN stood at stage left, the Barzón, for reasons of class affiliation, was mounted at stage right.

Self-preservation required that the Barzónistas cross class and political lines. They strode into the zócalo arm in arm with burly proletarians at mammoth May 1st marches staged by dissident unions. They went to the political parties, even the PRI, and requested laws that would save them from the bankers' avarice. When, in April 1996, the responses were scattered, El Barzón assembled thousands of members to block the legislators' entrance to the Mexican Senate, forcing modifications in a Zedillo-proposed law that would have reinstituted property confiscations. As usual, the Barzónistas brought mariachis to the protest.[74]

El Barzón went to the Catholic Church too and found a surprisingly open ear. Zacatecas Bishop Javier Lozano Barragán, a conservative, and now a member of Pope John Paul II's cabinet, was the first to offer a Debtors' Mass. By 1995, Norberto Rivera Carrera, once a lowly country priest in Río Grande, Zacatecas, and Quirino's neighbor, had become Archbishop of Mexico City, the most populous parish in the Roman Catholic world, and soon Rivera, also earmarked as a conservative, was condemning usury from the pulpit every Sunday and reminding the bankers that St. Thomas Aquinas defined this sin as charging anything over 2% interest. Now El Barzón has appealed to the Pope for an audience—"we want the old Pater Noster back," explains Quirino.

Before the Church went neo-liberal in the 1970s, he explains, the Pater Noster talked of forgiving "debtors," not "trespassers."[75]

El Barzón is looking past Mexico's borders for allies. Barzónistas trek to Washington to buttonhole congresspeople, meet with the Teamsters and Big Labor, and march on the IMF. There are Barzón chapters now on the other side of the river, along the Texas border. Barzónistas travel east—the women of El Barzón attended the Beijing summit. El Barzón travels south to Argentina and Brazil, where they have consolidated a common front with debtors' unions in those countries. "It's not just personal debt that we are talking about now—the foreign debt is the mechanism by which the IMF keeps us chained up. The second Latin American debt crisis is coming," Quirino prognosticates, "Latin American debtor nations missed the opportunity to unite after 1982. This time, we must be ready to fight for a continental moratorium."

"TWO WAGONS ON THE SAME TRAIN"

The dateline is July 1996. The tiny Mayan residents of that heroic Zapatista outpost, La Realidad, leaned cross-armed against the mud walls of their houses and studied the curiously-dressed strangers as they straggled in from the jungle. "They are very different from us," a compañera observed to *La Jornada's* Hermann Bellinghausen, the world's most diligent chronicler of the Zapatista revolution.[76] The Tojolabales of La Realidad see a lot of weird strangers—in just a few days they would play host to an invasion of European and North American anarchists and cyber-punks who would be in town for what Marcos was calling *La Intergaláctica.*

For the pink-faced, leather-jacketed, cowboy-booted Barzónistas who were holding their national congress at the EZLN's *Aguascalientes* jungle convention center, things were certainly different too. Civilized Barzón conclaves are conducted at air-conditioned hotels in Durango or Morelia, where cellular telephones work and there is plenty of cold beer at hand to wash down the dismal micro-economic forecast. Nonetheless, 317 delegates from 27 states, some from as far off as Sonora on the northern border, had journeyed to La Realidad, at the invitation of the ski-masked rebels, who readily loaned them the facilities because that is what they are for, to be used by fraternal organizations in solidarity.[77] The two groups would sign a treaty of *Intocabilidad* which means "if the Zapatistas are attacked, we will act," Quirino explains, "and vice versa."

"We are two wagons on the same train to justice, democracy, and dignity," Quirino enthused to the debtors and the Zapatistas assembled under the stars for the closing session.[78] Then Marcos, who the Barzónista leader likens to Mel Gibson in *Braveheart,* took over: "The government shows us that their war is really against the Different, to assimilate and annihilate the Other. We are two different Differents here today but what brings us together in spite of our differences is not just the bad government that has made us grow, but what the old books call the Patria."[79]

Both the Zapatistas and the Barzónistas have learned the history of Mexico much better than the technocrats who sadly are still managing this enterprise. "Juárez was the first to say 'No niego que debo—Pago el justo.' If he were alive today, he would be the director of the Barzón, not me," Quirino laughs.

"The story of our country is the big appetite the United States and other economic powers have to devour us. Back in 1848, their strategies to annex us were obvious—they are more subtle and more punishing now. Yet, in every epoch, there have been Mexicans who rose up to inspire us to resist annexation—Cuauhtémoc and Juárez, Zapata, Lázaro Cárdenas, Marcos. *Ahora, nos toca…* Now, it's our turn…"

THE GUERRILLA
VS. THE U.S.-MEXICAN MILITARY MACHINE:
THE GHOSTS IN THE TREES
(GUERRERO AND OAXACA, 1967-97)

In the full-color, *Acapulco Sun* front-page photo[80], the much-maligned then-governor of Guerrero and a brace of U.S. Pacific Northwest timber company execs smile amiably, as they sign a five-year, $10 million USD agreement that will bring the Boise Cascade Corporation, one of the ten top timber producers in North America, to the state's Costa Grande, the conflictive, guerrilla-ridden stretch of coastline winding between the luxury resorts of Zihuatenejo/Ixtapa and Acapulco, on the south.

For Rubén Figueroa, a politician with a spotty human rights record—100 political killings, 76 of the victims left-opposition PRD members[81], would be recorded during his abbreviated, three-year term in office—the agreement with Boise seemed salutary. The accord allowed the transnational to "associate" with local ejidos, under terms dictated by the North American Free Trade Agreement, and would probably translate to hundreds of jobs along the Costa Grande—unemployment in this rambunctious stretch of coastline and sierra is a source of perennial social ferment.

BIG TIMBER—PIONEER OF RESOURCE GLOBALIZATION
Boise Cascade had good reason to smile too. In recent years, the Idaho timber giant has been harried by intensified government regulation, an indecisive National Forest Service annual cut, thinning inventories, and dogged environ-

mentalists. Mills have been closed in Oregon and Idaho with hundreds of jobs lost for good. The move to Mexico pointed to sunnier prospects. Boise's wholly owned subsidiary, Costa Grande Forest Products, would have access to a million acres of old-growth white fir and sugar pine, an enormous pool of cheap labor, and environmental regulations that, even in the most stringent of times, can best be described as languid.

Big Timber is a pioneer in this rapidly globalizing world. Deprived of unimpeded access to clear-cut forests in the First World, the timber giants are filling out their inventories by erasing the Third. From the Siberian Taiga to the Amazon, transnational timber merchants have entered into similar agreements with similar tyrants as the deal struck between Boise and the killer governor. Boise itself is scouting New Zealand, Chilean, and Malaysian sites to complement its holdings in Guerrero and Oaxaca. 15 U.S. timber companies have launched Mexican enterprises since NAFTA took shape.[82] But rather than bringing sustainable growth to the regions where they have relocated, transnationals like Boise and International Paper in the Tarahumara sierra appear to be orchestrating rip-and-run operations that will leave the communities they have damned with their presence in worse shape once the trees are gone.

"THE FORESTS BRING US WATER"

If the Boise Cascade execs had only dug a little deeper into the *Sol de Acapulco* (assuming they could read the language), their smiles might have soured quickly. 30 miles north of Acapulco, above the Costa Grande in the sierra near Tepetixtla, a dirt-poor town of 20,000 with a reputation for hardcore violence, a tense stand-off between militant farmers from the Organization of Campesinos of the Southern Sierra (OCSS) and loggers, backed up by heavily armed state police, had entered its second day and was rolling to a boil.[83]

"We saw how this lumber company was taking out our forests without returning anything to the people and we decided to stop them. They had already taken out a hundred truckloads of pine and cedar," remembered 20-year-old Rocío Mesino, the daughter of a jailed OCSS director—Mesino herself has since been forced into hiding. "We stopped the trucks and took down the logs and returned the wood to the community." But the owner, a Figueroa crony, kept sending logging rigs into the mountain and the OCSS set fire to them. "We are farmers," Rocío explained, "the forests bring us water. We know that we can't allow them to be cut down."[84]

The farmers of Tepetixtla have been seared by drought before. Julián Rodríguez, a soft-spoken local PRD leader (but not an OCSS supporter) recalls that, in the early 1980s, the town's forests were clear-cut by outside loggers:

"The river dried up and then the cornfields. It just stopped raining for two years. We were afraid that logging would bring us drought."[85]

By April 25th, a confrontation seemed unavoidable. Arrest warrants had been sworn out against OCSS leaders and the motorized police was assembled down in the county seat of Coyuca de Benítez, poised to move in under the direction of its itchy-fingered Operations director, Manuel Moreno. Judicial Police honchos kept the Governor informed by cellular phone while he sealed the deal with Boise. Figueroa had repeatedly pegged the OCSS as violence-prone hotheads with ties to the long-dormant guerrilla movement of Lucio Cabañas. Time and again, they had refused to negotiate with him. "What wasn't negotiable was the forests," Rocío Mesino affirmed.[86]

Bloodshed was narrowly avoided when the Governor agreed to meet with the malcontents early in May. The agreement hammered out between them was not a propitious sign for the future of Boise Cascade's Costa Grande Forest Products division—all logging in the Sierra of Tepetixtla was curtailed. What had been cut would be used to build homes in the community. Figueroa agreed to supply the OCSS with shipments of fertilizer and agricultural chemicals. "We're farmers…" Rocío had explained.

AGUAS BLANCAS

But the tension remained taut and the agreement only postponed a showdown between the farmers and the killer governor's security forces. Just two months later, near 10:30 am on the rainy morning of June 28th, OCSS militants, descending the muddy road from Tepetixtla to denounce Figueroa for failing to deliver the fertilizer, were met by the motorized police at a swift-moving mountain wash now indelibly inked into the national consciousness as *Aguas Blancas* (White Waters). Under Commander Moreno's direction, the *Motorizados* opened fire without warning, killing 17 farmers and wounding 23 others. Those near death were finished off with coups de grace and weapons placed in their hands to justify the massacre.[87]

The killings ignited national outrage—the National Human Rights Network, Todos Por Todos, and virtually every independent human rights organization in the land cried genocide. Even the government's ever-cautious National Human Rights Commission (CNDH) called for heads to roll. Demonstrators marched in Mexico City and international observers from Amnesty, Human Rights Watch, and the Minnesota Advocates, were soon on the ground to conduct investigations. The Governor sought to justify the murders by producing a three-minute videotape that purported to show the farmers attacking the police. 10 months later, a 20-minute version of the same tape was displayed on national television and proved that the police had acted without provocation.

DOWNFALL OF A KILLER GOVERNOR

Suspicions about Figueroa's motives persisted. Had the governor ordered the massacre to prevent OCSS opposition to logging the sierra from spreading to other ejidos—with which Boise was about to sign contracts? "There's no connection whatsoever between what happened at Aguas Blancas and our efforts to bring investors to the Costa Grande," Figueroa's press secretary, an affable lackey named Carlos Carrillo, once assured me. "The OCSS people are common criminals."[88] Carrillo himself was reported to have helicoptered to the massacre scene around noon on June 28th, presumably to pick up the videotape, which was shot by a local police comandante, and return it to the state capital to be doctored at Guerrero state radio and television studios.

The horrors revealed by the new videotape, a fresh wave of mass killings around the state, and a finding by the Mexican Supreme Court that Figueroa had contributed to the violation of individual guarantees at Aguas Blancas, resulted in the governor's resignation in March 1996. For generations, the Figueroas had been governors of Guerrero—Rubén Figueroa's father, also named Rubén, was kidnapped by Cabañas's guerrilla in the '70s—but now their reign had come to an abrupt end. President Zedillo, a formal compadre of the governor, finally bowed to months of public pressure and asked him to step down. Although upwards of 40 police and public officials have been prosecuted for their role in the Aguas Blancas killings, Figueroa has never been brought before a court of law.

BOISE BOOMING

As the human rights workers fumed at the impunity extended the governor, business boomed for Boise Cascade. In 1995, Boise put out 20 million board feet and expected to double that in '96. The timber giant rented two mill sites midway between Zihuatenejo and Acapulco and installed a planer mill that, according to U.S. millwrights who pieced it together, could be easily taken apart and shipped elsewhere when the wood runs out on the Costa Grande. Despite the OCSS's influence, Costa Grande contracted with 24 sierra ejidos, a process permitted by the revisions to Article 27 that allowed the ejidos to form an "association" with Boise, and by mid-winter 1996, logs were pouring into its enormous patio at Papanoa, 24 hours a day.

"We are the salvation of the ejidos," boasted Papanoa superintendent Carlos Vega, his Boise Cascade cap riding high on his head. "Before we got here, they owed the banks so much money for machinery they had bought on credit, that they were going under." But the Boise operation was not quite that altruistic. Base pay was U.S. $4.75 a day, well above the Mexican minimum wage, but close to 30 times less than what the corporation pays north of the border.[89]

LUCIO

In the months after the Aguas Blancas killings, this reporter traveled the region, recording the fury of farmers and social activists on and above the Costa Grande. "We will never forget the color of blood!" it screamed, in loopy red spray paint, on the side of a white-washed wall up in Atoyaquillo, where 11 of those murdered at the mountain wash are buried, and men in wheelchairs, crippled for life by the bullets of the police, navigate the rutted, muddy streets.

One morning I found myself on the coast, in the tree-filled plaza of Atoyac, just before 8 am flag-raising at the General Juan A. Alvarez school. Chattering children in schoolgirl smocks and slicked-down hair scampered under the boughs. This moment of innocence and grace contrasted starkly with the horror that struck this same plaza in May 1967 when nine teachers and parents, protesting a dictatorial school director, were gunned down by Guerrero state police. The massacre at the General Alvarez school was a relatively minor one in a state with a legacy of collective killings that almost always total in the teens.

But what is most remembered about the schoolhouse murders was that the leader of the protesting teachers, the maestro Lucio Cabañas Barrientos, the son of campesinos from nearby San Juan de las Flores, survived the gunfire, rallied his compañeros to rise up in arms against the bad government, and set off for the sierra above Atoyac where his Party of the Poor guerrilleros fought 25,000 Mexican Army troops, reportedly advised by CIA trainers, for seven complicated years[90]—the present Secretary of Defense, Enrique Cervantes, won his stripes in the Cabañas campaign. Lucio's biographers record 16 clashes with the military during the years in the sierra.[91] 30 years ago, Comandante Lucio galvanized Mexico every bit as much much as Subcomandante Marcos.

Guerrero history is soaked in the guerrilla mystique. Native Chontales took on the Mexica empire and then the Mexicas took on the Españoles in this Pacific Coast state whose namesake, Vicente Guerrero, inherited Morelos's guerrilla army and eventually joined with Iturbide to defeat the Crown in 1821. General Juan A. Alvarez directed his guerrilleros against the Conservatives and the French. During the revolution, Emiliano Zapata took refuge in Guerrero where he fought many notable battles—Lucio Cabañas's grandfather, Pablo, was a Zapatista general. Even as Lucio rose above the Costa Grande, another rural maestro, Genaro Vázquez, was already mounting a parallel campaign in the sierra to the southwest.

Cabañas was supposed to have been killed by an Army ambush, cornered in a sierra ravine on December 2nd, 1974. Military and state security forces, under the command of General Mario Arturo Acosta Chaparro, with the tacit approbation of President Echeverría, conducted a reign of terror against suspected Party of the Poor partisans that cost hundreds of lives along the Costa

Grande and in the farming villages above—the Eureka group, which is dedicated to locating the victims of those "disappeared" for political reasons, concluded that more than 300 of the 550 "disappeared" on their books, were taken by security forces during this period (locals place the number between 600 and 900.[92] Many of the victims were executed after being imprisoned at Military Camp #1 in Mexico City, if the testimony of army deserter Zacarias Osorio to Canadian authorities is to be trusted.[93] Others were thought to have been tortured and died in secret prisons on military bases around Acapulco and their bodies thrown into the sea or the infamous Meléndez hole, near Iguala.

"They came here to kill me—I still don't know why they didn't. They killed three people right over there, one was an old man. Many more were never seen again—as many women as men." Doña Rafita Barrientos de Cabañas, Lucio's 81-year-old mother, remembers the 1971 police invasion of her community as if it was yesterday. A shriveled, frail old lady, Doña Rafa still lives in San Juan de los Flores, a tiny collection of rickety houses near a rumbling mountain river. Held herself for two years at Military Camp #1, she continues to defiantly denounce the Mexican government: "All the government knows how to do is kill. Look what they did to those poor boys at Aguas Blancas!"

Nearly 30 years after Lucio Cabañas's death, his ghost continues to haunt Atoyac and its sister towns up in the sierra. Because his grave has never been located, many insist he is still alive. "They say no one saw where they buried him—that it was another who was buried in his place," Doña Rafa considers. The old woman has lost three sons to the guerrilla—Lucio's half-brother, David, has been held for six years at a Mexico City penitentiary, accused (but never tried) of having shot down two security guards at La Jornada newspaper in an errant 1991 paramilitary action. Lucio's father was himself killed by a local police comandante: "He never knew what his son became."

"Look at me—I'm old and thin, so thin. Why didn't they just kill me instead of having to live so long with all this sadness," she weeps. Doña Rafita doesn't believe that Lucio still lives: "If my son was alive, he would have come to visit me by now. How could he still be alive?"[94]

But Lucio Cabañas—or at least his spiritual heirs—were a lot more alive than Doña Rafita was telling visitors that winter morning. In February, 1996, local farmers insisted that an armed group had been sighted on Guajalote hill, an old Cabañas hideaway just above Tepetixtla. "They have high-powered weapons and they wear paliacates (kerchiefs) to hide their faces, like the Chiapanecos (i.e. Zapatistas)," I was told by one campesino whose name is best not noted here.[95]

APOCALYPSE NOW

The ghosts became flesh in June. On the 28th of that month, a year to the day of the Aguas Blancas killings, during ceremonies at the white-washed monument that has been erected to the slain men at the massacre site, between 70 and 100 armed fighters, their faces draped, but displaying a tooth-rattling array of AK-47s and AR-15s, descended from the hills above and took center stage at the memorial service. Dressed in pressed olive green uniforms, the masked men trotted in military formation, raising both the Mexican flag and a flag of their own creation, bearing the initials EPR— "Ejercito Popular Revolucionario" or Popular Revolutionary Army.

The nearly 2,000 onlookers recoiled at first, imagining that the Mexican Army had launched a preemptive assault on the gathering. The guerrilleros sought to calm them. "We are compañeros," Captain Emiliano urged. They had come to place wildflowers upon the white marker where the men had been gunned down and to read their "Manifesto of Aguas Blancas," first in Spanish, then in Náhuatl. Then the self-proclaimed guerrilla army retired, firing 17 salvos for the dead from the hilltop, and disappearing into the mountain forest.[96]

Although Mexican Army troops were immediately ordered into the region, a furious hurricane named Boris blasted the coast that night, facilitating the EPR's escape into the high sierra with only one minor scrape—hours after their appearance at the memorial, a group of EPR fighters jackknifed a huge Corona beer rig just ten minutes from Chilpancingo, the state capital, and 70 miles northeast of Aguas Blancas, hung a banner condemning neo-liberalism on its side, and distributed their manifestos to stalled motorists. Three state police agents were wounded when they sped to the scene and the guerrilleros opened fire on them, then fled into the bush.[97] The EPR had drawn its first blood.

The following week, armed EPR fighters appeared twice in Acapulco slum colonies to distribute their manifesto as they would throughout the region for months, in a stage of their offensive the EPR's mystery leadership called "armed propaganda." The manifesto explains that impoverishment and government repression had left those who formed their army "no option but to turn our tools into weapons." "We have arisen from the sadness of the widows, from the disappearances of our loved ones, the pain of the tortured, the wrath of those unjustly imprisoned, misery, hunger, disease, the children of the street."[98]

Many, of course, were skeptical of this new-old guerrilla. Cuauhtémoc Cárdenas, who had just concluded a speech at the memorial site when the EPR appeared above on the hill, called the act "a grotesque pantomime" and suggested that the spectacle had been arranged by Figueroa to discredit popular struggle—the "grotesque pantomime" riff (without the Figueroa footnote) was later reiterated, ad nauseam, by the Mexican government.

The emergence of a second guerrilla front stunned Mexico but not reporters. Since 1994, we had been stumbling around the Guerrero outback chasing rumors of ghosts of guerrilleros. Everyone knew someone who had seen the guerrilla but no one would admit to ever having seen them with their own eyes.

In the days following the EPR show at Aguas Blancas, I scoured the southern sierra for clues to their identity. Fording the wide, muddy river near Barrio Nuevo one afternoon, I encountered a young man pushing his disabled bicycle up the far bank. We were slogging uphill from the river when a pair of Mexican army Bell 212 helicopter gunships broke from the mountains and spun in low over the wrecked road. It felt a little like *Apocalypse Now*. "They are looking for the guerrilla," the young man smiled. "The guerrilla is real now." No, he personally didn't know anyone in it. We parted company at a turn in the road, just outside of town. "What is your name?" I asked, for my notes. "Lucíano..." the young man smiled again, "you know, like Lucio." And he headed off into the forest.[99]

WHAT BOISE DIDN'T TELL ITS STOCKHOLDERS

For the next 60 days, the EPR staged a series of hit-and-run attacks on army and police targets, from one end of Guerrero to the Oaxaca border. Although the military, which had poured tens of thousands of troops into the state[100], counted only one casualty, the EPR claimed that it had taken out 59 of the enemy.[101] The rebels visited many communities. They stopped five times in Tecpán de Galiana, where Boise has located a mill—a sailor was shot on one foray and the EPR took credit for raking a Naval barracks with gunfire on another.[102] Then a bookkeeper at a Costa Grande mill was kidnapped and ransomed—the EPR is believed to have built up a multimillion-dollar war chest through such kidnappings, which included that of the president of Banamex, Alfredo Harp Helú (Carlos Slim's cousin), for whose freedom they reportedly received a Latin American record $30 million ransom, a sum that buys lots of AK-47s.

Boise seems unconcerned as to what its stockholders think of the risks it is taking with their money by operating a string of mills in so volatile a zone. But the timber giant keeps its U.S. supervisors and technicians under lock and key, lodging them at a villa with armed guards just inside the wrought-iron gate. "They watch us so close we can't even stand off the sidewalk," said one millwright, who was set to cash in his chips and head back to the states.[103]

ROCKING THE STOCK MARKET

On August 28th, 1996, two months to the day after their initial appearance at Aguas Blancas, and acting outside of Guerrero for the first time, the rebel fighters directed their fire at strategic targets in six states, attacking two luxury tourist resorts, six police and army headquarters, a military bank (in Oaxaca city) and three installations of the Federal Electricity Commission in Puebla and Mexico states. At least 16 members of security forces were killed in the assaults. The synchronized attacks, which reached across a broad swath of south central Mexico all the way to Chiapas, were unprecedented in the recent history of the Mexican guerrilla, for their scope and ferocity.

In its first months of operation, the EPR's shoot-and-run tactics had made little impression on financial markets. So long as the guerrilleros remained holed up in the Guerrero sierra, skirmishing with the army at remote outposts, they were just one more worrisome spot on the Mexican map for jumpy investors to watch, but did not threaten the market. This was how both a foreign bank analyst and a J.P. Morgan vice president explained it to me at a Cuernavaca picnic in July. The morning after the EPR offensive, both called from New York to determine the extent of the damage. Over the next 48 hours, the Mexican Bolsa would plunge more than 100 points, 3% of its total value, and the peso lose 11 cents against the dollar.[105] The EPR had finally made an impression on financial markets.

TOURIST TIPS

The August attacks constituted a significant escalation of the EPR's undeclared war on the Zedillo administration. But what the guerrilleros were capable of doing and chose not to do, was even more chilling than the dead and wounded they left behind.

By staging attacks at Acapulco and Huatulco, the posh tourist center on the Oaxaca coast, the EPR struck a body blow against crucial tourist revenues—the economy's fourth largest source of dollars (7 million tourist visits, generating $7.2 billion USD). In both Acapulco and Huatulco, the Popular Revolutionary Army struck at security forces rather than tourist locations although they could have easily invaded the five-star hotel districts at the two resorts.[106]

The EPR operates in a geographical range that includes six key tourist havens—both the U.S. and British embassies immediately issued travel warnings to their citizens in the zone. Most of these resorts are designated by the Mexican government as "poles of development" and have drawn tens of thousands of impoverished campesinos down to the coast to work as ill-paid maids and hod carriers, converting such servant quarters as La Crucecita, adjacent to Huatulco, into breeding grounds of discontent.

Prime oceanfront land in Huatulco was expropriated from fishermen a decade ago and concessioned to international hotel chains like Sheraton and Club Med, infuriating locals. In a communiqué issued the day after the

Crucecita-Huatulco attack (11 military, police and rebels killed)[107], the EPR demanded an end to such annexation, writing that it had acted "to stop the continual sale of our land to Yanqui investors" and promising that its fighters would soon visit the Caribbean resort of Cancún, the Mexican government's biggest tourist money-maker.[108]

COUNTERINSURGENCY

The bloody August 28th events embarrassed and enraged the Zedillo government. At his September 1st *Informe* three days later, the President pounded on the podium and swore an oath that the full force of the state would fall upon the "terrorists." In off-the-record briefings with correspondents, government officials compared the EPR to the German Baader-Meinhof gang[109] and U.S. Ambassador Jim Jones offered U.S. anti-terrorism expertise, which he claimed had been accumulated investigating right-wing militias, to track down the villains. Although the numbers are a closely held state secret, it is safe to assume that 40,000 Mexican troops were mobilized in the region.

The militarization of central and southern Mexico has been accompanied by a harsh counterinsurgency campaign reminiscent of the post-Lucio years. Troops terrorize Nahua villagers in the Huasteca mountains, along the Veracruz-Hidalgo border, setting up road blocks, conducting house-to-house searches for weapons and propaganda, and arbitrarily singling out townspeople for interrogation and arrest.[110] The same pattern is repeated in Guerrero and Oaxaca, Chiapas, Tabasco, wherever the EPR has shown itself.

BLOOD AND COFFEE

To follow this trail of blood, one tracks the trail of coffee production in Mexico. "The map of coffee is the map of hunger and extreme poverty, the map of armed insurrection," writes Luis Hernández Navarro, an advisor to the National Coordinating Body of Small Coffee Growers.[111] 60% of Mexico's small producers are indigenous peoples who are subjected to the aberrant fluctuations of a global coffee market over which they have absolutely no control, proof of which, as Hernández points out, is that 349 of the 400 coffee-producing municipalities in Mexico are also on the extreme poverty list.[112]

The chances are that a good part of the Mexican gourmet coffee inventory available at your local upscale real food emporium comes from a zone in which the EPR or the Zapatista Army of National Liberation is active. The massacre at Aguas Blancas splashed blood on the sacks of beans pouring out of the mountains above Coyuca and Atoyac on the Costa Grande. La Realidad, "Cleen-tone" 's hometown, depends on coffee production for survival. So does

San Agustín Loxicha, a traditional Zapotec town in Oaxaca's coastal sierra so poor that babies die in the priest's arms during baptism.[113]

Since the Huatulco attack, the State has fallen with full force upon the 32 communities of the Loxichas, beating, torturing, and detaining nearly a hundred Indians for allegedly harboring EPR sympathies—53 men remain jailed, including virtually the town's entire elected government and most of its schoolteachers. Rural teachers, like Lucio Cabañas and Genaro Vázquez, are still in the forefront of social struggle in Oaxaca and Guerrero. The Mexican government, perhaps abetted by U.S. advisers, does not look kindly on these rebel educators.

NEXT VIETNAM IN MEXICO?

In the spring of 1997, the jails in those two states were filling fast with political prisoners. The broad-based Front for the Construction of a National Liberation Movement (FAC-MLN), an amalgam of dozens of campesino, urban, and labor groups, counts over 200 militants taken since the EPR first came out of the trees. On this dreadful roster are at least 11 leaders of the OCSS.

Crouched in a Oaxaca jail cell at the Santa María Ixcotl penitentiary that they share with 30 other prisoners, two young men describe how they were tortured under the direction of advisers wearing FBI caps: first their faces were wrapped in rags, then gallons of water were poured down their gullets. Live electric wires were attached to their genitals and the juice turned on. They were beaten and, much as U.S. special forces often threatened in Vietnam, they were told they would be thrown into the sea from military helicopters. The U.S. embassy, of course, denies complicity.[114]

But Washington is already knee-deep in the Zedillo administration's counterinsurgency campaigns. FBI trainers were in Oaxaca in 1997, shaping up local security forces. Ambassador Jones' offer of anti-terrorism aid, while officially turned down by foreign minister Gurria[115], is very much in evidence throughout the region, as U.S.-supplied Hummer armored vehicles and helicopter gunships battle the ghosts in the trees.

"This all began up in the forests," Julián Rodríguez reminds himself softly, sinking against the chipped wall of his permanently unfinished house up in Tepetixtla. "Now many good men are dead. They were all good workers and valuable compañeros…"

THE INDIANS VS. THE FLAG OF MONEY
TWO JUNGLES, MANY WORLDS, ONE PLANET
(THE CHIMILAPAS AND THE LACANDÓN 1492-1997)

This is a tale of two jungles and how the Indians who dwell within these tropical forests resist annexation—not by a foreign state but by the free traders and the globalizers whose only patria, as Subcomandante Marcos calls it, is money.[116]

With a million acres of cloud forest and lowland jungle straddling the narrow neck of the Tehuantepec Isthmus, where the states of Veracruz, Oaxaca, and Chiapas form a land bridge between the Caribbean and the Pacific, the Chimilapas is Mexico's last great, untrammeled tropical stand. One of the most bio-diverse regions in the Americas, the "Chimis" teem with tapirs and toucans, ocelots, jaguars, boas, rare quetzal birds, and precious hardwoods. Rising from 600 feet to 8,000, its forests enclose hundreds of micro-environments that produce such divergent species as dwarf pines and hotland orchids. 900 species of flora and 200 kinds of fauna have been recorded in a single hectare here.[117] The region represents Mexico's last intact set of lungs, a vital oxygen bank for the nation. Most of the great rivers of the south—the Coatzacoalcos, the Usumacinta, the Grijalva, the Tonalá—rise here. Now, those who are sworn to defend this vast wilderness fear extinction by the geo-political onslaught that answers to the name of globalization.

GOURDS OF GOLD

The Chimilapas have long been coveted by those who would annex Mexico for their own global adventures. In 1529, Cortez commissioned his cousin to explore the Tehuantepec Isthmus for a water route to the Pacific. The Conquistadores worked their way inland, south from the Caribbean coast, laying their axes into the virgin hardwood forests to the dismay of the Zoque nation that had stewarded these mountains for millennia. Descendants of the Olmecs, like the Chontales, the Zoques became so vexed by the invasion that they assembled gourds full of cold coins (*juntar jícaras*) and, in 1689, bought back their ancestral lands from the Crown for 25,000 pesos—hence the nomenclature: *Chimilapas* = "gourd of gold." [118]

But the invaders would not let the Zoques live in peace in their immense solitude for very long. In the 19th century, the North Americans, driven mad by Manifest Destiny and already in a global mood, conceived that a canal across the Isthmus would open the gates to the Far East. The gringos invaded

Mexico in 1847 to that end, among others, but, pressed to achieve a speedy settlement pror to the U.S. election of 1848, Nicholas Trist sacrificed the isthmus in the Treaty of Guadalupe Hidalgo. While James Gadsden tried to inveigle the isthmus into his 1853 "purchase," he left town without clear title. But U.S. dreams of aggrandizement die hard. Finally, in 1857, the Tehuantepec Isthmus was ceded by the cash-strapped Juárez to the Yanquis, a deal that even allowed American troops to be stationed in the region to protect the U.S. investment—the U.S. Civil War derailed this foolhardy concession and it was never ratified by Congress.

The Gringos were not to be denied. The 49ers and those who followed them crossed the Isthmus to reach the gold fields of northern California from U.S. southern ports. A New Orleans outfit bought the Tehuantepec concession but could not come up with enough backing to build a railroad. Civil engineer James Buchanan Epps brought Yanqui know-how to the project and designed a series of rolling platforms that would have transported ships over the mountains, from Caribbean to blue Pacific. Under the Porfiriato, transnational wood poachers like William Randolph Hearst hacked away at the Chimilapas without restraint. In 1907, Weetman Pearson, Don Porfirio's favorite venture capitalist, finally completed a rail link between the port of Salina Cruz and Puerto México, now Coatzacoalcos, on the Gulf, hauling Hawaiian sugar to the U.S. east coast for great personal profit.

During the 1974-82 oil boom, the Japanese financed pipeline construction from PEMEX facilities in Coatzacoalcos, over the hump of the mountains, down to Salina Cruz, where the Olmeca light crude was pumped onto tankers headed for the Land of the Rising Sun—during the 1980s, Japan was buying up about 14% of Mexico's export oil platform. Now 1,613 kilometers of ducts push petroleum and natural gas, ammonia and a witches' brew of petrochemicals, through this environmentally-sensitive zone. Meanwhile, the Zoques have their hands full on the Chiapas flank of the forest, beating off caciques who would turn their surviving trees into sheets of plywood and run prize cattle on the emptied land.

"Little Taiwancito"

On the brink of Buck Rogers' 21st Century, the predators are globalizing and the Tehuantepec Isthmus has resurfaced as a potentially profitable right of way for those who would annex the planet. With the Panama Canal so congested that east-west traffic is sometimes backed up 64 ships deep, the free traders need new routes and the Tehuantepec is, once again, projected as an international corridor for commerce and shipping. As the Vision crystallizes, the Zedillo government solicits multibillion-dollar investments from Arab sheikhs and U.S. transportation conglomerates. Deep inside the Chimilapas, at Santa

María and San Miguel, the Zoques fear that the government's Trans-Oceanic Megaproject is not going to have a happy ending for their communities and their culture and the forests whose depredation they have resisted for so long.

According to leaked documents prepared for the Transportation and Communications Secretariat (SCT)[119], the megaproject will transform the newly-privatized ports into gargantuan hubs, much like Singapore or Rotterdam, where goods are transferred and distributed throughout the hemisphere. An electric rail link will speed 60-car container trains between coasts at 120 kilometers an hour—80 international transportation giants, many of them U.S.-based, are vying for 50-year concessions to run Mexico's rail system. To accommodate truck traffic, a four-lane highway, reportedly being financed by a member of the royal family of the United Arab Emirates[120], will be completed between Coatzacolacos and Salina Cruz by the year 2000.

Time is money and Zedillo's mega-project will save both—the new Tehuantepec "dry" canal offers the northernmost route to U.S. east coast markets, cutting days off the sailing time south to Panama, and getting the goods on the streets of New York City that much more rapidly.

The neo-liberals are thinking big on this one. The Trans-Oceanic will feature a maquiladora zone to be located on the sun-scrubbed Tehuantepec plain. Government flacks tout the poverty-stricken region for its abundant cheap labor (workers from the Isthmus now have to travel all the way to the northern border to slave in such assembly plants). Damming rivers that rise in the Chimilapas will generate hydroelectric energy to power the projected industrial zone. The transnationally-owned maqs would serve as final assembly points for parts that would be shipped in from all corners of the globe. "The Isthmus could become a little Taiwan ('Taiwancito')," one SCT official tells *El Financiero*.[121]

IN THE GLOBAL EYE

Although the Trans-Oceanic Megaproject has the globalizers salivating, the locals don't seem to want to have anything to do with it. After President Ernesto Zedillo came to the Isthmus in October 1996 to announce that the New Tehuantepec Canal was under sail, Leopoldo De Gyves, local congressional representative from the militant Juchitán district and a founder of the powerful, left-leaning, Coalition of Workers, Farmers, and Students of the Isthmus (COCEI), grew maximally indignant: "They sold us a project we didn't know anything about beforehand—as usual, we have never been consulted. With the revision of Article 27, they will buy and expropriate our ejido and communal lands. Who will have sovereignty over the Isthmus? Mexico or the extranjeros?" De Gyves asked his Zoque constituents at a gathering in Santa

María: "Will you have to put your gourds together again to buy your land back from the North Americans?"[122]

"These schemes are very old but also very new. Actually, they go all the way back to Cortez and Charles V. But, up until the 20th century, the Atlantic was the key to global ambitions—now it is the Pacific Rim," Andrés Barreda, a UNAM strategic resources researcher, explained to this reporter during a break in the Zapatistas' Continental Forum against Neo-Liberalism, held in another jungle not far removed from the Chimilapas. Barreda figures the Tehuantepec project is designed to connect up Chinese and Asian Tiger offshore production with prime consumer markets on the U.S. east coast, a replay of Pearson's Hawaiian sugar trade nearly a century ago. The U.S. midwest and south would be serviced via the Mississippi River and the intercoastal canal system that now extends from Florida to northeastern Mexico.

But not only east-west commerce would be facilitated by the megaproject, Barreda reflects—new petroleum finds on the west side of South America in Colombia and Peru will flow more efficiently to northern markets over the Tehuantepec. The development of the Isthmus into a super strategic zone for energy speculators—80% of all Mexican oil production and processing is centered in the zone—makes the region sensitive to foreign designs. Barreda recalls U.S. invasions of Panama and the Persian Gulf to put down threats to the world oil supply and worries about future U.S. interventions to protect the proposed Tehuantepec route. "We haven't progressed very far since Juárez tried to sell the Isthmus in 1857," the researcher remarks dourly.[123]

A DARKER VISION

Environmental worker Miguel Angel García has walked the Chimilapas for years, seeking to bring the forest's 34 non-Zoque agrarian communities together into alliance with the Indians to create a conservation-minded, campesino-run biosphere. In the years since García has labored here, his *pactos* (pacts) have halted the slashing and burning of forest lands for crop planting (organic alternatives are taking root in the Chimis) and fought off roads that threaten to perforate wilderness areas. "Every road built here represents a tremendous loss of resource," he frets, worrying that the Trans-Oceanic Megaproject will reduce the Chimilapas to the size of a park—"They'll probably give us the golf course that they don't want in Tepoztlán," he quips blackly.

The projected industrial park component of the Tehuantepec project will poison the air and drain the rivers on the Atlantic side if dams are built to siphon off hydroelectric energy. Increased immigration of impoverished Mexicans "will bring us everything the neo-liberal social pathology offers: inflation, contamination, prostitution, alcoholism. The Megaproject is a death sentence for these forests and Mexico cannot breathe without them."[124]

García's dark vision is shared by other defenders of the Indians and their right to live unimpeded on the land they have held for all of their histories. "The installation of the megaproject means that poverty is going to get worse on the Tehuantepec Isthmus and in the Chimilapas," deduces Samuel Ruiz, the harried Bishop of San Cristóbal de las Casas. "This isn't prophecy. This is just how neo-liberalism works."[125]

Violence in the Chimilapas has thus far been avoided but the clock is running. Government officials are always being taken hostage by the Zoques to emphasize their ownership of these forests and there are constant sightings of guerrilleros above the tree line. The Popular Revolutionary Army and the Zapatista Army of National Liberation express their opposition in communiqués today and, perhaps, in bullets tomorrow. "The eruption of two leftist guerrilla insurgencies in the region…makes possible investors skeptical…" that bugle of global commerce, the *New York Times*, concluded in a 1996 piece on Central American canal building.[126]

A JUNGLE FULL OF SOLDIERS AND CHAPOPOTE

200 miles northeast of the Chimilapas, as the Quetzal bird and the Zopilote fly, in the heart of the Lacandón rain forest, the largely Mayan Zapatistas—and their mascots—hold the neo-liberal proposition at bay. "We are not going to let them annex us to the express train of brutality and human imbecilism," writes Durito, the jungle beetle who is Subcomandante Marcos's constant companion.[127]

At the bottom of the Zapatista rebellion may well be a great lake of that sublimely global fluid, petroleum—or so concludes Father Mardonio Morales, who has spent three decades trekking the canyons (*cañadas*) and the *selva* (jungle) of Lacandónia, the EZLN's area of influence. "Great interests are at play in this jungle—the lives of the Indian communities as opposed to the unrestricted control of the natural resources that sustain neo-liberal structures," Father Morales wrote in a private paper distributed for discussion among fellow priests.[128] Everywhere the snowy-bearded, 70-year-old padre has traveled in the Lacandón, from the floor of the jungle to the Mayan highlands, he sees *chapopote* (oil) oozing from the earth.

Mardonio is certainly not the only one to notice the region's energy potential. PEMEX has surveyed deposits and drilled test holes throughout the jungle and surrounding countryside since the 1970s. Most of Petroleos Mexicanos' working wells in the Lacandón have been perforated just east of the Montes Azules Biosphere, the reserve to which the core of the jungle has been reduced. The wells suck from the same basin as Guatemalan fields in the Petén. Drilling has been accompanied by widespread deforestation and the stripping of remaining stands of priceless hardwoods. Mardonio Morales recalls hitching a

ride with a big rig from the denuded Pico de Oro PEMEX complex. To his dis-
belief, the driver was hauling illegally cut mahogany logs to mills in the north
of Chiapas.[129]

Padre Mardonio is suspicious of the government's stepped-up road-building
through the jungle. "Wherever PEMEX waves its magic wand, a road appears"
while communities with no oil-developing potential remain isolated. "The
strategy is clear," he writes. "It is not for nothing that this jungle is filled with
soldiers."[130]

The number of PEMEX wells in the actual jungle is known only within the
conglomerate's inner sanctum. "We have tried unsuccessfully for years just to
get PEMEX to give us a list of the sites," reports Ignacio March, director of the
Center for the Investigation and Study of the Southeast (CIES), a San
Cristóbal environmental research institute dedicated to conserving what's left
of the Lacandón. "PEMEX is not very forthcoming."[131]

NAZARET

One field which is known to both researchers and those who live in the
nearby jungle is the Nazaret complex, above the Zapatista community of La
Garrucha in the Sierra of Coralchén. The first recorded clash between the
EZLN and the Mexican Army took place at Las Calabazas on May 23rd, 1993,
just off the access road a few kilometers from the now-capped drilling station,
at the crest of the Coralchén, in whose caves the Zapatistas had camped for
years.[132]

By PEMEX's own standards, at 400 barrels a day, Nazaret added little to
Mexico's daily production platform (2.85 million barrels in 1996). The oil was
"heavy," say former workers and March considers that Nazaret was too high in
the sierra to be a big producer. Former oil field workers told UNAM researcher
Fabio Barbosa that the wells, drilled and capped in 1991, "cried and howled" at
night and threw up stones. Indian workers feared that the *Yegatchuatl*, a Mayan
devil woman who "cuts up" womanizers, dwelt in the well.[133]

But Nazaret also produced natural gas—more than a million cubic feet a
day.[134] Despite the wasteful burn-off after the 1996 Cactus blow-out, Mexico
needs new natural gas deposits—the Zedillo government is committed to natural gas conversion by 1998 and investment, particularly in the newly privatized energy generation and pipeline sector, depends on fresh resources and the
installation of infrastructure to collect and pump it out. The continued presence of the Zapatista Army of National Liberation in the Lacandón jungle, is
not conducive to such extraction.

THE ZAPATISTA DREAM

At the heart of their agonizing, now-suspended "peace" negotiations with the "bad government" is the Zapatistas' dream of autonomy. While demands for autonomy are both political (administrative control over their own affairs, election of officials through traditional community mechanisms) and judicial (jurisdiction over their own justice system), they are also eminently territorial. Autonomy means dominion over a very particular place and it is a fiction if it does not include the land and the air above that place, the water around it, and what minerals lie beneath the soil too—in short, access to, and, ultimately, control over, that place's natural resources.

Such pretensions appear to be in direct conflict with the Mexican Constitution Article 27 which stipulates that what minerals are found beneath the subsoil—and petroleum is a mineral—belong to the entire nation. But the Zapatistas are hardly asking for their own nation state—they ask only for a piece of the action. "In the Zapatista world, there is room for everyone," postulates Comandante Tacho.[135]

Autonomy, and the demand for it, startle the Neo-liberal Beast—the triumph of the local over the global is dangerously counterproductive to transnational interests. In response to the Zapatista demand, the Zedillo administration fosters the calamitous spectacle of secession and balkanization, a Mexican Bosnia in southeastern Chiapas. Behind this smokescreen of fear and authoritarianism, the regime is busily at work, selling bonds on the international market to promote what it calls development, drafting new forestry laws that allow transnational pulp and paper giants to occupy Indian and ejido land in Chiapas and adjoining southern states[136], preparing the roads and the infrastructure, moving in the troops to capture the EZLN leaders. Confrontation would appear to be inevitable. The globalizers know full well that they must first move the Zapatistas out in order to annex the Lacandón jungle and what lies above and below its leafy floor.

WHICH WORLD?

Globalization invades indigenous regions, destroys native culture, shrinks precious resources, and concentrates the wealth among the very few New Masters of the Universe. The term itself is a bald-faced misnomer—historically, the resource-greedy, technology-endowed North drains prime material from the undeveloped South and returns little except plastic family-size containers full of Coca-Cola. Technological advancement has only fine-tuned this centuries-old one-way flow—now, computer-manipulated satellites scout out resource hot spots and deep sea drilling units reach to the bottom of the world's most secret oceans to suck out petroleum.

As the process of "globalization" accelerates, the planet polarizes between up and down. High in the sky, the transnational eyes scan the earth's farthest-flung corners for fresh resources and markets. Down on the ground, indigenous peoples, rooted for millennia to their lands and their forests, huddle under the trees and resolve to defend what's theirs, with renewed vehemence, as the enemy draws near.

The Zapatistas remain in the forefront of resistance to annexation by that country without a flag, "that patria called money." In August, 1996, they summoned thousands of strangers to their jungle to dance in the mud beneath a big, orange moon and rally their energies for a battle that will not be won soon. All the Zapatistas want, Subcomandante Marcos demands, "is a New World."[137] But Marcos's globe is not the same as that of the globalizers, who would homogenize us into one faceless mass of producers and dispensers and consumers of sterile, efficient, fast food tacos. As the Sup says, "We want a world with all the many worlds that the world needs to really be the world."[138]

EPILOGUE
Annexing North America

The Wall moves east from the stained beach, past Coronado State Park, dips into a steep canyon, runs parallel to the sewage-stippled Tijuana River and the San Ysidro freight yards, breaks at the teeming border station, picks up on the east side and starts to climb for the Otay mesa. 14.5 miles inland, the Wall disappears into steep mountain brush, resumes its trajectory for a few miles on either side of the Tecate gate, vanishes once more behind the hairpin turns of the Rumorosa road, shows up at the city limits of Mexicali-Calexico and again between the two San Luis Río Colorados at the end of California. The Wall vanishes out in the parched desert east of Yuma where an undetermined number of *indocumentados* perish under the broiling sun each year, reasserts itself between the Nogaleses, then at Naco and Douglas—the last two lengths built with contributions from businesspeople on the northern side. The Wall skips most of New Mexico until one approaches Anapra-Sunland Park on the west Texas line, and continues on into El Paso-Ciudad Juárez. There the river with two names takes over as a natural boundary to keep the indocs out, running 900 miles to the Gulf at Matamoros-Brownsville. At this writing, the Wall covers less than a hundred miles (only 316 miles are even fenced) out of a possible 1,962 miles of border but more, much more, is to come.

The Wall signifies division. The Wall divides the Americas between north and south, demarcates the First World from the Third, white people from brown people, the modestly affluent from the extremely poor, the well-fed from the malnourished. The Wall makes it clear which side you are on. The Wall divides two nations and splits one biological region in half. Naturalists worry that habitat will be restricted by the Wall, migratory paths disrupted for snakes and lizards, jackrabbits, pronghorn deer, and indigenous peoples, like the Pai Pai, who have roamed freely across this border for all of their own biological history. One cactus collector tells of finding stands of ancient, night-blooming cereus cactus trampled and smashed by Wall-builders out in the Arizona-Sonora desert.[1]

The Wall is 12 feet high and is constructed, for the most part, of corrugated steel landing pads, originally designed for U.S. helicopter set-downs during Operation Desert Storm. The Wall was begun in 1990 as a huge ditch between the two countries that would have slowed illegal vehicle traffic north, but then Saddam Hussein threw in the towel in just 40 days and, suddenly, there were all these leftover landing pads with which to build a real barrier. The U.S. Army Corps of Engineers began construction in late 1991, one of the first signs that the border between Mexico and the United States was about to get militarized.

The Wall has begun to rust. The Wall has sharp barbs at the top, which tear at the clothes and tear at the flesh. Washington could have spent a little more and built a better wall. 2,000 miles of ten-foot-tall, standard prison chain-link fence, topped by razor wire, would have come in at $835 million—for $362 million more, the fence could be electrified from the Pacific to the Gulf. A 12-foot-high, two-foot-thick concrete wall, painted on both sides, would run about $3 billion—a half-billion could be shaved if only one side was painted. *New York Times* correspondent Sam Howe Verhovik suggests that additional savings could be made if the Migra hired undocumented Mexican workers to build the Wall.[2]

The Wall is an indictment of the pernicious xenophobia sweeping the United States, a land of immigrants. "Watch your immigration policy," an old Sioux chief once told his representative in Washington. "We didn't watch ours."[3]

On the weekend after NAFTA cleared the U.S. Congress in November 1993, the California National Guard and the Army Corps of Engineers were winching in the final slabs of wall, out at the beach by Playas de Tijuana. A huge pile-driver pounded pilings into the sand—the Wall was being built 340 feet into the filthy surf. "I guess this is so the fish can't get across to the Other Side," cackled a toothless old bracero, observing the Yanqui engineering feat in progress.

The Wall makes it hard for old people and fat people to get to "El Otro Lado" so hustlers come out in the afternoons and carve out tunnels under the Wall, charging a peso a head in the dark, when the Migra shift changes and there might be a few minutes to make it into North America. But now the Migra is building a triple Wall or rather, "multiple barrier system," with patrol roads running in between to trap the indocs like rats in a maze. San Diego right-wingers came out to celebrate the first day of work on the triple wall in March 1997, carrying banners that warned "Good Walls Make Good Neighbors."[4]

The Wall is a bulletin board. Murals are painted on the Mexican side, political slogans, shouts of pain and greeting, the names of lovers enclosed in spray-painted hearts. Near Playas de Tijuana, there is a crude portrait of Emiliano Zapata. "If this man was here, this wall would not be here," it reads above the fading caudillo's sombrero.

The Wall is an ideological barrier every bit as much as was the Berlin Wall—but the ideologies being disputed here are called The Universal

Desperation of the Underdeveloped World and the withering First World paranoias of Fortress America

ESCAPE INTO NORTH AMERICA

There was no wall yet when I first crossed this divide, illegally, in the dark, under the Migra helicopters—no physical wall yet, but a paper one, yes. It was early May 1987, 24 hours after the U.S. Immigration Reform & Control Act (IRCA) or, more popularly, the Simpson-Rodino bill (after its sponsors), became the law of both lands. We were among the first "Rodinos," as those who crossed illicitly in its wake, trying to slip in under the Amnesty deadline, came to be known. To reduce the number of illegals living within U.S. borders, IRCA proposed to "amnesty" or legalize those who could prove five years' residency in the U.S. Thousands of Mexicans who had once worked in El Norte returned to try and prove their claim. It was a much more innocent time.

My escape into North America began as a joke. A Mexico City TV crew had come to the Zapata canyon above Tijuana's Colonia Libertad, then the staging area for the charge north, and wanted to film a group of Mexicans setting out for the Other Side. I spoke to Chuy and Marco, two guides I'd been cultivating. Their people were crouched around them, waiting for a break in the Migra patrols up on the ridge. Bored with the long wait, the would-be indocs agreed to stage their departure for the cameras and even marched about 50 feet down the canyon, shouting slogans. Once the tape had been shot and wrapped, the little band of 13 men, women, and babies just kept on going. Chuy and Marco graciously let me trail along.

Darkness fell fast as we advanced, first down into the broad canyon and then up a bald hillside, webbed by a thousand narrow goat paths, all of them winding north. Whenever the Border Patrol helicopter veered over the ridge top, its huge beams dividing the onrushing night, we stood stock-still, frozen like shrubs, as if we were part of the scenery. A plump woman, who had been traipsing the trail in a red miniskirt and white spike heels, used the interval to change into pants and black basketball sneakers. Everyone giggled.

We resumed our climb towards the top of the mesa and a burly farmer from Zacatecas explained that he needed to get to Fresno to find some check stubs that he had hidden last year under a board in an improvised camp out in the woods. "They will prove my amnesty claim," he said, his voice lost in his big chest.

Marco, a skinny teenager who looked more like he should be shooting hoops down on the schoolyard than committing major crimes out here in this no-man's land between worlds, whistled urgently from up above. Everyone bunched up together as the chopper wheeled in low, hovering almost directly overhead and illuminating the dry grass all around us, but were huddled in the blind spot right beneath it and the Migra missed us. "*Papi, Papi, un helicóptero,*" squealed a four-year-old and her tall, serious father cautioned her to be silent. The family, from Michoacán, had been trying to cross for seven nights and had been turned back each time.

The scrawny woman they called *La Prieta* (the dark one) had five nights in. Twice the Migra had caught her and returned her to Tijuana on the nightly deportees' bus, and twice she had returned on her own rather than risk custody. She told me that she had gone home to Guerrero because her mother was dying and now she needed to get to Santa Anna, California where her sister-in-law, an "Americana," she said hopefully, had been watching her daughter for the past two months.

The chopper rumbled overhead for a long minute, could not locate its prey, and moved on down the canyon. We took off again, in groups of threes and fours, running low and close together across the stubbly land. In a plowed but unplanted tomato patch, we stumbled into barbed wire strung between the rows. La Prieta pulled the strands apart and we ducked under. Then she slipped her arm inside mine and let me drag her along—she was exhausted. La Prieta felt light, even airy on my arm. I wondered if encouraging her to hold onto me like this constituted a felony, "aiding an alien" to escape into North America.

The groups came together 50 feet from the county road and crouched in the brush, waiting for the Migra patrol van to pass. Chuy could sort out the dangers by the sound of the motors. Then we were off again, darting through a peeled-back chain-link fence, and sprinting downhill into a deep ravine at full tilt, La Prieta still clinging to me—this is where I break my leg for sure, I fretted—and then straight up, puffing hard, bathed in cold sweat. At the top, we emerged out on the mesa. The fragrance of wild sage rising from the tableland in the spring air filled our nostrils and invigorated us. At the edge of the bluff, we sat and gaped in wonder at the lights of the subdivisions and malls bathing the southern California night for miles and miles and miles before us.

One boy pointed at the golden arches of McDonald's down in Chula Vista and said he had a friend who once worked there. "Maybe, he can get me a job." The man from Zacatecas told me his patrón in Fresno was a good man. He was sure that he was still holding his job open for him. "I have gone with this man every year for 13 years now," he said solemnly.

We moved quickly, single file, down the embankment to California 805, a spur of U.S. 5, roaring towards San Diego. Through a mix of our guide's guile and the Virgin of Guadalupe's intervention, all 13 of us made it across ten lanes of killer freeway in one piece. The next year, after 17 Mexicans had been cut down trying to make it to the Other Side, the State of California would post "Migrant Crossing" motorist warnings on 805. The signs were like "Deer

Crossing" warnings, only they displayed a pictograph of a humble family, scurrying for their lives through treacherous freeway traffic.

I walked the path straddling the freeway and a Chula Vista subdivision with young Marco. He was going to call the car to come pick up the *pollos* (chickens) he had just delivered and take them away from the border. I was going to call a taxi to take me back to Tijuana so I could write this story.[5] We parted company at the Palm Avenue shopping center. Anything you want to add, I asked Marco before putting away my mini-recorder. "Just tell them that we're going to keep coming here no matter what kind of pinche laws you people pass," the kid grinned.

THE BALLAD OF PEDRO FABIÁN HUARUCO[6]

A decade later, even though Mexico has officially joined North America in the interim, getting in the door has become an infinitely grimmer and more painful ordeal.

Pedro Fabián Huaruco hunkers down in what passes for his front yard, on the outskirts of Cherán, Michoacán, a high mountain town of 30,000 mostly unemployed Purépecha Indians, and tells a story that sounds like a corrido, those sad border ballads that have traditionally chronicled the misfortunes of undocumented workers who travel north each year to toil in the fields and the factories on the Other Side.

Pedro Fabián's ballad was written in the year of one of the most intense U.S. government crackdowns on illegal immigration in memory, 1996, but it is a story of the danger and disappointment that have always dogged those driven to escape this *desgraciada pobreza* (disgraceful poverty—the title of a corrido written by the prolific Salomé Gutiérrez) that engulfs Deep Mexico.

"I left here with certain illusions," the 22-year-old remembers, his dark eyes sullen with rage. "Now I can't say that I have them anymore."

In Cherán, only 1,100 farmers out of 6,000 families, hold land, and Pedro Fabián's is not one of them, a demographic that forces 3,000 to 5,000 men and women—at least one from every second household in town—to go north each year. Perhaps 600 of them carry legal papers.[7] The rest risk their necks to get across. The money orders the workers send home are virtually Cherán's only source of income. But the traffic has not been all one way. Homeboys come back in cardboard coffins these days and there are gang tags—"Sur Trece," a tough San Francisco street mob—on the wall by the plaza now.

Pedro's "illusion" was to rebuild the shack that his family of six share in the poorest barrio of the town. "I thought it would go good. I borrowed to pay for my ticket and for the price of the coyote (the people smuggler). The loan shark charged me 20%." Salvador Chávez, a childhood friend who just lived a few houses down the rut that passed for a street, had invited Pedro Fabián to go to

Watsonville, California and work the strawberries. Joining the party would be Salvador's three brothers, Florentino (who had a legal green card), Jaime, just 19, and Benjamín—at 33, with 15 years in the fields around Watsonville, Benjamín qualified for resident status but had never filed, preferring to go as a *mojado* each season.

Their odyssey began April 1st at the Zamora, Michoacán terminal when they boarded a bus that would move them a thousand miles north to Tijuana. In California, on that same morning, Riverside County sheriff's deputies were filmed by a local television helicopter crew as they systematically clubbed two indocumentados into submission, following a high-speed chase. The message of the tape, which galvanized Mexicans on both sides of the border and generated a complaint by the Mexican government to the Organization of American States, was perfectly clear: don't get caught.

The coyotes prowl the ill-lit Tijuana Central Camionera bus depot. "We bargained with them. The best deal was for $350 apiece. We would not have to pay it until we came to Los Angeles," Pedro recalls. Florentino, whose papers were in order, would cross at the gate. The men from Cherán embraced. With any luck, they would meet again in Watsonville where there would be work in the strawberries through the fall.

Their coyote had lined up 25 clients for the journey further north. Guides would accompany them over the line. But the crossing could not be in Tijuana where the Migra had beefed up to over a thousand agents and the Wall slowed down the indocs long enough to boost the Border Patrol's capture rates to record levels. Now the traffic had moved 35 miles east, around Tecate, into a sparsely populated mountainous region that spreads over both sides of the border—since the traffic was pushed this way in 1996, scores of Mexicans have died from plunges into yawning ravines or from exposure to the freezing weather in this part of the border. Upping the risks of passage is a Migra strategy to stem the flow north.

The men started into the mountains at dusk. "We walked for seven hours until we came to a place where there was a house. We hid there during the day. The next night, a camper came for us. It had painted windows so you couldn't see out. We drove for a half-hour to another house where they fed us, which was good because we hadn't eaten the whole day. What was bad was that there were only two tortillas to go around. Around 4 am, they put us back in the camper."

At dawn, an hour up the highway, near Temécula, on the San Diego-Riverside County line, a Border Patrol unit slipped in behind the camper. Each time the driver of the truck picked up speed, the Migra stayed right on its tail. Meanwhile, the agents had radioed up ahead and a second patrol car, its lights flashing to slow them down, tried to block the camper's passage. The panicked driver shot right past. "We were frightened that we were going to die. We kept signaling the driver to stop but he wouldn't listen."

The camper went off the road at 90 miles an hour and flipped over twice. Pedro Fabián thinks a tire blew out but others have argued that the Migra shot them out. When he regained consciousness, Pedro Fabián tried to find his friends but the medics from the ambulance would not let him stand. From where he lay, he could see the rescue unit winch lift the truck motor off the mangled corpses of the three Chávez brothers. "I knew there was no use, they were dead already." In all, eight migrant workers were killed in the tragedy, one of many such crashes that have occurred around Temécula as the result of Border Patrol chases. 17 others were injured—and deported.

Pedro Fabián was bruised and scraped but otherwise in one piece. The deportation took several days. A Mexican consular official appeared at the Riverside hospital and handed out cookies to the survivors. Back in Tijuana, Pedro sadly got back on the bus. The price of the ticket exhausted all the money he had borrowed back home and left him without anything to eat during the 46-hour trip south to Michoacán.

The bodies of Pedro's neighbors had arrived in Cherán before Pedro did, courtesy of the Michoacán state government, in cardboard boxes, "to humiliate us even more," says a fifth brother who had been too ill to go north that spring. The dead were mourned in the cramped Chávez family compound at a traditional Purépecha wake. Their grandmother walked up and down in the so-called street all night, casting incense smoke so that the spirits of the men left behind by the side of a California highway could safely find their way.

ZEDILLO'S FORCED RETREAT

Cherán is prototypical of how México Profundo lives in the last years of the 20th century. There is no work there—even the town's teachers have to go north in the summertime to keep their families in tortillas. There is no infrastructure—the scent of raw sewage hangs in the clear mountain air and the PRI-run state government is reluctant to provide services because this is a solidly PRD town. Decapitalization of the agrarian sector in conformity with IMF and World Bank mandates to cut government subsidies in the 1980s has dead-ended farming, and deforestation is finishing off the resin industry.

Although mestizos from surrounding towns like Gómez Farias have been going north for more than a century (the first group of men left from Gómez Farias for Watsonville, California in 1879),[8] the Purépechas of the sierra have only begun to migrate in great number in the last 20 years. Now, the Purés vie with the Mixtecos of Oaxaca and the Nahuas of Mexico state for the highest out-migration of Mexico's 56 indigenous nations.

It is an old story. Political and economic turmoil have been driving Mexicans north since Don Porfirio's day. "The initial impetus for emigration resulted from attempts to achieve capitalist modernization of the countryside," writes Lawrence Cardoso,[9] an observation that might describe the Mexican emigration impasse a century later in the 1990s. Bound to the haciendas, which had gobbled up their village lands for the sake of efficiency and progress, peons worked for pennies (15 cents a day in 1910),[10] producing export crops for Europe and the U.S., a model again much in vogue today. Then, as now, the privatization of agrarian Mexico narrowed campesinos' options. They could *aguantar* in silence, shout "*¡basta ya!*" and rise up in rebellion, or catch one of the Dictator's railroads north, first to Sonora and Chihuahua—the closer one got to the border, the better the wages were—and then across that largely open frontier, where western growers and mine operators and the railroads put them to work at ten times the pay back home.

The revolution drove at least a million Mexicans into the U.S.[11]—whole towns like Villa Acuña just picked up and relocated in Texas.[12] The Cristiada impelled tens of thousands more to flee to the U.S. during the Roaring '20s. A half-million Mexicans were forced home by the Great Depression but most came back for the second world war. The 1982 debt crisis is thought to have been responsible for pushing a million more across the line. During 1983-4 stops went over a million for the first time on the INS books and the surge was so strong for so long that Simpson-Rodino had to be devised to deal with the illegals—either by deporting those who did not qualify for amnesty or by making citizens out of those who did. Simpson-Rodino did not solve the problem.

In 1997, 2.7 million undocumented Mexicans are thought to be living underground in the U.S.A.[13] NAFTA's rearrangements of the Mexican economy, and the "adjustments" the revision of Article 27 imposed upon farmers, were compounded by Zedillo's peso crisis. The 1995 stops topped out at 1.4 million, and 1996 stats were running 36% above 1994 when there was no crisis and no Wall to discourage their flight.

The peso crisis broke just six weeks after Pete Wilson's malicious ballot Proposition 187 carried California with two-thirds of the vote. By the winter of 1995, while those too distraught to go on flung themselves on the tracks before oncoming trains in the Mexico City Metro, the border was jumping. There were 625,000 stops made in the first five months of the year—2,000 a day were being taken in the San Diego sector.[14] Over 2.8 million stops were made in the first two years of the crisis, if INS extrapolations are to be trusted. A third of the escapees are thought to have made it to the Other Side—during this same period, according to National Immigration Council estimates, another 300,000 went home to Mexico.[15]

The stop figures (which combine deportations with voluntary returns) are, of course, useless, because they do not tell us how many actual people tried to come across, or how many times they tried. In the San Diego sector, five times was the average number of tries for each indoc in 1995—one woman from Sinaloa was detained a record 39 times, reported sector spokeswoman Ann Sommers, a true profile in determination.[16]

Young men and young women formed the nucleus of this latest exodus— Mexico must create 1.5 million jobs a year just to stay even with those entering the job market,[17] and during the 1995-6 nose dive, it created none. Although young and not-so-young men are still in the majority, out-migration counters at Tijuana's College of the Northern Frontier are increasingly seeing young women, often alone, unaccompanied minors, whole families, and old people too. The poor and the desperate still fill out the migration stream but now there are more and more delegates from Mexico's bruised middle class in the flow.

They leave for all the usual reasons: because they don't have a job or have a lousy job and want to step up or because they have no hope of ever having a job at all. To escape the hunger that the crisis has inflicted upon daily calorie counts. They leave because of political repression, because they are sick of the corruption and the impunity, or because they sense Mexico is collapsing behind them and its time to get out. They leave because of family troubles or because it is a family tradition, because they are running from the cops or to make their fortune, or because they broke up with their *novias* (girlfriends) and are just so depressed they didn't know what to do next.

Whatever the reason(s), the Zedillo-White House-IMF war on the poor sent perhaps 2,000,000 Mexicans running for the border in 1995 and '96. They ran as if in forced retreat, fleeing from a Mexico that only promised more pain if they stayed. On the Other Side, U.S. authorities would perceive this forced retreat as an invasion, squeezing the would-be escapees into an even tighter corner between countries.

QUICK, HONEY, GET THE BLACK FLAG!

"They keep coming..." It was the old "Red Dawn," neo-Cold War refrain, the revolutionaries streaming across the border dressed up like poor people. "They keep coming," the voice-over warned, with a squirrelly tremor. It was the scare pitch for California governor Pete Wilson's pet project, the 1994 ballot Proposition 187, which would strip undocumented workers of health and education services within the boundaries of the Golden State. "They keep coming..." On the screen, file footage flickered: a mad dash of determined Mexicans crashing right through the San Ysidro border station and loping on up the freeway, before three federal and state police agencies combine to corral them, amidst heavy border traffic. "They keep coming…" the script read, as if the invaders were pesky cockroaches or termites, some common household plague. "They keep coming…" Quick, honey, get the Black Flag!

The invasion psychosis is particularly virulent in San Diego, a city and a county that likes to pretend no poor people reside within its quiet, comfortable confines, and the town where Pete Wilson made his political bones. "It's an invasion from Mexico!" warned then-Mayor Roger Hedgecock, now-Senator Wilson's replacement, declaring a state of emergency back in 1984. Worried citizens reached for their automatic weapons. "It's an invasion—not of soldiers, but of sewage," the mayor clarified. 5,000,000 gallons of raw sewage had broken out of the Tijuana River and befouled the pristine coastline all the way to La Jolla.[18]

Hedgecock has a flair for activating the vigilante set—now a popular local shock jock, he instigated "Light Up the Border," in which good citizens drove their cars to the border fence and turned on their brights, as if they were attending a lynching on the levee. The Border Lighters were presumably seeking to aid the Migra in their pursuit of the always elusive enemy aliens.

More recently, Hedgecock assembled a posse of highly white San Diegans to patrol that city's airport for brown escapees into America—after all, this invasion is not only one of foot people. Many a Mixteco has been sighted boarding a red-eye to the east coast at this terminal. "This is a domestic Vietnam," Win Housley told a local reporter as he scoured the ticket counters for invading Indians. The "U.S. Citizens Patrol" advocates aggressive preemptive strikes: "We should seize one whole 727—that would wake them up."[19]

"I have no intention of being conquered by Latins, blacks, Asians, Arabs, or any other people who have come to claim my country," affirmed Ruth Coffey, a Hedgecock ally and a player in something bluntly called "STOP Immigration Now!"[20]

They keep coming—the platitudes about invasion, that is: this is a "silent invasion," an insidious "virus" violating America's boundaries, a "cancer." "Mexico is a trampoline for terrorism," warned the posthumously waterlogged CIA director, William Colby. Managua was only 48 hours from Harlingen, Texas by car, fretted Ronald Reagan, on the cusp of Alzheimer's. The Libyan hitmen are already in Laredo, the Red Chinese were marching in Baja California—a John Birch Society shibboleth back in the paranoid '50s. Only a nation that has never been invaded could go this nuts about its borders.

SAFEGUARDING AMERICA'S BORDERS

Any invasion worth its salt requires maximum preparedness. 52 military installations back up the U.S. side of the border from San Diego to the Texas gulf. The National Guard has served in an auxiliary capacity to the Migra and the Customs Service since the 1980s. Active army units were first sent to patrol the border in 1989, under a Department of Defense training program, which lists the G.I.'s as "observers." Since then, over 2,000 such missions have dug in along the dividing line.[21] The Army Corps of Engineers built the initial sections of the Wall in 1991. Troops on war games in the desert near Naco in August '92 were the first to make immigration stops.[22] By 1995, military members of Joint Task Force 6 were regularly stopping suspected undocumenteds around Sunland Park, New Mexico, according to neighbors.[23] Headquartered at Fort Hood, Texas, Joint Task Force 6 includes U.S. Special Forces units and has operated along the Texas border for several years, assisting civil authorities to track drug smugglers.

On the night of January 24th, 1997, the U.S. military recorded its first enemy hit on this intentional battlefield when one Cesario Vázquez was cut down east of Brownsville-Matamoros. 15-year Green Beret vet Christopher Lemmen, in full-camou and face paint, pumped 11 rounds at Vázquez, hitting him in the back.[24] Sergeant Lemmen, who is ordinarily stationed at Fort Campbell, Kentucky, was bivouacked above the Río Grande with five other members of a Special Forces "observation" team. Vázquez, who tints car windows for a living, was on his way to Houston to find work, and had just emerged from the river in his underwear when he was struck. The Matamoros native, who survived, now faces seven years in jail for supposedly assaulting a member of the U.S. military.[25]

Cesario Vázquez earned the dubious distinction of being the first Mexican downed by U.S. military fire in this very live "low-intensity war"—the Migra contracts with the Center for the Study of Low Intensity Conflict to coach its agents.[26] But the actual sources of the bullets that cut Vázquez down are less important than the direction from which they came. In 1997, Joint Task Forces blend the distinctions between military and civilian defenders of the border. The Migra, with its elite anti-terrorism squads, high-powered weaponry, and enormous number of service veterans among its majority-Latino troops, is indistinguishable from the U.S. armed forces.

Like the Green Berets, the Migra is not adverse to shooting down an unarmed invader or two. In June, 1992, Nogales sector agent Michael Elmer stopped Dario Miranda with three slugs in the back in a lonely desert wash west of the border gate, and then tried to drag his body back into Mexico to make everything all right again. Elmer, an ex-military man, was acquitted three times by Arizona juries, in a case that became known as the Border Patrol's "Rodney King."

Michael Elmer's license to kill is a custom for U.S. border guards that dates back to the Migra's founding—the Border Patrol was organized from former members of the Texas and Arizona Rangers, the *rinches* who cut down many a

Mexican in their day, as recorded in such border corridos, as "The Ballad of Gregorio Cortez." On the California end of the line, this homicidal tradition was kept alive by the San Diego Border Crimes Task Force—San Diego Police and Border Patrol agents who disguised themselves as indocumentados in order to entrap the border bandits who prey on the migrants. Between 1984 and 1989, the BCTF shot 30 Mexicans to death—40 other gunshot victims survived, according to the venerable Roberto Martínez of the American Friends Service Committee's San Diego Border Project, who has dozens of shooting cases in his voluminous archives.[27]

This "low-intensity" war is killing a lot of Mexicans. In the first six months of 1996, 58 would-be invaders were fished out of the Río Grande-Bravo.[28] 77 Mexicans died coming across in the San Diego sector in 1995-96, the year of the Zedillo-induced forced retreat.[29] Vehicle pursuits, forced desert treks, freeway roadkills, and desolate mountain trails, take a weekly toll that stocks common graves along the border. 50 coffins a month show up at Guadalajara International Airport, to be returned to the villages of Jalisco in place of the live men and women who once left home with all their "illusions" for El Norte.[30]

IMMIGRATION EMERGENCY

Sergeant Lemmens' M-16 and Michael Elmer's service revolver are pieces in the mindboggling arsenal trained upon the escapees: fleets of planes and helicopters, blimps, armored vehicles and green vans, horses, bicycles, dogs; operations code-named Gatekeeper or Hold the Line or Hard Hand that rival Desert Storm and Just Cause in their organization; the Wall, fences, barbed wire, vapor lamps, electronic sensors, night vision scopes, aluminum batons, plastic handcuffs, detention centers, new laws, Prop 187, Nazis, skinheads, cholos, the Klan.

And still they keep coming...

If things get really out of hand on the southern border, the U.S. president is mandated to declare an immigration "emergency." The anti-terrorism squads will slam shut the border gates. Mass round-ups of suspected aliens (read, all Mexicans) will be ordered and, under the FEMA contingency plan code-named "Vortex," the invaders will be concentrated at military bases for safekeeping. Such facilities are already being used for this contingency—in March 1996, a rebellion of Mexicans held in the Miramar California Marine brig was crushed by military authorities. 26 indocumentados had to be hospitalized. They were treated at ritzy Scripps Memorial in nearby La Jolla,[31] at great cost to U.S. taxpayers. Ironically, many wealthier Mexicans maintain second homes in La Jolla.

Both George Bush and Bill Clinton must have had an inkling NAFTA would cause "adjustments" in the Mexican economy sure to trigger "short-term" leaps in immigration to the U.S.—the famous Hinojosa study done for the Mexican agricultural secretariat put 670,000 farm families, perhaps 3,000,000 people, in the immigration stream as the result of such dislocation, an immigration emergency in the making. One might inquire if the Wall, and the militarization of the border between these two new free trade partners, was anticipated to meet the perfectly predictable forced retreat of millions of Mexican citizens.

THE SAFETY VALVE

The exodus north is often perceived as a safety valve, allowing the disillu-sioned young and the most dangerously dissatisfied citizens to escape into North America. Mexicans retreating to the U.S. have usually been catalogued as economic refugees—but for many, the malignancy of the PRI government has been the impulse which forced them to flee and, in the 1990s, more and more escapees have been applying for, and receiving, political asylum. At least 9,721 claims have been filed since two PAN members and a gay Mexican were awarded asylum during the Salinas years. 36 Mexicans have thus far achieved recognition that they were forced from their country by political repression—they include an Indian tortured by judicial police, a worker who fought his *charro* union and lost, and a waiter who accidentally spilled soup on a famous narco-lord.[32]

Exporting dissidents is an obligatory ritual for the rulers of Mexico. Don Porfirio forced Francisco Madero and the Flores Magón brothers across the border—Díaz himself had escaped to Texas to organize his coup. As the revolu-tion built a full head of steam, the Dictator at first encouraged migration north. "The outflow of unemployed removed potential rebels and converted them into workers with incomes Mexico could not provide," writes Cardoso.[33] But, criticized by the industrialists and hacenderos he served for favoring this drain of cheap labor, Don Porfirio reversed himself and tried to stanch the migrant stream with lurid tales of life across the line—those who were leaving because of the regime's brutal excesses paid little heed.

The generals who succeeded Díaz understood the merits of the safety valve soon enough. Obregón and Calles "believed that it was not in the best inter-ests of the country to halt the labor exodus."[34] Carranza insisted that all Mexican workers leaving the country carry signed contracts that were in con-formity with Article 123 of his new constitution, which guarantees labor rights and is, in many respects, far more progressive than U.S. labor codes. The restriction proved all bluster and, indeed, Mexican labor inspectors took advantage of the decree to extort migrants heading north. At the border, the inspectors handed them over to U.S. labor contractors, who were waiting to snatch up new crews. During the Depression years, Lázaro Cárdenas sent trains to the border to repatriate his country men and women and the Mexican Autonomous Publicity and Propaganda Commission plastered posters on public walls announcing the establishment of special "colonies" for those who came home,[35] but in his heart of hearts, Cárdenas knew that Mexico could not recover without those workers outside of the country, on the Other Side, if just for the money that they sent back. Sociologist Manuel Gameo, an early student of such matters, calculated that, in the month of July 1926, 12,000 Mexican workers in the U.S. sent home $300,000 USD. At least $14,000,000 in money orders was transmitted to Mexico between 1928 and 1930, $58,000,000 during the whole decade.[36] In 1996, the figure has swelled to $4 to $8 billion a year, according to a Western Union corporate spokesperson (Western Union carries half the load), Mexico's third or fourth most important source of Yanqui dollars.[37]

The 1997 model of immigration intolerance, "The Immigration Control and Responsibility Act," further shuts down the Mexican safety valve, preventing the most disgruntled from escaping into North America, and sending billions of dollars home to maintain their families and their communities. But physical law supersedes legislative law. The U.S. immigration clampdown is a surefire formula for violent combustion south of the river with two names.

WHAT'S ON THE WELCOME WAGON

The escapees have been welcomed and unwelcomed, depending on who was on the welcoming committee. Those who sought to exploit a ready pool of cheap labor lobbied for their admittance. Those who were looking for a job, strove to keep the Mexicans out.

The first braceros dueled with coolie labor. 132,000 Chinese lived on the Pacific Coast of the United States when the Mexicans began arriving in California in the 1880s.[38] The new source of cheap labor signaled the Chinese Exclusion. All sorts of racist excuses were proffered to insure their expulsion. The Chinese were too inscrutable for the nativists. They hoarded their gold and sent all their money home. They were said to dine on dogs and cats, and you could never understand what they were saying to each other. They came from far away and they overstayed their welcome. The Mexicans were transients, always returning to their country after the harvest was in, a country that was ruled by Don Porfirio Díaz, the American Friend. His people couldn't be all that bad.

Mexicans are "plentiful, generally peaceful, and satisfied with very low condition," boasted a 1907 *Pacific Fruit Grower*, the organ of California's new millionaire agribusiness set.[39] Agricultural work was the Mexicans' strong suit because, as former Hollywood song & dance man and U.S. senator from California, George Murphy, reportedly observed, "They are built closer to the ground."[40] Murphy's anatomical assessment had historical antecedents. "…[T]he Mexican, due to his crouching and bending habits, is fully adapted to agricultural tasks," was how Dr. George Clements, founder of the Los Angeles Chamber of Commerce, endorsed the exploitation of Mexican labor in 1917.[41]

"Nativism" is just a catchy name for racism. The rule of thumb in this land of adulterated milk and honey is that each new immigrant group arrives desperate and destitute on these shores and is only too willing to offer its labor for less than anyone else on the market—thus setting itself up to get bashed by the groups that were thrown into the U.S. melting pot before it. Nonetheless, in the American pecking order, the new immigrants will, in turn, dump on those who follow—and all will dump on black people, the only immigrant group to be brought to America against its will, in chains. The melting pot brews a redolent racism that keeps workers separated, at odds, and in their place.

Xenophobia is a staple on the North American Welcome Wagon but it is even more vicious when the pigmentation of the newcomers is a shade darker than pink. There is a direct line from the "Know Nothings" of the 1850s, jobless working class stiffs who sought to exclude Mexicans from the United States because they were Papist "apes"[42] to Tom Metzgar's WAR ("White Aryan Resistance"), a Nazi skinhead clique that frequently accompanies San Diego "nativists" when they "light up the border."

The rhetoric of the nativists of an earlier time is not much distinct from that of Hedgecock's airport posse. In the teens of the century, Frederick Russell Burnhem compared Mexican farm labors to "a creeping blight," akin to the boll weevil.[43] Albert Johnson feared for the health of the republic because Mexicans represented "an ever-recurring foci of infection".[44] Some suggested that Mexicans were coming to take revenge for 1848, that what was won by U.S. armed might then, would now be lost to "biological inundation."[45] Mexicans were not only brown, they were red too. Every Mexican immigrant was "potential revolutionary material because they were born communists,"[46] opined Theodore Lothrup Stoddard. Eugenics were responsible for the Mexican's lowly condition—"he is eugenically low-powered," analyzed C.M. Goethe of Sacramento, a frequent spokesperson for the American Coalition, one of a slew of nativist groups whose arguments enlivened immigration bigotry in the 1920s.[47] Dr. Roy Garis, professor of economics and eugenics at Vanderbilt University, could not fathom why some Americans wanted this filth in his country: "In every huddle of Mexican shacks, one meets the same idleness…disease…stench, fornication, and bastardy…these people sleep by day and prowl by night, like coyotes, stealing everything they can get their hands on...yet there are Americans clamoring for more of these human swine to be brought over from Mexico."[48]

Such stirring racism poured oil on the bonfires of the Klan—in 1919, the year of the Palmer Raids on the IWW and other immigrant radicals, and a period of maximum KKK activity, one Mexican was lynched each week in the state of Texas.[49]

Nonetheless, they kept coming. Other U.S. citizens wanted them—if only for their labor: sugar beet growers throughout the West, copper bosses in Arizona and Colorado, the Southern Pacific railroad. Base pay was $1 or $2 a day and there were moments in the 1920s when the cost of living in the U.S. was lower than in Mexico. A lot of money was sent south.

Between 1900 and 1910, 500,000 Mexicans crossed the border, that is, their crossing was registered by U.S. authorities. God only knows how many did not sign in. The long, lacerating years of the revolution thickened the flow. Both sides in that fratricidal struggle escaped north: those who had been stripped of their land by the revolutionaries and those who never had land in the first place and were just sick of the fighting. 100 to 150 families a day crossed the border at Juárez during peak moments of bloodshed.[50] Fortunately, World War I caught the U.S. short-handed and 72,000 Mexicans were invited in each year to fill the ranks of those who had been taken off to fight "the war to end all wars." Even without that seminal conflict, the U.S. suffered a chronic labor shortage down on the farm— between 1900 and 1920, 6,000,000 Americans abandoned their rural homesteads to find their fortune in the cities.[51]

The fleeing Mexicans did not just cluster at the border. They followed the crops into the Frozen North—Montana and Minnesota and Michigan. From the sugar beets, many stepped up to the railroads, laying ties all the way to Chicago, where the steel mills presented new opportunities. The Pilson barrio was founded by Michoacanos and Zacatecos who followed this trail.

But in 1921 the U.S. hit an economic bump. 100,000 businesses collapsed, putting millions of American workers on the street.[52] The downturn demonstrated just how fast Mexicans could become unwelcome. Stranded in the snow in Detroit (15,000) and Minneapolis without jobs or welfare to sustain them through the long winter, thousands of Mexican families begged their government to rescue them—Washington refused to pick up the transportation tab south for fear it would set a precedent. Spring brought merciful relief and, by the summer of 1922, the U.S. economy had righted itself and those who had managed to leave dutifully returned to their appreciative patrones. But 1921 was a forewarning of the hard times to come.

The nose-dive closed the American gate. Quota legislation was drawn up and the restrictive 1924 Immigration Bill slammed the door shut. The '20s version of the Immigration Responsibility Act was a clean victory for the nativists on every front—except the Mexican one. Although the measure placed severe and permanent quotas on non-whites seeking to enter the United States, those economic interests that profited by cheap Mexican labor beat back the nativists' drive to exclude their field hands from America. California agribusiness, which had grown into a half-billion-dollar business annually, threw its weight around to secure the exemption. To avoid complications, Mexicans registering at the border on the way into the country were checked off as "white."[53] In the U.S. capitalist model, predicated as it is on racism, bosses are empowered to convert brown people to Caucasians whenever it suits their pocketbooks.

The creation of the U.S. Border Patrol in the same year, 1924, also gladdened the hearts of the nativists and vindicated their dire predictions that the Mexicans were going to keep on coming.

MANY MOMENTS OF CRUELTY

Black Friday sank the Mexicans' stock in the U.S. for the next decade. Overnight, foreign workers became pariahs. 3,000,000 U.S. proletarians were laid off in the first two months of the 1929 Depression and the AFL demanded that Mexicans be "removed" from the country because they were taking up good American jobs. The Bureau of Immigration, then under the command of the U.S. Department of Labor, sent its agents into the field, staging coast-to-coast raids at workplaces, private homes, and public gathering spots like La Placita, in downtown Los Angeles.[54] Thousands were rounded up but only hundreds actually deported—among them, persons designated "American-born" Mexicans. Tens of thousands more voluntarily returned to Mexico due to the economic collapse and the anti-Mexican attitudes that nativist know-nothings sold the white working class.

In a concerted effort to drive the greasers out of town, the Los Angeles County Welfare Department cut Spanish surnames from its rolls. Between 1931 and 1933, the county sent 15 trainloads of Mexican welfare recipients and other indigents to the border, a total of 12,688 passengers (many went voluntarily).[55] The savings to L.A. county, welfare officials boasted, was in the neighborhood of $424,933.70.[56] Pete Wilson would have been proud.

The crusade to "remove" (Bureau of Immigration lingo) Mexicans, pervaded all states with sizable Mexican populations—Texas, with 700,000, was an easy target. One nativist propaganda technique was to associate Mexican nationals with marijuana use. Headline scare stories, featuring horrible crimes supposedly committed by Mexicans high on *mota*, appeared throughout the southwest—such propaganda later became a staple of the successful crusade for the 1938 federal law that made the use, cultivation, possession, and sale of marijuana, without an unobtainable federal tax stamp, a criminal felony.[57] "Marijuana, perhaps our most insidious narcotic, is a direct product of unrestricted Mexican immigration," wrote the American Coalition's C.M. Goethe.[58]

How many Mexicans the Great Depression sent home remains imprecise. 40,000 "eloped" (more Migra lingo) from Los Angeles in the first weeks of 1931 alone[59]—the business community objected to the city's efforts to drive the indocumentados out because, it was feared, credit payments would not be kept up once the deadbeats were back home, on the rancho.[60] 120,000 Mexicans probably left the U.S. side in 1931, the peak year for "repatriation." By 1935, an estimated 425,000 to 500,000 Mexicans had probably gone home.[61] U.S. census figures in 1930 record 1.5 million Mexicans living in the United States but do not make a clear distinction between citizens of Mexico and Mexican-American U.S. citizens.[62] The truth is that no one really knew how many Mexicans were living within the borders of the United States then—just as no one really knows now.

Those who had been hounded to go back to where they came from were not particularly happy in Mexico. Many wrote the U.S. State Department, complaining that they had been unjustly uprooted from jobs and homes they had held for years, that their children—not a few of whom were born in the United States and were, therefore, U.S. citizens—could not adjust to this strange land to which they had been returned.[63] The sense of dislocation is similar to that expressed by today's returnees. Living for long stretches in the States changes the way Mexicans look at Mexico. There are many who can't go home again.

But still they kept coming—back. "White men are doing work today that they will not do in better times," Professor James H. Batten of Clairmont College clairvoyantly wrote in 1933.[64] As Roosevelt's relief programs took hold and massive public works projects were embarked upon, Mexicans slipped back into the country, replacing the Dust Bowl Okies who had filled in for them out in the fields to keep agribusiness happy, during the darkest days of the Depression. Management was not displeased by the switch-over in its work force—there were too many Tom Joads and Preacher Caseys and Woody Guthries in the Oklahoma contingent.

In compliance with orthodox capitalist doctrine, the Depression could only be relieved by world war. Once again, the Mexican people were welcomed back to their home away from home across the Bravo River. Tata Marcelino marched north to win World War II for the *pinche gringos*. The push and pull factors pulse to the rhythms of capitalist needs. "Operation Wetback," under the direction of General Joseph Swing, a veteran of Pershing's "punitive expedition," chased 1.3 million Mexicans back across the river in the summer and fall of 1954.[65] The 1955 INS annual report boasted that "the wetback problem no longer exists—the border is secure."[66] Ha! Ha! Ha!

The bracero program, a creature of California agribusiness, brought them back. The raids began again in 1964. The debt crisis exodus of '82 was countermanded by IRCA in 1986. The openings and closings of the border were, and are, cyclical and depend on the machinations of industry and money. Racism, on the other hand, is constant.

Although the U.S. government has sought to wash every successive wave of immigrants back to Mexico when the need for their labor diminished, many have refused to be "removed," held on, like barnacles on a rock, up on Boyle Heights in East L.A. and in every barrio in the U.S. southwest and, by the time the Migra came back to pick them up, they had become Mexican-Americans and their children Chicanos, re-annexing a land that had, indeed, once been theirs. In 1966, the Los Angeles school district racial breakdown was 19% Hispanic and 56% white. 20 years later, Hispanics were the 56% and whites reduced to 18%.[67] Many Mexicans became citizens of the United States of Gringolandia to turn such demographics upside down—"for convenience, not because we love this country," says my friend Arnoldo, the poet son of a communist from Sonora, over morning coffee at the Café La Bohème in San Francisco's Mission barrio. "I'm always a Mexican here—they don't ever let you forget it."

A malignant meanness infuses nativist sentiment today. Hungry men congregating on California street corners at informal labor markets are harassed by citizens patrols and swept up by the Migra. Families are torn apart by deportations, kids threatened with expulsion from school, old people separated from the checks by which they live their threadbare lives, pregnant mothers refused service at the hospital door, just for being Mexican. Such moments of cruelty have always marked the Mexican presence in the U.S. History offers that much consolation. At least the knowledge that all this has happened before can make us feel less alone.

DEFINING THE BORDER

The Border is an annexed land but just who is annexing who is never very clear here. Both sides in this geographically ordained marriage invade each other's territory in massive numbers. Three-quarters of a million people cross the border north to south and south to north on a good day—the Tijuana-San Ysidro station clocks 40 million visits annually, the most traveled border crossing in the known universe.[68] The languages of this mutual invasion mingle on the tongue just as the coins of both nations mingle in the pocket. "Buey de la Barranca" (by Los Felinos) is on the jukebox at the Hollywood Café in El Paso and Snoop Doggy Dogg rattles from the discotheques in Juárez. When a hailstorm hits south Texas, northern Tamaulipas is going to catch hell, and when the sun goes down in the west, it goes down over both Californias. But not everything is contiguous and interchangeable.

Where does the Border begin and where does it end? The east-west coordinates are secure, defined by large bodies of water. But the north-south line has many different limits. Technically, the Border is demarcated by 20 sets of twin towns[69] where the immigration services of both nations have established stations, and the contiguous municipalities and counties that surround them on both sides of the line. 9 to 11 million people live within these confines, most on the southern side (at least 6 million).[70] These 40 border outposts, towns and cities represent gaps in a long barrier that is sometimes a Wall and sometimes a fence or just two strands of barbed wire or nothing at all except the knowledge of separation. This divide tracks 1,962 miles of mostly empty, mean-looking badlands. Many of the intervals in this continuum are extensions of each other, like Nogales, Arizona and Nogales, Sonora. The Imperial Valley changes its name to the Mexicali Valley at Calexico. Spooked by the phantom of Pancho Villa, Columbus, New Mexico and Las Palomas, Chihuahua are more distant, a long cab ride between them. The toxic canyons of Tijuana are light-years distant from the mirrored skyscrapers of San Diego.

The border does not necessarily move on a north-south bias—Tijuana is hundreds of miles north of El Paso, and Chihuahua City and San Antonio, Texas are in the identical latitude. Joel Garreau, in *The Nine Nations of North America*, has Houston and Sacramento and Los Angeles as border cities, anchoring a nation called MexAmerica that extends almost to Denver and as far south as Sinaloa and Monterrey.[71] The Border is much wider than its contiguous parts. The border states are as much a component of the Border as the border cities. And what of the states bordering the border states, all of which used to conform Mexico? Today, there are 150,000 Mexicans in Kansas, a wedge of which was deeded to the U.S. in the Treaty of Guadalupe Hidalgo.

The extension of Mexico's northern border follows the wanderings of its workers and Mexicans are everywhere in the U.S. and Canada these days.

New Border Nation?

Ever since border native Bill Moyers' landmark PBS documentary, "One River, One Country" in 1986, it has become fashionable to perceive of both sides of the immediate border as one region, biologically, topographically, linguistically, pop culturally, and above all, economically, welded together, as much by their distances from Mexico City and Washington as the two lands' proximity to each other, out here in the middle of this godforsaken desert.

But the New Border Nation that seemed to be coalescing in the 1980s is now divided by a foreboding Wall, a militarized Migra, and a fistful of harsh new laws that shout, "Stop right there!" and "Go back to where you came from!" Such rejection tends to accentuate the differences between the two sides, differences that, despite desired convergence, have always outweighed the similarities.

The border between the United States of America and the United States of Mexico is the only land border on earth separating the First World from the Third. Consequently, it is the longest land border between these two breathtakingly distinct spheres of affluence and misery. There is no border on the planet where the economic differentials between the two sides (salaries, prices, gross national products) are so steep. The inequities are often in plain sight of each other. The Third World of the Colonia Buenavista in Nuevo Laredo, where the swampy, feces-striped streets are named after the postmen who dare to deliver letters to the cardboard shacks that dot the desert there, is open for inspection through the picture-window portals of the impressively security-minded Holiday Inn in Laredo, right across the big river.

The Border often seems like a seesaw, with the U.S. side up and the Mexican slice permanently sitting on the ground, dragged down by the sheer weight of the population and the commerce that fill its streets. On trips along the border, I sometimes cross the line so often that I confuse the place name of the town I have entered—but I never mistake which world it is I am visiting. U.S. avenues are broad. Shiny automobiles move smartly over unwrinkled asphalt. The few pedestrians stop obediently on corners with molded wheelchair ramps. "Walk/Don't Walk" signs flash red and green. It no longer reads "No Mexicans or Dogs Allowed" above the mirrors in south Texas saloons, but there are plenty of other prohibitions. "No Smoking, No Drinking, No Musical Devices," you are warned when boarding buses. You can drink the water.

On the other side of the bridge, the pavement, where it remains, is cracked and stained and crowded wall to wall with *ambulantes* (street vendors) hawking the small things of life, a single hairpin, a few mangos. Bus drivers are disc jockeys, tuning in raucous corridos for their passengers, and legless men crawl the aisles, begging for spare change. Nothing is regulated by "Walk/Don't Walk" signals. Life seems cheaper but more valued over there.

Do the charms balance off the inequities? Most Mexican border dwellers would probably say no. The bottom line on the frontera is cold cash, not quaint paradoxes. This used to be a desert until "World War II picked it up at both ends and pulled the region's economy into a new age."[72] Military installations and defense industry in San Diego and El Paso set the pace of development and the industrial capacity on the northern side resonated on the southern one. Across the river, the infrastructure to service the sailors grew disproportionately. Jorge G. Castañeda writes that half the female work force in Tijuana during the second world war was employed in prostitution.[73]

NEW BORDER TIMEBOMB

The maquiladora industry has become so vital to Mexico's economic viability that it is hard to determine whether the maqs are here because of the border or the border is here for the maqs. Over 2,500 mostly foreign-owned assembly plants now employ 811,000 Mexicans and account for half of Mexico's manufacturing exports and 38% of total exports.[74] The maquiladoras are the engines of growth—not just for the border but for Mexico as a maquiladora nation in the global firmament.

But, as usual, there is a downside to such booming enterprise. The maquiladoras have pulled so many young people from the interior of Mexico to Nuevo Laredo and Juárez and Tijuana that there is no physical infrastructure along this narrow, waterless fringe of desert to accommodate them. Clusters of cardboard shacks break out on the parched hillsides or down in the garbage-filled ravines. Raw sewage pours into the Río Bravo and penetrates the plume of the aquifer that supplies both Nogaleses. Rusting drums of toxic chemicals glint in the blinding sunlight up on the Otay Mesa—the maquiladoras have trucked in tens of thousands of tons of toxic chemicals that are never returned to the Other Side, as the law requires them to be, and no one in Tijuana or Tecate or Mexicali knows where any of this lethal stew is buried. Airborne disease floats south to north—El Paso has one of the highest tuberculosis rates in the U.S. and bad water south of the border gives the city the shits. "It is not a question of will cholera get to El Paso, but when," a doctor at a public forum grimly announced as the epidemic swept up the continent from Peru and ravished Mexico, back in 1994.[75]

Now that NAFTA's a working fact of life and traffic has swelled to record levels (700,000 trucks going both ways on the Otay Mesa alone), such plagues are regarded as the cost of doing business on the border. But future scenarios are not sanguine. Already an environmental disaster zone, the border is being consumed by its own effluvia and precious resources, like water, are running out. What happens when the water—and the jobs dependent upon this vital fluid—dry up, and unfixable political instability and economic confusion drive the transnationals out of Mexico, to even cheaper wage shores? For nearly a million stranded, young, jobless workers and their families, drawn by conditions back home to come this far north, the only option will be to get over a Wall behind which a heavily-armed military is poised to open fire on all invaders from the south.

In this light, the maquiladora industry also represents an immigration emergency in the making. Old Agapito González, the CTM cacique who controls hiring and firing in the Matamoros maqs, put it on the line: "We insure social tranquility here."[76] "I can't stress enough how important it is that there is no disruption in this industry, because if there is, the consequences are not going to be pleasant for both of our countries," Raul García, the then-director of the Coastal Maquiladora Association remarked, as we studied a cluttered, chaotic Tijuana from his 12th-story offices.[77]

A LAND OF OPPORTUNITIES

The north has been going south for a good time ever since Prohibition—The ranch of Tía Juana (Aunt Joan's place) became a favorite watering hole between Californias. The cantinas, casinos, and Agua Caliente racetrack, lured the Hollywood stars and Al Capone reportedly bought in. The border has always presented golden investment opportunites.

The red light districts track the maquiladoras east from TJ's seedy *Zona del Norte* where the Mary Magadelene Vanguard of Free Women organizes the prostitutes and the swabbies still swarm the herky-jerky Norteña bars, to the walled city of tawdry clubs and one-bulbed cribs, across the tracks in Nuevo Laredo, which fun-loving gringos have christened "Boystown." A visit to a Mexican whorehouse is a rite of passage for young men on the Texas border. On Juárez Avenue, in the city of the same name, the maquiladora girls crowd the bar, competing for tricks to supplement their $4 a day take-home pay. Since 1995, 28 young women have disappeared from these bars, their strangled bodies dumped miles away in the Chihuahua desert.[78] The Border also presents such opportunities.

Banks deal in blood and money on the border and both flows are thriving. Green Cross's string of Alpha Plasma Centers has been snapped up by an even larger Japanese pharmaceutical conglomerate, to further globalize the blood supply. Carlos Hank Rhon, the son of the godfather of the PRI's dinosaur wing, owns three of the biggest money banks in Texas—Laredo National, South Texas National and the Mercantile Bank, with combined assets of $2.5 billion.[79] Banking institutions in the Lone Star state would collapse faster than the S&Ls did at the end of the '80s, if Mexican depositors suddenly withdrew their nest eggs. Mexicans have $31 billion USD, a third of their foreign debt, stashed in U.S. banks for safekeeping, much of it in Texas.[80]

The border offers commercial opportunities. Korean merchants have come to this border to make their fortunes, much like the Jews and the Chinese before them, dominating retail clothing and domestic appliance sales on the north side of the line. U.S. junk is big business on the southern side. Old clothes are trucked in in trailer rigs and sold by the kilo in the slums of Ciudad Juárez. Every old tire and broken household appliance ever discarded in Upper California seems to bottom out in Baja. My friend Gregorio Alvarez, who picks garbage up in Tijuana's hectic, smelly dump, shows me a collection of 37 Polaroid Land Cameras he has gleaned from the rotting slags of refuse, and wonders where he can sell them. The Border presents such opportunities.

For Juan Arana, his golden opportunity came when the body of DEA agent Enrique Camarena was discovered in a shallow Michoacán grave in February 1985. Camarena was a native of Calexico and to avenge his murder, U.S. customs officers slowed traffic to an agonizing crawl at the crossing from Mexicali. Juan jumped into the traffic jam to hawk his 8-foot bouncing balloons to the embittered motorists and their screaming kids. Business has been swell ever since.

For Refugio Olivares, her golden opportunity comes on the international bridge between Matamoros, Tamaulipas and Brownsville, Texas. A Tarahumara (Raramuri) Indian from "one side of Chihuahua," she squats against the low bridge wall with her infant daughter squirming in her lap, her hand upraised for hours, to receive the crumbs and the coins of passing pedestrians. "Sometimes, the Americans give me what they have left over," she tells an intruding reporter. "There is nothing to eat where I come from."

Refugio Olivares is often the last person that U.S. citizens will do business with in Mexico.

RUNNING FROM THE BORDER

The real business of borders is contraband. The *fayuca* (tons of smuggled toys, TVs and boom-boxes for the Tepitos of Mexican cities) and the firearms (the pistol that killed Colosio came across this border and the Zapatistas' limited arsenal was mostly purchased in El Paso gunshops)[81] move south, the freon and the parrots slip north—species smuggling from Mexico are a focus of U.S. federal wildlife investigators, and freon, banned as an ozone-layer killer in the U.S., is worth its weight in gold in southern California chop shops.[82]

But people and drugs are the staples of the subterranean traffic north. Sometimes the people are stuffed into locked boxcars and truck trailers and they suffocate to death, which is bad business for the traffickers. Drugs are less perishable and easier to move in bulk. La Droga rolls north from the Culiacán Valley under thousands of tons of winter tomatoes that are hauled through the Nogales station every February. The foot people bring some of it across in their shoes from Matamoros when the gringos crank up the War on Drugs and the big loads can't come across. Kilo-size bricks of heroin slip through inside the doors of Oldsmobiles and the cocaine is introduced in tins of Veracruz chilis, in piñatas, and strapped to the underbellies of cattle driven across the border in the New Mexico corridor. Moving vans haul mountains of mota through prearranged holes in desert surveillance. In the late 1980s, the DEA even claimed that Mexicans were firing missiles with marijuana payloads across the border.

Narco-tunnels are burrowed beneath the border—one subterranean passage uncovered between Agua Prieta, Sonora, and Douglas, Arizona, has nurtured a cottage industry in Douglas where you can buy a coffee cup that proves you "visited the narco-tunnel." Another tunnel burrowed between Tijuana and unincorporated San Diego county was an engineering marvel, complete with cart tracks and hydraulic systems. "We don't know how many more tunnels there may be out there," admitted a DEA spokesperson.

The War on Drugs has turned the Border into the hottest zone in Mexico. The Mexican Army patrols the highways running up to the border towns, setting up mobile checkpoints to shake down the motorists for drugs and money. Up ahead, on La Frontera, the cops are invariably on the payrolls of the Arellano Félixes or Amado Carrillos. In their spare moments, judicial and municipal police extort migrants and tourists for chump change.

Some Mexicans, when returning to their country, will cross in the dark, climbing the Wall in reverse, just so they can evade the ministrations of customs and police agents who rip off all they have accumulated during long months of hard labor on the Other Side. The Beta squad has been established by Mexican authorities to protect would-be mojados from the border bandits who rattle around in the no-man's land between nations—but many escapees into America wonder who will protect them from the Betas. The U.S. Migra, waiting for them across the line, is almost welcome relief after the persecution the indocumentados have endured just trying to leave their own country.

Across the river, on the other side of the triple Wall, are the helicopter gunships, the green vans, the plastic handcuffs, the overcrowded detention centers, a trip back to the border gate on the nightly deportee bus. The Border is a hot and traumatic place to land in the middle of the '90s. Today, the escapees' main concerns are first getting across the border, and then getting away from it, just as fast as one possibly can.

SPREADING INTO THE HEARTLAND

The Mexicans have broken out of the border corral for good. No longer confined to MexAmerica, the escapees have fled into the heartland, establishing colonies in every region and mid-level city in the U.S. Such communities often spring from a nucleus that has escaped from the same home town in Mexico, neighbor by neighbor. One cousin invites another cousin—as has always been the mechanism for immigration in the North American melting pot.

300,000 natives of the states of Puebla and Tlaxcala now work in the greater New York City area, where ten years ago, there was virtually no Mexican population—or Mexican restaurants at all.[83] The New York contingent maintains strong ties to the folks back home. Many return to attend and participate in town Carnival fiestas each winter—in Tepeyanco, Tlaxcala, feathers and sequins for costumes now come from Manhattan's garment district. During a frenetic fiesta in Papalotla several seasons ago, a young man named Jesús took time out from a wild whip dance, to regale me with a blow-by-blow account of the World Trade Center bombing—he works in the deli downstairs.

Mexico's new northern border is fast becoming all of North America. The geography of the Mexican annexation of its northern neighbor extends from coast to coast and border to border. Mexicans are picking mushrooms in central Pennsylvania, working the tobacco in North Carolina (Pedro Fabián Huaruco once labored there). Field workers venture as far north as Rochester, New York and Saginaw, Michigan and Turner, Maine, where fed up with working conditions at a huge egg farm, they risked their necks by calling in the authorities in the spring of 1997.[84] In the Olintepec colony, near Emiliano Zapata's birthplace in the Cuautla Valley of Morelos, young men used to commute to Bradenton, Florida. Then one cousin found work washing dishes in Atlantic City—now all the young men flock to the Jersey shore to find work.

Mexicans have long been citizens of the Great Midwest—with a little over a million Mexican and Mexican-American in residence, Chicago is second only to Los Angeles as a U.S. Mexican city. But now there are important communities in Omaha and Iowa City and Lawrence, Kansas. Despite being home to such enclaves of white supremacists as Bo Gritz and the Aryan Lakes encampment, Idaho has long had a residual number of Mexican-born laborers working the potato farms. Now, Boise has its own parade and queen on that quintessential Mexican-American holiday, Cinco de Mayo.

Up in the Yakima Valley, and all throughout eastern Washington, designated as an Aryan nation by the new nativists, Mexicans have become so numerous that politicians like Cuauhtémoc Cárdenas pay partisan visits. Rancheros and corridos blast from the boom boxes in Medford, Oregon, which has its own Spanish-speaking radio station.

The California collapse and Texas tumble in the '80s and '90s spread the Mexicans around. The peso crisis drove them further and further into North America. Now the Mexican government has opened consular outposts in Orlando, Florida and Portland, Oregon, Honolulu, Hawaii, where 15,000 Mexicans now work in the pineapple and sugar cane, and Anchorage, Alaska—20,000 Mexicans travel to that gelid region these days, many to work salmon boats out of Kodiak Island.[85]

Rich Mexicans set up homes away from home in La Jolla, California, and Vail, Colorado. Disgraced Mexican politicians often wind up in Washington. Although the U.S. has begun to award political asylum to Mexicans, many would-be refugees escape to Canada (Carlos Salinas found temporary sanctuary in Montreal). 900 Mexican citizens applied for political asylum in that most northern of North American nations in 1996.[86]

The most peripatetic of the Mexicans are the Mixtecs, the "cloud people" of northern Oaxaca, whose moon-scaped mountains have become so eroded that nothing grows there anymore. The Mixtecs first escaped to Culiacán and San Quentin in Baja California to pick winter tomatoes for transnational growers, then hopped over the border and spread into the San Joaquin Valley where they congregate around Merced. Radio Bi-Lingue, their local radio outlet, broadcasts in Mixteco and was founded by Hugo Morales, the first Mixtec to graduate from Yale—and, as he once told me while perched atop a denuded peak in the high Mixteca, the only Mixtec member of the Sierra Club.

Now the Mixtecs have discovered airplane travel and are expanding their enterprise into downtown Manhattan where they are reported to be forming a colony on the lower east side, the Big Apple's most traditional landing pad for new immigrants. Like many who proceeded them, the Mixtecs bring with them their saints and their fiestas. Although their villages back home in Oaxaca are often deserted, the houses boarded up, even in deepest, darkest Manhattan the Mixtecos are never very far from their mountain homes.

Indigenous Mexico is increasingly a current in the North American immigration stream. Purépecha is spoken on the streets of Cosa Mesa, California where Tanaco has established a beachhead, and Zapotec kids in Los Angeles are skipping Spanish as a second language and going straight to English.[87] While waiting on a bus in rural Humboldt County near the Oregon border with California, I strike up a conversation with Mam Indians from Tapachula, Chiapas who have come this far north to pick flowers and pack crab. It is the American Way.

The Migra is just catching on that the Mexicans are no longer at the border. Coordinated raids in six southern states in the summer of 1995 netted 4,044 indocs—the operation was cleverly code-named "Southpaw" ("Protect American Workers"). Mexicans were found to be filling in at American job sites throughout the south, in restaurants, as tree planters, baby sitters, and gardeners. Just as Morrocans had hotfooted it to Barcelona for the run-up to the '92 Olympics, Mexicans had come for construction jobs on the '96 Atlanta games. One 13-year-old was picked up busing tables in a Jackson, Mississippi Chinese restaurant for $21 a week, and others lost $15-an-hour carpenter jobs. INS chief Doris Meissner praised the raids and warned that they would be the first of many, admitting that concentrating her forces on the border was passé: "The border has become a pass-through zone."[88]

"MORALLY, IT'S VERY BAD HERE..."

Some Mexican refugees have come to stay for a season—Michoacanos from Zacapu fly in on six-week grape contracts—and some come to stay for a lifetime. Families dig in, the cousins and brothers come one by one, then the old people. They find out where the supermarkets and the schools and the churches and the soccer games are. Their neighbors frequently hail from the same home towns. They go to work on roofing crews with their *primos* (cousins) or as gardeners with their uncles, fall in love, have children; some become citizens, and their children remember Mexico only through the bitterness and the nostalgia of their elders.

But for others, the lifetime they envisioned in America is too short. Juan Mercado's, for example. At 24, Juan came to Oakland in 1989, after Sicarsa, the government steel plant he had been toiling in on the Michoacán coast was privatized and down-sized. He found a job at the Four Star Pizza Parlor in the free-fire zone of East 14th, where the crack dealers and the hookers provide valet parking. To Juan, life in America, even this violent wedge of it, was better than it was back in Bapácuaro, deep in the hot lands of Michoacán. Juan invited his three older brothers up; their mom and dad and younger siblings came next, ten family members in all, living in a cramped, upholstered apartment near the pizza parlor. They spent much of the day helping out the Chinese owners, baking pizzas, delivering them. Then, on a rainy February night, Juan and his father, Crispín, delivered a pie to an apartment cluster on the deep east side of Oaktown and the customer paid them in lead. Crispín was only beaten. Juan was dead, the 16th homicide of Oakland's young murder season.

The devastated family decided that they had enough of American violence. Neighbors took up a collection to get the family home to Bapácuaro where Juan Mercado would be buried.

With the California economy sinking in seemingly endless recession, a lot of Mexicans were packing up and cashing it in in 1993. Antonio Montes was one. For a decade, Montes had made a good living from his Taco Mágico truck, parked at 5th and Edison in Redwood City, California, a town of 60,000, fully a third of whom have emigrated from the Michoacán municipality of Aguililla. Now Montes said he too had had enough of life in El Norte. He didn't like the violence and he didn't like the moral climate and he didn't like the racism. "I go into the jails to visit prisoners and all I see are Mexicans locked up for crimes that don't exist for anyone else—I don't like the ideology here. There's no feeling of community anymore, even among the Mexicans. Everyone has a gun. Drugs are everywhere for the kids to get, and the parents don't have any control. Morally, its very bad here. I have daughters, if you know what I mean," Montes anguished to me one night on the phone. "I don't know why I stayed so long—I guess I got caught up in the American Dream, Now I'm going home to our Mexico."

But going home to Our Mexico in the neo-liberal '90s is as difficult an adjustment as it was back in the Depression-ridden '30s. Months after they had returned to Bapácuaro, an almost nonexistent hamlet high above a tributary of the Balsas River, I visited to see how the Mercados were doing. The setting was an overwhelmingly rustic one—when I jumped down off the cargo truck, the first action that caught my eye was a young man beating a four-foot-long blue snake to death. East 14th presented comparable dangers.

The Mercados were now living in a semi-enclosed wood and stick hut. The day was very hot. 16-year-old Imelda was home, looking at photos. The pictures hung on strings in the open front room and swayed slightly in the small breeze. They were mostly snapshots of the family baking, eating, boxing, and delivering pizzas in Oakland, California.

Crispín was out weeding another man's corn field. "We have no land here or anywhere," Emma Mercado, Juan's mother, sighed morosely. María Elena, the 12-year-old, brought more photos. It was a sweltering, melancholy afternoon. "We dream of having our own pizza parlor," Emma Mercado confessed to me, just before I jumped back up on the cargo truck for the return trip to civilization. Although the family was still wounded by the boy's death, what really had them depressed was a gnawing homesickness for East 14th Street in Oakland, California.[89]

MOTECUHZONA'S REVENGE

There are an estimated 18,000,000 Mexicans and Mexican-Americans presently living in the United States, around 6% of the total census. 11 million or so of them are U.S. citizens and another 3.7 million resident aliens[90]— Mexican citizens who legally live within the belly of the beast. 6.7 million of people of Mexican descent who live in the U.S. were born in Mexico, accounting for 28% of the U.S. foreign-born.[91] The undocumented numbers are more problematic—prior to IRCA amnesty, 3.2 million Mexican indocs were estimated to be living in the recesses of America—1996 studies put that number at 2.7 million undocumented Mexicans who have relocated, however temporarily, within U.S. borders.[92] How long they stay is being measured: two years is the average, say demographers,[93] hardly long enough to suck up the billions in illegal benefits that Pete Wilson is always kvetching about.

The demographics are uncertain but the economics are not. The average American household earns $37,000 a year, the average Mexican-American family (larger families) $23,000.[94] A quarter of those living in poverty in the U.S. are classified as "Hispanics"—a category that, in 1996, overtook black people as the poorest ethnic group in the U.S.[95]

Despite NAFTA, Mexicans who reside in the U.S. are not certain that they want to become North Americans. For generations, Mexicans have been the most resistant immigrant group to naturalization, on the INS books. Unlike the Italians, Jews, Germans, Irish, Polish, Filipinos, Palestinians, Russians, and Vietnamese, millions of Mexicans have refused to be assimilated into the U.S. citizen pool. Someday, they thought, Mexico would change. There would be jobs and democracy and they would at last go home and be an important person in town. But U.S. lynch-mob nativism in the '90s has melted that resolve. With benefits to legal immigrants about to be chopped, many families are signing up for citizenship classes and flocking to the chapels to marry American citizens in the mistaken belief that matrimony will keep the Migra at bay. "We became Americans for convenience," said Arnoldo the poet, "not because we love this place."

In the style of Porfirio Díaz, the PRI government seeks to win these expatriates back to the Patria. Mexico has abruptly offered "dual nationality" to Mexicans who give up their citizenship and naturalize as U.S. Americans—such status allows them to retain certain property rights in the old country.[96] A constitutional amendment, passed in 1996, would allow those émigrés who retain Mexican citizenship to vote in the 2000 AD presidential election, perhaps 5 million voters, enough to determine the outcome.[97] But the prospect of Mexican presidential candidates campaigning on U.S. soil for the votes of millions of their country men and women is an unlikely one—if only because the PRI, which continues to control the legislative process, will not win the votes of Mexicans who have been pushed into exile by government crimes and failures.

Nonetheless, former Mexicans will have an opportunity to vote for president in 2000—a U.S. president. Voter registration groups like the Southwest Voters Education and Research Project are signing up Mexicans who opt to cash in their birthright for U.S. citizenship the moment they are sworn in—or even before.

In a key November 1996 Orange County congressional race, an unknown Latina Democrat named Loretta Sánchez (she had run two years earlier under her Anglo married name, and as a Republican) upset B-1 Bob Dornan, long one of the most rabid right-wing kooks in the U.S. House (some constituents have tried to have him declared legally insane). She did it with new U.S. voters, former Mexicans like her own parents, who had delayed 40 years before becoming citizens and only did so because their Medicaid benefits were threatened.[98] B-1 Bob cried fraud—illegals had voted, he raged, and, sure enough, 17 new citizens who had received citizenship letters from the INS but had not yet stepped forward to swear the Pledge of Allegiance, were busted for jumping the gun in their zeal to exercise their newly-guaranteed franchise.[99]

Mexicans and Mexican-Americans were not limited to casting their ballots for gavachos like Clinton and Dole and Nader in the 1996 U.S. presidential race. Though many never knew it, they had their own candidate: Super Barrio Gómez. The Caped Crusader tossed his mask into the ring (so to speak) during memorial ceremonies at the foot of the international bridge in Ciudad Juárez, honoring more than 300 Mexicans who have drowned in the swirling currents of the Río Bravo, trying to get to the Other Side—Super would be the candidate of the indocumentados, those without voice or face who live so anonymously under America.[100] Perversely, the Urban Avenger opened his campaign at elite Harvard University in the spring of 1996 but it was all downhill from there. "What happens in the White House hurts us. We should have a representative in there. The North Americans are not the only Americans. In fact, thanks to NAFTA, we are North Americans too," the corpulent candidate emphasized in a Zócalo interview.[101] Goméz's platform read like a page from Genesis in reverse: "On the first day, I shall abolish the Migra. On the second day, I will revise NAFTA so that the rights of undocumented workers are respected." On the third day, he would turn his attentions to finance and dismantle the International Monetary Fund. On the fourth day, he would change the name of the White House to the Brown House...

Alas, the public-spirited Señor Gómez did not win the U.S. presidency. Young Cleen-tone's namesake did, however, taking 80% of all new Mexican votes in California, according to Southwest Voters Project data.[102] But Super's future as a U.S. presidential candidate has promise—by 2000, Mexican-Americans will constitute between 25% and 30% of the California electorate; by 2020, if the demographics keep ticking, they will constitute half.[103] By then, Caucasians will be a minority in their late great state. This is Motecuhzona's real revenge.

THE ANNEXATION OF NORTH AMERICA

The Mexicans travel light but they bring a lot with them. Their food has made a big impression on the gavachos. More salsa than ketchup is now consumed in the United States, brags Carlos Fuentes[104] and the tortilla has become a national dinner staple—Maseca, the Mexican corn conglomerate, has built the world's largest tortilla factory ($60 million investment) in Rancho Cucamonga, California.[105] Veggie burritos (the idea is enough to make a red-blooded Chihuahuan retch) have nourished a whole generation of San Francisco Generation Xers and the recycling centers of the U.S.A. are studded with dead Corona beer bottles.

Mexican chic is on the rise in El Norte. Frida Kahlo and La Macarena have enjoyed more than their 15 minutes in the American spotlight. So did Selena Quintanilla, the slain Tex-Mex-pop songstress, whose murder became the Latino "O.J." scandal. *Like Water for Chocolate*, the all-time best-selling Mexican movie and book in the U.S. market, has inspired gourmet regional restaurants in major North American metropolises, and fine mescals coax jaded Yuppie palates. A *New York Times* travel special assigns Chicana novelist Ana Castillo to tour the downtrodden Chicago barrio in which she grew up and point out the highlights for adventuresome tourists.[106] Richard Avedon welcomes an indoc to *The American West*, by shooting his portrait just as he emerges dripping from the Río Grande. Guillermo Gómez Peña is "a migrant performing artist" smuggling his ideas across borders, or so he boasts in the dangerously glossy *High Performance* magazine. After the L.A. riots, which, as Los Angeles writer Mike Davis pointed out in his excellent *Nation* reportage, were as much brown as black, the prestigious Getty Museum hired a Chicano administrator to keep an eye on the barrio (he got tired of being asked "What do your people think?" and quit). In San Diego, conceptualists stage an ephemeral piece, "re-BATE," in which they hand out $10 bills to startled border jumpers at street corner labor markets and in the dry hills above San Ysidro. The National Endowment for the Arts and the usual gaggle of congressional reactionaries go berserk and money is now banned as an art material in future NEA-funded projects.

But these are New Wave exceptions. Most of the art the escapees haul in is traditional and grounded in the geography they have left behind: feast days and fanciful piñatas, Day of the Dead altars, patriotic fiestas, the stylized murals of the Mexican masters that now blaze on the desolate walls of many U.S. barrios, the veneration of the Dark Madonna, replanted indigenous ritual. For years, we thought the thuds and blows that emanated from the apartment beneath a friend's San Francisco Mission district home were caused by Señor Durán's fists pummeling something, hopefully a punching bag. Then I saw him at a neighborhood street fiesta, a whirling bronze figure in a gold lamé loincloth, deer antler rattles wrapped around his calves, a member of the Xipe Totec Aztec dance troupe. In his apartment, Mr. Durán, a waiter at a private Jewish club, showed me his shrine to Xipe Totec, the Aztec god of renewal, whose priests danced in the zócalo each spring, wearing the skins of flayed virgins. There are, I learned, 50 such Aztec dance groups in California alone, swirling in hypnotic homage to Xipe Totec, Huitzilopochtli, and Tonatiuh, the Aztec sun god. Hey, is this annexation or what?

The Mexicans bring with them, too, another kind of culture, the one that I have most addressed throughout this volume, a culture of struggle and resistance. All over the country, all of a sudden, in the middle of the stultifying '90s, Mexicans pushed out of their Patria by the neo-liberal policies of the PRI's mal gobierno are standing up on North American soil and fighting back. Undocumented mushroom pickers in Pennsylvania launch a hopeless strike— and win it. Mixtec flower vendors on Manhattan's Upper West Side form a self-defense organization to battle police brutality. In Ohio, pickers and cannery workers take on Campbell's soup and come out with an historic contract. Out in California, Mexican-born Sprint workers, fired for trying to join the Communications Workers Union, file under the NAFTA labor side-accord to get their jobs back, and the Teamsters organize Mexican employees of Maseca's

Mission Guerrero Foods, threatening a tortilla strike, a potential southern California disaster. The year-long struggle of Orange County dry-wall workers results in the deportation of many strikers but the Mexicans finally gain recognition from the building trades unions. All over the state, Chicano and Mexican teenagers walk out of their classrooms to protest the passage of Proposition 187 and even the United Farm Workers, which under César Chávez's leadership often saw Mexican workers as a threat, now embrace their militancy, in its reinvigorated (by lots of AFL-CIO money) crusade to unionize the fields of California.

"Tell them we're going to keep coming," Marco, the young guide had laughed that first night, as we parted company at the Palm Avenue shopping center, Chula Vista, California, 1987. Despite 187, the Migra, the Klan, the military, the Immigration Responsibility Act, and the Light-Up-The-Borders, they do keep coming. They come to Mexicanize us, to Emiliano Zapata-ize us, to Chili Relleno-ize us, to Dia-de-los-Muertos-ize us, to humanize us. To tell us their history so that we can remember our own. They are coming to civilize us, to dazzle us with their art and seduce us with their molés. They are coming to wake up a North America that seems to be increasingly on automatic pilot as the next millennium dawns. Do not be alarmed. They come in peace. Relax. Go with this annexation. Join up.

NOTES

CHAPTER 1: THE FIRST ANNEXATIONS

1. Soustelle, p. 13 on, for complete cosmology.
2. CF Jennings for detailed novelization of Aztec conquests.
3. John Ross, *Por El Puro Gusto…*
4. The author is much indebted to Jonathan Kendell's informative *La Capital.*
5. Díaz del Castillo, p. 3
6. Alejandra Toscano Moreno in Cosio Villegas's *Compact History* p. 58
7. Fagan, p. 220
8. Cortez, p. 75
9. Martín, Jesús de la Coruña *Relación de los Indios de la Provincia de Michoacán*, quoted in *La Capital.*
10. Cortez, p. 83
11. Leon-Portilla, pp. 136-148
12. Luis González de la Alba, "*La Caída de Tenochtitlán*," *La Jornada*, August 12th, 1996
13. CF "The Map of Tepechpan," reprinted in Cortez, and see note 52, p. 518
14. This is the official story from Ixcateopán's point of view. Many dispute the authenticity of the bones. When I last checked into the town, the PRI and the PRD were battling over their possession.
15. Kendell, p. 135
16. Vasconcelos
17. CF Chapter 15 for a more detailed discussion of *La Malinche.*
18. Simpson, p. 135
19. John Ross, *Rebellion*, p. 63
20. Crosby, pp. 72-73
21. Benítez, pp. 82-83
22. Aguirre Beltrán, p. 219
23. Cf *Proceso*, May 8th, 1995
24. Kendell, op cit. p. 163
25. 12.5 million is the academically accepted low-end estimate, based on archeological evidence, tax rolls, and collected testimony. Other estimates range as high as 25 million to 100 million throughout the Americas.
26. Kendell, op cit. p. 137
27. Motolinia, pp. 34-35
28. John Ross, "The Hour of God," interview with Chiapas Bishop Samuel Ruiz, *Noticias Aliadas*, Lima, March 6th, 1996
29. First quoted in the "*Nichan Mopohua*," 1648, a Nahua account of the Miracle
30. *Proceso*, March 26th, 1990 pp. 6-13
31. Luis González de Alba, *La Jornada*, June 3rd, 1996
32. Callahan and Smith
33. *Proceso*, March 26th, 1990
34. Teresa Jardi, *La Jornada*, June 4th, 1996
35. Kendell, op cit. p. 214
36. Aguirre Beltrán, op cit. p. 214
37. Kendell, op cit. p. 241
38. Luis González y González, in Cosio Villegas's *Compact History*, p. 84
39. Cf von Humboldt
40. González y González, op cit. p. 89
41. Kendell, op cit. p. 271
42. Cf "Ghosts In The Trees," Chapter 16
43. González y González, op cit. p. 98

CHAPTER 2: AN AMERICAN OBSESSION: FROM THE FOUNDING FATHERS TO THE "HALLS OF MONTEZUMA"

1. Quoted in Kendell, op cit. p. 156
2. Vázquez, p. 3
3. Stourzh, p. 199
4. Weinberg, p. 62
5. Vázquez, op cit. p. 21
6. Weinberg, op cit. p. 47
7. Vázquez, op cit. p. 21
8. Weinberg, op cit. p. 62
9. Zinn, p. 129
10. Weinberg, op cit. p. 47
11. ibid, p. 65
12. ibid, p. 66
13. ibid, p. 62
14. Timmerman, pp. 150-152
15. Pastor, p.151
16. Weinberg, op cit. p. 61
17. ibid, p. 57
18. ibid
19. ibid, p. 68
20. ibid, p. 66

21. Vázquez, op cit. p. 43
22. Weinberg, op cit. p. 55
23. INAH: *1829 Intervención*, p. 7
24. Medina Castro, p. 17
25. Vázquez, op cit. p. 38
26. ibid, p. 34
27. Simpson, op cit. p. 244
28. Vázquez, op cit. p. 44
29. ibid
30. ibid, p. 43
31. Zinn, op cit. p. 151
32. Medina Castro, op cit. p. 64
33. Tyrner, p. 34
34. Zinn, op cit. p. 151
35. Williams, p. 156
36. Simpson, op cit. p. 250
37. ibid, p. 251
38. Medina Castro, op cit. p. 88
39. One alternative etymology attributes the term to Irish troops, perhaps the San Patricios, who sang "Green Grow the Rushes, Oh." Partridge. "Gringo" is also associated with "gibberish," the language of the gringos, perhaps through a corruption of "griego"—"Greek," as in "it's all Greek to me." Spears.
40. Williams, op cit. p. 182
41. Cf Chapter 9, "Cold Warriors" for details
42. Medina Castro, op cit. p. 89
43. Vázquez, op cit. p. 49
44. Raul Bringas, "*El Debate en el Congreso de los Estados Unidos*" *Estudios Parlamentarios del Congreso*, May-June 1991, Vol. 3
45. Williams, op cit. p. 144
46. Vázquez, op cit. p. 66
47. Cf Chapter 16, "Two Jungles, Many Worlds, One Planet" for more

CHAPTER 3: ANNEXATION BY COMIC OPERA

1. Quoted in Kendell, op cit. p. 233
2. ibid, p. 327
3. ibid, p. 332
4. González y González, *Compact History*, op cit. p. 112
5. Kendell, op cit. p. 334
6. Marx, p. 594
7. Kissinger, Chapter 4.
8. Tyrner, op cit. p. 73
9. ibid, pp. 57-58
10. Vázquez, op cit. p. 68
11. Kendell, op cit. p. 340
12. ibid, p. 243
13. ibid, p. 344
14. Tyrner, op cit. pp. 91-102

15. Rolle
16. Kendell, op cit. p. 351
17. Tyrner, op cit. p. 144
18. Telephone interview with U.C. Berkeley professor Carlos Muñoz, author of *Youth, Identity, and Power—the Chicano Movement* Verso, London, and a one-time member of the Chicano Student Union at Cal State.
19. John Ross, *El Puro Gusto…*, op cit.

CHAPTER 4: PAX PORFIRIANO AMERICAN DREAM

1. INAH, *Intervenciones*, p. 2
2. Vázquez, op cit. p. 89
3. ibid, p. 77
4. Turner, p. 67
5. Cf the "Montaria" novels of B.Traven, notably "The Rebellion of the Hanged"
6. Vázquez, op cit. p. 84
7. Kendell, op cit. p. 374
8. Tiscendorf, p. 39
9. ibid, p. 42
10. ibid, p. 94
11. Meyer, op cit. p. 98
12. Vázquez, op cit. p. 91
13. Tiscendorf, op cit. p. 130
14. Meyer, op cit. p. 92
15. Vázquez, op cit. p. 85
16. Tiscendorf, op cit. p. 42
17. Kendell, op cit. p. 372
18. John Ross, op cit. *El Puro Gusto...*
19. Tiscendorf, op cit. pp. 97-102
20. Kendell, op cit. p. 354
21. ibid, p. 355
22. Tiscendorf, op cit, p. 78
23. Cosio Villegas, *Compact History*, op cit. pp. 135-7
24. Kendell, op cit. p. 386
25. Stanley R. Ross, p. 3
26. Vanderwood, p. 79
27. Rockefeller, p. 135
28. Turner, op cit. pp. 170-173
29. *Pearson's Magazine*, XIX3, March,1908, p. 242
30. Antonio García de León, in *La Jornada*, undated article, July 1994
31. Kendell, op cit. p. 393
32. ibid, p. 403
33. ibid, p. 404

CHAPTER 5: MEXICAN REVOLUTION, U.S. NIGHTMARE

1. Cosio Villegas, "Historia General," Vl. III, p. 286

2. INAH, *1914*, p. 1
3. ibid
4. Ulloa, p. 6
5. Meyer, op cit. p. 108
6. Katz, p. 157
7. Barron, p. 48
8. ibid, p. 40
9. ibid, XI
10. ibid, p. 12
11. ibid, p. 8
12. ibid, p. 76
13. DeLeón, pp. 90-92
14. Shapiro, p. 47
15. Katz, op cit. p. 108
16. Grieb, p. 30
17. Kendell, op cit. p. 418
18. Meyer, op cit. p. 109
19. Pastor, op cit. p. 84
20. INAH, *1914*, p. 7
21. Katz, op cit. p. 157
22. Grieb, op cit. p. 132
23. ibid, p. 133
24. Katz, op cit. p. 157
25. ibid, pp. 165-167
26. Grieb, op cit. p. 150
27. *S.F. Examiner*, April 17th, 1914
28. Katz, op cit. p. 198
29. Grieb, op cit. p. 176
30. Katz, op cit. p. 199
31. ibid, p. 197
32. Berta Ulloa in Cosio Villegas' *Historia General* op cit. pp. 1127-28
33. Hoyt, p. 328
34. Katz, op cit. p. 199
35. Grieb, op cit. p. 172
36. Katz, op cit. p. 202
37. Grieb, op cit. p. 178
38. Tuchman, p. 66
39. *New York Times*, July 6th, 1915
40. Fuentes
41. Reed
42. Clendenen, p. 199
43. Meyer, op cit. p.124
44. Womack, p. 246
45. John Ross, *Rebellion* cf *Locura*
46. Meyer, op cit. p. 114
47. Clendenen, op cit. p. 210
48. ibid, p. 211
49. ibid, p. 230
50. ibid, p. 231
51. Hoyt, op cit. p. 352
52. Author's interview with M. Epps, May 1987
53. Clendenen, op cit. p. 266
54. ibid, p. 254
55. Katz, op cit. p. 309
56. Nalty, p. 99
57. Atkin, p. 62
58. Katz, op cit. p. 309
59. Clendenen, op cit. p. 242
60. Hoyt, op cit. p. 333
61. Tuchman, op cit. p. 68
62. Meyer, op cit. p. 122
63. ibid, p. 120
64. Krauze, *Carranza*, p. 88
65. Meyer, op cit. p. 120
66. ibid

CHAPTER 6: FROM INVASION TO INVESTMENT CO-OPTING THE REVOLUTION

1. Freeman Smith, p. 137
2. ibid
3. ibid, p. 178
4. ibid, p. 207
5. ibid, p. 201
6. ibid, p. 155
7. ibid, pp. 176-77
8. ibid, p. 159
9. Miguel Granados Chapa, "Leavenworth," *Reforma*, February 7th, 1997 p. 13
10. Freeman Smith, op cit. p. 163
11. ibid, p. 216
12. *El Universal*, May 6th, 1924
13. Meyer, op cit. p. 128
14. Freeman Smith, op cit. p. 202
15. Krauze, *Calles*, p. 128
16. Freeman Smith, op cit. p. 230
17. Sinclair, pp 265-66, citing Gaston Means on Mrs. Harding's involvement
18. Meyer, op cit. p. 135
19. Freeman Smith, op cit. p. 232
20. ibid, p.233
21. Cf *La Malinche*, for a fuller discussion
22. Freeman Smith, op cit. p. 143
23. Meyer, op cit. p. 135
24. Selser, p. 74
25. Freeman Smith, op cit. p. 238
26. Jean Meyer, pp. 10-15
27. Krauze, *Calles*, op cit. p. 120
28. Chalmers, p. 284
29. Meltzer, p. 9
30. Freeman Smith, op cit. footnote p. 195
31. ibid, p. 259
32. Meyer, op cit. p. 120
33. Barma, p. 163
34. Krauze, *Calles*, op cit. p. 122
35. ibid, p. 83

36. Meltzer, op cit. p. 9
37. Sergio Aguayo, *La Jornada*, August 28th, 1996
38. Meyer, op cit. p. 142
39. Miguel Angel Granados Chapa, *Punto*,
    December 21, 1987, p. 5
40. Cosio Villegas, *Compact History*, op cit. p. 157
41. Meltzer, op cit. p. 18
42. ibid, p. 15
43. Krauze, *Calles*, op cit. p. 93
44. ibid, p. 98
45. Meltzer, op cit. p. 17
46. Krauze, *Calles*, op cit. p. 113

CHAPTER 7: "GENERAL, PRESIDENT OF THE AMERICA:" THE REVOLUTION'S LAST GASP

1. Cosio Villegas, *Compact History*, op cit. p. 170
2. Meyer, op cit. p. 142
3. Berry, op cit. p. 155
4. Krauze, *Cárdenas*, p. 109
5. ibid, p. 113
6. Kendell, op cit. p. 477
7. Manchester, p. 144
8. ibid
9. Meyer, op cit. p. 144
10. Kendell, op cit. p. 477
11. ibid, p. 478
12. ibid
13. Meyer, op cit. p. 146
14. ibid
15. Krauze, *Cárdenas*, op cit. p. 177
16. ibid
17. Castañeda, *Proceso*, September, 19th, 1988, p. 35
18. José Emilio Pacheco, "*La Vida en el Momento de la Gran Expropriación*," *Proceso*, March 14th, 1988
19. Krauze, *Cárdenas*, op cit. p. 159
20. Meyer, op cit. p. 148
21. Pacheco, op cit.
22. ibid
23. Krauze, op cit. p. 154
24. Pastor, op cit. p. 52
25. Krauze, op cit. p. 155
26. Meyer, op cit. p. 149
27. Pacheco, op cit.
28. Klaus Volland, quoted in Erroll Jones
29. Pastor, op cit. p. 154
30. Krauze, op cit. p. 158
31. Ota Mishima, Chapter IV

CHAPTER 8: FIGHTING U.S. WARS

1. *Proceso*, July 20th, 1992
2. Cline, p. 266
3. Meyer, op cit. p. 158
4. Krauze, *Cárdenas*, op cit. p. 180
5. Meyer, op cit. p. 160
6. Morrison
7. Meyer, op cit. p. 156
8. Cosio Villegas, *Compact History*, op cit. p. 160
9. Cline, op cit. p. 169
10. Meyer, op cit. p. 159
11. Webber, pp. 69-73
12. Cline, op cit. p. 176
13. ibid
14. ibid, p. 177
15. Alsup
16. McRobbie
17. Cline, op cit. p. 177
18. Meyer, op cit. p. 160

CHAPTER 9: COLD WARRIORS: FROM THE TRUMAN DOCTRINE TO TLATELOLCO TO THE TEHERAN NEXT DOOR

1. Cline, op cit. p. 281
2. Cf Bethell-Roxbourough
3. Cline, op cit. p. 298
4. Cosio Villegas, *Compact History*, op cit. p. 161
5. Meyer, op cit. p. 165
6. ibid, p. 168
7. Cosio Villegas, *Compact History*, op cit. p. 161
8. Cline, *Revolution to Evolution*, p. 179
9. Cline, *The United States and Mexico*, op cit. pp. 324-25
10. Riding, p. 87
11. Sergio Aguayo, *Reforma*, February 26th, 1997, p. 17A
12. Meyer, op cit. p. 165
13. Agee, p. 527
14. Buendía, p. 103
15. ibid, p. 192
16. Gil Green, p. 100
17. ibid
18. Agee, op cit. p. 542
19. *New York Times*, September 14th, 1968, p. 38
20. Buendía, op cit. p. 37
21. ibid, p. 21
22. Cline, op cit. p. 297
23. ibid, p. 294
24. ibid, p. 314
25. Juan Ramón García
26. Martínez Abad, p. 60
27. Pastor, op cit. p. 90
28. Schlesigner & Kinzer, p. 76
29. Meyer, op cit. p. 169

30. ibid, 172
31. González, p. 45. Arturo Durazo was later Mexico City police chief.
32. Cline, *Revolution to Evolution*, op cit. p. 316
33. ibid, p. 322
34. Meyer, op cit. p. 177
35. *La Jornada*, March 13th, 1997
36. Krauze, *Cárdenas*, op cit. pp. 198-99
37. Meyer, op cit. p. 176
38. *New York Times*, July 1st, 1962, p. 3
39. *Proceso*, June 19th, 1995, p. 53
40. Cline, *Revolution to Evolution*, op cit. p. 327
41. ibid, p. 325
42. *Proceso*, June 24th, 1996
43. Castañeda, op cit. p. 126
44. ibid
45. Meyer, op cit. p. 179
46. ibid
47. *Proceso*, March 25th, 1996
48. Agee, op cit. p. 526
49. ibid
50. Paco Ignacio Taibo II, *La Jornada*, October 3rd, 1996, p. 28
51. Agee, op cit. p. 526
52. ibid, p. 550 etc.
53. ibid, p. 517
54. ibid, p. 554
55. ibid
56. Riding, op cit. p. 59
57. *Proceso*, March 25th, 1996
58. Kendell, op cit. p. 525
59. Riding, op cit. p. 60. The 337 total was cited by Eduardo del Valle, a student strike leader, in a personal interview during the 20th aniversary ceremonies of this national tragedy.
61. Agee, op cit. p. 553
62. *Proceso*, September 29th, 1996, pp. 32-33
63. Agee, op cit, p. 551
64. Sergio Sarmiento, "Cambiar Candidatos," *Reforma*, October 11th, 1996
65. Cf *Lucio Cabañas*
66. Cf Chapter 16, "The Ghosts in the Trees"
67. Riding, op cit. p. 338
68. Buendía, op cit. p. 71
69. Meyer, op cit. p. 185
70. ibid, p. 193
71. Woodward, p. 227
72. ibid, p. 138
73. ibid, p. 345
74. *New York Times*, June 11th, 1980, p. 31
75. Riding, op cit. p. 339
76. Document stamped "Top Secret," reprinted in Kolb, pp. 18-19
77. Castañeda, op cit. p. 186
78. *Proceso*, May 7th, 1987, p. 26

CHAPTER 10: WAR ON DRUGS: WHOSE NATIONAL SECURITY?

1. Clinton, p. XI
2. Aguayo and Baily, p. 298
3. Richard Chahener, "The National Security Policy from Truman to Eisenhower" in Graebner
4. ibid, p. 43, quoting Daniel Yergin
5. Rudolph, p. 332
6. Weinberger, pp. 163-216
7. Evinger
8. *La Jornada*, December 6th, 1996
9. Aguayo and Baily, op cit. p. 17
10. Shannon, p. 98
11. NSDD 221 "Narcotics and National Security" and cf NSDD 297 and NSD 18, all in Christopher Simpson, p. 640
12. Pastor, op cit. p. 276
13. Cf Chapter 12, "The Open Veins of Mexico"
14. Presidential Commission on Organized Crime, Washington, 1986, p. 473
15. Shannon, op cit. p. 26
16. María Celia Toro, in "En Busca de Seguridad Nacional," op cit, p. 370
17. *La Jornada*, March 15th, 1997
18. *La Jornada*, February 3rd, 1997, p. 23
19. Wherever one stands on the *San Jose Mercury-News*'s eyepopping 1996 "Dark Alliance" scoop that pinned the crack plague on CIA-Contra connivance, the chain of recrimination begins with one Norwin Menesis, a Company-sponsored operator, identified as a drug peddler as early as 1976 by U.S. authorities—cf Jonathan Marshall et al., p. 137. The facts are incontrovertible: Norwin Menesis *did* sell cocaine to Freeway Rickey Ross who *did* cook it into crack and distribute it in Crip-infested Los Angeles housing projects.
20. *El Financiero*, June 7th, 1994, p. 35
21. *La Jornada*, June 6th, 1995
22. Castañeda, op cit. p. 249
23. Liera
24. Castañeda, op cit. pgs. 244-45
25. Mezzrow
26. Paredes, p. 154
27. Musto, pp. 225-27
28. Cline, *The U.S. and Mexico*, op cit. p. 269
29. Meyer, op cit. p. 182
30. Berry, op cit. p. 330 footnote
31. John Ross, *Dreams Mulch*, unpublished history of Northern California sinsemilla trade, 1983
32. Shannon, op cit. p. 64

33. Castañeda, op cit. p. 245
34. *Proceso*, January 15th, 1990, p. 8
35. *L.A. Times*, November 15th, 1984, p. 1
36. Shannon, op cit. p. 195
37. *New York Times*, February 22nd, 1985
38. *L.A. Times*, March 12th, 1985
39. *Proceso*, April 23rd, 1990, p. 8
40. *Proceso*, January 11th, 1990, p. 9
41. *Proceso*, January 29th, 1990, p. 19
42. Castañeda, op cit. p. 246
43. "A Policy of Impunity," *Americas Watch*, New York 1991
44. Fazio, chapter 10
45. *La Jornada*, October 25th, 1995, p. 11
46. Fazio, op cit. p. 179
47. *Proceso*, October 30th, 1995, p. 8
48. *La Jornada*, October 25th, 1995, p. 4
49. Osorio Cruz, Zacarias vs. the Ministry of Employent and Immigration, ELEM88-20043X, Canadian Immigration Board, March 14-24th 1988, Vol. II
50. *New York Times*, February 19th, 1989, p. 1 and see John Ross, *San Francisco Examiner*, October, 1988, p. 1
51. Osorio Cruz, op cit. Vol. I
52. Rudolph, op cit. p. 334
53. ibid, p. 328
54. Secretario de Educación Pública, p. 143
55. Berry, op cit. p. 52, and cf *La Jornada*, October 9th, 1996, p. 56
56. Rudolph, op cit. p. 340
57. Meyer, *Excelsior*, September 6th, 1989, p. 1
58. Cf Chapter 16: "Whose Oil? Whose Rights?"
59. *El Financiero*, February 10th, 1995
60. *La Jornada*, November 4th, 1995
60. *Reforma*, November 6th, 1995
61. *La Jornada*, July 26th, 1995, p. 56
62. ibid
63. *La Jornada*, July 29th, 1995, p. 1
64. Fazio, op cit. p. 189
65. *Proceso*, November 11th, 1991, p. 19
66. Berry, op cit. p. 332
67. *La Jornada*, September 20th, 1996, p. 16
68. *La Jornada*, September 24th, 1996
69. *La Jornada*, August 28th, 1995, p. 5
70. *La Jornada*, April 14th, 1995, p. 11
71. *San Francisco Chronicle*, September 19th, 1995, p. A8
72. Berry, op cit. p. 333
73. ibid
74. *Proceso*, March 6th, 1995
75. February 13th, 1995 cable, labeled "Chiapas Update #5," declassified from State

Department U.S. embassy documents by the National Security Archive
76. John Ross, *Rebellion*, op cit p. 49
77. *La Jornada*, August 21st, 1995
78. *La Jornada*, February 14th, 1995
79. Cf "Ghosts In The Trees," Chapter 16
80. *La Jornada*, September 11th, 1996, p. 9
81. *La Jornada*, October 28th, 1995
82. *Proceso*, July 5th, 1993
83. John Ross, *L.A. Weekly*, March 21st-27th, 1997
84. *La Jornada*, January 11th, 1996, p. 5
85. *La Jornada*, August 31st. 1996, p. 1

CHAPTER 11: WAR ON DRUGS: OF COPS, CAPOS, BIG FISH, MADRINAS AND THE LORD OF THE SKIES

1. *El Financiero*, January 19th, 1996, p. 28
2. John Ross, "Hunger," *Mexico Journal*, February 27th, 1989, p. 6
3. *Proceso*, November 2nd, 1992, p. 7
4. This reporter was the interviewer.
5. *New York Times*, December 28th, 1996, p. 11
6. Flanagan, p. 209
7. Johns, pp. 87-90
8. *Proceso*, December 25th, 1989
9. ibid
10. *New York Times*, January 17th, 1996, p. 5
11. *Proceso*, January 22nd, 1996, p. 8
12. ibid
13. *El Financiero*, July 31st, 1994, p. 17
14. *New York Times*, May 12th, 1996, p. 8
15. *Reforma*, September 21st, 1996, p. 1
16. *New York Times*, December 23rd, 1996, p. 6
17. *Proceso*, January 22nd, 1996, p. 7
18. *New York Times*, January 17th, 1996, p. 5
19. *La Jornada*, January 17th, 1996, p. 1
20. ibid, p. 11
21. *La Jornada*, March 10th, 1996, p. 49
22. *Reforma*, March 11th, 1997
23. *New York Times*, May 24th, 1993, p. 1
24. *L.A. Times*, June 16th, 1995, p. 20
25. *La Jornada*, May 20th, 1996, p. 49
26. *La Jornada*, Decmber 13th, 1996, p. 3
27. *El Financiero*, January 17th, 1996, p. 32
28. *Reforma*, September 15th, 1996, p. 16
29. *Wall Street Journal*, October 7th, 1996
30. *Reforma*, February 6th, 1997, p. 4
31. *La Jornada*, March 18th, 1997, p. 1
32. *Reforma*, March 8th, 1996, p. 6
33. *La Jornada*, February 7th, 1996, p. 1
34. *La Jornada*, September 9th, 1996, p. 1

35. *La Jornada*, May 3rd, 1997, p. 45
36. *La Jornada*, August 17th, 1996, p. 1
37. *La Jornada*, August 18th, 1996, p. 3
38. *La Jornada*, August 9th, 1996, p. 9
39. *El Financiero*, August 4th, 1996, p. 24
40. Berry, op cit. p. 334
41. *Proceso*, December 21st, 1992, p. 13
42. *Reforma*, May 4th, 1997, p. 4
43. *La Jornada*, February 11th, 1995, p. 17
44. *Reforma*, September 26th, 1996
45. Corsen, p. 589
46. *La Jornada*, December 22nd, 1995, p. 10
47. ibid
48. *La Jornada*, July 14th, 1995, p. 50
49. *Proceso*, April 22nd, 1990, pp. 9-11
50. Castañeda, op cit. p. 252
51. White House figures, quoted in *La Jornada*, February 24th, 1997, p. 7
52. *La Jornada*, February 15th, 1996, p. 19

CHAPTER 12: GUSHERS & VAMPIRES: MEXICO'S OPEN VEINS

1. *New York Times*, February 27th, 1997, p. C7
2. John Ross, "Border Vampires," *Pacific News Service*, June 1987
3. *Proceso*, February 6th, 1996, p. 16
4. ibid
5. Calculations based on $16 billion USD paid out in 1994
6. U.S. State Department: FRUS 1955-57, VI. American Republics, p. 649
7. *Proceso*, February 6th, 1995, p. 28
8. Kendell, op cit. p. 537
9. Riding, op cit. p. 171
10. ibid
11. ibid, p. 175
12. ibid, p. 176, published in the UK as *Inside the Volcano*—page numbers are from the British edition.
13. ibid, p. 176
14. López Obrador, pp. 52-53
15. Riding, op cit. p. 171
16. ibid, p. 153
17. ibid, p. 155
18. ibid
19. *Proceso*, February 6th, 1995, quoting Darrell Delmaid's *Debt Shock*
20. Riding, op cit. p. 156
21. *Proceso*, February 6th, 1995, Delmaid.
22. ibid
23. Jackie Roddick, *The Dance of the Millions*, quoted in Green

24. *Proceso*, February 6th, 1996, p 19
25. Riding, op cit. p. 157
26. ibid, p. 158
27. ibid, p. 154
28. ibid, p. 161
29. *Proceso*, February 6th, 1995
30. Riding, op cit. p. 158

CHAPTER 13: CARLOS'S HOUSE OF CARDS

1. John Ross, "The Baja Wall," *San Francisco Bay Guardian*, December 29th, 1993
2. Cf *San Francisco Examiner*, June-September 1988 for this reporter's chronicle of events—also Alan Riding's revealing report in the August 13th, 1988, *New York Times*.
3. *New York Times*, July 11th, 1988
4. ibid
5. ibid
6. *Proceso*, November 2nd, 1992, p. 7
7. John Ross, "Locking Up Labor," *Texas Observer*, December 6th, 1996
8. *New York Times*, January 20th, 1989, p. 20
9. Cf Oppenheimer, pp. 201-202
10. Castañeda, op cit. p. 220
11. *Proceso*, March 20th, 1989, p. 9
12. Duncan Green, op cit. p. 63
13. Berry, op cit. p. 88
14. *La Jornada*, March 3rd, 1997, p. 49
15. *Wall Street Journal*, March 27th, 1990, p. 1
16. Fukayama
17. *Proceso*, November 2nd, 1992, p. 7
18. *Proceso*, Aug.ust17th, 1992, p. 8
19. Berry, op cit. p. 296
20. *Proceso*, August 17th, 1992
21. Berry, op cit. p. 98
22. ibid, p. 143, and cf *Reforma*, May 26th, 1997, p. 40A
23. *La Jornada*, April 28th, 1997, p. 25
24. *Proceso*, May 7th, 1990, pp. 7-9
25. *Proceso*, July 20th, 1990, p. 8
26. Berry, op cit. p. 131
27. Stauber
28. *Business Week*, November 12th, 1990
29. *McCleans*, April 8, 1991
30. *Forbes* Magazine, July 9th, 1990
31. *El Financiero*, April 17th, 1991
32. Duncan Green, op cit. p. 52
33. *Wall Street Journal*, March 30th, 1991, p. 1
34. *Proceso*, May 13th, 1991
35. *Proceso*, November 2nd, 1992, p. 6
36. John E. ("Jeb") Bush met "Colu" when he was a 16 year-old exhange student in her hometown. *L.A. Times*, July 31st, 1991

37. John Ross, "The Annexation of Mexico," Z *Magazine*, Summer 1991
38. *El Financiero*, April 13th, 1991
39. Agee, op cit, p. 533
40. Castañeda, op cit. p. 241
41. Carlos Fazio, *Proceso*, February 13th, 1989, p. 22
42. ibid
43. *Proceso*, May 13th, 1991
44. *El Financiero*, November 25th, 1995, p. 34
45. *Proceso*, August 17th, 1992
46. *Proceso*, October 8th, 1995, p. 72
47. ibid
48. *Proceso*, November 15th, 1993, p. 7
49. ibid
50. ibid
51. *Proceso*, November 22nd, 1993
52. Telephone conversation, April 21st, 1997
53. *Proceso*, November 22nd, 1993
54. *Proceso*, December 14th, 1992
55. This is the accepted figure, but estimates vary wildly from $4 billion to as high as $16 billion—see Epilogue for a more complete discussion.
56. Hinojosa now says this was a worst-case scenario, telephone conversation, April 22nd, 1997
57. *Proceso*, Decembe 9th, 1991, pp. 22-23
58. Cf John Ross, *Rebellion*, chapters 11-12
59. North American Free Trade Agreement, Vol. I
60. *Proceso*, January 31st, 1994
61. quoted in *Proceso*, November 15th, 1993
62. *Proceso*, June 24th, 1991
63. *Forbes* Magazine, July 7th, 1994
64. The number of "extreme poor," as opposed to merely "poor," is a function of what criteria are applied—daily earning power, nutrition, etc. Low-end estimates are Solidarity numbers; high end, United Nations data.
65. Cf John Ross, *Rebellion*, chapters two and three
66. *Proceso*, March 26th, 1994
67. ibid

CHAPTER 14: MEXICAN MELTDOWN

1. *Proceso*, December 26th, 1994 p. 10
2. Pazos, p. 55
3. Oppenheimer, op cit. pp. 227-28
4. *Proceso*, July 10th, 1995, p. 10
5. *Proceso*, December 26th, 1994, p. 12
6. Oppenheimer, op cit. p. 222
7. *Proceso*, January 2nd, 1995, p. 10
8. ibid
9. *Proceso*, December 26th, 1994
10. *Proceso*, July 10th, 1995
11. Oppenheimer, op cit. p. 222
12. *Proceso*, January 2nd, 1995, p. 14
13. *Proceso*, December 26th, 1994, p. 14
14. *New York Times*, December 22nd, 1994
15. Ortiz, p. 10
16. *Proceso*, January 30th, 1995, p. 8
17. ibid
18. ibid
19. ibid
20. Oppenheimer, op cit. pp. 219-222
21. ibid
22. *Financial Times*, February 2nd, 1995
23. *Proceso*, January 30th, 1995
24. *Los Angeles Times*, January 17th, 1995
25. *Ovaciones*, February 1st, 1995
26. *Proceso*, February 6th, 1995
27. Oppenheimer, op cit. p. 221
28. Duncan Green, op cit. p. 85
29. *Proceso*, January 2nd, 1995, p. 8
30. Weinberger, op cit
31. *Proceso*, February 27th, 1995, p. 10
32. *Proceso*, January 30th, 1995, p. 24
33. *Reforma*, December 18th, 1995, p. 9
34. *Proceso*, January 23rd, 1995, p. 11
35. *La Jornada*, January 16th, 1997, p. 3
36. John Ross, *México Bárbaro*, June 22-August 6th, 1996
37. Cf Oppenheimer, for an "insiders" view of Ruiz Massieu murder,
38. *Proceso*, February 19th, 1995, p. 10
39. *La Jornada*, February 13th, 1995, p. 8
40. *La Jornada*, February 11th, 1995, p. 23
41. Reported in *Proceso*, February 13th, 1995, p. 13
42. *La Jornada*, February 11th, p. 12
43. *La Jornada*, February 14th, 1995, p. 5
44. *El Financiero*, December 19th, 1995, pp. 5-10
45. *El Financiero*, June 19th, 1994, p. 37
46. Davd Márquez Ayala, *La Jornada*, March 31st, 1997
47. Cf "Throwing Off The Yoke," Chap. 16
48. *La Jornada*, January 10th, 1995, p. 48
49. *La Jornada*, July 23rd, 1996
50. *La Jornada*, May 3rd, 1996, p. 1
51. *La Jornada*, February 27th, 1997, p. 49
52. *Proceso*, July 10th, 1995
53. *Forbes* Magazine, July 17th, 1995
54. *La Jornada*, April 20th, 1995, p. 37
55. *La Jornada*, October 9th, 1995
56. John Ross, "Return of El Barzón," *Texas Observer*, July 14th, 1995.
57. *La Jornada*, October 22nd, 1995, p. 48
58. *El Financiero*, June 17th, 1995, p. 23
59. *La Jornada*, January 29th, 1996, p. 51

60. *La Jornada*, October 11th-12th, 1996
61. *La Jornada*, March 12th, 1996, p. 46
62. *La Jornada*, March 21st, 1996, p. 46
63. John Ross, *México Bárbaro*, April 15th-22nd, 1996
64. *La Jornada*, May 30th, 1996, p. 47
65. *New York Times*, June 13th, 1996, p. A9
66. John Ross, *El Financiero Internacional*, October 23rd, 1995
67. *Financial Times*, October 9th, 1995, p. 8
68. *Washington Post*, October 11th, 1995, p. B1
69. ibid
70. *Proceso*, July 10th, 1995, p. 10
71. Speech published by the U.S. Chamber of Commerce, Washington D.C. Dates for the petrochemical sales were subsequently changed.
72. *New York Times*, October 14th, 1995, p. C7
73. *El Financiero*, December 15th, 1995, p. 23
74. John Ross, *México Bárbaro*, June 11th-25th, 1996
75. ibid
76. *La Jornada*, April 16th, 1995, p. 43
77. *Wall Street Journal*, January 25th, 1996, p. 1
78. *New York Times*, May 7th, 1997

CHAPTER 15: LA MALINCHE

1. Although this figure is usually put at 300,000, a U.S. official in country for the Clinton visit in May 1997 gave the number as being 500,000.
2. *Mexico City News*, August 29th, 1990
3. Interview with Eduardo Morales, July 1993
4. *Reforma*, January 29th, 1997, p. 22
5. Cortez, p. 154, footnote 25
6. Paz, pp. 65-88
7. ibid, p. 87
8. ibid, pp. 71-72
9. ibid, p. 70
10. Alba, p. 249
11. Castañeda, op cit. p. 339
12. ibid, p. 340
13. Paz, op cit. p. 70
14. Bonfil, p. 205
15. *New York Times*, August 6th, 1996, p. 1
16. Castañeda, op cit. p. 243
17. Cardoso, p. 61
18. *Proceso*, May 13th, 1996, p. 26
19. John Ross, *Rebellion*, p. 221
20. Cf Stoll
21. *New York Times*, November 2nd, 1996, p. 4
22. ibid
23. quoted by Enrique Semo, *Proceso*, January 3rd, 1994
24. Castañeda, op cit. p. 339

25. Cf Richard
26. In reverse order, the three won the Mexican League home run championship from 1939-41
27. Cf Sheffield, Chapter VI
28. *La Jornada*, November 30th, 1996, p. 37
29. *Proceso*, December 23rd, 1991, p. 62
30. *Proceso*, January 16th, 1989, p. 60
31. *Proceso*, Noember. 13th, 1989, p. 20
32. *Reforma*, January 27th, 1997
33. *The New Yorker*, November 9th, 1992
34. *Proceso*, January 1, 1990, p. 48
35. ibid
36. EZLN documents, Vol I, letter from Subcomandate Marcos, January 13th, 1994
37. Bonfil, op cit. p. 199
38. EZLN documents, Vol. II, p. 283

CHAPTER 16: LA COYUNTURA

1. *La Jornada*, September 16th, 1995, p. 9
2. *Proceso*, September 11th, 1995
3. ibid
4. ibid
5. ibid
6. ibid
7. ibid
8. Womack, op cit. pp. 74-75
9. ibid, p. 373
10. Beals, p. 137
11. *Proceso*, April 29th, 1996, p. 28
12. *La Jornada*, September 24th, 1995
13. "*Resumen Historico de la Lucha del Pueblo Tepozteco*," Ayuntamiento Libre, Popular, y Constitutional, 1996
14. *El Financiero*, April 28th, 1996, pp. 20-21
15. *Proceso*, September 11th, 1995
16. *La Jornada*, September 11th, 1995
17. *Proceso*, April 29th, 1996
18. "*Resumen*," op cit
19. *La Jornada*, April 15th, 1996, p. 12
20. ibid
21. *Proceso*, April 29th, 1996, p. 28
22. *La Jornada*, April 14th, 1996, p. 5
23. José Antonio Ríojas Nieto, *La Jornada*, May 27th, 1997, p. 17
24. *La Jornada*, July 31st, 1996, p. 6
25. *Proceso*, February 19th, 1996, p. 8
26. La Jornada, July 31st, 1996, p. 6
27. *Comisión Nacional de Derechos Humanos*, Recommendación #90/86, August 29th, 1996
28. ibid
29. A shorter version of this piece appeared in NACLA, January-February, 1997
30. *Proceso*, February 19th, 1996
31. *La Jornada*, July 28th, 1996

32. ibid
33. *Reforma*, January 22nd, 1997, p. 27A
34. Oilwatch-Mexico, "*Análisis de Los Impactos de la Explosión en Cactus*", September 12th, 1996
35. *Proceso*, February 19th, 1996
36. "La Contaminación en La Zona Costera," Ecología, *La Jornada*, March 18th, 1996
37. John Ross, *México Bárbaro*, November 3rd-17th, 1996
38. Miguel Angel Granados Chapa, "Tabasco," *Reforma*, February 8th, 1996, p. 7
39. *Proceso*, February 19th, 1996, p. 8
40. ibid
41. López Obrador, op cit. Chapter 8 "Historia de las Cajas"
42. *El Financiero*, February 6th, 1996, p. 32
43. *La Jornada*, February 12th, 1996, p. 3
44. *Proceso*, February 19th, 1996
45. *La Jornada*, February 9th, 1996, p. 1
46. Conversation with López Obrador February 15th 1996, and cf *La Jornada*, February 17th, 1996, p. 13
47. *La Jornada*, December 17th, 1995
48. John Ross, *Sierra* Magazine, July-August 1992
49. ibid
50. *La Jornada*, January 31st, 1996, p. 8
51. John Ross, *México Bárbaro*, March 15th-23rd, 1996
52. *La Jornada*, October 14th, 1996, p. 1
53. *La Jornada*, September 27th, p. 48, and September 28th, p. 56
54. John Ross, *México Bárbaro*, November 3rd-17th, 1996
55. John Ross, *México Bárbaro*, March 15th-23rd, 1996
56. *La Jornada*, March 19th, 1996, p. 5
57. Song sheet distributed by El Barzón Debtors Union, Puebla
58. ibid
59. John Ross, "Return of the Barzónistas," *Texas Observer*, July 14th, 1995
60. ibid
61. *Proceso*, July 24th, 1995, p. 42
62. Ross, *Texas Observer*, op cit
63. ibid
64. ibid
65. *El Financiero*, June 19th, 1995, p. 5
66. *La Jornada*, June 5th, 1995, p. 37
67. Ross, *Texas Observer*, op cit.
68. *Reforma*, March 9th, 1997
69. Interview with Juan José Quirino, January 1997
70. *San Francisco Chronicle*, May 17th, 1996, p. 15
71. *El Financiero*, March 19th, 1996, p. 7

72. John Ross, "The Gods Must Be Angry," *The Nation*, December 18th, 1995
73. *La Jornada*, July 11th, 1996, p. 39
74. *El Financiero*, April 23rd, 1996, p. 5
75. Actually, according to the Catechism of the Catholic Church, Loyola University Press, 1994, Matthew, who was a publican and trafficked in such terms, wrote of forgiving their "debts." Luke, more concerned with public morals, spoke of forgiving their "sins." cf pgs. 664-666.
76. *La Jornada*, July 21st, 1996, p. 15
77. ibid
78. *La Jornada*, July 25th, 1996, p. 8
79. ibid
80. *El Sol de Acapulco*, April 24th, 1995, p. 1
81. *La Jornada*, February 20th, 1996, p. 13
82. *Los Angeles Times*, November 4th, 1995
83. *El Sol de Acapulco*, ibid. p. 7
84. John Ross, *Sierra* Magazine, July-August 1996, p. 24
85. ibid
86. ibid
87. John Ross, *México Bárbaro*, February 21st-28th, 1996
88. Interview with Carlos Carrillo, Acapulco, February, 1996
89. John Ross, *Sierra* Magazine, July-August, 1996
90. Cabañas, op cit.
91. ibid
92. John Ross, *México Bárbaro*, February 21st-18th, 1996
93. Osorio Cruz vs. Canadian Immigration Board, op cit.
94. John Ross, *México Bárbaro*, February 21st-28th, 1996
95. ibid
96. *La Jornada*, June 29th, 1996, p. 1
97. *Sur*, July 1st, 1996
98. *El Machete*, July 23rd, 1996
99. John Ross, *México Bárbaro*, July 7th-14th, 1996
100. La Jornada, Aug. 25th, 1996. Note: the EPR claimed 23,000 troops but this was prior to the August 28th attacks, after which Mexican Army troop strength in the region escalated.
101. ibid
102. *La Jornada*, August 2nd, 1996, p. 15 and February 19th, 1997
103. Interview at Villa San Luis, San Luis de las Lomas, Guerrero, February, 1996
104. John Ross, *México Bárbaro*, September 15th-23rd, 1996
105. *La Jornada*, September 3rd, 1996, p. 44

106. John Ross, *México Bárbaro*, February 21st-28th, 1996

107. *La Jornada*, August 30th, 1996

108. *Universal Gráfico*, September 3rd, 1996

109. John Ross, *México Bárbaro*, September 15th-23rd, 1996

110. *La Jornada*, July 9th, 1996

111. "*Café: El Reloj de la Inconformidad*," Luis Hernández Navarro Campo, *La Jornada*, November 1st, 1996

112. ibid

113. *New York Times*, September 19th, 1996

114. John Ross, *México Bárbaro*, February 21st-28th, 1996

115. *La Jornada*, September 11th, 1996, p. 9

116. EZLN, op cit. p. 284

117. John Ross, *Sierra*, July-August 1992

118. *Comisión Conciliadora de las Chimilapas*, "*Por la Defensa de las Chimilapas*" October, 1991

119. Felipe Ochoa & Socios, "*El Programa de Desarrollo Integral del Istmo de Tehuantepec*," *Resumen Executivo*, March 30th, 1996

120. *La Jornada*, July 22nd, 1996, p. 1

121. *El Financiero*, April 24th, 1996

122. Remarks made at *Foro Nacional en Defensa de las Chimilapas*, October, 1996, Santa María Chimilapas, Oaxaca

123. Interview with Andrés Barreda, La Realidad, Chiapas, April, 1996

124. John Ross, *México Bárbaro*, July 22nd-Aug. 6th, 1996

125. *La Jornada*, August 15th, 1996, p. 9

126. *New York Times*, November 10th, 1996, p. 6

127. EZLN documents, Vol II. p. 416

128. *Proceso*, June 5th, 1995, p. 32

129. ibid

130. ibid

131. John Ross, "Wellspring of Rebellion," *Texas Observer*, November 17th, 1995

132. John Ross, *Rebellion*, op cit. pp. 27-29

133. The Barbosa article appeared in Tiempo, San Cristóbal de las Casas, in the spring of 1993

134. Exploración y Producción, Ocosingo, PEMEX, Mexico City, p. 118, The author is grateful to George Baker, an adviser to small energy companies doing business in Mexico, for access to this document.

135. Comandante Tacho, opening remarks, Special Forum on Indigenous Rights and Culture, San Cristóbal de las Casas, January 4th, 1996

136. Cf Jaime Aviles, "*El Tonto del Pueblo*," *La Jornada*, beginning February, 1997

137. *La Jornada*, August 2nd, 1996, p. 8

138. *La Jornada*, August 4th, 1996

EPILOGUE: ANNEXING NORTH AMERICA

1. Gary Paul Nabham, "Cryptic Cactus On The Border" in Byrd

2. *New York Times*, March 3rd, 1996

3. Pastor, op cit. p. 284

4. *La Jornada*, March 23rd, 1997, p. 18

5. This story was written for *Pacific News Service*. I dictated it on the phone. It appeared soon after in the *San Francisco Examiner*—on the flip page of the Real Estate section.

6. This story, in a slightly altered form, appeared in the *San Francisco Bay Guardian*, June 1996

7. Interview with Salvador Campanur, mayor of Cherán, May, 1996

8. Conversation with Gustavo López, Colegio de Michoacán, Zamora, Michoacán, May 1996

9. Cardoso, op cit. p. 1

10. ibid, p. 10

11. ibid, p. 38

12. ibid, p. 40

13. *New York Times*, February 8th, 1997, p. 7

14. *El Financiero*, June 19th, 1995, p. 66

15. Simon

16. *El Financiero*, July 10th, 1995, p. 72

17. David Márquez Ayala, *La Jornada*, March 3rd, 1997, p. 50

18. Pastor, op cit. p. 295

19. *San Francisco Chronicle*, May 16th, 1995, p. C2

20. *New York Times*, March 10th, 1996

21. Brownsville, *Texas Herald*, January 29th, 1997

22. *El Financiero*, July 3rd, 1995, p. 76

23. *La Jornada*, July 4th, 1995, p. 9

24. *Brownsville Herald*, January 29th, 1997

25. *Brownsville Herald*, January 28th-29th, February 9th, 1997 and *San Antonio Express-News*, January 28th, February 8th, and April 10th, 1997

26. *El Financiero*, July 3rd, 1995, p. 76

27. Conversation with Roberto Martínez, April 1997

28. *La Jornada*, July 4th, 1996, p. 23

29. *La Jornada*, February 3rd, 1997, p. 18

30. *El Sol de Mexico*, May 27th, 1996, p. 2B

31. *La Jornada*, March 30th, 1996, p. 19

32. *Reforma*, March 31st, 1997

33. Cardoso, op cit. p. 97

34. ibid, p. 109

35. Hoffman, p. 153

36. Cardoso, op cit. p. 82

37. John Ross, *México Bárbaro*, January 15th-23rd, 1997

38. Cardoso, op cit. p. 20

39. ibid, p.20

40. A free copy of this book to the first reader who can source this quote.
41. Hoffman, op cit. p. 10
42. Calavita
43. Cardoso, op cit. p. 132
44. ibid, p. 133
45. ibid, p. 124
46. ibid
47. ibid, p. 132
48. ibid, p. 134
49. This claim seems extravagant—1919 was a peak year for Klan activity—race riots occurred in 10 U.S. cities and, according to *The Black Americans* (William Morrow, New York, 1970, p. 403), 76 blacks were lynched. While blacks and Mexicans were interchangeable in the eyes of Texas racists, 52 seems an unlikely number.
50. Cardoso, op cit. p. 26
51. ibid, p. 33
52. ibid, p. 121
53. ibid, p. 129
54. Hoffman, op cit. p. 61. Newspaper accounts of such raids were almost universally sprinkled with racist descriptives. Two notable exceptions were the Los Angeles-based *La Opinión*, still the leading Mexican daily in the U.S., and Carey McWilliams' valiant reporting for *The Nation*.
55. ibid, p. 106
56. Cardoso, op ct. p. 147
57. Musto, op cit. p. 219
58. ibid, p. 220
59. Hoffman, op cit. p. 70
60. ibid, p. 71
61. Cardoso, op cit. p. 144
62. ibid, p. 91
63. Hoffman, op cit. p. 148
64. ibid, p. 90
65. Juan Ramón García
66. Pastor, op cit. p. 348
67. ibid, p. 291
68. ibid, Castañeda. p. 302
69. Tijuana, Baja California-San Diego, but technically, San Ysidro, California; Tecate, Baja California-Campo, California; Mexicali, Baja California-Calexico, California; San Luis Río Colorado, Sonora-San Luis Río Colorado, Arizona; Sonoyita, Sonora-Lukeville, Arizona; Nogales, Sonora-Nogales, Arizona; Naco, Sonora-Naco, Arizona; Agua Prieta, Sonora-Douglas, Arizona; Las Palomas, Chihuahua-Columbus, New Mexico; Cuidad Juárez, Chihuahua-El Paso, Texas; Ojinaga, Chihuahua-Presidio, Texas; Boquillas, Chihuahua-Boquillas, Texas; Ciudad Acuña, Coahuila-Del Río, Texas; Piedras Negras, Coahuila-Eagle Pass, Texas; Nuevo Laredo, Tamaulipas-Laredo, Texas; Ciudad Alemán, Tamaulipas-Roma, Texas; Díaz Ordaz/Camargo, Tamaulipas-Río Grande City, Texas; Reynosa, Tamaulipas-McAllen, Texas; Matamoros, Tamaulipas-Brownsville, Texas
70. Castañeda, op cit. p. 300
71. Garreau, *see* MexAmerica
72. Pastor, op cit. p. 288
73. Castañeda, op cit. p. 289
74. *Reforma*, May 26th, 1997, p. 40A
75. Debby Nathan, "Love In The Time Of Cholera," p. 45, Byrd, op cit.
76. Interview with this reporter, May 1987
77. Interview with this reporter, May 1987
78. *La Jornada*, December 13th, 1997, p. 27
79. *Reforma*, September 11th, 1996, p. 6
80. *La Jornada*, May 16th, 1997
81. John Ross, *Rebellion*, op cit. p. 284
82. *Reforma*, April 26th, 1997
83. John Ross, *El Puro Gusto*, op cit.
84. *Reforma*, May 12th, 1997, p. 12A
85. *New York Times*, February 4th, 1997, p. A3
86. *Reforma*, February 12th, 1997, p. 21
87. Carlos Montemayor, *La Jornada*, April 9th, 1997, p. 12
88. *New York Times*, September 26th, 1995, p. 9
89. This story appeared in a slightly altered form in the *San Francisco Bay Gaurdian*, August 25th, 1993
90. *La Jornada*, May 27th, 1997
91. *New York Times*, February 4th, 1997, p. 3
92. *New York Times*, February 8th, 1997, p. 7
93. *Wall Street Journal*, January 29th, 1997
94. *El Financiero*, April 18th, 1996, p. 19
95. *La Jornada*, February 2nd, 1997, p. 55
96. John Ross, *México Bárbaro*, January 15th-25th, 1997
97. *New York Times*, June 16th, 1996, p. 4
98. *SF Weekly*, January 1st, 1997
99. *San Francisco Chronicle*, January 2nd, 1997, p. 15
100. John Ross, *México Bárbaro*, May 15th-25th, 1996
101. Interview, May 1st, 1996
102. *New York Times*, November 10th, 1996, p. 18
103. *SF Weekly*, January 1st, 1997
104. Carlos Fuentes, *La Jornada*, April 11th, 1996, p. 1
105. *La Jornada*, August 6th, 1995, p. 50
106. *New York Times Magazine*, November 12th, 1995

* Footnoting is a subjective science. I've footnoted direct quotes, references found only in one source, and an occasional elucidation on the text. Where possible, I've listed my own writings as source for materials gathered in the process of reporting. Most news stories are listed only by publication and date except for bylined editorial and op ed pieces.

BIBLIOGRAPHY

Agee, Philip, *Inside the Company: CIA Diary*, Penguin Books, London, 1975

Aguayo, Sergio and Bruce Michael Baily, eds., *En Busca de Seguridad Nacional*, Siglo XXI, Mexico, 1990

Aguirre Beltrán, Gonzalo, *La Población Negra de México*, Fondo de Cultura Económico, Mexico, 1972

Alba, Victor, *The Mexican*, Praeger, New York, 1967

Alsup, Carl, *The American GI Forum: Origins and Evaluation*, Center for Mexican American Studies, Austin, Texas, 1982

Atkin, Ronald, *Revolution!*, John Daly Co. New York, 1970

Barma, Yon, *Eisenstein*, Indiana University Press, Bloomington, 1966

Barron, Clarence, *The Mexican Problem*, Houghton Mifflin, New York, 1917

Beals, Carlton, *The Mexican Maze*, New York, 1931

Benítez, Fernando, *The Century After Cortez*, trans. Joan Maclean, University of Chicago Press, 1995

Berry, Tom, ed. *Mexico, A Country Guide*, Interhemispheric Education Resources Center, Albuquerque, New Mexico, 1992

Bethell, Leslie, with Ian Roxborough, *Latin America Between The Second World War and The Cold War*, Cambridge University Press, 1992

Bonfil, Guillermo, *México Profundo*, Grijalvo, Mexico City, 1987

Buendía, Manuel, *La CIA en México*, Oceanos, Mexico, 1984

Byrd, Bobby, ed. *The Late, Great Border*, Cinco Puntos Press, El Paso, 1996

Calavita, Kitty, *U.S. Immigration and the Control of Labor, 1820-1924*. Academic Press, London, 1984

Callahan, P. and J. Smith, *La Tilma de Juan Diego—¿Técnica o Milagro?*, Alhambra, Mexico, (no year)

Cardoso, Lawrence, *Mexican Emigration to the United States 1897-1931*, University of Arizona Press, Tucson

Catechism of the Catholic Church, Loyola University, 1994

Chalmers, David *Hooded America*, Franklin Watts, 1965

Clendenen, Clarence C., *The United States and Pancho Villa: A Study In Unconventional Diplomacy*, Cornell University Press, Ithaca, NY, 1961

Cline, Howard F., *Mexico: Revolution to Evolution 1940-1960*, Oxford University Press, 1992
   The United States and Mexico, Harvard University Press, Cambridge, Massachusetts, 1967

Clinton, Bill, *National Security Strategy for the United States: Engagement and Enlargement*, Brassey, Washington, DC, 1995

Corsen, William, *The Armies of Ignorance: The Rise of the American Intelligence Empire*, Dial Press, NY, 1977

Cortez, Hernán, *Letters From New Spain*, trans. A.R. Pagman, Orion Press, New York, 1971

Cosio Villegas, Daniel, ed. *A Compact History of Mexico*, El Colegio de Mexico, Mexico, 1985
   Historia General de México, Hermes, Mexico City, 1955-60

Crosby, Alfred *The Columbian Exchange: Biological and Cultural Conquerors of 1492*, Greenwood Press, Westport, Connecticut, 1973

de la Coruña Martín, Jesús, *Relación de los Indios de la Provincia de Michoacán*, Aguilar, Madrid, 1956

DeLeón, Arnoldo, *They Called Them Greasers*, University of Texas Press, Austin, 1983

Díaz del Castillo, Bernal, *The Discovery and Conquest of Mexico*, Farrar, Straus, & Cudahy, New York

Ejército Zapatista de Liberación Nacional, *EZLN: Documentos y Comunicaciones*, Vol, I & II, ERA, Mexico City, 1995

Evinger, William, *Directory of U.S. Military Bases Worldwide*, Oryx Press, Phoenix, 1995

Fagan, Brian N., *The Aztecs*, W.H. Freeman, NY, 1984

Fazio, Carlos, *El Tercer Vínculo*, Joaquín Mortiz, Mexico, 1996

Flanagan, Lt. Gen. Edward, *The Battle For Panama*, Brassey, Washington, 1993

Freeman Smith, Robert, *The United States and Revolutionary Nationalism in Mexico 1916-1932*, University of Chicago Press, Chicago, 1972

Fuentes, Carlos, *El Gringo Viejo,* Fondo de Cultura Económica, Mexico City

Fukayama, Francis, *The End of History,* Maxwell-MacMillan, New York, 1995

García, Juan Ramón, *Operation Wetback,* Greenwood Press, Westport, Connecticut, 1980

Garreau, Joel, *Nine Nations of North America,* Avon, New York, 1981

González, José, *Lo Negro del Negro Durazo,* Editorial Posada, Mexico, 1983

Graebner, Norman A., ed. *National Security: Its Theory and Practice 1945-1960,* Oxford University Press, 1985

Green, Duncan, *Silent Revolution: The Rise of Market Economies in Latin America,* Cassel-LAB, London, 1995

Green, Gil, *Cold War Fugitive,* International Publishers, New York, 1984

Grieb, Kenneth, *The United States and Huerta,* University of Nebraska Press, Lincoln, 1969

Hoffman, Abraham, *Unwanted Mexican-Americans in the Great Depression: 1929-1939,* University of Arizona, Tucson

Hoyt, Edwin, *America's Wars and Military Excursions,* McGraw Hill, New York

Instituto Nacional de Antropología y Historia (INAH). *Las Intervenciones en Mexico,* Museo Nacional de Intervenciones, Mexico, undated

 1829: Intervención Española, Museo Nacional de Intervenciones, Mexico, 1995

 1914: La Intervención Norteamericana, Museo Nacional de Intervenciones, Mexico, 1992

Jennings, Gary, *Aztec,* Avon Books, New York, 1980

Johns, Cristina Jacqueline, with R. Ward Johnston, *State Crime, The Medea, and The Invasion of Panama,* Praeger, Westport, Connecticut, 1994

Jones, Erroll D., *Bibliography: World War II and Latin America,* Boise State University, (undated)

Katz, Frederich, *The Secret War In Mexico,* University of Chicago Press

Kendell, Jonathan, *La Capital,* Random House,1988

Kissinger, Henry, *Diplomacy,* Simon & Schuster, New York, 1994

Kolb, Peter, and Malcomb Byrne, eds. *The Iran-Contra Scandal,* A National Security Archive Reader, The New Press, New York, 1993

Krauze, Enrique, *Plutarco Elías Calles,* Biografías de Poder, Fondo de Cultura Económica, Mexico, 1987

 *Lázaro Cárdenas,*Biografías de Poder, Fondo de Cultura Económica, Mexico, 1987

 Venustiano Carranza, Biografías de Poder, Fondo de Cultura Económica, Mexico, 1987

León-Portilla, Miguel, *The Broken Spear: The Aztec Account of the Conquest of Mexico,* Beacon Press, Boston, 1962

Liera, Oscar, *El Jinete de La Divina Providencia,* Universidad de Sinaloa

Long, Jeff, *Duel of Eagles,* William Morrow, New York, 1990

López Obrador, Andrés Manuel, *Entre La Historia Y La Esperanza,* Grijalbo, Mexico, 1995

Lucio Cabañas y el Partido de Los Pobres author unidentified, Nueva America, Mexico, 1987

McRobbie, Angela, *Zoot Suit & Second-Hand Clothes,* Unwyn Hyman, Boston, 1981

Manchester, William, *The Glory and The Dream,* Bantam, New York, 1974

Marshall, Jonathan, with Peter Dale Scott and Jane Hunter, *The Iran-Contra Connection,* South End Press, Boston, 1987

Martínez Abad, Carlos, *El Henriquismo: Una Piedra en el Camino,* Martín Casillas Editores, Mexico, 1986

Marx, Karl, *The 18th Brumaire* from *The Marx-Engels Reader,* ed. Robert Tucker, W.W. Norton, New York, 1972

Medina Castro, Manuel, *El Gran Despojo,* Editorial Diogenes, Mexico City, (undated)

Meltzer, Richard, *Ambassador Simpatico: Dwight Morrow In Mexico 1927-1930* in *Ambassadors In Foreign Policy.* Ronnig C. Neale and Albert Vannuck, Praeger, 1987

Meyer, Jean, *The Cristero Rebellion: The Mexican People Between Church and State, 1926-29,* Cambridge University Press, 1976

Mezzrow, Milton "Mezz," *Really The Blues,* Dell, New York, 1946

Morrison, Samuel Elliot, *The Battle of The Atlantic 1939-1943,* Little, Brown, Boston, 1948

Motolinia, Fray Torribio de Benavente, *El Libro de las Cosas de Nueva España,* UNAM, Mexico City, 1971

Musto, David, *The American Disease: Origins of Narcotic Control,* Yale University Press, New Haven, 1991

Nalty, Bernard C., *Strength for the Fight,* The Free Press, New York, 1988

North American Free Trade Agreement, Vol. I U.S. Government Printing Office, Washington D.C. 1994

Oppenheimer, Andrés, *Bordering on Chaos*, Little, Brown, Boston, 1996

Ortiz, Guillermo, *La Reforma Financiera y La Desincorporacíon Bancaria*, Fondo de Cultura Economica, Mexico, 1994

Ota Mashima, María Elena, *Siete Migraciones Japoneses, 1870-1978*, El Colegio de Mexico, 1982

Paredes, Americo, *A Texas-Mexico Cancionero*, University of Illinois, Urbana, 1946

Partridge, Eric, *Dictionary of American Slang & Unconventional English*, MacMillan, 1961, 8th edition

Pastor, Robert with Jorge Castañeda, *Limits Of Friendship*, Vintage Press, New York, 1988. Footnotes indicate whether Pastor or Castañeda is the author cited.

Paz, Octavio, *The Labyrinth of Solitude*, trans. Lysander Kemp, Grove Press, New York, 1985 edition

Pazos, Luis, *Devaluación*, Editorial Diana, Mexico, 1995

Reed, John, *Insurgent Mexico*, Penguin Books, London

Richard, Alfred Charles, *Censorship & Hollywood's Hispanic Image*, Greenwood Press, Westport, Connecticut, 1995

Riding, Alan, *Inside The Volcano*, published in the U.S. as *Distant Neighbors*, Coronet Books, London, 1987

Rockefeller, John D., *Random Reminiscences of Men and Events*, Ayer Company, Salem, New Hampshire, reprinted 1985

Rolle, Andrew F., *The Lost Cause: The Confederate Exodus to Mexico*, University of Oklahoma Press, Norman, 1965

Ross, John, *Rebellion From the Roots: Indian Uprising in Chiapas*, Common Courage Press, Monroe, Maine, 1994

    Dreams Mulch, unpublished manuscript tracing the history of the Northern California sensimilla trade

    Por El Puro Gusto, unpublished manuscript describing Carnaval fiestas in Tlaxacala and Puebla, 1994

Ross, Stanley R., *Francisco Madero: Apostle of Mexican Democracy*, Columbia University Press, New York, 1955

Rudolf, James, ed. *Mexico, A Country Guide*, The American University Press, Washington, D.C., 1985

Schlesinger Stephen, with Stephen Kinzer, *Bitter Fruit*, Anchor Books, New York, 1982

Secretaria de Educación Pública, *Mi Libro de Historia*, quinto grado, 1992 (withdrawn)

Selser, Gregorio, *Sandino, General of the Free*, Monthly Review Press, New York, 1984

Shannon, Elaine, *Desperados*, Viking, New York, 1988

Shapiro, Herbert, *White Violence and Black Response*, University of Massachussetts Press, 1988

Simon, Julian L., *Immigration: The Demographic and Economic Factors*, National Immigration Council, Washington, DC, 1996

Simpson, Christopher, *National Security Directives: The Reagan and Bush Administrations*, Westview Press, Boulder, Colorado

Simpson, Leslie Byrd, *Many Mexicos*, University of California, Berkeley, 1967, 4th edition

Sinclair, Andrew, *The Available Man*, MacMillan, New York, 1965

Soustelle, Jacques, *El Universo de los Aztecas*, Fondo de Cultura Economica, Mexico City, 1986

Spears, Richard A., *Slang & Euphemism*, Jonathan David, Middle Village, New York, 1981

Stauber, John, and Sheldon Rampion, *Toxic Sludge Is Good For You*, Common Courage Press, Monroe Maine, 1995

Stoll, David, *Fishers of Men or Finders of Souls*, Zed Press, London, 1982

Stourz, Gerald, *Benjamin Franklin and American Foreign Policy*, University of Chicago, 1954

Timmerman, Wilbert, *Morelos of Mexico*, Texas Western Press, 1963

Tiscendorf, Alfred, *Great Britain and Mexico in the Era of Porfirio Díaz*, Duke University Press, 1961

Tuchman, Barbara, *The Zimmerman Telegram*, MacMillan, New York, 1958

Turner, John Kenneth, *Barbarous Mexico*, University of Texas, Austin, 1969

Tyrner-Tyrnauer, A.R., *Lincoln and the Emperors*, Harcourt Brace, New York

Ulloa, Berta, *La Revolución Intervenida*, El Colegio de Mexico, Mexico City, 1976

Vanderwood, Paul, *Disorder & Progress: Bandits, Police, and the Mexican Revolution*, University of Nebraska, Lincoln, 1981

Vasconcelos, José, *La Raza Cosmica*, Aguilar, Madrid, 1961

Vázquez, Joséfina Zoraida, with Lorenzo Meyer, *The United States and Mexico*, University of Chicago Press, 1985. Footnotes indicate whether Vázquez or Meyer is the author of the cite.

von Humboldt, Alexander, *Political Essays on the Kingdom of New Spain*, Riley, New York, 1811

Webber, Burt, *Retaliation: Japanese Attacks on the Pacific Northwest in World War II*, Oregon State University Press, Corvallis, Oregon, 1975

Weinberg, Albert K., *Manifest Destiny: A Study of Nationalistic Expansion*, Quadrangle Books, Chicago

Weinberger, Caspar, with Peter Schweitzer, *The Next War*, Regnery Publishing Inc., Washington DC, 1996

Williams, T. Harry, *The History of American Wars*, Knopf, New York, 1981

Womack, John, *Emiliano Zapata and the Mexican Revolution*, Vintage, New York, 1966

Woodward, Bob, *Veil: The Secret Wars of the CIA*, Simon & Schuster, New York, 1987

Yergin, Daniel, *The Shattered Peace*, Houghton Mifflin, Boston, 1977

Zinn, Howard, *A Peoples' History of the United States*, Harper & Row, New York, 1980

PERIODICALS CONSULTED

Mexico

Estudios Parlimentarios del Congreso Mexicano
Excelsior
El Financiero
La Jornada
Ovaciones
Punto
Proceso
Reforma
El Sol de México
El Sol de Acapulco (Sur Acapulco)
Tiempo (San Cristóbal de las Casas)
El Universal
El Universal Gráfico

U.S. and other English Language

Business Week
Financial Times
Forbes Magazine
Latin America Press (Lima)
México Bárbaro*
Mexico City Times
The Nation
The News (Mexico City)
Pacific News Service
Pearson's Magazine
San Francisco Bay Guardian
San Francisco Chronicle
San Francisco Examiner
SF Weekly
Sierra Magazine
Texas Observer
Wall Street Journal
Washington Post
Z Magazine

*México Bárbaro is published electronically from New York City at nicadlw@earthlink.net. The dates cited may not coincide with the order in which the stories were published.

INDEX

National Chamber of Commerce (U.S.): 213
National Coordinating Body of Small Coffee Growers (Mexico): 272
National Defense Agency (U.S.): 163
National Drug Enforcement, Education and Control Act of 1986 (U.S.): 133, 140
National Endowment of the Arts (NEA): 313
National Football League (NFL): 232
National Human Rights Commission (NDH; Mexico): 249, 265
National Human Rights Network (Mexico): 249, 265
National Imaging and Mapping Agency (NIMA; U.S.): 163
National Immigration Council (U.S.): 289
National Institute for drug Control (INCD; U.S.): 151, 158
National Polytechnic Institute (Mexico): 232
National Railroad Corporation of Mexico: 57
National Real Estate Clearing House (Mexico): 259
National Security Act (U.S.): 130
National Security Agency (NSA; U.S.): 163
National Security Archives (U.S.): 147, 158
National Security Council (U.S.): 147, 187, 202
Nature's Fingerprints, Inc.: 221
Navarro, Gen. Alfredo: 160
nazis/nazism: 293, 296
Negro League, the: 231
Negro Modelo, Inc.: 221
Negroponte, John: 177, 186-8
Neruda, Pablo: 99
Neutrality Act (U.S.): 70
New Tehuantepec Canal: 276
Newman, Gray: 199
Newsweek magazine: 185
New Yorker magazine: 233
New York Times: 39, 46, 128, 139, 140, 179, 213, 219, 228, 283, 312
Next War, The: 203
Nickerson, Hiram: 54
Nicklaus, Jack: 240, 242
Nicole Miller Salons, Inc.: 220
Nike Corp.: 223
Nine Nations of North America, The: 301
North American Free Trade Agreement (NAFTA): 24, 29, 39, 83, 106, 130, 135, 147, 153-5, 157, 178, 185, 189, 194-6, 198, 199, 201-5, 210, 212, 216, 218, 219, 222, 228, 230, 231, 238. 241, 249, 257, 253-4, 283, 289, 294, 303, 310, 312, 313; Chapters 6 and 7 of: 253-4; "Fast Track" of: 185-6; Helms-Burton Amendment to: 212; industrial park of: 176, 178, 193-5; U.S. passage of: 190-2
Nissan Corp.: 219
Nixon, Pres. Richard M.: 126, 137, 199
Noriega, Manuel: 75, 155
Norte del Corazon tv series: 234, 235
North, Oliver: 129, 187
Northwest Border Rapid Response Team (Mexico): 151

O

Obregón, Pres. Alvaro: 71-2, 77, 80, 82, 84, 86, 90, 294; and Villa assassination: 80; assassination of: 89; Bucareli Agreement of: 85
Ocampu, Melchor: 38
O'Dwyer, William O.: 113
Ojinaga, Battle of: 70
Oil Watch: 250

Olivares, Refugio: 305
Olmedo, Marcos: 246-7
One River, One Country (documentary film): 301
OPEC boycott: 171
"Operation Aztec," *see* "Rainbow War Plan"
"Operation Desert Storm," *see* Persian Gulf War
"Operation Intercept," *see* Drug Enforcement Administration
"Operation Just Cause," *see* Panama, U.S. invasion of
"Operation Wetback," *see* U.S. Border Patrol
Oppenheimer, Andrés: 202
Organization for Commerce and Development (Mexico): 196
Organization of American States (OAS): 116-8; Caracas meeting of: 118; Punte del Este meeting of: 118; 1960 Declaration of San José by: 117
Organization of Campesinos of the Southern Sierra (OCSS): 264-6
Orol, Juan: 229
Orosco, Enrique: 176
Ortega, Daniel: 127
Ortiz Rubio, Pascual: 91-2, 214-5
O'Shaughnessy, Ambassador: 66, 84
Osario, Zacarias: 142-3, 268
O'Sullivan, John: 28
Oswald, Lee Harvey: 120
Ouchi Sushi Co.: 221
Ousmanski, Constantino: 114
Ovaciones magazine: 203
Ovando, Xavier: 179
Overseas Male catalogue: 224

P

Pacheco, José Emilio: 99
Pacific Fruit Grower magazine: 295
Page, Walter: 65
Palestino Liberation Organization (PLO): 123
Palma, Héctor ("Guerro"): 156, 160-1
Palmer Raids, the: 297
Pan American Petroleum Corp.: 82
Panama, U.S. invasion of: 155, 277, 293
Pancho Villa Museum: 74
Pancho Villa State Park: 75
Panetta, Leon: 202
Pantex Corp.: 132
Pantoja, Jorge: 234
Party of Democratic Revolution (PRD): 93, 145, 171, 184, 187, 205, 252-3, 263-4, 288
Party of Institutionalized Revolution (PRI): 91, 93, 98, 109, 111, 112, 115, 123, 126, 144, 146, 153, 177, 179, 180, 183, 184, 187, 191, 206, 207, 215, 216, 234, 235, 243, 244, 246, 252, 253, 254-5, 288, 294, 304, 313; Honor and Justice Committee of: 207
Party of the Mexican Revolution (PRD): 91, 111
Party of the National Revolution (PNR): 90-2, 97
Pastor, Robert: 133
"Pastry War," the: 177
Patriotic Sons of America: 83
"Pax Porfiriano," *see* Díaz, Pres. Porfirio
Paz, Octavio: 216, 221, 222, 224, 237
Pazos, Luis: 125, 198
PBS, *see* Public Broadcasting Service
Pearson, Weetman ("Lord Cowdry"): 53-5, 55, 61, 64, 66, 70, 82, 275

ABOUT THE AUTHOR

Photo by Marcia Perskie

Acclaimed by top Mexican journalist Blanche Pertrich of *La Jornada* as "the new John Reed covering a new Mexican revolution," John Ross has been reporting on popular struggle in Mexico and Latin America for the better part of two decades. A social activist and poet as well as a working correspondent (*Noticias Aliadas*-Lima, *Gemini*-London), Ross resides in Mexico City's old quarter, once the Aztec island of Tenochtitlan. John Ross's work has been featured in the *Nation* and *Sierra* magazine in addition to his regular contributions to the *Los Angeles Weekly* and *San Francisco Bay Guardian*. His weekly electronic reportage, "Mexico Barbaro" is widely praised. He is the author of *Rebellion From the Roots-Indian Uprising in Chiapas*, a 1995 American Book Award winner, in addition to *In Focus: Mexico*, a political guide book, and editor of *We Came to Play*, and anthology of basketball writings, with Q.R. Hand. Ross's seventh chapbook of poetry, *jazzmexico*, will be published this fall by Calica de Pelon, in Mexico City.

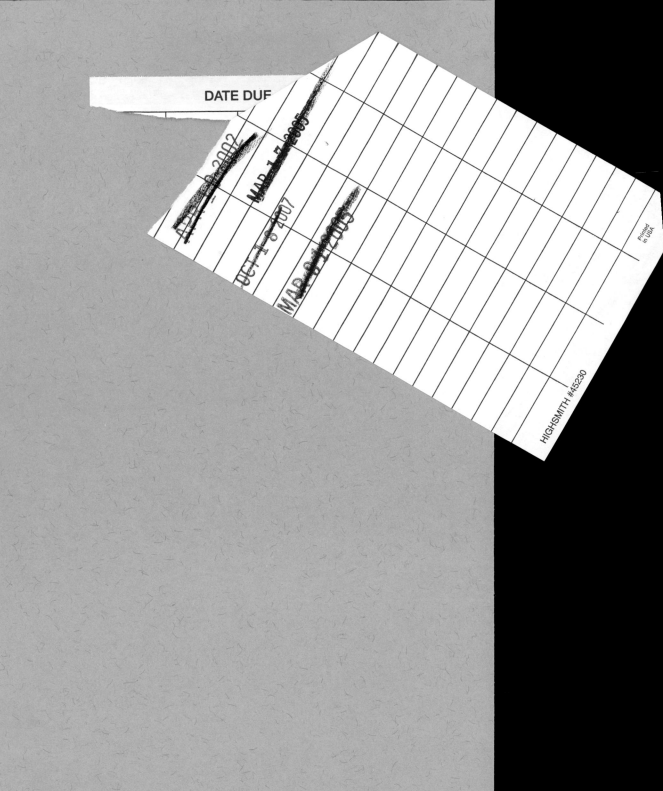

DATE DUE

HIGHSMITH #45230

Printed
in USA